Lecture Notes in Computer Science   5022

Commenced Publication in 1973
Founding and Former Series Editors:
Gerhard Goos, Juris Hartmanis, and Jan van

Anu G. Bourgeois   S. Q. Zheng (Eds.)

Algorithms and Architectures for Parallel Processing

8th International Conference, ICA3PP 2008
Cyprus, June 9–11, 2008
Proceedings

 Springer

Volume Editors

Anu G. Bourgeois
Georgia State University, Atlanta, GA 30303, USA
E-mail: anu@cs.gsu.edu

S. Q. Zheng
University of Texas at Dallas, Richardson, TX 75080, USA
E-mail: sizheng@utdallas.edu

Library of Congress Control Number: Applied for

CR Subject Classification (1998): D, F.1-3, C, I.6

LNCS Sublibrary: SL 1 – Theoretical Computer Science and General Issues

ISSN   0302-9743
ISBN-10   3-540-69500-1 Springer Berlin Heidelberg New York
ISBN-13   978-3-540-69500-4 Springer Berlin Heidelberg New York

Springer is a part of Springer Science+Business Media

springer.com

© Springer-Verlag Berlin Heidelberg 2008

Typesetting: Camera-ready by author, data conversion by Scientific Publishing Services, Chennai, India
Printed on acid-free paper   SPIN: 12323395   06/3180   5 4 3 2 1 0

Preface

Welcome to the proceedings of the 8th International Conference on Algorithms and Architectures for Parallel Processing (ICA3PP 2008).

ICA3PP 2008 consist of two keynote addresses, seven technical sessions, and one tutorial. Included in these proceedings are papers whose authors are from Australia, Brazil, Canada, China, Cyprus, France, India, Iran, Israel, Italy, Japan, Korea, Germany, Greece, Mexico, Poland, Portugal, Romania, Spain, Switzerland, Taiwan, Tunisia, UAE, UK, and USA. Each paper was rigorously reviewed by at least three Program Committee members and/or external reviewers, and the acceptance ratio is 35%. These papers were presented over seven technical sessions. Based on the paper review results, three papers were selected as the best papers.

We would like to thank the many people who helped make this conference a successful event. We thank all authors who submitted their work to ICA3PP 2008, and all Program Committee members and additional reviewers for their diligent work in the paper review process ensuring a collection of high-quality papers. We are grateful to Hong Shen University of Adelaide, Australia and Kleanthis Psarris University of Texas at San Antonio, United States, for their willingness to be the keynote speakers. Our thanks go to Hai Jin and George Papapodoulos, the conference General Co-chairs, and Andrzej Goscinski, Wanlei Zhou and Yi Pan, the conference Steering Committee Co-chairs for help in many aspects of organizing this conference. Finally, we thank all the conference participants for traveling to Cyprus. Without your participation, this conference would not have been a success. We hope you find the proceedings of ICA3PP 2008 enjoyable and stimulating.

Anu Bourgeois
S.Q. Zheng

Conference Organization

General Chairs

Hai Jin, Huazhong University of Science and Technology, China
George A. Papadopoulos, University of Cyprus, Cyprus

Steering Committee Chairs

Andrzej Goscinski, Deakin University, Australia
Yi Pan, Georgia State University, USA
Wanlei Zhou, Deakin University, Australia

Program Chairs

Anu G. Bourgeois, Georgia State University, USA
S.Q. Zheng, University of Texas at Dallas, USA

Organizing Chair

George A. Papadopoulos, University of Cyprus, Cyprus

Organizing Committee

Pyrros Bratskas, University of Cyprus, Cyprus
Pericles Cheng, University of Cyprus, Cyprus
Constantinos Kakousis, University of Cyprus, Cyprus
Nearchos Paspallis, University of Cyprus, Cyprus

ICA3PP Program Committee

Jemal Abbawajy	Deakin University, Australia
Selim Akl	Queen's University, Canada
Joseph Arul	Fu Jen Catholic University, Taiwan
Mark Baker	The University of Reading, UK
Amnon Barak	Hebrew University of Jerusalem, Israel
Maarten Boasson	University of Amsterdam, The Netherlands
Arndt Bode	Technical University of Munich, Germany
Xiaojun Cao	Georgia State University, USA
Jiannong Cao	Hong Kong Polytechnic University, Hong Kong

Peter Cappello	University of California, Santa Barbara, USA
Jianer Chen	Texas A&M University, USA
Yingying Chen	Rutgers University, USA
Francis Chin	University of Hong Kong, Hong Kong
Kenneth Chiu	State University of NY at Binghamton, USA
Jose Cunha	New University of Lisbon, Portugal
Alfredo Cuzzocrea	University of Calabria, Italy
Erik D'Hollander	Ghent University, Belgium
Eliezer Dekel	IBM Haifa Research Laboratory, Israel
Robert Dew	Deakin University, Australia
Marios Dikaiakos	University of Cyprus, Cyprus
Jack Dongarra	University of Tennessee, USA
José A. Fernández-Zepeda	CICESE, Mexico
Len Freeman	University of Manchester, UK
Chryssis Georgiou	University of Cyprus, Cyprus
Ching-Hsien Hsu	Chung Hua University, Taiwan
Zvi Kedem	New York University, USA
Ken Hawick	Massey University, New Zealand
Michael Hobbs	Deakin University, Australia
Bo Hong	Drexel University, USA
Susumu Horiguchi	Tohoku University, Japan
Shi-Jinn Horng	National Taiwan University of Science and Technology, Taiwan
Ali Hurson	Pennsylvania State University, USA
Weijia Jia	City University of Hong Kong, Hong Kong
Hong Jiang	University of Nebraska at Lincoln, USA
Krishna Kavi	The University of North Texas, USA
Ashwin Gumaste	Indian Institute of Technology, Bombay, India
Teofilo Gonzalez	University of California, Santa Babara, USA
Wayne Kelly	Queensland University of Technology, Australia
Tohru Kikuno	Osaka University, Japan
Jacek Kitowski	AGH University of Science and Technology, Cracow, Poland
Michael Langston	University of Tennessee, USA
Laurent Lefevre	INRIA, France
Kuan-Ching Li	Providence University, Taiwan
Keqin Li	State University of NY at New Paltz, USA
Cho-Chin Lin	National Ilan University, Taiwan
Thanasis Loukopoulos	University of Thessaly, Greece
Praveen Madiraju	Marquette University, USA
Christine Morin	IRISA/INRIA, France
Koji Nakano	Hiroshima University, Japan
Michael Palis	Rutgers University, USA
Marcin Paprzycki	SWPS and IBS PAN, Poland
Weizhong Qiang	Huazhong U. of Science and Technology, China
Rajeev Raje	Purdue University, USA

Michel Raynal	IRISA, France
Justin Rough	Deakin University, Australia
Barry Rountree	University of Georgia, USA
Srinivas Sampalli	Dalhousie University, Canada
Eunice Santos	Virginia Tech. University, USA
Yiannakis Sazeides	University of Cyprus, Cyprus
Edwin Sha	University of Texas at Dallas, USA
Chengzheng Sun	Nanyang Technological University, Singapore
Rajshekhar Sunderraman	Georgia State University, USA
Yong-Meng Teo	National University of Singapore, Singapore
Gabor Terstyanszki	University of Westminster, UK
Jerry Trahan	Louisiana State University, USA
Ramachandran Vaidyanathan	Louisiana State University, USA
Vassos Vassiliou	University of Cyprus, Cyprus
Jianping Wang	City University of Hong Kong, Hong Kong
Greg Wickham	GrangeNet, Australia
Yue Wu	University of Electronic Science and Technology, China
Jie Wu	Florida Atlantic University, USA
Roman Wyrzykowski	Czestochowa University of Technology, Poland
Dong Xiang	Tsinghua University, China
Chengzhong Xu	Wayne State University, USA
Laurence T. Yang	St. Francis Xavier University, Canada
Chao-Tung Yang	Tunghai University, Taiwan
Albert Zomaya	University of Sydney, Australia
Jun Zou	Chinese University of Hong Kong, China

External Reviewers

Waleed Alsalih	Marius Nagy
Sriram Chellapan	Sudhir Naswa
YJing Chen	Yinfei Pan
Kevin Chen	Jin Park
Eunjung Cho	Andy Perkins
John Eblen	Charles Phillips
Harald Gjermundrod	Gary Rogers
Lily Jia	Chaman Sabharwal
Asterios Katsifodimos	Jiro Sumitomo
Tao Li	Daniel Tauritz
Kai Lin	Theocharis Theocharides
Fei Liu	Marco Valero
Naya Nagy	Navin Viswanath

Table of Contents

Smart Content Delivery on the Internet

Hong Shen

School of Computer Science
The University of Adelaide

Abstract. As the ever-growing Internet applications in the emerging e-society are centered in sharing of various types of digital contents, content delivery on the Internet as a hot topic has been attracting most attentions. Web caching is an important technology for improving the efficiency of content delivery. As an emerging technology en-route caching computes locations among caches on access paths to store copies of an object such that specified objectives (such as satisfying future access demands to the object) are achieved. In this talk, I will first give an overview on recent developments in efficient content delivery. I will then introduce our recent work in tackling this problem by applying the technique of en-route caching, and present efficient solutions to the problem in systems containing single server and multiple servers respectively. While the problem is NP-hard in the general case, our solutions apply dynamic programming technique and run in polynomial-time in the worst case for both unconstrained and constrained cases in the network topologies of trees (for broadcast delivery) and linear arrays (for point-to-point delivery) respectively. They are shown theoretically either optimal or convergent to optimal. Finally, I will show some possible extensions of our solutions to other system settings.

A. Bourgeois and S.Q. Zheng (Eds.): ICA3PP 2008, LNCS 5022, p. 1, 2008.
© Springer-Verlag Berlin Heidelberg 2008

Parallel Query Processing in Databases on Multicore Architectures

Ralph Acker[1], Christian Roth[1], and Rudolf Bayer[2]

[1] Transaction Software, Willy-Brandt-Allee 2, D-81829 München, Germany
{Ralph.Acker, Christian.Roth}@transaction.de
[2] Institut für Informatik, TU-München, Boltzmannstr. 3, D-85747 Garching, Germany
rdlf.bayer@informatik.tu-muenchen.de
http://www.transaction.de

Abstract. In this paper we present a novel and complete approach on how to encapsulate parallelism for relational database query execution that strives for maximum resource utilization for both CPU and disk activities. Its simple and robust design is capable of modeling intra- and inter-operator parallelism for one or more parallel queries in a most natural way. In addition, encapsulation guarantees that the bulk of relational operators can remain unmodified, as long as their implementation is thread-safe. We will show, that with this approach, the problem of scheduling parallel tasks is generalized, so that it can be safely entrusted to the underlying operating system (OS) without suffering any performance penalties. On the contrary, relocation of all scheduling decisions from the DBMS to the OS guarantees a centralized and therefore near-optimal resource allocation (depending on the OS s abilities) for the complete system that is hosting the database server as one of its tasks. Moreover, with this proposal, query parallelization is fully transparent on the SQL interface of the database system. Configuration of the system for effective parallel query execution can be adjusted by the DB administrator by setting two descriptive tuning parameters. A prototype implementation has been integrated into the Transbase® relational DBMS engine.

Keywords: relational dbms, parallel query processing, encapsulation, intra-operator, inter-operator, scheduling, optimization.

1 Introduction and Related Work

Computer architecture is currently shifting, making concepts formerly restricted to supercomputers available on inexpensive server systems, desktop and laptop computers. Hardware-parallelism, in form of multicore computing and RAID-controlled access to secondary storage has apparently become the most promising cure for stagnation in the constant longing for more computing power.

Based on this trend, it has become tempting to revisit the concepts of database parallelism in the light of those emerging hardware architectures, and of modern operating system characteristics that support this hardware.

A. Bourgeois and S.Q. Zheng (Eds.): ICA3PP 2008, LNCS 5022, pp. 2..13, 2008.
© Springer-Verlag Berlin Heidelberg 2008

Over the last two decades parallel query processing in database systems was the topic of considerable research. Its outcome is now undoubtedly in daily use as part of major commercial DBMSs. Most of the work was concentrated on shared nothing (SN) architectures, e.g. the research prototypes Gamma [1] and Bubba [2]. Now it is applied in modern grid and cluster computing. Other approaches focus on symmetric multiprocessing architectures (SMP), such as XPRS [3] and Volcano [4], [5]. Extensive additional efforts on scheduling parallel tasks have been made, e.g. [6], [7]. The most recent work published in this field focuses on the special requirements of simultaneous multithreading (SMT), e.g. [8], and especially on the well-known problem of stalls in the memory hierarchy [9].

However, the fundamental concepts of task identification and resource scheduling were not revised recently to honor emerging technologies in modern SMP systems. Our approach adopts the evident idea of encapsulating asynchronous relational query execution as an opaque relational operator. All implementation details are hidden within this operator while its usage poses minimal requirements to other relational operators, allowing them to remain unaffected. This idea of an asynchronous relational operator was originally proposed in [10] and [4], but it appears that it never reached maturity. Our parallel operator differs from the Volcano *exchange operator*, as it inherently supports intra-operator parallelism and also addresses the problem of order preservation. Tandem s *parallel operator* is a commercial solution and no details were published, but according to [4] it seems to be very similar to Volcano s exchange operator.

We combine the encapsulation of parallelism with a two-phase query plan optimization. The first phase is common static optimization by the DMBS optimizer. The optimizer drafts a plan on how a query should be carried out in parallel. The additional complexity of parallelization adds to the complexity of the NP-hard problem of query plan optimization. We completely evade this complexity by using an approach to query plan parallelization that is based on a minimal set of boundary conditions. The second phase of optimization dynamically refines the query plan during the query execution phase, rebalancing the threads of execution into an equilibrium that guarantees maximum resource utilization. This in itself is also a common concept for maximizing parallelism on restricted resources. This form of two-phase optimization was first applied to the problem of parallelism in database systems by [11]. The original concept identifies (generates) tasks, and schedules them such that resources (I/O and CPU) are optimally utilized. Therefore the tasks are categorized based on criteria such as I/O or CPU boundedness, tuple size, tuples per page and estimated execution time. These estimates can be inaccurate or vary over time, e.g. due to data skew. So resource utilization is constantly monitored and whenever it is not optimal rescheduling is used. Our work diverges strongly from this approach in the aspect that we understand parallelization as a concurrency problem. In our approach all tasks are strictly data-driven, i.e. they are runnable at any time, provided that input data is available. They all apply for limited resources at the same time, while they are collaboratively calculating the result of a relational query. There is no requirement to actively interfere with the scheduling or prioritization of tasks, or to act on assumptions on these tasks. Slow tasks are accelerated by assigning additional threads. Fast tasks will wait on empty input buffers, consuming no resources at all. So permanent, automatic and data-driven rebalancing of resources takes place, always striving to achieve optimal resource allocation through concurrency.

To the best of our knowledge, this is the only work that covers both aspects of general parallelization of relational queries, i.e. query plan optimization and load balancing. It refers to the only implementation ready for integration into a relational database system. Therefore this discussion of an asynchronous relational operator is unique and complete.

2   Encapsulation of Parallelism

We model parallelization as a new operator (ASYNC) in the query execution plan (QEP). Without loss of generality, we presume query plans consisting of operators based on the well-known iterator model, i.e. each operator in the operator tree exposes an open(), next(), and close() method to other operators, while all implementation details are hidden within the operator. The ASYNC operator is an abstraction of thread boundaries in the operator tree, i.e. data moving through an ASYNC node is passed from one thread to another. An ASYNC node may be placed between any pair of operators in a sequential QEP, i.e. on any edges of the operator tree, as long as it has no side-effect compromising the functional integrity of the QEP. As an example for such a side effect, imagine an ASYNC node allowing out-of-order execution below a relational grouping operation. The GROUP operator relies on an input order on the grouping field, which is arranged by a sequential QEP (SORT before GROUP in Figure 1a). But in a parallelized QEP the ASYNC operator might disrupt the order (Figure 1b).

Exchange of data (tuples) over thread boundaries is done via a buffer that is encapsulated and operated on by every ASYNC operator and thereby shared among the two adjacent threads. Access to this buffer is synchronized, resembling the classic consumer-producer problem. In order to minimize synchronization overhead, the buffer is not locked for every tuple insertion/retrieval, but it is divided equally into three partitions, which are used in a round-robin fashion. Consumer and producer need to be synchronized only when they acquire access to a new partition. We chose partitioning into three regions in order to allow one thread to switch partitions without necessarily having to wait for the other thread. Thereby the first thread has the opportunity to completely utilize its time slice rather than to give it up when its partition is exhausted. A higher number of partitions would further improve this behavior, but it would also induce additional synchronization operations for switching partitions. Experimental results have confirmed that partitioning into three regions is optimal for common database operations.

Calling the open() routine of the ASYNC operator assigns a new producer thread that evaluates the QEP sub-tree below this ASYNC node. The new thread propagates the open() call to its sons and afterwards *asynchronously* starts evaluating its sub-tree. It retrieves all input data by calling next() and copying results into its current buffer partition, until end-of-data is reached and the lock on the current buffer partition can be released. Finally a call to close() frees all resources and terminates the thread. The ASYNC nodes operate strictly in FIFO mode, so any ordering of the input data will be retained.

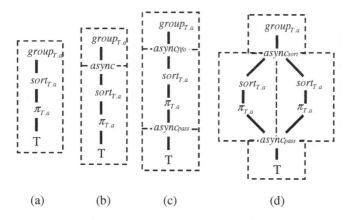

Fig. 1. Different parallelized QEPs for the query *SELECT T.a FROM T GROUP BY T.a*. Dotted lines represent thread boundaries. (a) Sequential plan (b) Example for ASYNC placement, (c) Inter-operator parallelism and order preservation, (d) Intra-operator parallelism and sorting.

Using an ASYNC operator yields three valuable advantages. First, it is entirely consistent with the recursive programming paradigm of the iterator model. Second, existing operators do not need any modification, provided that they are thread-safe. Third, ASYNC nodes can be placed (almost) freely in the QEP by the optimizer, allowing for arbitrary forms of parallelization. An algorithm for parallelization will be presented in Section 3.

Obviously, inter-operator parallelism can be easily modeled with this approach by simply inserting ASYNC nodes into any given operator tree. In order to reduce the costs for creating and terminating threads, the established concept of thread pooling is used. The system maintains a pool of worker threads. Threads from this pool can be assigned to all sorts of tasks. If the operation is completed, i.e. the ASYNC operator is closed, the thread will return into the pool where it can be reused for another task.

Intra-operator parallelism is modeled by identifying *pipeline fragments* in the operator tree that are suitable for parallel execution. These fragments are enclosed by two ASYNC nodes, i.e. execution is to be carried out by three threads (e.g. Figure 1c). Each of these fragments is logically replicated and its clone is executed in parallel as a data pipeline (Figure 1d). At each thread boundary a partitioned buffer is installed. The lower ASYNC node acts as data partitioner, i.e. it distributes its input data among the pipelines input buffers, while the upper ASYNC merges the result from the different pipelines output buffers. Here special attention has to be paid to data ordering. Partitioning and merging can be organized in two ways, reflected as two operating modes of the involved ASYNC nodes. In pass-through mode (PASS) the pipeline is adjusted for maximum throughput. Input data is written to any pipeline that currently accepts more input and the upper ASYNC passes processed data on as soon as it becomes available. So a pipeline in PASS mode is likely to process data in an out-of-order fashion.

In some cases however, it is preferable to retain a given input order of the data, e.g. if this order can be exploited by a consecutive operation. Therefore the pipeline may also operate in FIFO mode, at the expense of losing some throughput (Figure 1c). In this mode, data may also be inserted into any pipeline. But, as a meta information, a partition is also marked with a sequential number that is also accessible for the upper end of the pipeline. The upper ASYNC will then arrange its output along this sequence, thereby preserving the original order. Throughput is lost compared to the PASS variant at the upper end of the pipeline, where the ASYNC potentially has to wait for data with the next sequence number to become available. This might cause the other pipelines to stall, because data is not retrieved fast enough. Another problem of FIFO pipelining is that the amount of data is typically not constant in a pipeline, as a pipeline might produce dramatically lesser (e.g. pipeline contains a restriction or projection) or greater (e.g. pipeline contains a JOIN operator) amounts of data than the input amount. For relational operators it is particularly hard to estimate how the data size will change. This presents a profound problem in buffer space allocation for FIFO pipelines. However, the problem is attenuated by roughly estimating changes in data size where this is possible, e.g. for a projection eliminating one column. And it is completely overcome by adding an additional flag of meta information into the pipeline buffers. This flag specifies whether all data from the source partition with the current sequential number was retrieved, i.e. whether more data from a source partition has to be processed from this particular pipeline, or if the upper ASYNC can move on to the next partition with the next sequence number. With this simple modification, one input partition of the pipeline may evolve to one, possibly empty, or more output partitions of the same pipeline.

Finally, parallelizing SORT operations (Figure 1d) in a pipeline is a particularly attractive feat. To achieve this, the lower end of the pipeline operates in PASS mode, as any input order becomes irrelevant at the upcoming SORT operation in the pipeline. The upper end operates in SORT mode, i.e. the ASYNC performs a heap-merge operation with all input pipeline tuples. Thereby a SORT operation sorting n tuples can be performed in m parallel pipelines with an estimated complexity of $n/m*log(n/m)$ for each pipeline, i.e. $n*log(n/m)$ for m pipelines. The final heap merge has a complexity of $n*log(m)$, so the final *linear* complexity of the pipelined SORT operation remains $n*log(n)$, just like for the sequential operation.

It is also important to emphasize, that the static parallelization, as well as dynamic load balancing discussed in the next sections, are not based on any assumptions or statistics such as data sizes or distributions, estimations on operators such as number of machine instructions per operation, number of I/Os or classification in CPU- or I/O-bound query plan fragments. Statistics regularly tend to be compromised by data skew and the constant activities of monitoring and refining their validity induces unwanted additional computational costs.

3 Optimization for Parallel Execution

As proposed in many other approaches, we also adopt a two phase optimization. The first phase performs static optimization and takes place during general query optimization. The DBMS SQL compiler and optimizer generate a QEP. This constitutes what the DBMS considers an optimal plan for sequential processing. Afterwards, this sequential plan is statically parallelized, i.e. the sequential execution plan is split up into tasks that can be executed in parallel.

In order to reduce the complexity of this famous NP-hard problem of query plan optimization, the query optimizer will generally consider only left-deep operator trees. It is well understood [12] that these plans are not always optimal, especially for parallel execution, where under certain circumstances (size of intermediate results, available memory) bushy join trees may perform better, because joins are performed in parallel. Considering all forms of operator trees is still an open research field and will not be addressed in this paper. Without loss of generality, we assume in the following, that the result of the optimizer for a sequential query evaluation is also near-optimal for parallel processing, while we emphasize the fact that our approach to encapsulation of parallelism applies to arbitrary operator trees without restrictions.

3.1 Static Parallelization

Two configuration parameters are of importance in static parallelization. The first is the total size of memory available per ASYNC operator (*async_max_buffer*). Every ASYNC operator requires a buffer for inter-thread communication. If this buffer is chosen too small, a lot of synchronization has to be performed when large amounts of data are passed through it. If the buffer is too large, memory might be wasted. The optimal size would allow a thread to process one partition of the buffer and release its locks on it. Given the versatile forms of relational operators and their numerous combinations, this goal is very difficult to achieve. However, a buffer partition should be at least big enough, that most threads cannot process it in a mere fraction of their time slices. Thus synchronization and scheduling overhead is limited reasonably.

The second parameter is the maximum number of parallel *pipeline fragments* that should be active at any time (*async_max_threads*). QEPs for complex statements tend also to be complex, involving several thousands of operators. If such a plan is evaluated sequentially, only one single operator is active and consuming CPU and/or I/O resources at any point in time, and typically only operators in the immediate vicinity are likely to demand massive memory allocation. Parallel query execution behaves contrarily. Here it is actually desired to have many fractions of the tree running in parallel, each fragment having one active operator consuming CPU and/or I/O and each with potentially heavy memory requirements. Obviously some precautions, like limiting the number of ASYNC operators, have to be taken in order to cope with this problem.

Yet there exists a special class of relational operators, the so-called *blocking* operators. These operators have to process all input data before any output can be generated, e.g. SORT/ AGGR. They represent a rupture in the data flow, i.e. the plan below and above such a blocking node will be executed mutually exclusively, even by a parallel QEP. By identifying these blocking operators, the parallelizer can apply maximum parallelism by inserting *async_max_threads* ASYNC nodes below and above such a blocking node.

With these two configuration parameters, we can devise an algorithm for static parallelization. Its task is to identify QEP fragments that can be split off for asynchronous execution. To limit memory consumption, synchronization and communication overhead, we choose to find QEP portions of maximum length, i.e. the number of initial ASYNCs is minimized. We can rely on dynamic load balancing, which is discussed below, to increase the number of ASYNCs for optimal parallelism.

Additionally an ASYNC is always placed at the root of the QEP (not shown in Figure 1) to ensure, that the server will work ahead on a bulky query result set, while the database client is processing the last portion of the result. More ASYNCs are always placed above any leaves of the QEP, i.e. data sources (relation or index accesses) that are likely to perform I/O, so asynchronous I/O is maximized. Pipelines (intra-operator parallelism) contain only unary operators. The subtrees of n-ary operators are split into several threads by inserting ASYNCs below this operator, so n input streams are calculated independently in n threads. The only exception to this rule is NL-JOIN (nested-loop) operator, because of its strong functional dependency in looking up join partners; it may reside in one pipeline as a whole.

The static parallelization is essentially a depth-first traversal of the initially sequential QEP. While moving down the QEP, we keep an account if the current operator (or a parent operator) relies on the current data order, so we can later apply the optimal mode to an ASYNC. When we reach a leaf of the QEP we insert the first ASYNC to encourage asynchronous I/O. Then we retrace our steps upwards over any unary operators. When we reach an n-ary operator (not NL-JOIN), we insert another ASYNC node and thereby build a pipeline. Finally for these two associated ASYNCs the operation mode is set to PASS/ FIFO or SORT (if the pipeline contains a sort operation). A pipeline may be executed *async_max_threads* times in parallel and each ASYNC may allocate as much as *async_max_buffer* memory for its buffer.

These are the basic steps of our algorithm to parallelize a sequential QEP. Obviously its complexity is determined by the complexity of the tree traversal O(n), and is therefore linear with the number of operators in the QEP.

3.2   Dynamic Load Balancing

The second phase of optimization is carried out during query run-time. While one, or possibly several, queries are executed in parallel, the system resources must be constantly reallocated to ensure optimal utilization of CPU, memory and disk resources. We distinguish three phases of query execution, each with its own special requirements to load balancing.

3.2.1   Phases of Query Execution

During the first phase, execution startup, all portions of operator trees (separated by ASYNC nodes) are initiated and start computation one by one. As calculation is data-driven, in this phase only the leaf -threads will run. All other threads are currently waiting for input. This fact exhibits two important problems. The leaves of the operator trees are the data sources and typically involve mostly I/O, while the inner operator nodes of a tree are more biased towards CPU utilization. This brings about a heavy load imbalance in the earliest phase of query execution.

In the second phase all parts of the operator tree are active. In this phase, if we temporarily assume uniform data distribution, the tasks will automatically be rebalanced for maximum data throughput and optimal resource utilization. Data skew will constantly disturb this balance, making permanent rebalancing necessary. In this phase however, it is most likely to achieve the target of full resource utilization.

In the third stage, the leaf nodes are already exhausted. Now, all input data is available and stored in various buffers across all involved operators, and no more I/O is necessary, balance shifts again for a massive CPU shortness. Thus, the second phase has most potential to compensate for the incurred overhead of parallelization by maximized resource utilization. Moreover, if this phase is too short, parallelization is likely not to pay off. Particularly in the presence of simple and short-running queries we will show in our experimental results, that this fact alone can already make parallelization disadvantageous over sequential query execution without further precautions.

We therefore propose a robust approach of gradually increasing parallelism using *retarded pipeline activation* and *dynamic buffer size*. As in the first phase of query execution only the leaf threads are running, there is no point in activating all pipelines, as they would immediately block on their empty input buffers. In addition we artificially limit the memory in the input buffers on our ASYNC buffers. Immediately after startup only a small fraction of the buffer region is used. Therefore, a buffer partition fills up relatively fast and a producer is forced to switch to the next partition. The consumer is signaled that input data has become available and begins work much earlier, i.e. the startup phase is shortened dramatically at the expense of some additional synchronization on the input buffers. When the producer has to wait on a full input buffer (imbalanced consumer-producer relationship), it increases the fraction of its buffer that it may use next time. This is repeated until either a balance between producer and consumer is reached or the buffer is used completely. In the latter case, if the buffer in question is at the lower end of a pipeline, one additional pipeline is activated. In combination, these two simple techniques guarantee a very agile and short query startup. They make sure that asynchronous execution of short-running queries has only a negligible overhead compared to sequential query execution while optimal balance between consumers and producers is established quickly.

In conclusion, data-driven load balancing as proposed here, is fully adaptive to all forms of hardware configurations, i.e. it is not limited to any specific number of CPU cores, particular memory hierarchies or disk configurations. On the contrary, it will automatically scale to the system parameters it is confronted with. This is solely achieved by its ability of finding the equilibrium of optimal data-flow and thereby optimal resource allocation. This is done completely independent from the particular hardware situation.

3.2.2 Asynchronous I/O System

In our approach, I/Os are issued against the centralized asynchronous I/O system of the operating system. They are issued one at a time as the threads in the QEP move along. Unlike other approaches where I/O is classified into sequential and random I/O and the DBMS decides on I/O serialization, the decision which I/O request to serve first is postponed to the operating system s I/O system. This is where all information for optimal global scheduling (physical I/O system layout, current position of head(s), complete system wide I/O request queue, physical addresses of all I/Os in queue) is available. This is particularly true, when several processes are competing for disk resources. Our only requirement to the I/O system is fairness in scheduling, i.e. no starvation and active I/O reordering. If the operating system would simply serve I/O request in FIFO order, this would severely undermine all efforts for efficiency. These requests are satisfied by all modern operating systems. As for task scheduling, prioritization of I/O requests is not a requirement. However, the DMBS could exploit a second, lower priority. By constantly interspersing low priority write requests, it utilizes an otherwise idle I/O system for writing ahead modified pages from the database cache to disk. So these pages become replaceable at low costs [13].

Our results prove that this concept works well in most cases. But strict fairness in scheduling I/O requests affects the performance of sequential I/O. If one thread, performing sequential I/O, issues only one request at a time and another thread issues additional, possibly random I/Os, the former sequential I/O is permanently disturbed and becomes in fact random. This effect can be lessened, if both threads issue not only one request at a time, but a set of read-ahead requests against the I/O system. Then sequential requests are completed as batches without the overhead of positioning, resulting in near sequential I/O performance for sequential I/O while concurrent random I/O requests are still reasonably served.

4   Experimental Results

In the following, we will present the experimental findings of our parallelization approach. All measurements were made on a 2 CPU Intel Xeon server running both Linux 2.6.18 and Windows 2003 Server as operating systems. The results are equivalent for both operating systems.

Overall performance gain is examined using a query mix of partially complex ad-hoc queries that were extracted from a productive real-world data warehouse application.

This query suite is consisting of a total of 387 retrieval queries. For this presentation the queries were sorted along ascending elapsed times for sequential execution. In addition to the sequential time, the estimated optimal parallel query performance for a two-CPU system (Sequential/2) is shown as a theoretical lower boundary for parallel execution. A direct comparison to other RDBMS parallelization approaches is too extensive to fit in the given space constraints.

The following two diagrams of Figure 2 intend to clarify the interaction of the various components of our prototype. They do not show the full capabilities of our approach, but exhibit the outcome if critical features are disabled.

On the left side of Figure 2 only inter-operator parallelism is used, i.e. the QEP is parallelized as discussed but no pipelines are built. The first 219 are very short running queries (below 10 ms), with little or no potential for parallelization. Most of the measured elapsed time here is actually spent for client-server communication, SQL query compilation, and optimization. Query evaluation, although multithreaded, induces only a minor fraction to overall calculation time. These queries represent over 50% of this query suite. Note, that the cumulated difference graph ($CumDiff_n = \sum_{i=1}^{n} Par_i - Seq_i$, referring to the secondary axis) stays close to zero, meaning that parallelization has neither a positive, nor a negative impact for these queries.

Approximately 100 (queries 220-318) are medium-runners (10 to 600 ms), where parallelization is attempted. Most of them incur some minor overhead. The cumulated difference graph is rising slowly to its peak at 10.772 seconds. This indicates that this restricted parallelization is causing a performance penalty for medium-runners. Only

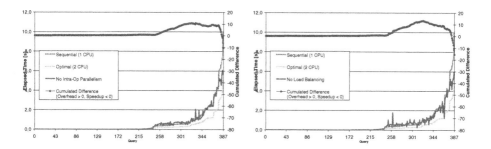

Fig. 2. Performance of *limited* parallel query execution. Left side: Intra-Operator Parallelism disabled. Right side: No load balancing. Queries are sorted by ascending sequential elapsed times. Cumulated Difference always refers to the secondary Y-axis.

the long-runner queries (elapsed times over 600 ms) show potential for parallelization. Here the cumulated difference falls monotonously below 0, i.e. this represents the total speedup of 4.5%. Clearly inter-operator parallelism is not sufficient for speeding up relational queries, because it offers no mechanism to eliminate performance bottlenecks. Only complex queries with extensive independent tasks can benefit.

The second measurement was carried out without load balancing. Data pipelines are established and immediately activated. This measurement shows more distinct peaks, depending on how near the fully parallel QEP happens to be to the optimally balanced plan. Some queries are close to the optimal performance but in total the cumulated difference peaks at 13,124 ms for medium runners. Again, this is compensated by the long-runners leading to a total speedup of 6.9%.

Both results are not very satisfactory as the medium-runners in both cases account for a perceptible overhead. In the next step we will examine the combination of all discussed proposals. The left diagram in Figure 3 shows elapsed times of queries 1 to 318. The right diagram shows the remaining queries in a different scale. Once again the short running queries are almost unaffected by parallelization. However, in this scenario the medium-runners sometimes pay off and sometimes incur some minor overhead. In total both effects almost eliminate each other, as the cumulated difference graph is rising only very slightly above zero, i.e. parallelization is causing a negligible performance penalty for medium-runners. The cumulated difference rises as high as 1.651 seconds, and is falling later on. It is adding up to an average penalty of 10 ms per query for the medium runners. However, an integral examination shows that the average overhead per medium-runner is only about 3%, which we consider acceptable. Moreover, a total of 1.651 seconds of overhead seems negligible compared to a cumulated runtime of 34.852 s for the short and medium-runners and a total elapsed time of over 226.5 seconds for the compete query suite. The long-runner queries (Figure 3, right hand side, elapsed times over 600 ms) consistently show good potential for parallelization. In this phase the cumulated difference falls monotonously far below 0. Clearly the performance of the parallel query execution is close to the estimated optimum. Only few long-runners stay close to the sequential performance. The reason for this would-be poor parallelization is that the involved relational operators in these queries are inherently barely parallelizable. Still, it is noteworthy that

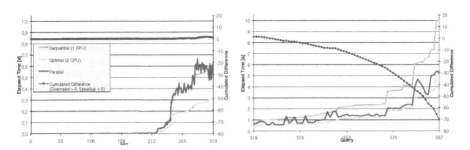

Fig. 3. Overall performance of parallel query execution. Left side: Short-runners (queries 1-219) and medium-runners (220-318). Right side: Long-Runners (319-387). Queries are sorted by ascending sequential elapsed times. Note the different scale on the primary Y-axis. Cumulated Difference always refers to the secondary Y-axis.

parallel query execution never surpasses sequential performance and that those that come close to sequential behaviour are very few.

In total, parallelization reduces the total elapsed time for the whole query suite from 226.5 to 156 seconds, i.e. below 70 %. If only the long-runners are accounted for, the ratio sinks even below 63%. Similar results where produced on several other multicore machines without changing any parameters. This emphasizes our claim that the ASYNC operator is adaptive and universally applicable, independently from any particular hardware configuration.

5   Conclusion

We presented a complete evaluation of an approach to parallel relational query execution that is based on encapsulation of parallelism into the relational ASYNC operator. This work includes an algorithm that is capable of efficiently parallelizing sequential execution plans. Parallelization provided by this algorithm is sufficient to generate query execution plans that reach maximum resource utilization during query execution. Continuously high resource utilization in the presence of data skew and varying machine workloads is guaranteed by the robust and powerful dynamic load balancing capabilities of the ASYNC operator. Measurements in a productive environment have proven the capabilities and maturity of this concept and its implementation. They confirm near-linear speedup for queries that are well-suited for parallelization and a respectable average run-time reduction by over 30% for an extensive ad-hoc query suite. On the other hand, our approach incurs no noteworthy performance loss for queries that are adverse to parallelization, because they run too shortly or their relational calculus offers no possibility for parallelization.

Future work on the ASYNC operator will concentrate on further improving interaction with an asynchronous I/O system. Another field is the extension of parallelization of selected relational operators, such as GROUP and AGGR. Finally some fine-tuning is planned to improve the cooperation of the ASYNC operator and the main memory cache hierarchy, in order to reduce memory stalls in SMT environments by implementing aggressive data prefetch into the ASYNC node.

References

1. DeWitt, D.J., Ghandeharizadeh, S., Schneider, D.A., Bricker, A., Hsaio, H.I., Rasmussen, R.: The gamma database machine project. IEEE Transactions on Knowledge and Data Engineering 2(1), 44..62 (1990)
2. Copeland, G., Alexander, W., Boughter, E., Keller, T.: Data Placement in Bubba. In: Proceedings of the 1988 ACM SIGMOD international conference on Management of data, Chicago, Illinois, USA, June 01-03, pp. 99..108 (1988)
3. Stonebraker, M., Katz, R.H., Patterson, D.A., Ousterhout, J.K.: The Design of XPRS. In: Proceedings of the 14th International Conference on Very Large Data Bases, August 29-September 01, pp. 318..330 (1988)
4. Graefe, G.: Encapsulation of parallelism in the volcano query processing system. In: SIGMOD 1990: Proceedings of the 1990 ACM SIGMOD international conference on Management of data, pp. 102..111. ACM Press, New York (1990)
5. Graefe, G., Cole, R.L., Davison, D.L., McKenna, W.J., Wolniewicz, R.H.: Extensible Query Optimization and Parallel Execution in Volcano. Morgan-Kaufman, San Mateo (1994)
6. Lu, H., Tan, K.: Dynamic and load-balanced task-oriented database query processing in parallel systems. In: Pirotte, A., Delobel, C., Gottlob, G. (eds.) EDBT 1992. LNCS, vol. 580, pp. 357..372. Springer, Heidelberg (1992)
7. Mehta, M., DeWitt, D.J.: Managing intra-operator parallelism in parallel database systems. In: VLDB 1995: Proceedings of the 21th International Conference on Very Large Data Bases, pp. 382..394. Morgan Kaufmann Publishers Inc., San Francisco (1995)
8. Zhou, J., Cieslewicz, J., Ross, K.A., Shah, M.: Improving Database Performance on Simultaneous Multithreading Processors. In: Proc. VLDB Conference, pp. 49..60 (2005)
9. Ailamaki, A., DeWitt, D.J., Hill, M.D., Wood, D.A.: DBMSs on a modern processor: Where does time go? The VLDB Journal, 266..277 (1999)
10. Englert, S., Gray, J., Kocher, R., Shah, P.: A Benchmark of NonStop SQL Release 2 Demonstrating Near-Linear Speedup and Scaleup on Large Databases, Tandem Computer Systems Report (1989)
11. Hong, W., Stonebraker, M.: Optimization of parallel query execution plans in XPRS. In: PDIS 1991: Proceedings of the first international conference on Parallel and distributed information systems, pp. 218..225. IEEE Computer Society Press, Los Alamitos (1991)
12. Hong, W.: Exploiting inter-operation parallelism in XPRS. In: SIGMOD 1992: Proceedings of the 1992 ACM SIGMOD international conference on Management of data, pp. 19... 28. ACM Press, New York (1992)
13. Hall, C., Bonnet, P.: Getting Priorities Straight: Improving Linux Support for Database I/O. In: Proc. VLDB Conference (2005)

Evaluation of a Novel Load-Balancing Algorithm with Variable Granularity

Yi Dai and Lei Cao

National University of Defense Technology, Changsha, Hunan, 410073, P.R. China
y_dai@163.com, dai_guacl@sina.com

Abstract. In this paper, we propose a Uniform Fine-grain Frame Spreading (UFFS-k, where k is the aggregate factor) algorithm to guarantee packet ordering in load-balanced switches by assigning k cells of the same flow to the fixed k successive intermediate inputs. The UFFS-k algorithm first guarantees packet ordering at input linecards without any computation and communication overhead. As the simulation results demonstrate, UFFS-k offers improved delay performance among existing scheduling algorithms that guarantee packet ordering.

1 Introduction

Recently, there has been considerable interest in a class of switch architectures called load-balanced routers. A problem with the load-balanced router is that different packets of the same flow can take different paths, possibly leading to packet reordering [1]. Packet reordering is a widespread property among load-balanced systems and can be detrimental to Internet traffic [2]. Consequently, packet reordering is strongly necessary in Internet routers when packets become mis-sequennced. In this paper, we introduce a novel Uniform Fine-grain Frame Spreading (UFFS-k) algorithm that spreads arriving packets evenly among intermediate input linecards by constructing a fixed mapping relationship between flows and intermediate input linecards in a round-robin manner. By spreading cells in a fine-grained way, UFFS-k can offer improved delay performance compared to existing approaches.

2 The UFFS-k Algorithm

The load-balanced switch architecture applied in the UFFS-k algorithm is shown in Fig. 1. The intermediate inputs $1, 2, ..., N$ are divided into N / k groups in order, each containing k consecutive intermediate inputs that constitute a region. For each input linecadrd, there are k flows mapped to a fixed region, and these k flows constitute a flow branch. In order to distribute traffic equally among the intermediate inputs, the fixed mapping relationship between flow branches of different input ports and regions varies in a round-robin fashion. In the load-balanced switch, reordering occurs when two OQs destined to the same output in different intermediate inputs have different lengths. UFFS-k always assigns k cells of the same flow to the fixed region according to the preset mapping relationship. Due to this fixed mapping relationship, all the OQs of the same region destined to the same output having the same length thus packet ordering being guaranteed.

A. Bourgeois and S.Q. Zheng (Eds.): ICA3PP 2008, LNCS 5022, pp. 14..17, 2008.
© Springer-Verlag Berlin Heidelberg 2008

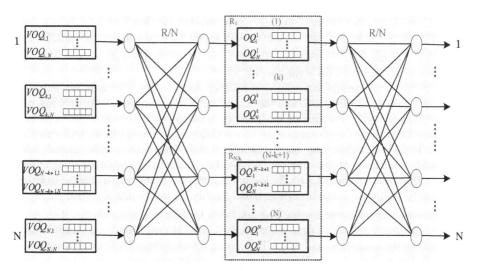

Fig. 1. The load-balanced switch architecture. The intermediate inputs are divided into N/k regions, and the VOQs at each input are also divided into N/k groups corresponding to N/k regions.

As shown in Fig. 1, in order to reduce the memory bandwidth requirement the two stages of meshes in the load-balanced router usually run at rate R/N. Then we have the following definitions:

Definition 1. *External Cell Slot:* Refers to the time taken to transmit or receive a fixed length cell at link rate of R.

Definition 2. *Cell Slot:* This is the time taken to transmit or receive a fixed length cell at link rate of R/N.

According to the link constraints described in Ref. [3], each input is constrained to send a cell to specific intermediate input at most once every N external time slots. If input i starts sending a cell to intermediate input l at external time slot t, then the first time it can again send a cell to intermediate input l again is at external time slot $t+k$. So during each external cell slot, the UFFS-k algorithm at most selects a cell for transmission. UFFS-k is distributed and can operate independently in each input. UFFS-k services flow branches in a round-robin manner and dispatches cells according to the mapping relationship between flow branches and regions. For each flow branch, UFFS-k always sends k cells for the VOQ with the longest length during consecutive k external cell slots. If the longest VOQ whose length less than k, the UFFS-k algorithm will choose next flow branch to service.

3 Performance Simulation and Analysis

We modified SIM simulator developed by Stanford University to observe the performance of UFFS-k[4]. In this section, we present the simulation results of a 16×16 UFFS-k for $k = 8, 4, 2, 1$ and analyze the effect of different aggregate factor of

UFFS-k on delay performance. We also compare the performance of UFFS-k, the originally-proposed load-balanced switch with no packet ordering guarantees [5], the full-ordered frame first (FOFF) algorithm[1] with a reordering buffer of N^2 cells at each output [1], and the UFS algorithm[1].

Fig. 2 shows the simulation results on average delay under Bernoulli_iid_uniform traffic of UFFS-k, FOFF, UFS, and the basic load-balanced switch [5]. UFS has the poorest average delay because of the need to accumulate full frames. By reducing aggregate factor k, the performance of UFFS-k can be improved by a large margin. For the FOFF algorithm, the large portion of cell delay still occurs in the cell-reassembly operation at the output. UFFS-4 has lower average delay than FOFF above 0.3 offered load and UFFS-2 clearly outperforms FOFF for all loads. UFFS-1 surprisingly performs better than the basic load-balanced switch for load $\rho \le 0.2$.

UFFS-1 sends each flow through a dedicated link to the intermediate input. This may result in poor utilization of first stage mesh, but works well under uniform traffic especially at light loads. That s why UFFS-1 outperforms other UFFS-k algorithms of k=2, 4, 8. We will show later UFFS-1 has poor performance under bursty traffic. The performance of the basic load-balanced switch is better than UFFS-1 under heavy load. However, unlike the basic load-balanced switch that can badly mis-sequence packets, UFFS-k guarantees packet ordering.

Fig. 3 shows the simulation results for bursty traffic. The average delays of most algorithms become unstable at 0.99 offered load. For smaller aggregate factor k, the reduction in delay is less. In an extreme case, take UFFS-1 for example, of which the delay performance gets worse under heavy load and has the poorest performance at 0.99 offered load even compared with UFS. Due to spreading each flow via a dedicated link, UFFS-1 cannot spread traffic evenly among intermediate inputs under bursty traffic. Unfortunately, under bursty traffic, this uneven distribution of traffic gets worse as load increases. Therefore, UFFS-1 has better performance under Bernoulli_iid_uniform

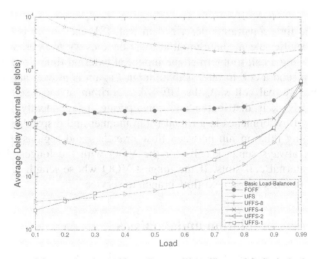

Fig. 2. Average delay under the uniform Bernoulli traffic model. Switch size is N = 16.

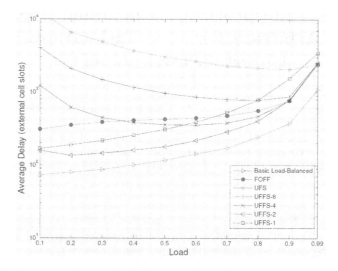

Fig. 3. Average delay under the bursty traffic model. Switch size is N = 16.

traffic but much poorer under bursty traffic. UFFS-4 has poorer performance than FOFF for load $\rho \leq 0.4$, but it outperforms FOFF at higher loads. UFFS-2 shows the best delay performance among algorithms that guarantee packet ordering.

4 Conclusion

In this paper, we proposed the UFFS-k algorithm for performance guarantees in load-balanced switch. We compare the performance of UFFS-k to existing scheduling algorithms for load-balanced switches through simulation. The simulation results demonstrate that generally the performance of UFFS-k is improved as aggregate factor decreases. UFFS-2 outperforms existing scheduling algorithms that guarantee packet ordering. Furthermore, UFFS-2 shows close performance compared to the basic load-balanced switch without packet ordering guarantees under bursty traffic model so do UFFS-1 under uniform Bernoulli traffic model.

References

1. Keslassy, I.: The Load-Balanced Router, Ph.D. Thesis, Stanford University (2004)
2. Fomenkov, M., Keys, K., Moore, D., Claffy, K.: A longitudinal study of internet traffic from 1998-2001: a view from 20 high performance sites. In: Proc. of WISICT 2004, Mexico (2004)
3. Iyer, S., McKeown, N.: Analysis of the parallel packet switch architecture. IEEE/ACM Transactions on Networking, 314.324 (2003)
4. Chang, C.S., Lee, D.S., Jou, Y.S.: Load balanced Birkhoff-von Neumann switches, Part I: one-stage buffering. Computer Communications 25, 611.622 (2002)
5. http://klamath.stanford.edu/tools/SIM/

A Static Multiprocessor Scheduling Algorithm for Arbitrary Directed Task Graphs in Uncertain Environments

Jun Yang[1,2,*], Xiaochuan Ma[1,**], Chaohuan Hou[1], and Zheng Yao[3]

[1] Institute of Acoustics, Chinese Academy of Sciences
[2] Graduate University, Chinese Academy of Sciences
[3] Department of Electronic Engineering, Tsinghua University, China

Abstract. The objective of a static scheduling algorithm is to minimize the overall execution time of the program, represented by a directed task graph, by assigning the nodes to the processors. However, sometimes it is very difficult to estimate the execution time of several parts of a program and the communication delays under different circumstances. In this paper, an uncertain intelligent scheduling algorithm based on an expected value model and a genetic algorithm is presented to solve the multiprocessor scheduling problem in which the computation time and the communication time are given by stochastic variables. In simulation examples, it shows that the algorithm performs better than other algorithms in uncertain environments.

Keywords: scheduling, parallel processing, stochastic programming, genetic algorithm.

1   Introduction

Given a program represented by directed acyclic graph (DAG), the objective of a static scheduling algorithm is to minimize the overall execution time of the program by properly assigning the nodes of the graph to the processors before executing any process. This scheduling problem is known to be NP-complete in general, and algorithms based on heuristic search, such as [1] and [2], have been proposed to obtain optimal and suboptimal solutions.

There are several fundamental flaws with those static scheduling algorithms even if a mathematical solution exists, because the algorithms assume that the computation costs and communication costs which denoted by the weights of nodes and edges in the graph are determinate.

In practice, sometimes it is very difficult to estimate the execution times of various parts of a program without actually executing the parts, for example, one

* The author would like to thank Yicong Liu (LOIS, Chinese Academy of Sciences) for her valuable comments and suggestions.
** This paper is supported by commission of science technology and industry for national defence, China (No. A1320070067).

A. Bourgeois and S.Q. Zheng (Eds.): ICA3PP 2008, LNCS 5022, pp. 18–29, 2008.

part has an iterative process and the actual times of iteration is data-dependent. Therefore, scheduling these parts without using actual execution times is innately inaccurate. In addition, some systems may also have communication delays that vary under different circumstances, and it could also be difficult to incorporate variable communication delays in static scheduling problem. If we turn to dynamic scheduling, it does incur an additional overhead which constitutes a significant portion of the cost paid for running the scheduler during execution.

In this paper, we address only the static scheduling problem, and assume that all the computation costs and communication costs are random variables, the multiprocessor system is non-preemptive and can be heterogeneous. This paper presents an uncertain intelligent scheduling algorithm based on stochastic simulation and genetic algorithm to solve the multiprocessor scheduling problem in uncertain environments.

2   Problem Description

2.1   The DAG Model

In static scheduling, a program can be represented by a DAG [3] $G = (V, E)$, where V is a set of v nodes and E is a set of directed edges. A node in the DAG represents a task which is a set of instructions that must be executed sequentially without preemption in the same processor. The weight of a node, which represents the amount of time needed for a processor to execute the task, is called the *computation cost* of the node. The edges in the DAG correspond to the communication messages and precedence constraints among the nodes. The weight of an edge, which represents the amount of time needed to communicate the data, is called the *communication cost* of the edge.

The source node of an edge incident on a node is called a *parent* of that node. Similarly, the destination node emerged from a node is called a *child* of that node. A node with no parent is called an *entry* node and a node with no child is called an *exit* node. The precedence constraints of a DAG dictate that a node cannot start execution before it gathers all of the messages from its parent nodes. The communication cost among two nodes assigned to the same processor is assumed to be 0.

The processors in the target system may be heterogeneous or homogeneous. Heterogeneity of processors means that the processors have different speeds. We assume the processors can be heterogeneous, which means every part of a program can be executed on any processor though the computation time needed on different processors may be different. However, we simply assume the communication links are always homogeneous.

The notations used in the paper are summarized in Table 1. Computation costs and communication costs are considered as uncertain variables. Specially, $\omega_k(n_i)$ denotes uncertain computation cost of node n_i on processor k in heterogeneous environments. An example DAG, shown in Fig. 1, will be used as an example later.

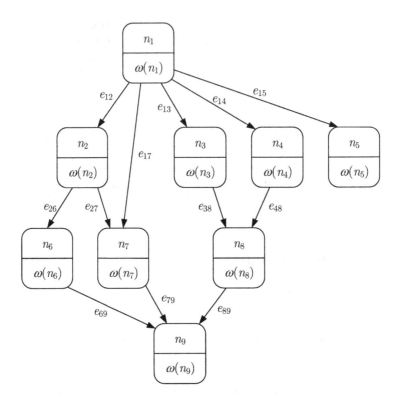

Fig. 1. Example of a DAG

Table 1. Definitions of Some Notations

Symbol	Definition
n_i	Node number of a node in the task graph
v	Number of nodes in the task graph
p	Number of processors in the target system
$\omega(n_i)$	Uncertain computation cost of n_i
$\omega_k(n_i)$	Uncertain computation cost of n_i on processor k
e_{ij}	Directed edge from n_i to n_j
$c(n_i, n_j)$	Uncertain communication cost of e_{ij}
$Parent(n_i)$	The set of parents of n_i
$Child(n_i)$	The set of children of n_i
$\mathbf{x}, \mathbf{y}$	Integer decision vectors
$\mathbf{x'}, \mathbf{y'}$	Legal integer decision vectors
$t(n_i)$	T-level of node n_i
$l(n_i)$	Legal-order-level of node n_i
$FT(n_i)$	Finish-time of node n_i
f	Makespan of a schedule

2.2 Computing Top Levels

The top level [3] (*t-level*) of a node n_i is the length of a longest path (there can be more than one longest path) from an entry node to n_i excluding n_i.

An algorithm for computing the t-levels is shown below. Because computation costs and communication costs are supposed to be stochastic variables in this paper, notations in the algorithm, like $\omega(n_i)$ and $c(n_i, n_j)$, denote *samples* of computation costs and communication costs. In the algorithm, t is a vector for storing t-levels.

. Construct a list of nodes in topological order. Call it *Toplist*.
. for each node n_i in *Toplist* do
. $max = 0$
.   for each node $n_x \in Parent(n_i)$ do
.   if $t(n_x) + \omega(n_x) + c(n_x, n_i) > max$ then
. $max = t(n_x) + \omega(n_x) + c(n_x, n_i)$
.   endif
.   endfor
. $t(n_i) = max$
. endfor

3 Scheduling Representation

The scheduling in this paper is represented by Liu's[4] formulation via two decision vectors [4] $\mathbf{x}$ and $\mathbf{y}$, where $\mathbf{x} = (x_1, x_2, \ldots, x_v)$ is an integer decision vector representing v nodes with $1 \leq x_i \leq v$ and $x_i \neq x_j$ for all $i \neq j$ and $i, j = 1, 2, \ldots, v$. That is , the sequence $\{x_1, x_2, \ldots, x_v\}$ is a rearrangement of $\{1, 2, \ldots, v\}$. And $\mathbf{y} = (y_1, y_2, \ldots, y_{p-1})$ is an integer decision vector with $y_0 \equiv 0 \leq y_1 \leq y_2 \leq \ldots \leq y_{p-1} \leq v \equiv y_p$.

We note that the schedule is fully determined by the decision vectors $\mathbf{x}$ and $\mathbf{y}$ in the following way. For each $k(1 \leq k \leq p)$, if $y_k = y_{k-1}$, processor k is not used; if $y_k > y_{k-1}$, processor k is used and processes nodes $n_{x_{y_{k-1}+1}}, n_{x_{y_{k-1}+2}}, \ldots, n_{x_{y_k}}$ in turn. Thus the schedule of all processors is as follows:

Processor 1: $n_{x_{y_0+1}} \rightarrow n_{x_{y_0+2}} \rightarrow \ldots \rightarrow n_{x_{y_1}}$;
Processor 2: $n_{x_{y_1+1}} \rightarrow n_{x_{y_1+2}} \rightarrow \ldots \rightarrow n_{x_{y_2}}$;

$\ldots$

Processor p: $n_{x_{y_{p-1}+1}} \rightarrow n_{x_{y_{p-1}+2}} \rightarrow \ldots \rightarrow n_{x_{y_p}}$.

3.1 Generating Legal Schedule

For a given random integer decision vectors $(\mathbf{x}, \mathbf{y})$, we have to rearrange them to guarantee that the precedence constraints are not violated. For example, if there are precedence relations between two nodes n_i and n_j, $e_{ij} \in E$, and both of them are assigned to the same processor, we should guarantee that n_i will be executed before n_j. If there are no precedence relations between two nodes, however, they can be executed in any order in that processor.

We can get a legal schedule by rearranging the list of nodes within each processor by ascending order of t-levels. However, the t-level ordering condition is only a necessary condition, so the optimal schedule may not satisfy it. To reduce the likelihood of this happening, we define legal-order-levels which is generated from t-levels of nodes. The algorithm to compute legal-order-levels is shown below. In the algorithm, t is a vector of t-levels and l is a vector for storing legal-order-levels.

- . Construct a list of nodes in topological order. Call it *Toplist*.
- . for each node n_i do
- .   Initialize $l(n_i) = t(n_i)$
- . endfor
- . for each node n_i in *Toplist* do
- .   Compute $max = \max\{l(n_j)\}, n_j \in Parent(n_i)$
- .   Compute $min = \min\{l(n_j)\}, n_j \in Child(n_i)$
- .   Generate a random $l(n_i)$ which satisfies $min < l(n_i) < max$
- . endfor

Finally we can compute legal integer decision vectors $(\mathbf{x}', \mathbf{y}')$ by rearranging nodes of the scheduling which is determined by $(\mathbf{x}, \mathbf{y})$. The steps are listed as follows.

- . Compute t-level $t(n_i)$ for each node n_i
- . Compute legal-order-levels $l(n_i)$ for each nodes n_i
- . for each integer k, $1 \le k \le p$ do
- .   if $y_k > y_{k-1}$ then
- .   Resort $(x_{y_{k-1}+1}, x_{y_{k-1}+2}, \ldots, x_{y_k})$ by ascending order of legal-order-levels
- .   endif
- . endfor
- . $\mathbf{x}' = \mathbf{x}$
- . $\mathbf{y}' = \mathbf{y}$

3.2   Stochastic Programming Model

For the multiprocessor scheduling problem, we can consider factors such as throughput, makespan, and processor utilization for the objective function. The objective function used for our algorithm is based on makespan, the overall finish-time of a parallel program. The makespan of a schedule is defined as follows:

$$f(\omega, c, \mathbf{x}', \mathbf{y}') = \max_{n_i \in V} FT(n_i) \tag{1}$$

$FT(n_i)$ denotes finishing time of node n_i. For a given DAG, the makespan is a function of computation costs ω, communication costs c and the legal schedule $(\mathbf{x}', \mathbf{y}')$.

In this paper, the makespan of a schedule is also uncertain because all the computation costs and communication costs are given by stochastic variables. We introduce an stochastic expected value model which optimizes the expected makespan subject to some expected constraints. We assume that the expected makespan $E[f]$ should not exceed the target value b. Thus we have a constraint $E[f] - b = d^+$, in which $d^+ \vee 0$ (the positive deviation) will be minimized. Then, we have the following stochastic expected value model:

$$
\begin{cases}
\min d^+ \vee 0 \\
\text{subject to:} \\
\quad E[f(\omega, c, \mathbf{x}', \mathbf{y}')] - b = d^+ \\
\quad \omega(n_i), n_i \in V, \text{stochastic variables} \\
\quad c(n_i, n_j), e_{ij} \in E, \text{stochastic variables} \\
\quad (\mathbf{x}', \mathbf{y}'), \text{legal integer decision vectors}
\end{cases}
\tag{2}
$$

In order to compute the uncertain function $E[f]$, first, a legal schedule $(\mathbf{x}', \mathbf{y}')$ is generated from $(\mathbf{x}, \mathbf{y})$. Second, we repeat N times to generate ω and c according to their probability measure and use the samples to compute $f_i = f(\omega, c, \mathbf{x}', \mathbf{y}'), i = 1, 2, \ldots, N$. Finally, the value $E[f]$ is estimated by $\frac{1}{N} \sum_{i=1}^{N} f_i$ provided that N is sufficiently large, which is followed from the strong law of large numbers.

Note that other stochastic models such as stochastic chance-constrained model and stochastic dependent-chance model can also be used under different circumstances for modeling different stochastic systems. Stochastic simulations based on those stochastic models will be used. In this paper, without loss of generality, we only discuss the simplest one, stochastic expected value model.

4   Uncertain Intelligent Scheduling Algorithm

In this paper, we present an uncertain intelligent scheduling algorithm based on stochastic simulation and genetic algorithm to solve the stochastic expected value programming problem. From the mathematical viewpoint [4], there is no difference between deterministic mathematical programming and stochastic programming except for the fact that there exist uncertain functions in the latter. If the uncertain functions can be converted to their deterministic forms, we can obtain equivalent deterministic models. However, in general, we cannot do that. It is thus more convenient to deal with them by stochastic simulations. Genetic algorithm is a stochastic search method for optimization problems based on the mechanics of natural selection and natural genetics and it has demonstrated considerable success in providing good solutions to many complex optimization problems. The standard genetic algorithm is shown below.

. Generate initial population
. while number of generations not exhausted do
  .   for $i = 1$ to *PopulationSize* do
  .   Randomly select two chromosomes and crossover

·   Randomly select one chromosome and mutation

·   endfor

·   Evaluate chromosomes and perform selection

· endwhile

· Report the best chromosome as the final solution

The initialization, evaluation, crossover and mutation operations, which are used in our algorithm, are revised as follows.

4.1   Initialization

We encode a schedule into a chromosome $(\mathbf{x}, \mathbf{y})$, where $\mathbf{x}, \mathbf{y}$ are the same as the decision vectors. For the gene section $\mathbf{x}$, we define a sequence $\{x_1, x_2, \ldots, x_v\}$ with $x_i = i$, $i = 1, 2, \ldots, v$. In order to get a random rearrangement of $\{1, 2, \ldots, v\}$, we repeat the following process from $j = 1$ to v: generating a random position v' between j and v, and exchanging the values of x_j and $x_{v'}$. For each i with $1 \leq i \leq p - 1$, we set y_i as a random integer between 0 and v. Then we rearrange the sequence $\{y_1, y_2, \ldots, y_{p-1}\}$ from small to large and thus obtain a gene section $\mathbf{y} = (y_1, y_2, \ldots, y_{p-1})$. Finally, $(\mathbf{x}, \mathbf{y})$ is used to generate and replaced by legal integer decision vectors $(\mathbf{x}', \mathbf{y}')$ to guarantee that the produced schedule is legal. In this way, we can ensure that the produced chromosome $(\mathbf{x}, \mathbf{y})$ is always feasible.

4.2   Evaluation

Evaluation function is to assign a probability of reproduction to each chromosome so that its likelihood of being selected is proportional to its fitness relative to the other chromosomes in the population. That is, the chromosomes with higher fitness will have more chance to produce offspring by using roulette wheel selection.

We define the rank-based evaluation function as $a(1 - a)^{i-1}$, $i = 1, 2, \ldots,$ *PopulationSize*, where $a \in (0, 1)$ is a given parameter. Note that $i = 1$ means the best individual, $i = PopulationSize$ the worst one.

4.3   Crossover

Let us illustrate the crossover operator on the pair $(\mathbf{x}_1, \mathbf{y}_1)$ and $(\mathbf{x}_2, \mathbf{y}_2)$. First, we generate legal integer decision vectors for $(\mathbf{x}_1, \mathbf{y}_2)$ and $(\mathbf{x}_2, \mathbf{y}_1)$, which are denoted as $(\mathbf{x}_1', \mathbf{y}_2')$ and $(\mathbf{x}_2', \mathbf{y}_1')$. Then, two children are produced by the crossover operation as $(\mathbf{x}_1', \mathbf{y}_2')$ and $(\mathbf{x}_2', \mathbf{y}_1')$. Note that the obtained chromosomes $(\mathbf{x}_1', \mathbf{y}_2')$ and $(\mathbf{x}_2', \mathbf{y}_1')$ in this way are always feasible.

4.4   Mutation

We mutate the parent $(\mathbf{x}, \mathbf{y})$ in the following way. For the gene $\mathbf{x}$, we randomly generate two mutation positions v_1 and v_2 between 1 and v. If $v_1 \leq v_2$, we rearrange the sequence $x_{v_1}, x_{v_1+1}, \ldots, x_{v_2}$ at random to form a new sequence $x'_{v_1}, x'_{v_1+1}, \ldots, x'_{v_2}$. Else, we rearrange the sequence $x_1, x_2, \ldots, x_{v_2-1}$, $x_{v_1+1}, x_{v_1+2}, \ldots, x_v$ at random to form two new sequences $x'_1, x'_2, \ldots, x'_{v_2-1}$ and $x'_{v_1+1}, x'_{v_1+2}, \ldots, x'_v$.

Similarly, for the gene $\mathbf{y}$, we generate two random mutation positions v_1 and v_2 between 1 and $p-1$, and set y_i as a random integer number y'_i between 0 and v for $i = v_1, v_1+1, \ldots, v_2$ if $v_1 \leq v_2$. Or $i = 1, 2, \ldots, v_2-1, v_1+1, v_1+2, \ldots, v$ if $v_1 > v_2$. We then rearrange the sequence from small to large and obtain a new gene section $\mathbf{y}$. Finally, we generate legal integer decision vectors $(\mathbf{x}', \mathbf{y}')$ and replace the parent with the offspring $(\mathbf{x}', \mathbf{y}')$.

5   Performance Results

In this section, we use the DAG shown in Figure 1, and assume that the number of processors is 4. Note that the problem is NP-hard even if the variables are constants. So the solution of our algorithm may be near-optimal, as other genetic algorithms. In this section, we focus on the differences between stochastic environments and constant environments. The simulation results show that our algorithm often succeed in finding best schedule that fit more to the real applications from those schedules which are considered the same in other algorithms that use constant computation costs and communication costs.

Example 1. In the first example, we assume that processors in target system are homogeneous, and all of the computation costs and communication costs are normally distributed variables, which may fit more than other distributions to real applications. An normally distributed random variable is denoted by $N(\mu, \sigma^2)$, where μ and σ are given real numbers. If we use the *means* of computation costs and communication costs in Table 2 instead of the random variables, we can get schedules produced by several list scheduling algorithms [3] such as dynamic critical path (DCP) algorithm[5], modified critical path (MCP) algorithm[6] and so forth. The schedule generated by the DCP algorithm is shown below,which is an optimal schedule (makespan = 16) under determinate costs assumption. We denote it as *DCP-1*.

Table 2. Normally distributed computation costs and communication costs

Symbol	Definition	Symbol	Definition	Symbol	Definition
$\omega(1)$	$N(2,1)$	$\omega(2)$	$N(3,1)$	$\omega(3)$	$N(3,1)$
$\omega(4)$	$N(4,1)$	$\omega(5)$	$N(5,1)$	$\omega(6)$	$N(4,1)$
$\omega(7)$	$N(4,1)$	$\omega(8)$	$N(4,1)$	$\omega(9)$	$N(1,1)$
$c(1,2)$	$N(4,1)$	$c(1,3)$	$N(1,1)$	$c(1,4)$	$N(1,1)$
$c(1,5)$	$N(1,1)$	$c(1,7)$	$N(10,1)$	$c(2,6)$	$N(1,1)$
$c(2,7)$	$N(1,1)$	$c(3,8)$	$N(1,1)$	$c(4,8)$	$N(1,1)$
$c(6,9)$	$N(5,1)$	$c(7,9)$	$N(6,1)$	$c(8,9)$	$N(5,1)$

Processor 1: $n_4 \rightarrow n_8 \rightarrow n_6 \rightarrow n_9$;
Processor 2: $n_1 \rightarrow n_2 \rightarrow n_7$;
Processor 3: $n_3 \rightarrow n_5$;
Processor 4: is not used.

Actually there are some more optimal schedules in this problem. Another optimal schedule produced by DCP with different scheduling list [2] is denoted by *DCP-2* shown below.

Processor 1: $n_1 \rightarrow n_2 \rightarrow n_7$;
Processor 2: $n_4 \rightarrow n_8 \rightarrow n_9$;
Processor 3: $n_3 \rightarrow n_5$;
Processor 4: n_6.

The schedule produced by MCP algorithm which is not an optimal schedule (makespan = 20) is shown below and denoted by *MCP*.

Processor 1: $n_1 \rightarrow n_4 \rightarrow n_2 \rightarrow n_7 \rightarrow n_9$;
Processor 2: $n_3 \rightarrow n_6$;
Processor 3: n_8;
Processor 4: n_5.

We suppose that the target value of expected makespan is $b = 0$. A run of the uncertain intelligent scheduling (UIS) algorithm (10000 cycles in stochastic simulation, 400 generations in genetic algorithm) shows that the optimal schedule which is denoted by *UIS-1* is

Processor 1: $n_1 \rightarrow n_2 \rightarrow n_7 \rightarrow n_8 \rightarrow n_9$;
Processor 2: $n_4 \rightarrow n_5$;

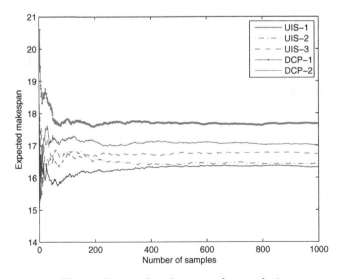

Fig. 2. Expected makespans of example 1

Processor 3: n_3;
Processor 4: n_6.

Note that the schedules DCP-1, DCP-2 and UIS-1 are all optimal schedules under determinate costs assumption, but they perform differently when costs have uncertainty. In uncertain environment, simulation results show that the expected makespans (10000 samples in simulation) of MCP, DCP-1, DCP-2 and UIS-1 are 20.34, 17.59, 16.97 and 16.41.

Example 2. In the second example, one processor in target system is heterogeneous and a little faster than the other three. Without lose of generality, we assume that Processor 1 is a little faster. The computation costs on this processor are listed in Table 3. A run of UIS Algorithm (10000 cycles in stochastic simulation, 400 generations in genetic algorithm) shows that the optimal schedule is

Processor 1: $n_1 \rightarrow n_2 \rightarrow n_7 \rightarrow n_8 \rightarrow n_9$;
Processor 2: $n_3 \rightarrow n_5$;
Processor 3: n_4;
Processor 4: n_6.

We denote the schedule as *UIS-2*. The 4 schedules in the former example are also used in simulation. To guarantee that the best schedule is obtained, we suppose that the processor to which most nodes are assigned is the faster one. In uncertain environment, simulation results show that the expected makespans (10000 samples in simulation) of MCP, DCP-1, DCP-2 ,UIS-1 and UIS-2 are 19.11, 16.91, 15.76, 15.39 and 15.32.

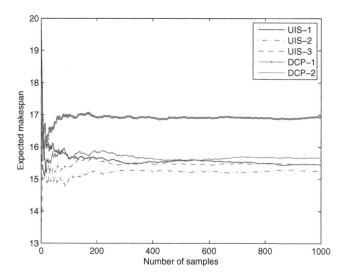

Fig. 3. Expected makespans of example 2

Table 3. Computation costs on Processor 1 in heterogeneous system

Symbol	Definition	Symbol	Definition	Symbol	Definition
$\omega_1(1)$	$N(1.5, 1)$	$\omega_1(2)$	$N(2.5, 1)$	$\omega_1(3)$	$N(2.5, 1)$
$\omega_1(4)$	$N(3.5, 1)$	$\omega_1(5)$	$N(4.5, 1)$	$\omega_1(6)$	$N(3.5, 1)$
$\omega_1(7)$	$N(3.5, 1)$	$\omega_1(8)$	$N(3.5, 1)$	$\omega_1(9)$	$N(1, 1)$

Example 3. In the third example, we also use the heterogeneous system in the second example. But all the real numbers σ^2 in $N(\mu, \sigma^2)$ are changed from 1 to 0.5. A run of UIS Algorithm (10000 cycles in stochastic simulation, 400 generations in genetic algorithm) shows that the optimal schedule is

Processor 1: $n_1 \rightarrow n_2 \rightarrow n_7 \rightarrow n_5$;
Processor 2: $n_6 \rightarrow n_8 \rightarrow n_9$;
Processor 3: n_4;
Processor 4: n_3.

We denote the schedule as *UIS-3*. In uncertain environment, simulation results show that the expected makespans (10000 samples in simulation) of MCP, DCP-1, DCP-2 ,UIS-1, UIS-2 and UIS-3 are 18.58, 16.23, 15.24, 15.04, 15.02 and 14.77.

The results of the three examples are listed in Table 4. We can see that MCP performs poor because the schedule is not optimal even in the constant costs assumption. However, the other 5 schedules are all optimal (makespan=16) in the case that the costs are constant. They performs differently in uncertain environments. Part of the results are shown in Fig. 2, Fig. 3 and Fig. 4. The curves show the first 1000 samples in the simulation results and MCP is not

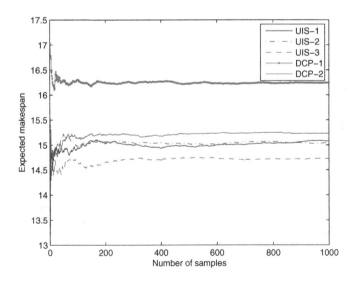

Fig. 4. Expected makespans of example 3

Table 4. Simulation Results (10000 samples in simulation)

Example	System	σ^2	MCP	DCP-1	DCP-2	UIS-1	UIS-2	UIS-3
1	homogeneous	1	20.34	17.59	16.97	*16.41*	16.45	16.66
2	heterogeneous	1	19.11	16.91	15.76	15.39	*15.32*	15.42
3	heterogeneous	0.5	18.58	16.24	15.24	15.04	15.02	*14.77*

included because the schedule is not optimal even in the case that the costs are constant.

6 Conclusions

In this paper, we present an uncertain intelligent scheduling algorithm to solve the multiprocessor scheduling problem in uncertain environments. We introduce an expected value model based on stochastic simulation and devise a genetic algorithm to obtain optimal solution. In simulation examples, it shows that our algorithm performs better than other algorithms in uncertain environments.

References

1. Hou, E.S.H.: A genetic algorithm for multiprocessor scheduling. IEEE Transaction on Parallel and Distributed Systems 5(2), 113–120 (1994)
2. Kwok, Y.K., Ahmad, I.: Efficient scheduling of arbitrary task graphs to multiprocessors using a parallel genetic algorithm. Journal of Parallel and Distributed Computing (47), 58–77 (1997)
3. Kwok, Y.K., Ahmad, I.: Static scheduling algorithms for allocating directed task graphs to multiprocessors. ACM Computing Surveys 31(4), 406–471 (1999)
4. Liu, B.: Theory and Practice of Uncertain Programming, 1st edn. Physica-Verlag, Heidelberg (2002)
5. Kwok, Y.K., Ahmad, I.: Dynamic critical-path scheduling: An effective technique for allocating task graphs to multiprocessors. IEEE Tran. Parallel Distrib. Syst. 7(5), 506–521 (1996)
6. Wu, Gajaki: Hypertool: A programming aid for message-passing systems. IEEE Trans. Parallel Distrib. Syst. 1(3), 330–343 (1990)

An ACO Inspired Strategy to Improve Jobs Scheduling in a Grid Environment

Marilena Bandieramonte, Antonella Di Stefano, and Giovanni Morana

Dept. of Computer Science and Telecommunication engineering,
Catania University, Italy
{marilena.bandieramonte,ad,gmorana}@diit.unict.it

Abstract. Scheduling is one of the most crucial issue in a grid environment because it strongly affects the performance of the whole system. In literature there are several algorithms that try to obtain the best performance possible for the specified requirements; taking into account that the issue of allocating jobs on resources is a combinatorial optimization problem, NP-hard in most cases, several heuristics have been proposed to provide good performance. In this work an algorithm inspired to Ant Colony Optimization theory is proposed: this algorithm, named Aliened Ant Algorithm, is based on a different interpretation of pheromone trails.

The goodness of the proposed algorithm, in term of load balancing and average queue waiting time, has been evaluated by mean of a vast campaign of simulations carried out on some real scenarios of a grid infrastructure.

Keywords: scheduling algorithms, grid computing, simulation, ant colony optimization, aliened ant.

1 Introduction

Grid[8][9][10] is a distributed infrastructure that concurs to connect various type of resources (in terms of power of calculation, memory, etc) and to share them. Grids offer different types of resources belonging to scalable groups of research organizations without a particular geographic characterization named Virtual Organization(VO)[8][9]. Grids are used for High Performance Computing (HPC) applications and, also, for business applications. In the HPC scenarios typically, grid users are scientists that need instrumentation for HPC and cooperate on experiments done on a huge quantity of data. The grid services allow e-scientists to approach calculation power, storage capability and information stages, guaranteeing an access co-ordinated and controlled to them, offering to these customers the visibility of a unique computation system to which submit the jobs.

In a grid environment the jobs scheduling strategy plays a crucial role since it influences the effective usage of system resources, that can be expressed by queue waiting time, job throughput and fair load balancing.

In this work, we propose an algorithm inspired from ACO[1] heuristic to face the scheduling problems in a grid environment. In particular we show how this

A. Bourgeois and S.Q. Zheng (Eds.): ICA3PP 2008, LNCS 5022, pp. 30–41, 2008.

algorithm allows to obtain good performance on two main scheduling issues: the first one is related to queue waiting time perceived by resources users, the second one is related to resources usage (load balancing and jobs throughput) perceived by resources managers.

The rest of the paper is organized as follows. Section 2 presents the main issues related to jobs allocation in grid. Section 3 introduces the Ant Colony Optimization theory and the concepts related to an ACO algorithm model. Then the Aliened Ant Algorithm is depicted. Section 4 presents the simulation results. Finally, Section 5 briefly concludes the work.

2   The Scheduling Issues in Grids

Generally, grid environments are composed by a wide quantity of different types of processing nodes, storage units, scientific instrumentation and information, belonging to different research organizations, exploited by users of a virtual organization (VO[8][9]). Each time a VO user submits a job in the grid, it has to make reference to a Resource Broker (in the follow RB). The aim of RB is to receive all job submission requests, to analyze the job requirements and features, to map jobs to the resources required for their execution and, finally, to dispatch them to the most suitable Computing Element (in the follow CE). Each CE handles the job management system (JMS) of the underlying cluster of Worker Nodes (in the follow WN). The aim of WNs is to execute jobs and to return their results to VO users. Scheduling policies are an essential part for the functioning of a Grid. The scheduling issue, on a grid environment, has many unique characteristics that make it different compared to traditional scheduling on parallel and distributed computing systems. For example, unlike the counterparts in traditional parallel and distributed systems, Grid schedulers usually cannot control Grid resources directly, but work like brokers or agents; also, in a Grid, resources are distributed in multiple domains then not only the computational

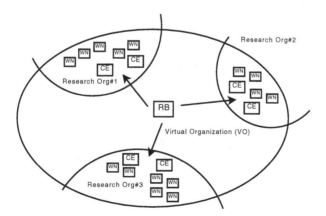

Fig. 1. Grid organization

and storage nodes, but also the underlying networks connecting them are heterogeneous.

Fig. 1 shows a typical example of grid deployment. In this type of hierarchical
organization it is possible to identify three scheduling layers. The first one is
related to the algorithm used by RB to distribute jobs among CEs; this algorithm
influences in a strong manner the performance of the whole system. The second
scheduling layer manages the jobs allocation done by the CE on its underlying
WNs. Finally lowest scheduling activity is related to the mechanism used by
the operating system(OS) of each WN to schedule jobs on its CPU. In the
following will be taken into account only the first two levels of scheduling: it has
been assumed that the OS scheduling is constituted by non preemptive FIFO
schedulers that link only one job per CPU at time (as used in HPC systems).

3   Aliened Ant Algorithm

In 1996 M. Dorigo [1,2,6,7] introduced the Ant Colony Optimization (ACO) theory . The main target of this algorithms class, that is inspired from the behavior
of real ants, is to solve several types of combinatorial optimization problems exploiting the self-organizing ability of these little bugs. The ants are able to solve
the issues related to colony survival communicating indirectly with each other.
A known example is represented by their ability to find minimum paths from
the colony to food in a brief time. This is possible because each ant marks the
found path with a chemical trail, called *pheromone*, in a quantity proportional
to quality and proximity of food. As greater is the amount of pheromone of a
path, as greater will be the probability that another ant, in looking for food, will
choose it reinforcing the pheromone quantity. Thus, while the level of pheromone
of the best path slowly grows, because of evaporation[1], the level of pheromone
of the other paths decreases. Following this algorithm, after a certain number of
iterations, all ants will follow the path with higher concentration of pheromone,
identifying it as the minimum path from the colony to food. The ACO class algorithms follow a theoretical formalization of the above mentioned ants behavior.
As expressed in [1], every ACO algorithm focuses on a parametric probabilistic
model, known as *pheromone model*. This model is characterized by parameters
vectors that store the tracks of pheromone, called *pheromone trail parameters*.
The steps of a generic ACO algorithm are the following: firstly the pheromone
tracks are initialized for each path(*step 0*); next, for each iteration, the ant a_i
builds a set of solutions for the combinatorial optimization problem (*step 1*) on
the basis of the value of pheromone tracks (that are updated, every time, with a
mechanism simulating the evaporation). From this solution set (*step 2*) the best
one is probabilistically extracted[2]. Finally, before the beginning of next cycle,
the ant releases the pheromone (*step 3*) on the selected path, to mark its choice.

---

[1] Over time, the pheromone trails start to evaporate, reducing their attractive
strength.

[2] This is done through a specific policy related to application context.

Doing so, for each iteration, the algorithm is able to find the best solution for the considered problem.

Recently, several studies investigate the ACO theory, both producing theoretic formulation about this issue and proposing application to face several problems. In this paper it is proposed an algorithm, freely inspired from ACO theoretical formulation, that allows to obtain a suboptimal solution for the scheduling problem in a Grid environment: the *Aliened Ant Algorithm*. The aim of this algorithm is to perform a scheduling policy that:

- guarantees a good load balancing,
- provides a reasonable response time,
- is able to adjust itself on changing of jobs load and network conditions.

Also, referring to grid environments explained in Section 2, this algorithm can be used both in the first and in the second scheduling layers. There are many versions of ACO based algorithms, each different from the others because of the mechanisms used to update pheromone: some examples in literature are AS-update rule (*ant-system*) used in AS algorithm [4], and IB-update rule (*iteration-best*) and BS-update rule (*best-so-far*) used in ACS (Ant Colony System)[5] and MMAS (Max-Min Ant System) algorithms [3].

The proposed solution differentiates itself from other approaches since it is based on a reverse interpretation of pheromone trails.

3.1   Algorithm Description

The proposed solution, inspired from mentioned ACO algorithm, takes into account the behavior of an ideal aliened ant.

This ant stays away from tussle and prefers the paths where it can found the least number of other ones. In order to achieve this it smells pheromone trails but, instead of following the path where the pheromone trail is stronger (as the other normal ants), it takes the path with the lighter one. For the aliened ant, in fact, a tenuous pheromone trails on a path means that either only few ants have taken the path or much time has passed from the last use of the path.

Doing a comparison between the aliened ant and a job and considering resources as paths, it is possible to transform the behavior of the aliened ant in a job scheduling algorithm.

Referring to the sequence of steps describing the functioning of generic ACO depicted in the previous section, the proposed algorithm can be explained as follows:

Step 0: pheromone trails initialization Vectors, representing all links between the scheduler and the resources, are created: in our model this is done linking RB with CEs and each CE with its WNs. The pheromone trails in each vector are initialized with a value that is inversely proportional to the computational power of the linked resource; this allows to reach speedily the steady state condition.

Step 1 and Step 2: trails evaluation (construction and selection of solution) and pheromone evaporation Each time a job arrives at the scheduler, it has to decide in which node the job has to be allocated. In our algorithm this decision is taken basing on pheromone trails, following the strategy of the aliened ant. The scheduler assigns a probability value to the underlying resources, basing on the value of the relevant entry in the trails vector. The probability for the *ith* resource is calculated as:

$$1 - \frac{phres_i}{phresTOT} \tag{1}$$

where $phres_i$ is the value of pheromone trail related to the ith resource and $phresTOT$ is the sum of pheromone trails of all resources.

The lower is the pheromone value the greater is the probability to select the resource. In order to simulate pheromone evaporation, at each scheduling cycle there is an update of trails vector entries value. Each entry is updated basing on:

- computational power of the relevant resource: this assures that the greater is the resource power the greater is the speed of pheromone evaporation and, consequently, the probability to select the resource.
- the elapsed time: this guarantees the logical consistency between the pheromone evaporation mechanism and the time spent in jobs scheduling.

The evaporation mechanism, that is applied to all entries of trails vector, follows the formula below:

$$\Delta PhT = -(elTime * compPower_i) \tag{2}$$

where ΔPhT^3 represents the updating value of pheromone trail, $elTime$ is the time (in minutes) elapsed since last update operation and $compPower_i$ is a value related to the computational power of ith resource.

Step 3: trails updating The mechanism used to update the trails values is very simple and it is based on the estimation of tasks duration (obtained either from scheduler job profiling or from user indication). Each time a job is scheduled, the trail value, related to resource in which the job has been sent, is increased by a quantity equals to the estimation of the job execution time, expressed in minutes.

$$\Delta PhT = jobExTime \tag{3}$$

The pseudo-code below summarizes the Aliened Ant Algorithm:

Aliened Ant - C style pseudo code

---

[3] It should be noted that the PhT value can not be less than zero. If the PhT, after the updating process has a negative value, it is rounded to zero.

```
trailInit(pherVector[]);

void AlienedAnt(pherVector[], taskTimeEval){
    //evaporation step
    for (i=0;i<pherVectorLenght;i++){
    pherVector[i] = pherVector[i] - evap(elasedTime,resNumber);
    }
    //solution creation->resource selection step
    res = evalPher(pherVector);
    //pheromone trail update step
    pherVector[res] = pherUpdate(TaskTimeEval);
    return;
}
```

4   Simulations Campaign

The performance evaluations of the proposed algorithm and the comparisons with other solutions have been done on a real grid model using the Simgrid[11] simulator. Simgrid is a toolkit that provides core functionalities for the simulation of distributed applications in heterogeneous distributed environments; it enables the simulation for the specific purpose of developing and evaluating scheduling algorithms on distributed resource infrastructure defined by the user. The measures have been done considering:

- the system behavior when changing of load in terms of (i) submitted jobs number and (ii) composition of jobs type (i.e. proportion among short, medium and long jobs)
- the system behavior in case of wrong estimation of jobs execution time.

In order to evaluate the performance, two evaluation concerns have been taken into account: the first one is related to queue waiting time perceived by resource users, the second one is related to resources usage (load balancing and jobs throughput) perceived by resource managers. In the following, we shortly depict the grid model, the algorithms compared with the proposed one and, finally, we show the results.

4.1   Reference Infrastructure

The grid model used for the simulations, reproduces a realistic scenario: the Cometa PI2S2 grid infrastructure[4]. This grid infrastructure involves 3 sites (in the cities of Catania, Palermo and Messina, including Universities and Research Centers) where 7 clusters of Worker Nodes are managed by the relevant Computing Elements, coordinated by a single Resource Broker, related to the various research organizations forming part of the consortium. The

---

[4] Cometa is a multi-entity consortium for the promotion and adoption of advanced computing technologies: www.consorzio-cometa.it.

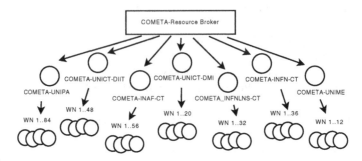

Fig. 2. PI2S2 grid infrastructure

number of these Worker Nodes changes from a Computing Element to another one. The grid and the jobs flow model were created considering the information related (i) to the types and the distribution of resources in the real PI2S2[5] grid infrastructure and (ii) to the dimension of the waiting queues for different type of jobs typically submitted by the users.

4.2   The Scheduling Algorithms Used for a Comparison

The Aliened Ant Algorithm has been compared with other algorithms, which are briefly described below.

Random-based scheduling. This algorithm (in the follow *RbS*) is used only to demonstrate that the adoption of an intelligent scheduling algorithm is a necessary condition to obtain good performances. Although causality makes this algorithm insensible both to load increasing and to all possible errors considered, simulations show that it is always convenient to adopt intelligent scheduling mechanisms.

RoundRobin scheduling. This algorithm (in the follow *RR*) aims to be fair in distributing jobs between CEs or WNs. Used at both RB and individual CE level, this algorithm ensures an equal jobs distribution on underlying resources. This algorithm is very simple: the scheduler (RB or CE) keeps (i) a list of all the suitable resources (CE or WN) and (ii) the position of the last resource scheduled (initially the first resource of the list); every time a job has to be scheduled, the scheduler (RB or CE) takes from the list the resource positioned immediately after the last one used.

Scheduling based on resources availability. This algorithm (in the follow *RA*), used at RB level, ensures that the jobs are submitted to the various CEs based on the number of the available underlying resources (WN). This means that, unlike the previous two algorithms, the RB is aware of the overall structure of the network[6] and gives more jobs, in a proportional manner, to CE with more

---

[5] These information can be found at www.pi2s2.it.
[6] The RB knows how many WNs there are on each CE.

available resources. While the RR algorithm assigns $\frac{m}{nCEs}$ jobs to each CE (m is the number of jobs and $nCEs$ is number of CEs), this one assigns to each CE $nWN_i * \frac{m}{nWN_{TOT}}$ job (m is the number of jobs, nWN_i is the number of WNs of ith CE and nWN_{TOT} is the number of all WNs in the considered grid). This ensures a fair resources distribution at the level of CE and tends to reduce the queue waiting times if compared to the RR algorithm. In practice the RB assigns to each CE a probability of being chosen by the scheduling mechanism that is proportional to the number of underlying WNs.

CE_dedicated scheduling. This algorithm (*CED* in the follow) maps specific types of jobs to a specific CE used, exclusively, to execute these types of jobs. In order to do this, the RB has to know more information, about resources distribution and jobs types, respect to the previous ones; in fact, it is necessary that the RB, besides the knowledge of the WNs number of each CE (also needed in the last proposed one) must have an estimation of the execution time of each job (estimation obtained from profiling operation or from user indication).

Considering three different types of jobs (small<10min, medium<100m and long>100 min), the CED scheduling algorithm assigns a set of CEs (consequently a set of WNs) to each type of job based on a prediction of the workload composition. Using a job load composed by 15% of long, 75% of medium and 10% of short, it has been decided to order the CEs by number of its WNs and to reserve the two most powerful CE to long jobs, the two less ones to short jobs and the remaining ones to medium jobs. At CE scheduling level, the jobs are distributed on underlying WNs in a round robin way.

WN_dedicated scheduling. This algorithm (*WND* in the follow), similarly to the previous, assigns a number of different resources to different types of jobs but, unlike the previous one, the distinction is done locally at each CE. This algorithm is built on the real one used in the PI2S2 grid infrastructure where each CE presents a queue for each specific job type. In practice, each CE reserves a certain number of WNs to the various types of job based on load type expectation; in the adopted configuration, every CE reserves the 50 % of its WNs to long jobs, the 30 % to medium jobs and the remaining 20 % to short jobs. The proportion job-WNs is chosen on the basis of the same considerations made for the previous algorithm. At the RB scheduling level, the jobs are distributed on underlying CEs in a round robin way.

4.3   Performance Evaluations Results

This section briefly discusses the results of the measures obtained by led simulations to evaluate the proposed Aliened Ant (AA) algorithm.
The considered evaluation scenarios make reference to:

- the real grid deployment, described above (see Fig. 2), which consists of 69 WNs (276 CPUs) distributed on 7 CEs under a single RB that receives jobs from 3 load generators (called User Interfaces into grid systems); one generator for each type of jobs.

– a workload consisting of three types of jobs, distinguished according to their execution time and named (i) "short" if their duration varies on range between 1 and 10 minutes, (ii) "medium" if varies between 10 and 100 minutes and (iii) "long" if their duration is more than 100 minutes. The jobs are composed using short(10%):medium(75%):long(15%) ratio, but other ratios are also considered to observe the general behavior.

The measures refer for each simulation to steady state condition. For each algorithm are evaluated:

– *the load balancing capability*. For each scheduling algorithm it will be shown the trend of jobs distribution among the CEs in terms of standard deviation (σ, named σlb): using this parameter, the performance of the algorithm is better when the value of σ is small (i.e $\sigma lb = 0$ means an equal jobs distribution on each CE, $\sigma lb >> 0$ means bad load balancing capability) .
– *the average queue waiting time*. For each scheduling algorithm the job average queue waiting time (named μqwt) is measured on each CE.

Behavior when changing the workload in terms of quantity of submitted jobs. The Fig. 3 shows the average queue waiting time and the standard deviation of load balancing when the number of jobs put in the grid grows. The measures have been done respectively from 1000 to 5000 jobs (1000 jobs per step), maintaining constant the jobs rate (jobs/s) and the proportion between jobs types short(10%):medium(75%):long(15%). In terms of μqwt, the AA, CED and RA algorithms give good results. In particular, the Aliened Ant Algorithm shows the best behavior. The other three algorithms present bad results: in particular,

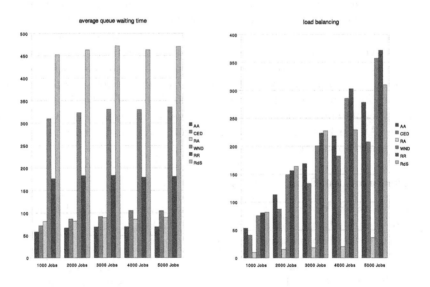

Fig. 3. μqwt and σlb when changing the workload in terms of quantity of submitted jobs

the Random algorithm gives the worst result, demonstrating the importance of a good scheduling algorithm. In terms of σlb, instead, all algorithms present the same behavior: their trend worsens with increasing workload size. As it is foreseeable, the RA algorithm shows the best load balancing capability.

Behavior when changing the ratio between jobs types. The Fig. 4 shows the average queue waiting time and the standard deviation of load balancing when it changes the proportion between short, medium and long jobs. The measures have been done with 3000 jobs respectively divided[7] in (1)2100: 600 :300, (2)1800: 600: 600, (3)1000: 1000, 1000, (4)600: 600: 1800, (5)300: 600: 2100. Generally, these results confirm what has been observed previously. The only exception is represented by CED algorithm since its behavior is related to the jobs types proportion in the workload: when there are a large amount of long jobs ((3),(4) and (5) measures), the performance of this algorithm is better than others in terms of μqwt but it shows bad behavior in terms of σlb. It should be noted that, also in this case, Aliened Ant presents very good performance in terms of μqwt.

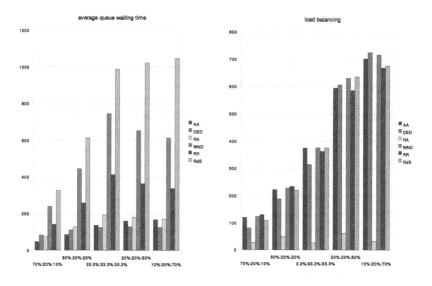

Fig. 4. μqwt and σlb when changing the ratio between jobs types

Behavior in presence of wrong jobs execution time estimation. The Fig. 5 shows the average queue waiting time and the standard deviation of load balancing when there are errors in the estimation of jobs execution time. Measures have been done when the estimation error is, respectively, 5, 10, 20, 25 and 30% of total execution time. In the figure are shown only the trends related to Aliened

---

[7] short:medium:long.

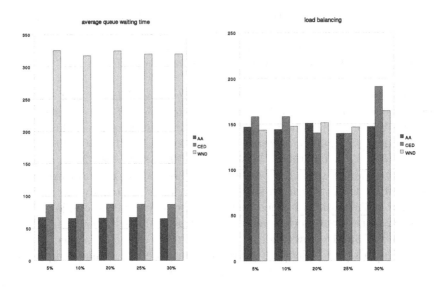

Fig. 5. μqwt and σlb in presence of wrong jobs execution time estimation

Ant, CED and WND (WND only in the μqwt fig.) algorithms since their behavior is related to jobs size estimation: other algorithms are insensitive regarding these types of errors. Measures have demonstrated that all algorithms taken into account present an high error tolerance since their performance remains approximately constant for considered errors percentage. This happens because, although an estimation could be wrong, it is very difficult to mistake a job belonging to a class with one belonging to another class (due to the different magnitude order).

5   Conclusion

This paper proposes the Aliened Ant algorithm, a heuristic technique freely inspired from Ant Colony Optimization theory that, in order to reduce the average queue waiting time, exploiting own interpretation of pheromone trails, is able to identify the least loaded computational resource among ones available in a Grid environment. In particular, here they were given a general algorithm description and a simulation campaign results to show the algorithm performance when it is used to face the jobs scheduling issues in a grid environment. Also, in the lead tests, a comparison with other scheduling algorithms performance is done.

As shown in Section 4.3 the proposed solution allows to obtain very good performance in term of average queue waiting time (measured on each CE composing the grid model used for simulation).

In the future our research will be focused (i) on discovery of new techniques to update pheromone trails and evaporation mechanism, (ii) on comparison between Aliened Ant algorithm and other bio-inspired heuristics and (iii) on evaluation of AA Algorithm with a distributed Resource Broker.

References

1. Dorigo, M., Blum, C.: Ant colony optimization theory: a survey. Journal Theoretical Computer Science 344(2-3), 243–278 (2005)
2. Sun, K.M.S.W.H.: Ant colony optimization for routing and load-balancing: survey and new directions. IEEE Trans. on Systems, Man and Cybernetics, Part A 33(5), 560–572 (2003)
3. Stytzle, T., Hoos, H.H.: MAX-MIN Ant system. Future Generation Computer Systems 16(9), 889–914 (2000)
4. Dorigo, M., Maniezzo, V., Colorni, A.: Ant system: optimization by a colony of cooperating agents. IEEE Trans. on Systems, Man and Cybernetics, Part B 26(1), 29–41 (1996)
5. Dorigo, M., Gambardella, L.M.: Ant colony system: a cooperative learning approach to the traveling salesman problem. IEEE Trans. on Evolutionary Computation 1(1), 53–66 (1997)
6. Merkle, D., Middendorf, M., Schmeck, H.: Ant colony optimization for resource-constrained project scheduling. IEEE Trans. on Evolutionary Computation 6(4) (2003)
7. Blum, C., Sampels, M.: An ant colony optimization algorithm for shop scheduling problems. Journal of Mathematical Modeling and Algorithms 3(3) (2004)
8. Kesselman, C., Foster, I., Tuecke, S.: The Anatomy of the Grid - Enabling Scalable Virtual Organizations. International Journal of High Performance Computing Applications 15(3), 200–222 (2001)
9. Foster, I., Kesselman, C., Nick, J., Tuecke, S.: The Physiology of the Grid: An Open Grid Services Architecture for Distributed Systems Integration. Open Grid Service Infrastructure WG, Global Grid Forum (2002)
10. Foster, I., Kesselman, C.: The Grid: Blueprint for a New Computing Infrastructure. Morgan Kaufmann Publishers (1999) ISBN: 1-558660-475-8
11. http://simgrid.gforge.inria.fr/

Architecture Aware Partitioning Algorithms*

Irene Moulitsas[1,2] and George Karypis[1]

[1] University of Minnesota, Department of Computer Science and Engineering
and Digital Technology Center and Army HPC Research Center
Minneapolis, MN 55455
[2] The Cyprus Institute, P.O. Box 27456, 1645 Nicosia, Cyprus
{moulitsa,karypis}@cs.umn.edu

Abstract. Existing partitioning algorithms provide limited support for
load balancing simulations that are performed on heterogeneous parallel
computing platforms. On such architectures, effective load balancing can
only be achieved if the graph is distributed so that it properly takes into
account the available resources (CPU speed, network bandwidth). With
heterogeneous technologies becoming more popular, the need for suitable
graph partitioning algorithms is critical. We developed such algorithms
that can address the partitioning requirements of scientific computations,
and can correctly model the architectural characteristics of emerging
hardware platforms.

1 Introduction

Graph partitioning is a vital pre-processing step for many large-scale applications that are solved on parallel computing platforms. Over the years the graph
partitioning problem has received a lot of attention [3, 12, 5, 1, 2, 7, 10, 11, 14, 15,
18, 19, 23, 20]. Despite the success of the existing algorithms, recent advances in
science and technology demand that new issues be addressed in order for the
partitioning algorithms to be effective.

The Grid infrastructure [9, 4] seems to be a promising viable solution for satisfying the ever increasing need for computational power at an affordable cost.
Metacomputing environments combine hosts from multiple administrative domains via transnational and world-wide networks into a single computational
resource. Even though message passing is supported, with some implementation
of MPI [8], there is no support for computational data partitioning and load

* This work was supported in part by NSF EIA-9986042, ACI-0133464, ACI-0312828,
and IIS-0431135; the Digital Technology Center at the University of Minnesota;
and by the Army High Performance Computing Research Center (AHPCRC) under
the auspices of the Department of the Army, Army Research Laboratory (ARL)
under Cooperative Agreement number DAAD19-01-2-0014. The content of which
does not necessarily reflect the position or the policy of the government, and no
official endorsement should be inferred. Access to research and computing facilities
was provided by the Digital Technology Center and the Minnesota Supercomputing
Institute.

A. Bourgeois and S.Q. Zheng (Eds.): ICA3PP 2008, LNCS 5022, pp. 42–53, 2008.
© Springer-Verlag Berlin Heidelberg 2008

balancing. Even on a smaller scale, clusters of PCs have become a popular alternative for running distributed applications. The cost effectiveness of adding new, and more powerful nodes to an existing cluster, and therefore increasing the cluster potential, is an appealing solution to a lot of institutions and researchers. We can clearly see that upcoming technologies have introduced a totally new class of architectural systems that are very heterogeneous in terms of computational power and network connectivity.

Most of the graph partitioning algorithms mentioned above compute a data partitioning that is suitable for homogeneous environments only. Recently there has been some work on partitioning for heterogeneous architectures, namely PaGrid [16,24], JOSTLE [22], MiniMax [21], and DRUM [6].

In the context of the widely used MeIIS [17] library, we have developed graph partitioning algorithms for partitioning meshes/graphs onto heterogeneous architectures. Our algorithms allow full heterogeneity in both computational and communication resources. We use a more accurate model to describe the communication cost instead of the notion of edgecut used in the algorithms mentioned above. We also do not solve the expensive and unscalable quadratic assignment problem, and we do not enforce a dense processor-to-processor communication.

In the remainder, Section 2 discusses the modeling of the computational graph and the heterogeneous architecture system. In Section 3 we present the problem formulation. In Section 4 we describe our proposed algorithms. Section 5 presents a set of experimental results. Finally Section 6 provides some concluding remarks.

2   Problem Modeling

The graph partitioning problem can be defined as follows: Given a graph $G = (V, E)$, where V is the set of vertices, $n = |V|$ is the number of vertices, and E is the set of edges in the graph, partition the vertices to p sets $V_1, ..., V_p$ such that $V_i \cap V_j = \emptyset$ for $i \neq j$ and $\bigcup V_i = V$, for $i, j = 1, ..., p$. This is called a p-way partitioning and is denoted by P. Every one of the subsets V_i is called a partition or subdomain. P is represented by a partition vector of length n, such that for every vertex $v \in V$, $P[v]$ is an integer between 1 and p, indicating the partition which v is assigned to.

2.1   Computational Graph Modeling

The graph G is a weighted graph if every vertex v is associated to either or both weights $w(v)$ and $c(v)$. If no specific weights are provided, we can assume that all vertices, have uniform weights. The first vertex weight w is assigned depending on the amount of computations performed by a vertex. The second weight c reflects the amount of data that needs to be sent between processors i.e., communication.

The majority of multilevel graph partitioning formulations have primarily focused on edgecut based models and have tried to optimize edgecut related objectives. In the edgecut model all the edges split between different partitions account as multiple communication messages. The edgecut metric is only an

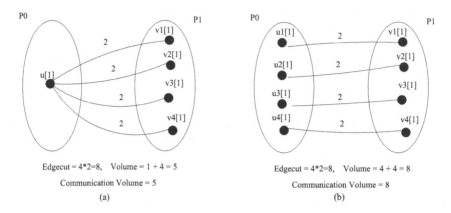

Fig. 1. Comparison between the edgecut and volume models

approximation of the total communication cost [13]. The actual communication may be lower and depends on the number of boundary vertices. For this reason we will focus on the **Volume** of a partitioning which we define as the total communication volume required by the partition. This measure is harder to optimize [13] than the edgecut.

Look at the two different scenarios presented in Figure 1(a) and (b). Let's assume vertex u and vertices u_1, u_2, u_3, u_4 are assigned to partition P_0, while vertices v_1, v_2, v_3, v_4 are assigned to partition P_1. We have noted the communication weights of every vertex in square brackets in the figure (i.e., $c(u_i) = 1$ and $c(v_i) = 1$ for all i). If the edgecut model was used, each one of the cut edges would have an edge weight of 2, as each one of the incident vertices to the edge has communication size of 1. Both of the partitionings presented in Figure 1, would incur an edgecut of 8. However, in Figure 1(a) the actual communication volume is only 5, as processor P_0 will send a message of size 1 to P_1, and P_1 will send four messages of size 1 to P_0. Only if the volume model is used, will we have an accurate estimate of the actual communication for both cases.

2.2   Architecture Graph Modeling

Partitioning for a heterogeneous environment requires modeling the underlying architecture. For our model we use a weighted undirected graph $A = (P, L)$, that we call the *Architecture Graph*. P is the set of graph vertices, and they correspond to the processors in the system, $P = \{p_1, \ldots, p_p\}$, $p = |P|$. The weights $w^*(\cdot)$ associated with the architecture graph vertices represent the processing cost per unit of computation. L is the set of edges in the graph, and they represent communication links between processors. Each communication link $l(p_i, p_j)$ is associated with a graph edge weight $e^*(p_i, p_j)$ that represents the communication cost per unit of communication between processors p_i and p_j.

If two processors are not "directly" connected, and the communication cost incurred between them is needed, we sum the squares of the weights of the shortest path between them. This is called a *quadratic path length* (QPL). In [22] it is shown that a *linear path length* (LPL) does not perform as well as the QPL. The insight is that LPL does not sufficiently penalize for cut edges across links that suffer from slower communication capabilities.

For our model we assume that communication in either direction across a given link is the same, therefore $e^*(p_i, p_j) = e^*(p_j, p_i)$, for $i, j = 1, \ldots, p$. We also assume that $e^*(p_i, p_i) = 0$, as the cost for any given processor to retrieve information from itself is incorporated in its computational cost $w^*(p_i)$.

Although the existing heterogeneous partitioning algorithms assume a complete weighted architecture graph, we find that this approach is not scalable and therefore avoid it. We provide more details in Section 4.

3   Metrics Definition

Given the proposed models for the computational graph and the architecture graph, we now define several metrics that will be used in our partitioning algorithms.

Computational Cost. This first metric is the cost a processor p_i will incur to perform computations, over all its assigned portion of vertices V_i:

$$CompCost_{p_i}^{V_i} = w^*(p_i) \times \sum_{v \in V_i} w(v)$$

The computational cost reflects the time needed by a certain processor to process the vertices assigned to it.

Communication Cost. This metric is the cost a processor p_i will incur for communicating, sending and receiving, any necessary information.

Each partition can distinguish between three types of vertices: (i) interior (local) vertices, those being adjacent only with local vertices, (ii) local interface vertices, those being adjacent both with local and non–local vertices, and (iii) external interface nodes, those vertices that belong to other partitions but are coupled with vertices that are assigned to the local partition. In the context of a parallel application, communication is performed only due to the internal and external interface vertices. Specifically, vertices that belong to category 2 will need to be sent to the corresponding neighboring processors, and vertices belonging to category 3 will need to be received from their hosting processor/partition.

The cost that a processor p_i will incur for communicating any information associated to its assigned portion of the vertices V_i of the computational graph:

$$CommCost_{p_i}^{V_i} = \sum_{v \in V_i} \left(\sum_{P(w), w \in adj(v)} e^*(p_i, P(w)) \times c(v) \right) +$$

$$\sum_{v \in V_i} \left(\sum_{w \in adj(v)} e^*(p_i, P(w)) \times c(w) \right)$$

where $adj(v)$ indicates the vertices adjacent to vertex v, and $P(w)$ is the processor/partition a vertex w is assigned to. In the above equation, please note that no communication links are double counted.

Processor Elapse Time. For every processor p_i, its elapse time (**ElTime**) is the time it spends on computations plus the time it spends on communications. Therefore, using the above definitions, the elapse time of processor p_i is:

$$ElapseTime_{p_i}^{V_i} = CompCost_{p_i}^{V_i} + CommCost_{p_i}^{V_i}$$

Processor Overall Elapse Time. By summing up the elapse times of all individual processors, we have an estimate of the overall time (**SumElTime**) that all processors will be occupied:

$$TotalElapseTime = \sum_{p_i \in P} ElapseTime_{p_i}^{V_i}$$

Application Elapse Time. The actual run time of the parallel application (**MaxElTime**) will be determined by that processor that needs the most time to complete. Therefore, no matter how good the quality of a partitioning is, its overall performance is driven by its "worst" partition:

$$ElapseTime = \max_{p_i \in P}\{ElapseTime_{p_i}^{V_i}\}$$

4   Framework for Architecture-Aware Partitioning

One of the key ideas of our architecture-aware partitioning algorithms is that they follow the two-phase approach. The purpose of the first phase is to focus entirely on the computational and memory resources of each processor and compute a problem decomposition that balances the demands on these resources across the different processors. The purpose of the second phase is to take into account the interconnection network characteristics (and its potential heterogeneity) and modify this partitioning accordingly so that it further optimizes the final problem decomposition. We will refer to this as the *predictor-corrector* approach, since the purpose of the second phase can be thought of as *correcting* the decomposition computed by the first phase. The motivation behind this approach is that it allows us to leverage existing high-quality partitioning algorithms for achieving the first phase, which even though in the context of network heterogeneity they tend to produce suboptimal partitionings, these partitionings are not arbitrarily poor. As a result, these partitionings can be used as building blocks for constructing good architecture-aware partitionings.

In all of our algorithms, the partitioning for the first phase is computed using the *kvmetis* algorithm from the MΞΤIS [17] library. This algorithm computes a p-way partitioning that takes into account the resource capabilities of each processor and minimizes the total communication volume. The partitioning for the second phase is computed by utilizing a randomized greedy refinement algorithm (similar to those used in MℰℐℐS's p-way partitioning algorithms) that moves vertices between partitions as long as such moves optimize the quality of the resulting decomposition.

We used two different approaches to assess the quality of the architecture-aware partitioning. The first is based on the maximum communication volume and the second is based on the application elapsed time. This leads to two different objectives functions that drive the refinement routines of the second phase. The first objective function tries to minimize the maximum communication volume while keeping the computational load proportional to the computational power of each processor. The second objective function couples the communication and computational requirements and tries to directly minimize the application elapsed time (i.e., the maximum elapsed time across the p processors). Note that both of these formulations attempt to compute decompositions that will be balanced. However, they use a different notion of "balance". The first treats computation and communication as two different phases and attempts to balance them individually, whereas the second one treats them in a unified way and attempts to balance them in a coupled fashion.

Our discussion so far assumed that each processor has full information about the communication cost associated with sending data between each pair of processors (i.e., $e^*(p_i, p_j)$). This is required in order to properly compute either the maximum communication volume or the application elapsed time. If the number of processors is small, this is not a major drawback, as the cost associated with determining and storing these values is rather small. However, for large number of processors, such an approach creates a number of problems. First, if we need to have accurate estimates of these costs, these values need to be determined during the execution of the partitioning algorithm (e.g., by using a program to send messages between all pairs of processors to explicitly measure them). This will increase the time required by the partitioning algorithm and impose a quadratic memory complexity, which in some cases can be the determining factor of the scalability of these algorithms. Second, if we rely on a network topology model to infer some of these communication costs, then we introduce a level of approximation in our models, which their inherent errors may nullify any improvements that can potentially be achieved by architecture-aware partitionings.

To overcome this problem, we augmented the maximum volume- and application elapsed time-based formulations to operate on a *sparse* representation of the architecture graph. The idea behind these formulations is to constraint the refinement algorithms of the second phase so that not to create decompositions that require communication between any additional pairs of processors beyond those required by the first phase decomposition. By imposing this addition constraint, then our two-phase algorithm needs to only estimate the communication costs associated with the pairs of communicating processors of the first phase, and use those to accurate evaluate the maximum communication volume and application elapsed time objectives. Since the first-phase decomposition was obtained using state-of-the-art graph partitioning algorithms, the pairs of processors that need to communicate is rather small and independent of the number of processors in the system. On the average, each subdomain will need to communication with a constant number of other subdomains. This greatly reduces the memory and time complexity associated with constructing the architectural graph, and leads to scalable architecture-aware partitioning algorithms.

In summary, using the above predictor-corrector framework, we developed four different architecture-aware partitioning algorithms that differ on the objective function that they use (maximum communication volume or application elapsed time) and whether or not they use a dense or a sparse architectural graph. We will refer to these algorithms using the names *VolNS* (maximum volume, non-sparse), *VolS* (maximum volume, sparse), *ElTNS* (elapsed time, non-sparse), and *ElTS* (elapsed time, sparse).

5   Experimental Results

We evaluated the performance of our algorithms using a wide variety of graphs and architecture topologies. The characteristics of the computation graphs are presented in Table 1. The size of these graphs ranged from 14K to 1.1M vertices.

The architecture graphs we used are presented in Figure 2. Figure 2(a) presents a one dimensional array. Figure 2(b) is a two dimensional array. Figure 2(c) presents an 8–node, 32–processor cluster. Each node has four tightly connected processors, and a fast interconnection network among its 4 processors. Communication between different nodes is slower Finally, Figure 2(d) shows a typical grid architecture. The top and bottom part may each be physically located in the same geographical location and each is a metacomputer. The intra-communication across the two parts is slower than the inter-communication locally for each one.

5.1   Quality of the Results

We compared the characteristics of the partitionings produced by the four algorithms described in Section 4 by looking at four performance metrics: maximum elapsed time (i.e., application elapsed time), sum of elapsed time over all processors, (total) edgecut, and total communication volume. Due to space constraints,

Table 1. Characteristics of the test data sets

	Name	# Vertices	# Edges	Description
1	144	144, 649	1, 074, 393	Graph corresponding to a 3D FEM mesh of a parafoil
2	auto	448, 695	3, 314, 611	Graph corresponding to a 3D FEM mesh of GM's Saturn
3	brack2	62, 631	366, 559	Graph corresponding to a 3D FEM mesh of a bracket
4	cylinder93	45, 594	1, 786, 725	Graph of a 3D stiffness matrix
5	f16	1, 124, 648	7, 625, 318	Graph corresponding to a 3D FEM mesh of an F16 wing
6	f22	428, 748	3, 055, 361	Graph corresponding to a 3D FEM mesh of an F22 wing
7	finan512	74, 752	261, 120	Graph of a stochastic programming matrix for financial portofolio optimization
8	inpro1	46, 949	1, 117, 809	Graph corresponding to a 3D stiffness matrix
9	m6n	94, 493	666, 569	Graph corresponding to a 3D FEM mesh of an M6 wing

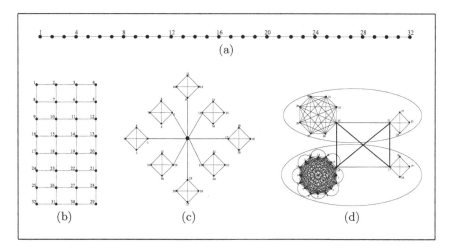

Fig. 2. (a) Arch32_1: 1D Array Processor Graph, (b) Arch32_2: 2D Array Processor Graph, (c) Arch32_3: Cluster of 8 compute nodes, (d) Arch32_4: Metacomputer

for each one of the architectures and algorithms, we report the average of these metrics over the nine graphs. These results are summarized in Figure 3.

From these results we can see that all four proposed algorithms lead to decompositions that have a lower application elapsed time than those computed by kvmetis (Figure 3(a)). This is true for both the maximum volume- and the application elapsed time-based formulations. These results show that non trivial reductions (10%–25%) in the applications elapsed time can be obtained by explicitly modeling and optimizing the communication characteristics of the architecture and problem. Comparing the two different objective functions, we see that the one that explicitly minimizes the application elapsed time leads to consistently better results than the one that just tries to minimize the maximum volume. This is not surprising, as the former is capable of better trading communication and computational costs towards the goal of reducing the maximum elapsed time. The results comparing the sum of the elapsed times over all processors (Figure 3(b)) provide some additional insights on the type of solutions produced by the two objective functions. In general, the volume-based objective function achieves lower values than those achieved by its elapsed time-based counterpart. This suggests that the dramatic improvements at the application elapsed time (i.e., maximum elapsed time) come at the expense of uniformly increasing the amount of time spent by all the processors.

Comparing the edgecut and volume of the resulting partitions (Figures 3(c) and(d)), we see that in general, the architecture-aware algorithms produced decompositions that have higher edgecuts than those produced by kvmetis, but lower communication volumes. This is not surprising, as the refinement algorithms used in the corrector phase, entirely ignore the edgecut and focus either on the maximum volume or the application elapsed time. These two objective functions better correlate with the total volume and as the results suggest, in

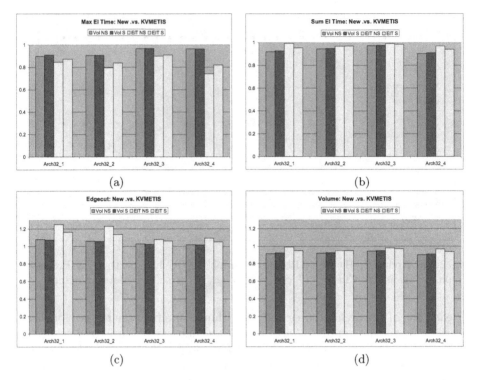

Fig. 3. Characteristics of the induced 32-way partitioning for Arch32_1, Arch32_2, Arch32_3, and Arch32_4

some cases it is at odds with minimizing the edgecut. This is also an indirect verification of the argument that eventhough the edgecut gives an indication of the communication volume, it is by no means an accurate measure of it. Indeed, by looking at Figure 3(c) we would have been misled as to say that our algorithms would have higher communication needs, which is not true as shown in Figure 3(d).

5.2   Comparison between Sparse and Non-sparse Algorithms

As discussed in Section 4, one of the main contributions of this work is that it also proposes sparse algorithms that are more scalable compared to the non-sparse refinement ones. Of course there lies a question regarding how much we have sacrificed in quality in order to achieve this scalability.

In Figure 4 we compare the sparse volume refinement algorithm with its non-sparse counterpart, and the sparse elapse time refinement algorithm with the non-sparse one. We have taken the ratio of the application elapse times of the sparse algorithms, over the application elapse times of the non-sparse ones. We have a total of 72 comparisons. We can see that in only 5 of the cases, did the

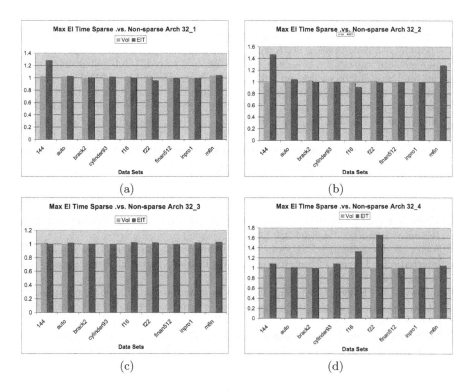

Fig. 4. Comparison of the sparse and non sparse approaches

sparse scalable algorithms produce worse results. In the remaining 67 cases, the qualities were comparable, and therefore we did not see any degradation.

6   Conclusions

The field of heterogeneous graph partitioning is a very new field and there is a lot of room for improvement. However the approaches described above represent a scalable solution that merits further investigation and development. We were able to produce partitions of high quality that can correctly model architecture characteristics and address the requirements of upcoming technologies.

References

1. Barnard, S.T.: Pmrsb: Parallel multilevel recursive spectral bisection. In: Supercomputing 1995 (1995)
2. Barnard, S.T., Simon, H.: A parallel implementation of multilevel recursive spectral bisection for application to adaptive unstructured meshes. In: Proceedings of the seventh SIAM conference on Parallel Processing for Scientific Computing, pp. 627–632 (1995)

3. Bui, T., Jones, C.: A heuristic for reducing fill in sparse matrix factorization. In: 6th SIAM Conf. Parallel Processing for Scientific Computing, pp. 445–452 (1993)
4. Chapin, S.J., Katramatos, D., Karpovich, J., Grimshaw, A.S.: The Legion resource management system. In: Feitelson, D.G., Rudolph, L. (eds.) Job Scheduling Strategies for Parallel Processing, pp. 162–178. Springer, Heidelberg (1999)
5. Diniz, P., Plimpton, S., Hendrickson, B., Leland, R.: Parallel algorithms for dynamically partitioning unstructured grids. In: Proceedings of the seventh SIAM conference on Parallel Processing for Scientific Computing, pp. 615–620 (1995)
6. Faik, J., Gervasio, L.G., Flaherty, J.E., Chang, J., Teresco, J.D., Boman, E.G., Devine, K.D.: A model for resource-aware load balancing on heterogeneous clusters. Technical Report CS-03-03, Williams College Department of Computer Science (2003), Submitted to HCW, IPDPS 2004
7. Fiduccia, C.M., Mattheyses, R.M.: A linear time heuristic for improving network partitions. In: Proc. 19th IEEE Design Automation Conference, pp. 175–181 (1982)
8. Message Passing Interface Forum. MPI: A message-passing interface standard. Technical Report UT-CS-94-230 (1994)
9. Foster, I., Kesselman, C.: Globus: A metacomputing infrastructure toolkit. The International Journal of Supercomputer Applications and High Performance Computing 11(2), 115–128 (1997)
10. Gilbert, J.R., Miller, G.L., Teng, S.-H.: Geometric mesh partitioning: Implementation and experiments. In: Proceedings of International Parallel Processing Symposium (1995)
11. Goehring, T., Saad, Y.: Heuristic algorithms for automatic graph partitioning. Technical report, Department of Computer Science, University of Minnesota, Minneapolis (1994)
12. Heath, M.T., Raghavan, P.: A Cartesian parallel nested dissection algorithm. SIAM Journal of Matrix Analysis and Applications 16(1), 235–253 (1995)
13. Hendrickson, B.: Graph partitioning and parallel solvers: Has the emperor no clothes (extended abstract). In: Workshop on Parallel Algorithms for Irregularly Structured Problems, pp. 218–225 (1998)
14. Hendrickson, B., Leland, R.: An improved spectral graph partitioning algorithm for mapping parallel computations. Technical Report SAND92-1460, Sandia National Laboratories (1992)
15. Hendrickson, B., Leland, R.: A multilevel algorithm for partitioning graphs. Technical Report SAND93-1301, Sandia National Laboratories (1993)
16. Huang, S., Aubanel, E.E., Bhavsar, V.C.: Mesh partitioners for computational grids: A comparison. In: Kumar, V., Gavrilova, M.L., Tan, C.J.K., L'Ecuyer, P. (eds.) ICCSA 2003. LNCS, vol. 2669, pp. 60–68. Springer, Heidelberg (2003)
17. Karypis, G., Kumar, V.: METIS 4.0: Unstructured graph partitioning and sparse matrix ordering system. Technical report, Department of Computer Science, University of Minnesota (1998), http://www.cs.umn.edu/~metis
18. Karypis, G., Kumar, V.: Multilevel k-way partitioning scheme for irregular graphs. Journal of Parallel and Distributed Computing 48(1), 96–129 (1998), http://www.cs.umn.edu/~karypis
19. Karypis, G., Kumar, V.: A fast and highly quality multilevel scheme for partitioning irregular graphs. SIAM Journal on Scientific Computing 20(1) (1999); A short version appears In: Intl. Conf. on Parallel Processing 1995, http://www.cs.umn.edu/~karypis
20. Schloegel, K., Karypis, G., Kumar, V.: Graph partitioning for high performance scientific simulations. In: Dongarra, J., et al. (eds.) CRPC Parallel Computing Handbook, Morgan Kaufmann, San Francisco (2000)

21. Kumar, R.B.S., Das, S.K.: Graph partitioning for parallel applications in heterogeneous grid environments. In: Proceedings of the 2002 International Parallel and Distributed Processing Symposium (2002)
22. Walshaw, C., Cross, M.: Multilevel Mesh Partitioning for Heterogeneous Communication Networks. Future Generation Comput. Syst. 17(5), 601–623 (2001) (originally published as Univ. Greenwich Tech. Rep. 00/IM/57)
23. Walshaw, C., Cross, M.: Parallel optimisation algorithms for multilevel mesh partitioning. Parallel Computing 26(12), 1635–1660 (2000)
24. Wanschoor, R., Aubanel, E.: Partitioning and mapping of mesh-based applications onto computational grids. In: GRID 2004: Proceedings of the Fifth IEEE/ACM International Workshop on Grid Computing (GRID 2004), Washington, DC, USA, pp. 156–162. IEEE Computer Society, Los Alamitos (2004)

A Simple and Efficient Fault-Tolerant Adaptive Routing Algorithm for Meshes

Arash Shamaei[1,2], Abbas Nayebi[1,3], and Hamid Sarbazi-Azad[1,3]

[1] IPM School of Computer Science
[2] Payeme Noor University
[3] Sharif University of Technology, Tehran, Iran
shamaei@ipm.ir, nayebi@ce.sharif.edu, azad@{ipm.ir,sharif.ir}

Abstract. The planar-adaptive routing algorithm is a simple method to enhance wormhole routing algorithms for fault-tolerance in meshes but it cannot handle faults on the boundaries of mesh without excessive loss of performance. In this paper, we show that this algorithm can further be improved using a flag bit introduced for guiding misrouted messages. So, the proposed algorithm can be used to route messages when fault regions touch the boundaries of the mesh. We also show that our scheme does not lead to diminish the performance of the network and only three virtual channels per physical channels are sufficient for tolerating multiple boundary faulty regions.

1 Introduction

Communication between processing nodes in mulicomputer is performed by message passing mechanism through the interconnection network. The nodes in the interconnection network, named routers, support a certain number of input and output channels. Links between routers connect output channels of one router to input channels of its neighboring routers, defining the network topology. The most popular topologies are orthogonal structures, e.g. n-dimensional meshes and k-ary n-cubes. A message is divided into packets and a packet is divided into flow control digits (flits). The flits are transmitted through the network one after another in a pipeline fashion called wormhole switching technique [1]. A flit of the message is designated as the header flit, which leads the message through the network. When the header flit is blocked due to lack of output channels, all of the flits wait at their current nodes for available channels.

A routing algorithm specifies how packets choose the path to their destinations. There are two types of routing algorithms: deterministic and adaptive. In deterministic routing only one path is determined through source to destination, while adaptive routing algorithms allow multiple paths. Although deterministic routing is generally simple and fast, but it cannot tolerate even single node or link failure. Since adaptive routing algorithms can use multiple paths from source to destination, it is appropriate to have fault-tolerant routing algorithms based on adaptive routing. Adaptive routing usually requires additional network resources. To avoid using extra physical channels, a physical channel can be shared by several virtual channels. Multiple buffers per each physical channel are used and share the bandwidth among several packets in

A. Bourgeois and S.Q. Zheng (Eds.): ICA3PP 2008, LNCS 5022, pp. 54–57, 2008.

time multiplex. In adaptive routing, deadlocks are usually avoided by using virtual channels and by separating network topology into several logical subclasses [2].

A well-known adaptive routing algorithm, planar-adaptive routing algorithm, was presented by Chen and Kim [3]. Their method uses three virtual channels per physical channel to handle fault blocks in n-dimensional meshes. Also planar-adaptive routing is very efficient and simple to use, but it cannot handle faults on the boundaries of mesh without excessive loss of computational power. For example, to handle a node fault in the tip row of a 2D mesh, all other nodes in that row must be labeled faulty. In this paper, we address the issue of improving planar-adaptive routing algorithm in order to handle boundary fault situation.

2 Planar-Adaptive Routing

The idea in planar-adaptive routing is to provide limited adaptivity by routing adaptively in a series of two-dimensional planes. Planar-adaptive routing restricts packets to be routed in plane A_0, then moving to plane A_1 and so on. Each adaptive plane A_i involves only two dimensions; d_i and d_{i+1}, while the order of dimensions is arbitrary. Within each adaptive plane, packets route adaptively with respect to first and second dimensions by choosing any channel that take it closer to the destination. In order to prevent deadlock, the traffic is divided into two classes: packets which need to increase (increasing) and decrease (decreasing) their d_i address. The virtual channels in A_i are divided into increasing and decreasing virtual networks which are completely disjoint. Routing in adaptive plane A_i reduces the distance in d_i to zero. If in plane A_i, the d_{i+1} distance is reduced to zero first, routing continues in d_i exclusively, until the d_i distance is reduced to zero.

Planar-adaptive networks can be augmented with misrouting around fault blocks to support fault-tolerance. The basic idea is to use the flexibility of the adaptive routing algorithm to circumvent any faulty channels. It assumes that both node and link fault model are detected. If faulty regions are not naturally convex, healthy nodes and channels are marked as faulty until the regions become convex. In fault-tolerant planar-adaptive routing, packets route in adaptive plane A_0 to A_{n-1}. For each adaptive plane A_i, if packets are not blocked by fault, route as in the fault-free case. If packets are blocked by fault only in one dimension, then routing continues in another dimension. If packets are blocked by a fault in d_i, and the d_{i+1} distance has already been reduced to zero, it is necessary to misroute. Misrouting around faulty region continues until d_{i+1} distance is reduced to zero again.

3 Improving the Fault-Tolerant Planar-Adaptive Routing

In this section, we present a scheme to handle faulty regions with boundary nodes. For the sake of clarity, we consider two dimensional meshes, while extensions to n-dimensional meshes can be done similarly. It is sufficient to apply the introducing method in each adaptive plane A_i.

To do so, we use the concept of f-chain similar to [4]. F-chain is a set of fault-free nodes adjacent to faulty regions which includes nodes on the boundary of the network. Each boundary node that resides on the f-chain is called end-node. So each f-chain has two end-nodes.

A one-bit flag is maintained by each node on the f-chains to facilitate fault-tolerant routing. After f-chains are constructed for the boundary fault regions, the following flag setting procedure is executed by each node on the f-chains to set the associated flag bit:

1. Initially, a node sets its flag to 0.
2. Each end-node of f-chain sets its flag to 1 and sends a set-1 message to its neighbor that is on the same f-chain.
3. If a node receives a set-1 message, sets its flag to 1. If the set-1 message is sent to it from a neighbor on dimension D and its neighbor on the opposite direction of the same dimension is also on the same f-chain, forward the set-1 message. Otherwise, consume the set-1 message.

After running the above procedure, some flag bits of some nodes residing on f-chains will change to 1 as shown in figure 1..Each node on the f-chains (except boundary nodes) saves the direction from which the set-1 message is received. This direction is called as forbidden direction.

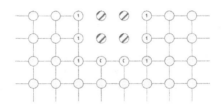

Fig. 1. The status of flag bits in f-chain

The modified fault-tolerant planar-adaptive routing acts as the preceding algorithm with the following changes when normal message encounters a node with flag bit 1:

- If there is only one optimal channel (the channel that leads a message to its destination on the optimal path) and it is faulty, the message misroutes around faulty region in the direction opposite to the forbidden direction. This case is shown in Figure 2a.
- If there are two optimal channels that one of them is faulty and the other one is in the same direction as the forbidden direction, the message misroutes around faulty region in the direction opposite to the forbidden direction as shown in Figure 2b.
- If there are two optimal channels that both of them are nonfaulty and one of them is in the same direction as the forbidden direction, the message chooses the other optimal channel as shown in Figure 2c.

We evaluate our method by a continues-time event-based flit-level simulator (Xmulator [5]) which is developed by the authors to achieve various results. Simulations are performed under various boundary fault regions with different message lengths and two different size of network to show that performance of the method does not degrade in contrast to the main method.

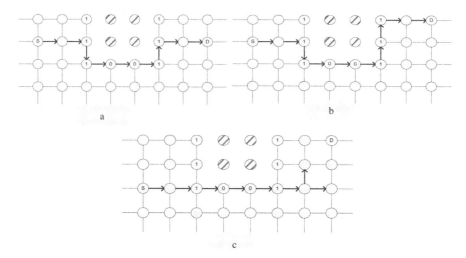

Fig. 2. Circumventing faulty regions when flag bit of node is 1.S: Source D: Destination

4 Conclusion

In this paper, we have presented a method to improve the fault-tolerant planar-adaptive routing. We used the concept of f-chain for each boundary faulty region of the network. A one-bit flag was maintained by each node on the f-chains to facilitate fault-tolerant routing and each node resides on f-chains saved the direction called forbidden direction. Routing decision was made according to the forbidden direction. We also showed how the proposed method can improve the performance of the network by saving many nodes wasted in the original routing algorithm.

References

1. Dally, W.J., Seitz, C.L.: Deadlock-free message routing in multiprocessor interconnection networks. IEEE Trans. Computers 36(5), 547..553 (1987)
2. Duato, J., Yalamanchili, S., Ni, V.: Interconnection Networks, an Engineering Approach. Morgan Kaufmann Publishers, USA (2003)
3. Chen, A.A., Kim, J.H.: Planar-Adaptive routing: Low-cost adaptive networks for multiprocessors. In: Proc. 19th Ann Int l Symp Computer Architecture, pp. 268..277 (1992)
4. Boppana, R.V., Chalasani, S.: Fault-tolerant wormhole routing algorithms for mesh networks. IEEE Trans. Computers 44(7), 848..864 (1995)
5. Nayebi, A., Meraji, S., Shamaei, A., Sarbazi-Azad, H.: XMulator: A Listener-Based Integrated Simulation Platform for Interconnection Networks. In: Asia Int l Conf. on Modelling and Simulation, pp. 128..132 (2007)

Deadlock-Free Adaptive Routing in 2D Tori with a New Turn Model

Dong Xiang*, Qi Wang, and Yi Pan

[1] School of Software
Tsinghua University
Beijing 100084, China
[2] Dept. of CS,
Tsinghua University
Beijing 100084, China
[3] Dept. of CS
Georgia State University
Atlanta, GA 30302, USA

Abstract. A new deadlock-free partially adaptive routing algorithm is proposed for 2− dimensional (2D) tori with only two virtual channels. The deadlock avoidance technique is presented based on a new turn model for 2D tori. In order to avoid cyclic channel dependencies completely, we propose the new odd-even turn model for 2D tori. The new model is an improved algorithm of the original turn model, and sets some constraints for some special turns. As far as we know, there is no existing algorithm for deadlock-free partially adaptive routing in 2D tori using only two virtual channels in the literature up to now. Sufficient simulation results are presented to demonstrate the effectiveness of the proposed algorithm by comparing with several previous methods.

Keywords: Deadlock avoidance, deadlock-free adaptive routing, odd-even turn model, torus, turn model.

1 Introduction

Torus-connected networks have been widely used in recent experimental or commercial multicomputers and processor-memory interconnects [1] [7] [9]. The number of virtual channels for deadlock-free routing and adaptivity provided by the routing scheme have great impact on performance of a routing algorithm.

Dally [3] presented the sufficient and necessary conditions for deadlock-free routing in an interconnection network. Sullivan, *et al.* [11] proposed a deadlock-free deterministic routing method for tori with two virtual channels. Duato's

---

* This work is supported in part by the National Science Foundation of China under grants 60373009, 60573055 and the Key Fundamental Research grant of School of Information Science, Tsinghua University from 985 grant of the Education Ministry under grant SIST3006.

A. Bourgeois and S.Q. Zheng (Eds.): ICA3PP 2008, LNCS 5022, pp. 58–69, 2008.

protocol [4] presented a fully adaptive deadlock-free routing method by using a combination of a base routing algorithm and additional adaptive virtual channels.

Linder and Harden [6] proposed a fully adaptive deadlock-free routing algorithm for k-ary n-cubes based on virtual network partitioning. The required number of virtual channels is $O(2^n)$. Puente, et al. [8] proposed novel routing method for virtual cut-through switched tori, which avoids deadlocks inside rings established by different dimensions by preventing packets from using the potentially last free buffer. The T3E [9] is a commercial machine based on the 3-dimensional torus topology. A fully adaptive routing scheme for 3-dimensional torus network with five virtual channels based a new dimension-order routing scheme and the Duato's protocol [4]. A load-balanced, non-minimal adaptive routing algorithm called GOAL for tori was proposed by Singh and Dally [10] with three virtual channels.

Glass and Ni [5] proposed an interesting partially adaptive routing algorithm call turn model to implement deadlock-free routing in meshes. This method removes cyclic channel dependencies by preventing some turns. The odd-even turn model proposed by Chiu [2] implements deadlock-free routing for 2D meshes by restricting the EN and NE turns on even columns and the ES and SE turns on the odd columns.

In this paper, we introduce a new partially adaptive algorithm for torus networks. This algorithm just uses two virtual channel to route the message, and improves the adaptability. The method is deadlock-free by using the new odd-even turn model

A new scheme for determination of the direction to route the message along both dimensions in 2D tori is introduced by using only two virtual channels in Section 2. A new odd-even turn model is proposed for 2D tori in Section 3. The new deadlock-free routing adaptive routing algorithm is presented in Section 4. Deadlock-freedom of the proposed routing scheme is presented in Section 5. Extensive simulation results are presented to compare with the dimension-order routing algorithm, some partially adaptive routing schemes in Section 6. The paper is concluded in Section 7.

2 Determination of the Routing Directions in 2-Dimensional Torus Networks

A Deadlock represents each of the packets that occupies some resource and waits for some other resource, which establish a cyclic dependency [3]. Adaptivity presents more flexibility for packet routing by presenting more choices at each intermediate node. A partially adaptive routing algorithm presents limited adaptivity at any intermediate nodes [2,5], while a fully adaptive routing algorithm allows a message to be routed along any possible paths, usually, all minimum paths [4]. A column is called an even (or odd) column if coordinate of the column is even (or odd) [2].

We shall present a deadlock avoidance technique for 2D tori with only two virtual channels. In this paper, two virtual channels are used for each physical channels. Two directions of a message must be determined when injecting into the network. Directions of a message can be determined by the procedure as presented Fig. 1.

The virtual channel assignment scheme can be stated as follows. Let a message be delivered along dimension x or y in direction $+$ according to the procedure in Fig. 1, the virtual channel $c_{x,1}+$ (or $c_{y,1}+$) must be used if $x_1 < x_2$ (or $y_1 < y_2$); otherwise, the virtual channel $c_{x,1}+$ (or $c_{y,1}+$) must be used. Let a message be delivered along dimension x or y in direction $-$ according to the procedure in Fig. 1, the virtual channel $c_{x,1}-$ (or $c_{y,1}-$) must be used if $x_1 > x_2$ (or $y_1 > y_2$); otherwise, the virtual channel $c_{x,2}-$ (or $c_{y,2}-$) must be used.

Determine-Route-Direction()
Input: Coordinates of source (x_1, y_1) and destination (x_2, y_2).
Output: Determined routing directions.

1. $A = x_2 - x_1$, $B = y_2 - y_1$;
2. Let $A \geq 0$ and $B \geq 0$, if $A \geq k/2$, $B \geq k/2$, $d_x = -$, $d_y = -$; if $A < k/2$, $B \geq k/2$, $d_x = +$, $d_y = -$; if $A \geq k/2$, $B < k/2$, $d_x = -$, $d_y = +$; if $A < k/2$, $B < k/2$, $d_x = +$, $d_y = +$.
3. Let $A \geq 0$ and $B < 0$, if $A \geq k/2$, $B \geq -k/2$, $d_x = -$, $d_y = -$; if $A < k/2$, $B \geq -k/2$, $d_x = +$, $d_y = -$; if $A \geq k/2$, $B < k/2$, $d_x = -$, $d_y = +$; if $A < k/2$, $B < k/2$, $d_x = +$, $d_y = +$.
4. Let $A < 0$ and $B \geq 0$, if $A \leq -k/2$, $B \geq k/2$, $d_x = +$, $d_y = -$; if $A \leq -k/2$, $B < k/2$, $d_x = +$, $d_y = +$; if $A > -k/2$, $B \geq k/2$, $d_x = -$, $d_y = -$; if $A > -k/2$, $B < k/2$, $d_x = -$, $d_y = +$.
5. Let $A < 0$ and $B < 0$, if $A \leq -k/2$, $B \leq -k/2$, $d_x = +$, $d_y = +$; if $A \leq -k/2$, $B > -k/2$, $d_x = +$, $d_y = -$; if $A > -k/2$, $B \leq -k/2$, $d_x = -$, $d_y = +$; if $A > -k/2$, $B > -k/2$, $d_x = -$, $d_y = -$.

Fig. 1. Determination of the routing directions

The procedure in Fig. 1 returns the directions of a message, inside which the message should be routed. Let A and B be the offsets of the destination (x_2, y_2) and source (x_1, y_1), where $A = x_2 - x_1$, and $B = y_2 - y_1$. In the procedure as shown in Fig. 1, d_x and d_y stand for the directions along dimensions x and y. Four separate cases are considered: (1) $A \geq 0$ and $B \geq 0$, (2) $A \geq 0$ and $B < 0$, (3) $A < 0$ and $B \geq 0$, and (4) $A < 0$ and $B < 0$. Let us consider case (4). The directions d_x and d_y should be $+$ and $+$, respectively when $A \leq -k/2$ and $B \leq -k/2$, and $+$ and $-$ when $A \leq -k/2$ and $B < k/2$. The directions d_x and d_y along dimensions x and y should be $-$ and $+$ when $A > -k/2$ and $B \leq -k/2$, and they are $-$ and $-$ when $A > -k/2$ and $B > -k/2$. Determination of the directions for other cases is similar.

After determining directions for both dimensions, a message can be delivered via the given virtual channels. The potential cyclic channel dependencies can be removed easily. The message is routed via the first virtual channel for a hop along a dimension if no wraparound channel along the dimension should be traversed to reach the destination; otherwise, the message must be delivered via the second virtual channel if a wraparound link has to be traversed.

There may exist enough cyclic channel dependencies in a 2D torus based on the above virtual channel assignment scheme. There may exist some potential cyclic channel dependency in any rectangular structure in the submesh, the rectangular structure constructed by some links in the submesh and some wraparound links can also establish some cyclic channel dependency. As for the cycles constructed by the four boundary wraparound links, cyclic channel dependencies can also be established. We would like to propose a deadlock-free routing method by using a new odd-even turn model for 2D tori.

3   Odd-Even Turn Model for 2D Tori

Virtual channel assignment scheme introduced above can easily remove cyclic channel dependencies produced by the rings along the same dimension. However, there may still exist some cyclic channel dependencies. In this section, we propose a new odd-even turn model for 2D tori [2]. These cyclic channel dependencies are completely removed by using our new odd-even turn model.

Definition 1. *A column is called an even (or odd) column if the coordinate of dimension x of the column is an even (or odd) number; a row is called an even (or odd) row if the coordinate of dimension y of the row is an even (or odd) number.*

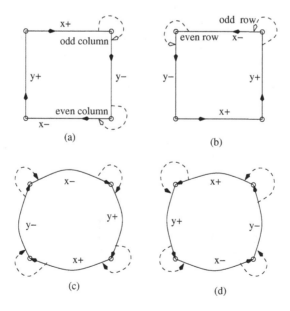

Fig. 2. Removal cyclic channel dependencies by a new turn model

As shown in Fig. 2, there can exist clockwise cycles and counter clockwise cycles. As for a clockwise cycle, an $x+$ channel turns to a $y-$ channel only at the odd column; a $y-$ channel turns to an $x-$ channel only at an even column. As for a counter clockwise cycle, a $y+$ channel turns to an $x-$ channel only at an odd row while an $x-$ turns to a $y+$ channel only at an even row. In this paper, any channel is in the same row or column as the router it leads to.

Constraining a turn from an $x+$ channel to a $y-$ channel only at the odd column and a turn from a $y-$ channel to an $x-$ channel only at an even column can make more messages staying in the x channels. Therefore, there may exist traffic conjestion on the x channels. Our method constrains a turn from a $y+$ channel to an $x-$ channel only at an odd row, and a turn from an $x-$ channel to a $y+$ channel only at an even row. Compared with the odd-even turn model in a 2D mesh, more balanced load can be obtained.

There may exist some extra cyclic channel dependencies contained two adjacent wraparound links as shown in Fig. 3. As shown in Fig. 3(a), wraparound links h and e can establish a cyclic channel dependencies h-e-i-c and h-e-b-c; the wraparound links g and f can also construct a cyclic channel dependencies g-f-i-c and g-f-d-c. We would like to introduce some special technique to avoid the above cyclic channel dependencies. As for the cyclic channel dependencies h-e-i-c and h-e-b-c, a turn from the wraparound link h along direction $y+$ to another wraparound link e along direction $x+$ uses virtual channel $c_{x,1}+$ instead of $c_{x,2}+$, where $c_{x,2}+$ channel should be used according to the virtual channel assignment scheme. Cyclic channel dependencies g-f-i-c and g-f-d-c can be avoided for the turn from the wraparound link g along direction $x+$ to another wraparound link f along direction $y+$ uses virtual channel $c_{y,1}+$ instead of $c_{y,2}+$.

The following two rules can be used to implement the new odd-even turn model in a 2D torus: (1) A message turns from an $x+$ channel to a $y-$ channel only at the odd columns, and a message turns from a $y-$ channel to an $x-$ channel only at even columns. and (2) A message turns from a $y+$ channel to an $x-$ channel only at odd rows, and a message turns from an $x+$ channel to a $y+$ channel only at the even rows.

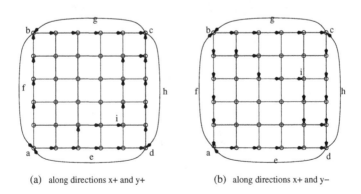

(a) along directions x+ and y+   (b) along directions x+ and y−

Fig. 3. Avoidance of cyclic channel dependencies with two adjacent wraparound links

Deadlock-free-route-in-2D-torus()
Input: Coordinates of the source (x_1, y_1) and the destination (x_2, y_2).
Output: A selected output channel.
{

   1. Call *Determine-Route-Direction*();
   2. if $d_x =+$, and $d_y =+$, *route1*();
   3. if $d_x =+$, and $d_y =-$, *route2*();
   4. if $d_x =-$, and $d_y =+$, *route3*();
   5. if $d_x =-$, and $d_y =-$, *route4*().

}

Fig. 4. Deadlock-free adaptive routing in 2D tori

As shown in Fig. 2(a), a turn from an $x+$ channel to a $y-$ channel happens only at the odd columns, and a turn from a $y-$ channel to an $x-$ channel only happens at the even columns when Rule 1 meets, which removes the clockwise cyclic channel dependencies. When Rule 2 is satisfied, the counter clockwise cyclic channel dependencies as presented in Fig. 2(b) can be removed.

4 Routing Algorithm

The procedure *Determine-Route-Direction*() returns the parameters d_x and d_y for the message classification given a pair of the source (x_1, y_1) and destination (x_2, y_2). The algorithm calls the routing procedures *route1*(), *route2*(), *route3*(), and *route4*() when the message falls into the message classes $d_x =+$ and $d_y =+$, $d_x =+$ and $d_y =-$, $d_x =-$ and d_y+, and $d_x =-$ and $d_y =-$, respectively.

Let A and B be offsets along dimensions x and y. The procedure in Fig. 5 presents the details to deliver a message in message class $d_x =-$ and $d_y =-$. There exist two kinds of constrained turns for this message class as shown in Figs. 2(a) and (b). Potential cyclic channel dependencies produced by the boundary wraparound channels as presented in Fig. 2(c) and (d), and the potential cyclic channel dependencies as presented in Fig. 3 should also be removed.

Let $A < 0$ and $B < 0$, and a message occupy a $y-$ channel in an even row, the next hop can be one of $c_{x,1}-$ and $c_{y,1}-$ channels because it does not need to traverse a wraparound link along dimensions x and y. Otherwise, the message selects $c_{y,1}-$ as the next hop if it is in an odd row. The message selects one of $c_{x,1}-$ and $c_{y,1}-$ as the next hop if it occupies an $x-$ channel in an even column; the message is delivered via channel $c_{x,1}-$ if it occupies an $x-$ channel in an odd column.

Let $A < 0$ and $B > 0$, the message must traverse a wraparound link along dimension y. One of $c_{x,2}-$ and $c_{y,1}-$ can be the next hop if the message occupies an $x-$ channel in an even row; let the message occupy an $x-$ channel in an odd row, the channel $c_{y,1}-$ should be the next hop. Assume the message occupies a $y-$ channel in an even column, one of $c_{x,2}-$ and $c_{y,1}+$ can be the next hop;

route4()
Input: The current node (x_1, y_1) and destination (x_2, y_2), $A = x_2 - x_1$, $B = y_2 - y_1$.
Output: A selected output channel.

1. Let $A < 0$ and $B < 0$, channel:= select($c_{x,1}-, c_{y,1}-$) if the message occupies a $y-$ channel in an even row; channel:= $c_{y,1}-$ if the message occupies a $y-$ channel in an odd row; channel:= select($c_{x,1}-, c_{y,1}-$) if the message occupies an $x-$ channel in an even column; otherwise, channel:= $c_{x,1}-$ if the message occupies an $x-$ channel in an odd column.

2. Let $A < 0$ and $B > 0$, channel:= select($c_{x,1}-, c_{y,2}-$) if the message occupies a $y-$ channel in an even row; channel:= $c_{y,2}-$ if the message occupies a $y-$ channel in an odd row; channel:= select($c_{x,1}-, c_{y,2}-$) if the message occupies an $x-$ channel in an even column; otherwise, channel := $c_{x,1}-$ if the message occupies an $x-$ channel in an odd column.

3. Let $A > 0$ and $B < 0$, channel:= select($c_{x,2}-, c_{y,1}-$) if the message occupies an $x-$ channel in an even row; channel:= $c_{y,1}-$ if the message occupies an $x-$ channel in an odd row; channel:= select($c_{x,2}-, c_{y,1}+$) if the message occupies a $y-$ channel in an even column; otherwise, channel := $c_{x,2}-$ if the message occupies a $y-$ channel in an odd column.

4. Let $A > 0$ and $B > 0$, if the message occupies a boundary wraparound link $x-$, channel:= select($c_{x,2}-, c_{y,1}-$); if the message occupies a boundary wraparound link $y-$, channel := select($c_{x,1}-, c_{y,2}-$); if the message occupies an $x-$ link in an odd column, channel:= select($c_{x,2}-, c_{y,2}-$); channel:= $c_{x,2}-$ if the message occupies a channel in an even column; if the message occupies an $y-$ channel in an even row, channel:= select($c_{x,2}-, c_{y,2}-$); channel:= $c_{y,2}-$ if the message occupies a link in an odd row.

5. If $A = 0$, channel := $c_{y,2}-$ if $B > 0$, and channel := $c_{y,1}-$ if $B < 0$; if $B = 0$, channel := $c_{x,2}-$ if $A > 0$, and channel := $c_{x,1}-$ if $A < 0$; return internal channel if $A = 0$, $B = 0$.

Fig. 5. Deadlock-free adaptive routing for a message along directions $x-$ and $y-$

let the message occupy a $y-$ channel in an odd column, $c_{x,1}-$ must be the next hop. The situation for $A > 0$ and $B < 0$ is similar, where a wraparound link along dimension x must be traversed.

Let $A > 0$ and $B > 0$, the message must traverse a wraparound link along both dimensions. Therefore, potential cyclic channel dependencies that contain two adjacent boundary wraparound links must be removed, which also include the ones as shown in Figs. 2(c) and (d). If a message occupies a boundary wraparound link $x-$, one of the channels $c_{x,2}-$ and $c_{y,1}-$ should be the next hop, while one of $c_{x,1}-$ and $c_{y,2}-$ can be the next hop if the message occupies a boundary wraparound link $y-$. Let the message occupies an $x-$ link in an odd column, one of the channels $c_{x,2}-$ and $c_{y,2}-$ should be the next hop; otherwise, $c_{x,2}-$ should be the next hop if the message occupies a channel in an even column. Let the message occupies an $y-$ channel in an even row, one of the channels $c_{x,2}-$ and $c_{y,2}-$ should be the next hop; otherwise, $c_{y,2}-$ must be the next channel if the message occupies a channel in an odd row. Deadlock-free adaptive routing for other two classes when $d_x =-$ and $d_y =-$, and $d_x =+$ and $d_y =-$ are similar.

5 Deadlock-Freedom Proof of the Deadlock Avoidance Technique in 2-Dimensional Tori

We would like to prove that a combination of the proposed virtual channel assignment scheme and new turn model truly presents a deadlock-free routing scheme for 2D tori. We need to prove that no cyclic channel dependency can be established based on the proposed adaptive deadlock-free routing algorithm.

Lemma 1. *There exists no cyclic channel dependency on the boundary wraparound links of the 2-dimensional torus based on the virtual channel assignment scheme and the routing algorithm.*

Proof: Fig. 6(a) presents the cyclic boundary wraparound links. We would like to show that the cycles does not establish any cyclic channel dependency.

As shown in Figs. 6(a) and (b), four messages can form cyclic channel dependencies. All channel dependencies can be illustrated as follows according to the routing algorithm introduced in Figs. 4 and 5: m_1 occupies $c_{y,2}-$ and requests $c_{x,1}-$, m_2 occupies $c_{x,2}-$ and requests $c_{y,1}+$, m_3 occupies $c_{y,2}+$ and requests $c_{x,1}+$, and m_4 occupies $c_{x,2}+$ and requests $c_{y,1}-$. As shown Fig. 6(b), no cyclic channel dependency can be established. □

Lemma 2. *There exists no cyclic channel dependency in any ring along the same dimension based on the virtual channel assignment scheme.*

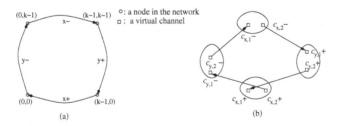

Fig. 6. Acyclic channel dependencies among the boundary wraparound links

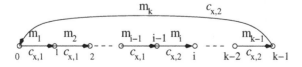

Fig. 7. Acyclic channel dependency of a ring

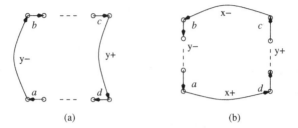

Fig. 8. Acyclic channel dependencies for directed cycles with wraparound links

Proof: Without loss of generality, let us consider the $x+$ rings as presented in Fig. 7. Situations for the $x-$ rings are similar. Two message classes (1) $d_x =+$ and $d_y =+$, and (2) $d_x =+$ and $d_y =-$ contain $x+$ rings. Both message classes use the same virtual channels to deliver a message along the $x+$ hops. That is, $c_{x,1}+$ is used for a message that does not need to traverse a wraparound channel, and $c_{x,2}+$ is used for messages that need to traverse a wraparound channel.

As shown in Fig. 7, the message m_1 occupies the virtual channel $c_{x,1}+$ of link $(0,1)$. There exists a virtual channel $c_{x,1}+$ dependency chain from 0 to $i - 1$. There exists at least one message m_{k-1} that occupies a virtual channel $c_{x,2}+$ and requests the same virtual channel on the wraparound link (k-1,0). The message m_k must occupy the $c_{x,2}$ virtual channel on the wraparound link and request the virtual channel $c_{x,1}$ of the wraparound link $(k-1,0)$ in order to establish a cyclic channel dependency. The potential cyclic channel dependency has been broken at the link $(i-1,i)$ because the message m_{i-1} requests the virtual channel $c_{x,1}+$ in any case.   □

Lemma 3. *Cyclic channel dependencies cannot be formed by the directed cycles as shown in Fig. 8, which contain two wraparound links.*

Proof: Let us consider the directed cycle as shown in Fig. 8(a), where the label at a channel shows the direction of that physical channel. Let us consider the corners c and d in Fig. 8(a), where a turn is allowed at an odd column and a turn is allowed at the corner d at an odd column m_1. Therefore, no cyclic channel dependency can be established.

As for a counter clockwise cycle as shown in Fig. 8(b), the proposed odd-even turn model allows a turn from a $y+$ channel to an $x-$ in an odd row, and a turn from an $x-$ channe to a $y-$ channel in an even row. Therefore, potential cyclic channel dependencies as presented in Fig. 8(b) cannot be established. Potential cyclic channel dependencies with two wraparound links also cannot be established similarly.   □

Theorem 1. *The proposed virtual channel assignment scheme and adaptive routing algorithm route() in 2D tori can avoid all potential cyclic channel dependencies.*

Proof: As presented in Lemmas 1-3, any potential cyclic channel dependencies as shown in Figs. 2, the potential cyclic channel dependencies as shown in Fig. 3, the potential cyclic channel dependencies established inside rings along the same dimension as presented in Fig. 7, and any potential cyclic channel dependencies with two wraparound links as shown in Fig. 6 can be removed completely. Therefore, no cyclic channel dependencies cannot be established.   □

6   Simulation Results

We have implemented the new deadlock-free adaptive routing algorithm in 2D tori. We have also extended the original west-first and negative-first deadlock-free routing algorithm for meshes [5] of the turn model [5] to 2D tori, where two virtual channels are used. The idea of the extended west-first, the negative-first, and the dimension-order [11] routing algorithms for any hop along a dimension in 2D tori is that the first virtual channel is used when no wraparound link is necessary to traverse along the dimension. The second virtual channel is used when a wraparound link along the dimension must be traversed to reach the destination.

The message length is set to 32 flits in all cases. All simulation results are presented for the 32×32 torus. The buffer size for each node is set to 24 flits in all cases for all methods. We present performance comparison with the dimension-order routing and the partially adaptive routing algorithms.

Fig. 9 presents performance comparison of the four methods based on the uniform communication pattern. The proposed new deadlock-free adaptive routing algorithm needs less latency to deliver a message in all cases. Latency to deliver a message for the proposed algorithm is much less than that of the dimension-order routing algorithm, the west-first algorithm and the negative-first algorithm after the normalized applied load is greater than 0.5. As for the normalized accepted traffic, the proposed algorithm does not show apparent advantage before the normalized applied load is greater than 0.8.

Fig. 10 presents performance comparison among four different methods for the transpose communication pattern, where a message at the source (i, j) must be sent to the destination $(31 - j, 31 - i)$. The source is selected randomly in all cases. The proposed method needs the least latency to deliver a message ind obtains much better normalized accepted traffic in all cases.

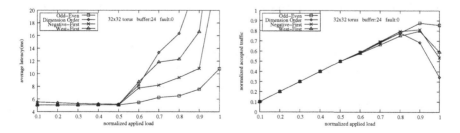

Fig. 9. Performance comparison with the partially adaptive routing and the deterministic routing scheme under the uniform communication pattern

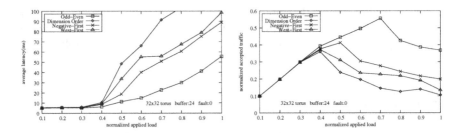

Fig. 10. Performance comparison with the partially adaptive or deterministic routing schemes under the transpose communication pattern

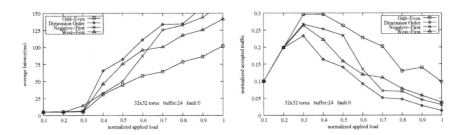

Fig. 11. Performance evaluation for the hotspot communication pattern with previous methods

Fig. 11 presents performance comparison of the four algorithms based on the hotspot communication pattern with two hotspot nodes. Fig. 11 shows performance of the four algorithms with 10% hotspot messages. The remaining 90% are injected under the uniform communication pattern. The proposed routing algorithm works the best in all cases, where the advantage of the proposed algorithm on both parameters over the previous methods is quite apparent.

7   Conclusions

A new adaptive deadlock-free routing algorithm for 2D tori is proposed based on a new turn model and virtual channel assignment scheme. The new virtual channel assignment scheme can successfully remove potential cyclic channel dependencies in rings along the same dimensions. The new odd-even turn model completely removes potential cyclic channel dependencies related to the mesh sub-network, where some techniques are introduced to avoid load-unbalancing. Extensive simulation results are presented by comparison with the dimension-order routing algorithm [11], and two partially adaptive routing algorithms, such as the west-first routing [5], and the negative-first routing [5] algorithms for 2D tori. The results indicate that our proposed method outperforms other related routing algorithms on 2D torus in all cases.

References

1. Allen, F., et al.: Blue gene: A vision for protein science using a petaflop supercomputer. IBM Systems Journal 40, 310–327 (2001)
2. Chiu, G.M.: The odd-even turn model for adaptive routing. IEEE Trans. on Parallel and Distributed Systems 11(7), 729–738 (2000)
3. Dally, W.J., Seitz, G.L.: Deadlock-free message routing in multiprocessor interconnection networks. IEEE Trans. on Computers 36(5), 547–553 (1987)
4. Duato, J.: A new theory of deadlock-free adaptive routing in wormhole networks. IEEE Trans. Parallel and Distributed Systems 4(12), 1320–1331 (1993)
5. Glass, C.J., Ni, L.: The turn model for adaptive routing. Journal of ACM 41(5), 874–902 (1994)
6. Linder, D., Harden, J.: An adaptive and fault-tolerant wormhole routing strategy for k−ary n−cube. IEEE Trans. Computers 40(1), 2–12 (1991)
7. Mukerhjee, S., Bannon, R., Lang, S., Spink, A.: The Alpha 21364 network architecture. IEEE Micro 22, 26–35 (2002)
8. Puente, V., Izu, C., Beivide, R., Gregorio, J., Vallejo, F., Prellezo, J.: The adaptive bubble router. Journal of Parallel and Distributed Computing 61, 1180–1208 (2001)
9. Scott, S., Thorson, G.: The Cray T3E network: Adaptive routing in high performance 3D torus. In: Proc. of Int. Symp. on Hot Interconnects, pp. 147–156 (1996)
10. Singh, A., Dally, W.J., Gupta, A., Towles, B.: GOAL: A load-balanced adaptive routing algorithm for torus networks. In: ACM/IEEE Int. Symp. on Computer Architecture, pp. 194–205 (2003)
11. Sullivan, H., Bashkow, T., Klappholz, D.: A large scale, homegeneous, fully distributed parallel machine. In: Proc. of ACM/IEEE Int. symp. on Computer Architecture, pp. 118–124 (1977)
12. Xiang, D., Zhang, Y., Pan, Y., Wu, J.: Deadlock-free adaptive routing in meshes based on cost-effective deadlock avoidance schemes. In: 36th Int. Conference on Parallel Processing (2007)

Neighbourhood Broadcasting and Broadcasting on the (n, k)-Star Graph

L. He[1], K. Qiu[1], and Z.Z. Shen[2]

[1] Department of Computer Science
Brock University
St. Catharines, Ontario, L2S 3A1 Canada
[2] Dept. of Computer Science and Technology
Plymouth State University
Plymouth, NH 03264
U.S.A.

Abstract. The (n, k)-star graph is a generalization of the star graph. We first present an optimal neighbourhood broadcasting algorithm for the (n, k)-star, which is then used to develop an optimal broadcasting algorithm for it. Both algorithms are for the single-port model of the network. While our neighbourhood broadcasting is the first such algorithm designed for the network, our optimal $O(\log(n!/(n - k)!))$-time $(=O(k \log n))$ broadcasting algorithm improves previous algorithms with $O(kn)$ running time. For the all-port model, we first identify a minimum dominating set for the (n, k)-star. We then use it to find an optimal broadcasting algorithm on the all-port model of the (n, k)-star. The running time of this algorithm matches those of previous ones but the algorithm is simpler by using a dominating set instead of spanning trees. In addition, the algorithm has no redundancy in that no node receives the same message more than once.

Keywords: broadcasting, neighbourhood broadcasting, star, (n, k)-star, disjoint cycle, dominating set.

1 Introduction

The star graph was proposed to be an attractive alternative to the hypercube topology for interconnecting processors in a parallel computer (interconnection network), and compares favourably with it in several aspects [1]. A star graph of dimension n is a regular graph with degree $n - 1$. It has $n!$ nodes, but both its degree and diameter are $O(n)$, i.e., sub-logarithmic in the number of vertices, while a hypercube with $O(n!)$ vertices has a degree and diameter of $O(\log(n!)) = O(n \log n)$, i.e., logarithmic in the number of vertices. Other attractive properties include their symmetry properties, as well as many desirable fault tolerance characteristics [1]. However, a major limitation to its feasibility as a topology in which processors are connected in an interconnection network is the requirement that the number of nodes in an n-star be $n!$, resulting in a huge gap

A. Bourgeois and S.Q. Zheng (Eds.): ICA3PP 2008, LNCS 5022, pp. 70–78, 2008.

between the n-star and the $(n+1)$-star. For the very popular hypercube, a similar problem exists since an n-cube contains 2^n nodes while the next one has 2^{n+1} nodes. It is for this reason that *incomplete hypercube* was proposed [9]. To achieve scalability, *incomplete stars* have also been proposed [15,10]. Similarly, (n,k)-star graph was proposed to overcome the drawback of the star [4]. The (n,k)-star graph is a generalization of the star graph without the restriction that the total number of nodes be $n!$ while preserving many properties of the star graph [4,5].

For any interconnection network, we can classify it as either a weak model or a strong model, depending on how a node communicates with its neighbours. In a weak model (single-port model), in one time unit, a node can send (receive) at most one datum of fixed length to (from) one and only one of the nodes to which it is directly connected. On the other hand, in a strong model (all-port model) in one time unit, a node can send (receive) one datum of fixed length to (from) any number of nodes to which it is directly connected.

One of important operations on a parallel computer is broadcasting where one node (source) sends a message to all nodes. A similar problem that has been studied is the problem of *neighbourhood broadcasting* which is defined as sending a fixed sized message from the source node to all its neighbours where in one time unit, a node can send to or receive from exactly one of its neighbours a datum of constant size [6]. In other words, it is to simulate a single step of the strong model on a weak model. This problem has been considered for several interconnection networks [2,6,7,8,13,14]. Clearly, for any interconnection network with N nodes, on a single-port model, the problem of broadcasting has a trivial lower bound of $\Omega(\log N)$ since the number of nodes receiving the message can at most double after each step. Similarly, the problem of neighbourhood broadcasting has a trivial lower bound of $\Omega(\log n)$ where n is the degree of the source node. On an all-port model, clearly, a trivial lower bound for the problem of broadcasting is the diameter of the network and the neighbourhood broadcasting can be done in constant time.

For the single-port model, we first present an optimal neighbourhood broadcasting algorithm for the (n,k)-star, which is then used to develop an optimal broadcasting algorithm for the interconnection network. Our neighbourhood broadcasting is the first such algorithm to the best of our knowledge while our broadcasting algorithm achieves the optimality, improving the previous results which are not optimal. For the all-port model, we first identify a minimum dominating set for the (n,k)-star. We then use it to find an optimal broadcasting algorithm. This time complexity matches the results of previous work but our algorithm is much simpler. We organize the paper as follows. Section 2 defines the (n,k)-star graph and presents its relevant properties. We then develop the optimal neighbourhood broadcasting and broadcasting algorithms on the network for the two models in Section 3. Note that throughout this paper, we use nodes and vertices interchangeably to refer to processors in an interconnection network (graph).

2   Properties of the (n, k)-Star Interconnection Network

For $1 \leq k \leq n - 1$, an (n, k)-star graph is defined as follows. The vertex set is $\{p_1 p_2 \cdots p_k | 1 \leq p_i \leq n,\ and\ for\ i \neq j,\ p_i \neq p_j\}$ such that each node $p_1 p_2 \cdots p_k$ is adjacent to $k - 1$ nodes $p_i p_2 \cdots p_{i-1} p_1 p_{i+1} \cdots p_k$, $2 \leq i \leq k$ (these edges are called *i-edges* and we call these connections *dimensions*) and to $n - k$ nodes $p p_2 p_3 \cdots p_k$ for $p \in \{1, 2, \cdots, n\} - \{p_1, p_2, \cdots, p_k\}$ (1-edges). An (n, k)-star is also denoted as $S_{n,k}$. Fig. 1 shows a $(4, 2)$-star.

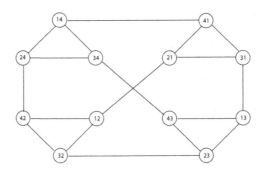

Fig. 1. A $(4, 2)$-star $S_{4,2}$

The (n, k)-star graph is an $(n - 1)$-regular graph with $n!/(n - k)!$ number of nodes. In addition, it is vertex symmetric, and $S_{n,n-1}$ is isomorphic to the n-star S_n [4]. The vertex symmetry of the graph implies that routing between two arbitrary nodes reduces to routing from an arbitrary node to the identity node $e = 123 \cdots k$. We use the notation $i*$ to represent a node whose first symbol is i. Similarly, $*i$ represents a node whose last symbol is i. The diameter of $S_{n,k}$ is $O(k)$ [4].

Let $S_{n-1,k-1}(i)$ be a subgraph where all the nodes are of the form $*i$, $1 \leq i \leq n$, then $S_{n-1,k-1}(i)$ is isomorphic to an $(n - 1, k - 1)$-star. This gives us one way to decompose an (n, k)-star into n $(n - 1, k - 1)$-stars $S_{n-1,k-1}(i)$, for $1 \leq i \leq n$ [4].

3   Broadcasting and Neighbourhood Broadcasting on the (n, k)-Star

3.1   Broadcasting on the Single-Port Model

Neighbourhood Broadcasting on $S_{n,k}$. Because the (n, k)-star is vertex-symmetric, without loss of generality, we assume that the source node is $12 \cdots k$. For this node, its i-edge neighbours are

$$21345 \cdots k$$
$$32145 \cdots k$$
$$42315 \cdots k$$

$$\cdots$$
$$k2345\cdots 1$$

and its 1-edge neighbours are

$$(k+1)234\cdots k$$
$$(k+2)234\cdots k$$
$$\cdots$$
$$n234\cdots k$$

Our algorithms are based on the following observations on structural properties of the (n,k)-star:

Observation 1. *For any $m \neq 1$, $S_{m,1}$ is a clique K_m (a complete graph of size m).*

Observation 2. *In $S_{n,k}$, for any node u, u and all its 1-edge neighbours form a clique K_{n-k+1}.*

Observation 3. *For any two i-edge neighbours $i * k = i23\cdots(i-1)1(i+1)\cdots k$ and $j * k = j23\cdots(j-1)1(j+1)\cdots k$ of the node $12\cdots k$ (we assume that $i < j$ without loss of generality), they are on the same cycle of length 6 as follows,*

$$123\cdots i\cdots j\cdots k \leftrightarrow$$
$$i23\cdots 1\cdots j\cdots k \leftrightarrow$$
$$j23\cdots 1\cdots i\cdots k \leftrightarrow$$
$$123\cdots j\cdots i\cdots k \leftrightarrow$$
$$i23\cdots j\cdots 1\cdots k \leftrightarrow$$
$$j23\cdots i\cdots 1\cdots k \leftrightarrow$$

where $\leftrightarrow$ represents a bi-directional link (edge) between two nodes. This cycle involves only i-edges.

In fact, the above observation also holds true when $k + 1 \leq j \leq n$:

Observation 4. *For any i-edge neighbour $i * k = i23\cdots(i-1)1(i+1)\cdots k$ and 1-edge neighbour $j * k = j23\cdots k$ of of the node $12\cdots k$, where $k + 1 \leq j \leq n$, they are on the same cycle of length 6 as follows,*

$$123\cdots(i-1)i(i+1)\cdots k \leftrightarrow$$
$$i23\cdots(i-1)1(i+1)\cdots k \leftrightarrow$$
$$j23\cdots(i-1)1(i+1)\cdots k \leftrightarrow$$
$$123\cdots(i-1)j(i+1)\cdots k \leftrightarrow$$
$$i23\cdots(i-1)j(i+1)\cdots k \leftrightarrow$$
$$j23\cdots(i-1)i(i+1)\cdots k \leftrightarrow$$

This cycle involves both i-edges and 1-edges.

Observation 5. *Any two 6-cycles formed as in Observations 3 and 4 with distinct* $2 \leq i_1, j_1, i_2, j_2 \leq n$ *are disjoint except that they share the source node* $123 \cdots k$.

The proofs for these observations are fairly straightforward and thus omitted.

Note that Observations 3, 4, and 5 allow us to view the source node together with its $n - 1$ neighbours as a de facto complete graph in the sense that any two nodes are connected by a path of constant length.

Based on the above observations and the technique of recursive doubling where at each step, we double the number of neighbours with the message by using a set of disjoint cycles of constant size in $S_{n,k}$, a simple neighbourhood broadcasting algorithm (given below) for $S_{n,k}$ can be designed.

Initially, the source node is the only one with the message. In one step, it sends the message through the direct link to one of its neighbours. Now two nodes have the message and they in turn send the message to two other neighbours of the source node in such a way that the source sends its message to a neighbour in one step and the neighbour who just received the message in previous step sends the message to another neighbour of the source node via a length-4 path that is part of a 6-cycle. The number of nodes with the message is now 4 (the source node and three of its neighbours) and these four nodes send the message to another four neighbours of the source node in the same fashion. That is, three neighbours of the source node with the message send the message to another three neighbours of the source node by disjoint paths of length four that are parts of three disjoint 6-cycles and the source node sends its message to a neighbour directly. The algorithm continues until all neighbours of the source node receive the message.

One possible implementation is given as follows (assuming that the neighbours of node $12 \cdots k$ are ordered such that $213 \cdots k$ is the first, $321 \cdots k$ is the second, etc.):

Broadcast (n)
    $N = 1$ /* the number of nodes currently with the message */
    for $i = 0$ **to** $\lceil \log \frac{n}{2} \rceil$ **do**
        if $1 \leq n - N \leq 3$
            source node $12 \cdots n$ sends the message to the remaining nodes
            (neighbours) that have not received the message yet by direct
            links /* nodes $2^i + j$, $1 \leq j \leq n - N$ */ **stop**
        else in parallel
            each node u that has the message sends its message to node
            $u + 2^i$, if node $u + 2^i$ exists (source node does this through
            the direct link while others through paths of the form
            $u* \rightarrow (u + 2^i)* \rightarrow 1* \rightarrow u* \rightarrow (u + 2^i)*$
            (a neighbour of the source) of length 4 on disjoint cycles)
            $N \leftarrow 2 \times N$
end Broadcast (n)

Another possible implementation is to first do a (neighbourhood) broadcasting in the $(n-k)$-clique formed by all the 1-edge neighbours of the source node, then start the recursive doubling. Many other implementations are also possible since the source and its neighbours form a de facto complete graph from a practical point of view.

This algorithm works correctly because the 6-cycles used in the routing are all disjoint (except at the source node). As for the running time, we first consider the case where $n \bmod 2^{\lfloor \log n \rfloor} > 3$. In this case, $\lceil \log n \rceil$ steps are needed where each step requires routing of length 4 except the very first step where the source sends its message directly to node 2. Thus,

$$\begin{aligned} t(n) &= 4\lceil \log n \rceil - 3 \\ &= 4\lceil \log n \rceil - 4\log 2 + 1 \\ &= 4\lceil \log(n/2) \rceil + 1. \end{aligned}$$

The analysis for the other case is similar. Therefore, the running time for the algorithm is

$$t(n) = \begin{cases} 4\lfloor \log(n/2) \rfloor + 1 + x & if\ 1 \le x = n \bmod 2^{\lfloor \log n \rfloor} \le 3 \\ 4\lceil \log(n/2) \rceil + 1 & otherwise \end{cases}$$

which is $O(\log n)$.

Note that when n is relatively small, it is better for the source node to simply send its message to each of its $n - 1$ neighbours one at a time, requiring $n - 1$ steps.

To the best of our knowledge, this neighbourhood broadcasting is the first such algorithm for the (n, k)-star graph.

Broadcasting on $S_{n,k}$. The problem of broadcasting has been studied for the (n, k)-star previously [3,11] where $O(nk)$ time algorithms are obtained.

With our algorithm for neighbourhood broadcasting just developed, broadcasting on an (n, k)-star can now be done easily. Once again, without loss of generality, assume that node $123 \cdots k$ wants to broadcast a piece of message. The algorithm proceeds as follows:

Broadcast$(S_{n,k})$
    if $k = 1$ (the network has become a clique), simply perform a standard
        broadcasting algorithm
    else the source node $12 \cdots k$ performs a neighbourhood broadcasting so that
        nodes $2*k, 3*k, ..., (k-1)*k$, and $k*1$ (all i-edge neighbours, $2 \le i \le k$),
        and $(k+1)*k, (k+2)*k, ...,$ and $n*k$ (all 1-edge neighbours) all have
        the message. Now, all (except node $k*1$) send their message to their
        k-dimension neighbours $*2, *3, ..., *n$ so that every $S_{n-1,k-1}(i)$ has
        a node with the message
        In parallel, for all $1 \le i \le n$, **do** Broadcast$(S_{n-1,k-1}(i))$.

Let $t(n, k)$ be the running time for broadcasting on (n, k)-star, then $t(n)$ is easily seen to be

$$
\begin{aligned}
t(n, k) &= C \log n + t(n - 1, k - 1) \\
&= C \log n + C \log(n - 1) + t(n - 2, k - 2) \\
&\ \ \vdots \\
&= C \log n + C \log(n - 1) + \cdots + C \log(n - k + 2) + t(n - k + 1, 1) \\
&= C \log n + C \log(n - 1) + \cdots + C \log(n - k + 2) + C_1 \log(n - k + 1) \\
&= O(\log(n!/(n - k)!)) \\
&= O(k \log n),
\end{aligned}
$$

which is optimal in view of the $\Omega(\log(n!/(n - k)!))$ lower bound.

The key to the broadcasting algorithm is the neighbourhood broadcasting algorithm that first sends the message to $n - 1$ neighbours of the source node that are of the forms $2 * k$, $3 * k$, ..., $(k - 1) * k$, $k * 1$, $(k + 1) * k$, $(k + 2) * k$, ..., and $n * k$. Similar idea has been used before in deriving a broadcasting algorithm for the star, for example, in [12]. The main difference is that instead of being neighbours of the source node, these $n - 1$ nodes are in a binary tree rooted at the source node. It is also worth pointing out that there is a binomial tree rooted at the source node (thus any node due to the vertex symmetry of the star graph) containing nodes of these forms.

3.2   Broadcasting on the All-Port Model

In addition to the time (the number of communication steps) required, one of the considerations in developing a broadcasting algorithm in a parallel computer is the traffic, i.e., the total number of messages exchanged [16]. This means that it is desirable to minimize both the time and traffic [16]. To minimize the traffic is equivalent to minimizing the redundancy, i.e., the number of times a node receives the same message.

Broadcasting on the all-port (n, k)-star has been considered before and optimal algorithms whose running times are proportional to the diameter of the network have been obtained using spanning trees [11] . Here, we present another approach to the problem using a minimum dominating set to relay the message such that no node receives the same message more than once. Its running time is $O(k)$, thus optimal, and is arguably simpler.

A *dominating set* of vertices in a graph $G = (V, E)$ is a set $V' \subseteq V$ such that every vertex of G belongs to V' or has a neighbour in V'.

Let $D_{n,k}$ be a minimum dominating set of $S_{n,k}$. Since the graph is a regular graph of degree $n - 1$, and each vertex in a minimum dominating set dominates itself and up to $n - 1$ of its neighbours, we have $|D_{n,k}| \geq (n!/(n - k)!)/n$, i.e., $D_{n,k}$ contains at least $(n - 1)!/(n - k)!$ vertices.

Let D be the set of all the nodes of the form $i*$. Clearly, any node in the graph is adjacent to one node of this form. In addition, the number of nodes of this form is $(n-1)!/((n-1)-(k-1))! = (n-1)!/(n-k)!$. Therefore, D is a minimum dominating set of $S_{n,k}$.

A simple broadcasting algorithm on all-port $S_{n,k}$ can now be found based on the minimum dominating set as follows:

Algorithm Broadcast $(S_{n,k})$
   if $n = 2$ **then**
      Source sends the message along dimension 2
   else if $k = 1$ **then**
      Source sends the message to all its neighbours (all 1-edge neighbours)
   else
      Broadcast$(S_{n-1,k-1}(k))$
      Each node $*k$ (in $S_{n-1,k-1}(k)$) sends its message to neighbour $k*$
      along dimension k (the set of the nodes of the form $k*$ is a
      minimum dominating set)
      Each node in the dominating set sends its message along
      all dimensions except k
End Algorithm

It is easy to see from the algorithm that each node receives the message exactly once, thus there is no message redundancy. As to the analysis, let $t(n,k)$ be the time required to broadcast in $S_{n,k}$, then we have

$$t(n,k) = \begin{cases} 1 & n = 2 \text{ or } k = 1 \\ t(n-1, k-1) + 2 & else \end{cases}$$

Solving it gives us that $t(n,k) = 2k = O(k)$.

4 Conclusion

We presented an optimal neighbourhood broadcasting algorithm for the (n,k)-star under the single-port model, a generalization of the star graph. This algorithm was then used to develop an optimal broadcasting algorithm for the interconnection network. Both algorithms are the first optimal algorithms for the (n,k)-star. For the all-port model, we developed an optimal algorithm using the minimum dominating set whose performance matches those obtained earlier. In developing these algorithms, some interesting properties of the (n,k)-star are also found. We hope to find more algorithms that can run on this interconnection network in the future.

References

1. Akers, S.B., Krishnamurthy, B.: A Group Theoretic Model for Symmetric Interconnection Networks. IEEE Transactions on Computers c-38(4), 555–566 (1989)
2. Bermond, J.C., Ferreira, A., Pérennes, S., Peters, J.G.: Neighbourhood broadcasting in hypercubes, Technical Report, SFU-CMPT-TR 2004-12, School of Computing Science, Simon Fraser University, Canada

3. Chen, Y.S., Tai, K.S.: A Near-Optimal Broadcasting in (n,k)-Star Graphs. In: ACIS International Conference on Software Engineering Applied to Networking and Parallel/Distributed Computing (SNPD 2000), pp. 217–224 (2000)
4. Chiang, W.K., Chen, R.J.: The (n,k)-Star Graph: A Generalized Star Graph. Information Processing Letters 56, 259–264 (1995)
5. Chiang, W.K., Chen, R.J.: Topological Properties of (n,k)-Star Graph. International Journal of Foundations of Computer Science 9(2), 235–248 (1997)
6. Cosnard, M., Ferreira, A.: On the real power of loosely coupled parallel architectures. Parallel Processing Letters 1, 103–111 (1991)
7. Fujita, S.: Neighbourhood Information Dissemination in the Star Graph. IEEE Transaction on Computers 49(12), 1366–1370 (2000)
8. Fujita, S.: Optimal Neighborhood Broadcast in Star Graphs. Journal of Interconnection Networks 4(4), 419–428 (2003)
9. Katseff, H.P.: Incomplete Hypercubes. IEEE Trans. Compu. C-37(5), 604–608 (1988)
10. Latifi, S., Bagherzadeh, N.: Incomplete Star: An Incrementally Scalable Network Based on the Star Graph. IEEE Trans. on Parallel and Distributed System 5(1), 97–102 (1994)
11. Li, J.L., Chen, M.L., Xiang, Y.H., Yao, S.W.: Optimum Broadcasting Algorithms in (n,k)-Star Graphs Using Spanning Trees. In: Li, K., Jesshope, C., Jin, H., Gaudiot, J.-L. (eds.) NPC 2007. LNCS, vol. 4672, pp. 220–230. Springer, Heidelberg (2007)
12. Mendia, V.E., Sarkar, D.: Optimal Broadcasting on the Star Graph. IEEE Trans. on Parallel and Distributed System 3(4), 389–396 (1992)
13. Qiu, K., Das, S.K.: A Novel Neighbourhood Broadcasting Algorithm on Star Graphs. In: IEEE 9th International Conference on Parallel and Distributed Systems (ICPADS 2002), Taiwan, December 2002, pp. 37–41 (2002)
14. Qiu, K.: On a Unified Neighbourhood Broadcasting Scheme for Interconnection Networks. Parallel Processing Letters 17(4), 425–437 (2007)
15. Ravikumar, C.P., Kuchlous, A., Manimaran, G.: Incomplete Star Graph: An Economical Fault-Tolerant Interconnection Network. In: Proc. International Conference on Parallel Processing, vol. 1, pp. 83–90 (1993)
16. Sheu, J.P., Wu, C.T., Chen, T.S.: An Optimal Broadcasting Algorithm without Message Redundancy in Star Graphs. IEEE Transactions on Parallel and Distributed Systems 6(6), 653–658 (1995)

Fault Tolerance in the Biswapped Network

Wenhong Wei and Wenjun Xiao

Department of Computer Science, South China University of Technology,
510641 Guangzhou, China
hquwwh@tom.com, wjxiao@scut.edu.cn

Abstract. Biswapped network (BSN) is a new topology for interconnection networks in multiprocessor systems. BSN is built of $2n$ copies of an n-node basic network and total nodes are $2n^2$, and its basic network may be hypercube, mesh and other networks, hence we can construct BSN-Hypercube and BSN-Mesh by using hypercube and mesh as basic network. Some topological properties of BSN have been investigated, and some algorithms have been developed on the BSN such as sorting and matrix multiplication etc. In this paper, we discuss the fault tolerant issue of the BSN including network connectivity and fault diameter.

Keywords: Biswapped network (BSN), Cayley graphs, Network connectivity, Fault diameter.

1 Introduction

The swapped network is also called as the OTIS-network and has important applications in parallel processing [1,2]. In this network architecture, n^2 processors are divided n groups where there are n processors, and processors in the same group are connected by intra-group link, simultaneously, these groups are connected by inter-group link. But swapped network is not a Cayley graph, and then it is not a symmetrical network architecture, so some algorithms on it are not always convenient. For remedying this limitation about swapped network, [3] proposed Biswapped network (BSN), the new network is a class of Cayley graph if the basic network is a Cayley graph and is tight related to the swapped network. BSN is of more regularity than the swapped network. BSN is built of $2n$ copies of an n-node basic network using a simple rule for connectivity that ensures its regularity, modularity, fault tolerance, and algorithmic efficiency. Some topological properties of BSN have been investigated [3], and some algorithms have been developed on the BSN such as sorting and matrix multiplication etc [4].

A central issue in the design of interconnection networks is fault tolerance as it is essential for a large parallel system to work properly even when some processors fail, and fault tolerance is one of the central issues in today s interconnection networks, which has been discussed extensively [5-6]. In this paper, we analyze the fault tolerance aspects of BSN, including network connectivity and fault diameter of BSN. The remainder of this paper is organized as follows. Section 2 describes BSN and related

A. Bourgeois and S.Q. Zheng (Eds.): ICA3PP 2008, LNCS 5022, pp. 79..82, 2008.

terms used in its definition. Section 3 discusses the network connectivity of the BSN; link and node connectivity are covered, and proves that BSN is maximally fault toler-ant when its basic network is maximally fault tolerant. Section 4 describes fault-diameter of the BSN. The conclusion is made in Section 5.

2 Biswapped Network

Definition 1. Let Ω be a graph with the vertex set $V(\Omega) = \{h_1, h_2, ..., h_n\}$ and the arc set $E(\Omega)$. Our biswapped network $\Sigma(\Omega) = \Sigma = (V(\Sigma), E(\Sigma))$ is a graph defined as follows [3]:

$$V(\Sigma) = \{\langle g, p, 0\rangle, \langle g, p, 1\rangle \mid g, p \in V(\Omega)\}$$

and

$$E(\Sigma) = \{(\langle g, p_1, 0\rangle, \langle g, p_2, 0\rangle), (\langle g, p_1, 1\rangle, \langle g, p_2, 1\rangle) \mid (p_1, p_2) \in E(\Omega), g \in V(\Omega)\}$$
$$\cup \{(\langle g, p, 0\rangle, \langle p, g, 1\rangle), (\langle g, p, 1\rangle, \langle p, g, 0\rangle) \mid g, p \in V(\Omega)\}$$

Intuitively, if we regard the basis network as group, the definition postulates $2n$ groups, each group being an Ω digraph: n groups, with nodes numbered $\langle$group#, processor#, $0\rangle$, form part 0 of the bipartite graph, and n groups constitute part 1, with associated node numbers $\langle$group#, processor#, $1\rangle$. Each group p in either part of Σ has the same internal connectivity as Ω (intra-group edges, forming the first set in the definition of $E(\Sigma)$). In addition, node g of group p in part 0/1 is connected to node p in group g of part 1/0 (inter-group or swap edges in the second set in the definition for $E(\Sigma)$). The name biswapped network (BSN) arises from two defining properties of the network just introduced: when group are viewed as super-nodes, the resulting graph of super-nodes is a complete $2n$-node bipartite graph, and the inter-group links connect nodes in which the group number and the node number within group are interchanged or swapped.

When $\Omega = C_4$ is a circle of order 4, an example of the network $\Sigma(C_4)$ is denoted in Fig. 1.

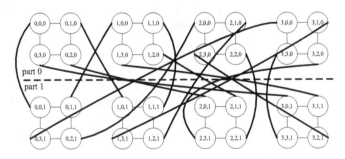

Fig. 1. An example of BSN whose basic network is C_4

Similar to swapped network (or OTIS), links between vertices of the same group are regarded as intra-group links, and links between vertices of between two groups follow the swapping strategy, which are regarded as inter-group links.

3 Network Connectivity

Connectivity is the minimum number of nodes or links that must fail for the network to be partitioned into 2 or more disjoint sub-networks. In one network, if any less than k-1 nodes are removed but the network isn t disconnected, and when this network is separated by removing k nodes, this network becomes disconnected, the connectivity of this network is k. Node (link) connectivity is the minimum number of nodes (links) which should be removed for a network of being divided into at least two sub-networks. A network that has the same node-connectivity, link-connectivity and degree can be said that it is maximally fault tolerant.

Consider the BSN as a 2-level structure, and hence the connectivity of BSN is corresponding to the basic network. For example, if basic network is hypercube, the connectivity of BSN-Hypercube is derived from hypercube.

Theorem 1. The node-connectivity of BSN-Ω is $n+1$ if node-connectivity of Ω is n.

Proof: Omitted.   □

In any network, the node-connectivity is smaller than or equal to the minimum degree since removal of a node whose degree equal to the minimum degree results in a disconnected network. Also, the node-connectivity must always be smaller than or equal to the link-connectivity [8], because removing a node effectively removes all links connected to that node. Thus, a node failure is more damaging to network-connectivity than a link failure, and fewer node failures could be necessary to disconnect the network.

Corollary 1. The link-connectivity of BSN-Ω is $n+1$ if link-connectivity of Ω is n.

Theorem 2. BSN-Ω is maximally faulty tolerant if Ω is maximally faulty tolerant.

Proof: Let the degree of Ω be n, because Ω is maximally faulty tolerant, the node-connectivity and link-connectivity of Ω is n, hence the node-connectivity and link-connectivity of BSN-Ω is $n+1$. As we know, the degree of BSN-Ω is $n+1$, so BSN-Ω is maximum faulty tolerant.   □

When the node-connectlivity of one network is n, the network provides n disjoint paths between every pair of nodes in the network and can tolerate n-1 faulty nodes. Hence, higher node-connectivity or link-connectivity increases the resiliency of the network to failure. New routing paths can be established based on the proofs of theorem 1. Of course, longer paths have to be used to avoid faulty nodes and links. In addition to being a measure of network reliability, connectivity is also a measure of performance. So designing a network with higher connectivity is especially important.

4 Fault Diameter

A fault diameter of a network G is defined as the diameter of a new network G generated after the faulty nodes and links are removed from network G [5]. An f-fault diameter of a network is defined to be the maximum of distances over all possible networks that can occur with at most faults. In a regular network of degree d, d-faulty diameter is equal to ∞ since if all neighbors of any node fail, the network becomes disconnected. Hence, particular interest is $(d$-1$)$-fault diameter, and we consider $(d$-1$)$-fault diameter as fault diameter in a general way. When the fault diameter of network G is the diameter+constant value, we can say G to be strongly resilient [7]. Now, calculate the fault diameter for BSN.

Theorem 3. The n-fault diameter of BSN-Ω is $2D(\Omega)+2+\varepsilon$ if the fault diameter of Ω is $D(\Omega)+\varepsilon$ ($\varepsilon \geq 0$).

Proof: Omitted.   □

Corollary 2. BSN-Ω is strongly resilient if Ω is strongly resilient.

Proof: According to theorem 3 and [7], corollary 2 is proved easily.   □

5 Conclusion

BSN is a two-stage network, the fault tolerant of BSN is decided by its basic network. In this paper, we analyzed the fault tolerance of BSN with knowing the fault tolerance of its basic network. We proved that node-connectivity and link-connectivity of BSN was n+1 when of its basic network was n, and BSN was maximally fault tolerant when its basic network was maximally fault tolerant. We also derived the fault diameter of BSN and proved BSN was strongly resilient. Because of our conclusion, we know that BSN is a good fault tolerant network, and what we will do is develop the fault tolerant routing algorithm of BSN.

Acknowledgments. This work is supported by the Doctorate Foundation of South China University of Technology and Open Research Foundation of Guangdong Province Key Laboratory of Computer Network.

References

1. Parhami, B.: Swapped Interconnection Networks: Topological, Performance, and Robustness Attributes. Journal of Parallel and Distributed Computing 65, 1443..1452 (2005)
2. Day, K., Al-yyoub, A.: Topological Properties of OTIS-networks. IEEE Transactions on Parallel and Distributed Systems 13(4), 359.366 (2002)
3. Xiao, W.J., Chen, W.D., He, M.X., Wei, W.H., Parhami, B.: Biswapped Network and Their Topological Properties. In: Proceedings Eighth ACIS International Conference on Software Eng., Artific. Intelligence, Networking, and Parallel/Distributed Computing, pp. 193..198 (2007)
4. Wei, W.H., Xiao, W.J.: Matrix Multiplication on the Biswapped-Mesh Network. In: Proceedings Eighth ACIS International Conference on Software Eng., Artific. Intelligence, Networking, and Parallel/Distributed Computing, pp. 211..215 (2007)
5. Pan, Y.: Fault Tolerance in the Block-Shift Network. IEEE Transactions on Reliability 50(1), 88..91 (2001)
6. Cao, F., Hsu, D.F.: Fault Tolerant Properties of Pyramid Networks. IEEE Transactions on Computers 48(1), 88..93 (1999)
7. Akers, S.B., Krishnamurthy, B.: On Group Graphs and Their Fault Tolerance. IEEE Transactions on Computer c 36(7), 885..888 (1987)
8. Bondy, J.A., Murty, U.S.R.: Graph Theory with Applications. North-Holland (1979)

3D Block-Based Medial Axis Transform and Chessboard Distance Transform on the CREW PRAM

Shih-Ying Lin[2,*], Shi-Jinn Horng[1,3,4,7], Tzong-Wann Kao[5], Chin-Shyurng Fahn[3], Pingzhi Fan[1], Cheng-Ling Lee[6], and Anu Bourgeois[7]

[1] Institute of Mobile Communications, Southwest Jiaotong University, 610031, Chengdu
[2] Department of Electrical Engineering, National Taiwan University of Science and Technology, Taipei, Taiwan
[3] Department of Computer Science and Information Engineering, National Taiwan University of Science and Technology, Taipei, Taiwan
[4] Department of Electronic Engineering, National United University, Miaoli, Taiwan
[5] Department of Electronic Engineering, Technology and Science Institute of Northern Taiwan, Taipei, Taiwan
[6] Department of Electro-Optical Engineering, National United University, Miaoli, Taiwan
[7] Department of Computer Science, Georgia State University Atlanta, GA 30302-4110

Abstract. Traditionally, the block-based medial axis transform (BB-MAT) and the chessboard distance transform (CDT) were usually viewed as two completely different image computation problems, especially for three dimensional (3D) space. We achieve the computation of the 3D CDT problem by implementing the 3D BB-MAT algorithm first. For a 3D binary image of size N^3, our parallel algorithm can be run in $O(\log N)$ time using N^3 processors on the concurrent read exclusive write (CREW) parallel random access machine (PRAM) model to solve both 3D BB-MAT and 3D CDT problems, respectively. In addition, we have implemented a message passing interface (MPI) program on an AMD Opteron Model 270 cluster system to verify the proposed parallel algorithm, since the PRAM model is not available in the real world. The experimental results show that the speedup is saturated when the number of processors used is more than four, regardless of the problem size.

Keywords: parallel algorithm, image processing, CREW, PRAM model, block-based medial axis transform, chessboard distance transform, Euclidean distance transform.

* The revision of this paper was completed by the second author while visiting Georgia State University. This work was supported in part by the Southwest Jiaotong University Visiting Professor Fellowship and the University Doctorial Research Foundation under grant No.20020613020, Ministry of Education. It was also supported in part by National Science Council under the contract number NSC 95-2221-E-011-020-, NSC 95-2221-E-011-032-MY3 and NSC 96-2918-I-011-002. Currently, S.-Y. Lin is a full instructor at Lan Yang Institute of Technology, I-Lan, Taiwan. E-mail: max@mail.fit.edu.tw. Corresponding author: Prof. Shi-Jinn Horng, Email: horngsj@yahoo.com.tw

A. Bourgeois and S.Q. Zheng (Eds.): ICA3PP 2008, LNCS 5022, pp. 83.96, 2008.
© Springer-Verlag Berlin Heidelberg 2008

1 Introduction

Consider a two dimensional (2D) or a three dimensional (3D) binary image consisting of foreground (black) pixels and background (white) pixels. The extraction of the information about the shape and the position of the foreground pixels relative to each other are frequently used in the fields of image processing and computer vision. This can be done by two common techniques. One is the distance transform (DT) introduced by Rosenfeld and Pfaltz [1]. The other is the medial axis transform (MAT) originally explored by Blum [2]. The DT is an operation that converts a binary image to an image, where each pixel has a value corresponding to the distance to the nearest foreground pixel. The chessboard distance transform (CDT) and the Euclidean distance transform (EDT) are both DTs based on the chessboard distance metrics and the Euclidean distance metrics, respectively. Given an $N \times N$ binary image M with $m(i, j) \in \{0,1\}$, $0 \le i$, $j \le N\text{-}1$, where 1 denotes a foreground pixel, 0 denotes a background pixel. Let $B_1 = \{b_1(i, j) \mid m(i, j) = 1$ of $M\}$ be the set of all foreground pixels of M, and $B_0 = \{ b_0(i, j) \mid m(i, j) = 0$ of $M\}$ be the set of all background pixels of M. Then the 2D EDT of an image M can be computed by

$$EDT(m(i, j)) = (\min_{(x, y) \in B_1} (i..x)^2 + (j..y)^2)^{1/2}, \text{ for } 0 \le i, j \le N\text{-}1.$$

The two dimensional distance function of L_k metric of the plane by d_k as defined in [3] is listed as follows:

$$d_k((i, j), (x, y)) = (|i - x|^k + |j - y|^k)^{1/k} \text{ where } 1 \le k < \infty,$$

$$d_\infty((i, j), (x, y)) = \max(|i - x|, |j - y|).$$

d_1 is called the city block distance , d_2 is called the Euclidean distance and d_∞ is called the chessboard distance . Then the 2D CDT of an image M is to find an array

$$CDT(m(i, j)) = \min_{(x, y) \in B_1} \{\max(|i - x|, |j - y|)\}, \text{ for } 0 \le i, j \le N\text{-}1. \tag{1-1}$$

1.1 Related Work

The block-based MAT is denoted as BB-MAT [4], which is a recovering of the object by maximal square (cube) blocks of pixels (voxels) in a 2D (3D) space. A maximal square (cube) block of pixels (voxels) is a square (cube) block that is not contained in any other square (cube) block. In this paper, the MAT is defined as the BB-MAT. Similar to [5, 6], we define the 2D MAT of an image M as follows:

$$MAT(m(I, j)) = \begin{cases} \text{the height of the largest square} \\ \text{in the lower - right direction,} & \text{if } m(i, j) \in B_1 ; \\ \\ 0, & \text{if } m(i, j) \in B_0 \end{cases} \tag{1-2}$$

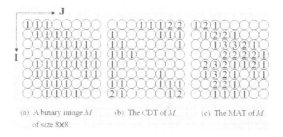

(a) A binary image M (b) The CDT of M (c) The MAT of M
of size 8×8

Fig. 1. An example for the chessboard distance transform and the medial axis transform of a binary image M. An empty circle is a pixel whose value is 0.

An example for the chessboard distance transform and the medial axis transform of a binary image M of size 8×8 is shown in Fig. 1.

There are some practical applications for the MAT developed either in two or three dimensional space. Ramanathan and Gurumoorthy [7] proposed an algorithm for generating the MAT of 3D objects with free form boundaries that are obtained by extrusion along a line or revolution about an axis. This algorithm uses the 2D MAT of the profile being extruded or revolved to identify the limiting entities (junction points, seams and points of extremal maximum curvature) of the 3D MAT. Morrison and Zou [8] proposed a non-pixel-based skeletonization technique and showed many advantages over traditional pixel-based methods such as thinning. These advantages include superior efficiency and faster processing time. Remy and Thiel [9, 10] proposed an algorithm that computes the look-up table and the neighborhood to be tested in the case of chamfer distances.

For the theoretical research domain, very few parallel algorithms have been developed for the 3D distance-based MAT (DB-MAT) or 3D BB-MAT problem. Wang and Horng [11, 12] showed that the task of computing the 3D DB-MAT of a binary image of size $N \times N \times N$ can be performed in $O(1)$ time using $N^{3+\delta+\varepsilon}$ processors on the CRCW PRAM, and in $O(1)$ time using $N^{3+\varepsilon}$ processors on the array with reconfigurable optical buses (AROB), respectively, where $\delta = 1/(2^{c+1}-1)$, $\varepsilon = 1/d$, d and c are constants and positive integers. Recently, Wang [13] proposed the 3D BB-MAT of a binary image of size $N \times N \times N$ in $O(1)$ time on an Linear array with a reconfigurable pipelined bus system (LARPBS) of size $\max\{N^3, S_3, S_{3i}, S_{3j}, S_{3k}\}$ processors, where $0 \leq S_3, S_{3i}, S_{3j}, S_{3k} \leq N^{4+\delta}$, $0 < \delta = 1/(2^{c+1}-1) \leq 1$. The worst case would result in using N^5 processors. Lin and Horng et al. [14] developed a parallel algorithm that can solve the 3D BB-MAT of a binary image of size $N \times N \times N$ in $O(1)$ time using N^4 processors on the AROB. In this paper, we present a parallel algorithm for solving the three dimensional block-based medial axis transform problem on the CREW PRAM model. Based on the relationships of the 2D CDT and the 2D MAT derived by Lee and Horng [15], we compute the 3D CDT by use of the 3D BB-MAT algorithm. For a 3D binary image of size N^3, our parallel algorithm can be run in $O(\log N)$ time using N^3 processors on the CREW PRAM model to solve both 3D BB-MAT and 3D CDT problems. To the best of our knowledge, the presented results are the first 3D CDT algorithm known. The

Table 1. Comparison results for parallel 3D BB-MAT algorithms

Algorithm	Time Complexity	Processor	Architecture
Wang [13]	O(1)	max{ N^3, S_3, S_{3i}, S_{3j}, S_{3k} } , where $0 \le S_3$, $S_{3i}, S_{3j}, S_{3k} \le N^{4+\delta}$, $0 < \delta = 1/(2^{c+1}-1) \le 1$.	LARPBS
Lin et al.[14]	O(1)	$N \times N \times N \times N$	AROB
This paper	O(logN)	$N \times N \times N$	CREW

Table 2. Comparison results for parallel 3D CDT algorithms.

Algorithm	Time Complexity	Processor	Architecture
No previously published results			
This paper	O(logN)	$N \times N \times N$	CREW

comparison results for the 3D BB-MAT and 3D CDT are shown in Table 1 and Table 2, respectively.

1.2 Organization

The paper is organized as follows. In Section 2 we present computation models of the CREW PRAM and basic operations. In Section 3 we state the 3D BB-MAT problem and propose the corresponding 3D BB-MAT algorithm. Section 4 shows the 3D CDT problem that is related to the 3D BB-MAT problem and also develops the 3D CDT algorithm. In Section 5 we implement an MPI program to verify the 3D CDT algorithm on an AMD Opteron Model 270 (2.0 GHz/1M L2) cluster system located at National Taiwan University of Science and Technology (http://www.ntust.edu.tw/). Finally, some concluding remarks are included in the last section.

2 The Computation Model and Basic Operations

We first present the CREW PRAM computation model in Section 2.1. In the following section, we describe several basic data operations and lemmas useful for the medial axis transform problem.

2.1 The Computation Model

The parallel shared-memory model is an extension of the sequential model, where the parallel shared-memory model consists of a number of identical processors, each of which has its own local memory to execute its own program and to access its own data. All processors communicate and exchange data through a common global memory that is referred to as shared memory. In this paper, we use the single instruction multiple data stream (SIMD) model for the parallel random access machine (PRAM). That is, all processors operate synchronously under the control of a common clock, and in each unit of time, all active processors execute the same instruction, but with different data. There are several variations of the PRAM model. The most common three models are the exclusive read exclusive write (EREW) PRAM, the concurrent read exclusive write (CREW) PRAM and the concurrent read concurrent write (CRCW) PRAM. In the EREW PRAM model, a single memory location cannot be simultaneously accessed by more than one processor. The CREW PRAM model allows multiple processors to simultaneously access a single memory location for reading, but not simultaneously to write. The CRCW PRAM model allows multiple processors to simultaneously access a single memory location for either read or write instructions. For simplicity, we assume that it takes a unit of time to do either an arithmetic instruction or a shared memory access for any PRAM model. The parallel computation model upon which our algorithms are based is the CREW PRAM.

2.2 Basic Operations

In this section, we describe several basic data operations and lemmas that are useful in developing the 3D BB-MAT algorithm given in Section 3.

- Prefix Sums (PS): Given a data sequence ds_0, ds_1, f, ds_{N-1}, the operation of computing the Prefix Sums (PS) of N partial sums is to find $PS_i = ds_0 + ds_1 + f + ds_i$, where $0 \leq i \leq N-1$.
- Postfix Sums (POS): Given a data sequence ds_0, ds_1, f, ds_{N-1}, the operation of computing the Postfix Sums (POS) of N partial sums is to find $POS_i = ds_i + ds_{i+1} + f + ds_{N-1}$, where $0 \leq i \leq N-1$.
- Summation Operation (SO): Given a data sequence ds_0, ds_1, f, ds_{N-1}, the operation of computing the summation of N-item data is to find $SO = ds_0 + ds_1, f, + ds_{N-1}$.

Lemma 1 [16]. The Prefix Sums (PS) can be computed in $O(\log N)$ time for a data sequence of size N on the EREW and CREW PRAM. Lemma 1 leads to the following corollary.

Corollary 1. The Postfix Sums (POS) can be computed in $O(\log N)$ time for a data sequence of size N on the EREW and CREW PRAM.

Assume that we have a 2D $N \times N$ binary image M, with $m(i, j) \in \{0,1\}$, $0 \leq i, j \leq N-1$, and a pixel of value 0 (resp. 1) is denoted as a white (resp. black) pixel correspondingly. Let a specified pixel p with coordinates (i_p, j_p) be denoted as $p(i_p, j_p)$, where i_p and j_p are the coordinates along I-axis and J-axis of the 2D coordinate system, respectively. The origin of the 2D coordinate system is at the top-left corner of the image M and the corresponding pixel is $m(0, 0)$. The 2D dominance is defined as follows:

Definition 1. In a 2D binary image, pixel p_1 *dominates* pixel p_2 (denoted by $p_2 \prec p_1$) if $i_{p2} \leq i_{p1}$ and $j_{p2} \leq j_{p1}$, where (i_{p1}, j_{p1}) and (i_{p2}, j_{p2}) are the coordinates of pixels p_1 and p_2, respectively.

Definition 2. The number of pixels $Q(p)$ of black pixels from B_1 which is satisfied with $i \leq i_p$ and $j \leq j_p$ in a 2D rectangle (or square) with sides parallel to the coordinate axes I and J is determined by p. That is, $Q(p)$ is the number of pixels in B_1 which are dominated by p, where $B_1 = \{b_1(i, j) \mid m(i, j) = 1 \text{ of } M\}$ is a set of all black pixels of a binary image M.

For a pixel $p(i_p, j_p)$, $0 \leq i_p, j_p \leq N\text{-}1$, Q(p) can be computed by the following equation.

$$Q(p) = \sum_{j=0}^{j_p} \sum_{i=0}^{i_p} b_1(i, j) \tag{2-1}$$

From Definition 1 and Definition 2, we have the following equation for the 2D dominance counting.

• 2D Dominance Counting [17]: The number $H(p_1, p_2, p_3, p_4)$ of pixels contained in a 2D rectangle (or square) $p_1\ p_2\ p_3\ p_4$ is given by $H(p_1, p_2, p_3, p_4) = (Q(p_3) + Q(p_1)) - (Q(p_2) + Q(p_4))$. $\tag{2-2}$

Based on the definition of the 2D dominance (i.e., Definitions 1 and 2), the 3D dominance can be extended to add K-axis for the 3D coordinate system. Given a 3D $N{\times}N{\times}N$ binary image V, where $V = \{v(i, j, k) \in \{0,1\}, 0 \leq i, j, k \leq N\text{-}1\}$, then a voxel of value 0 (resp. 1) is defined as a white (resp. black) voxel in the image V. The origin of the 3D coordinate system is at the top-left-front corner of the image V and the corresponding voxel is $v(0, 0, 0)$. Let $D_1 = \{d_1(i, j, k) \mid v(i, j, k) = 1$ of $V\}$ be a set of all black voxels of V. A specified voxel v with coordinates (i_v, j_v, k_v) can be denoted as $v(i_v, j_v, k_v)$, where i_v, j_v and k_v are the coordinates along the I-axis, J-axis and K-axis of the 3D coordinate system, respectively. We say that a 3D_Q(v) is the number of voxels in D_1 which are dominated by v, where, $0 \leq i_v, j_v, k_v \leq N\text{-}1$. Then 3D_Q(v) can be computed by the following equation:

$$3D\_Q(v) = \sum_{k=0}^{k_v} \sum_{j=0}^{j_v} \sum_{i=0}^{i_v} d_1(i, j, k) \tag{2-3}$$

Definition 3. The number of voxels 3D_Q(v) of black voxels from D_1 that are satisfied with $i \leq i_v, j \leq j_v$ and $k \leq k_v$ in the rectangular parallelepiped area (or cube) with sides parallel to the coordinate axes I, J, and K is determined by v. That is, 3D_Q(v) is the number of voxels in D_1 that are dominated by v, where $D_1 = \{d_1(i, j, k) \mid v(i, j, k) = 1$ of $V\}$ is a set of all black voxels of a 3D binary image V.

From Definition 3 and Eq. (2-3), we have the following lemma for the 3D dominance counting.

Lemma 2. The 3D dominance counting for the number $H(v_1, v_2, v_3, v_4, v_5, v_6, v_7, v_8)$ of voxels contained in a 3D rectangular parallelepiped (or cube) $v_1\ v_2\ v_3\ v_4\ v_5\ v_6\ v_7\ v_8$ is given by $H(v_1, v_2, v_3, v_4, v_5, v_6, v_7, v_8) = (3D\_Q(v_7) + 3D\_Q(v_4) + 3D\_Q(v_5) + 3D\_Q(v_2)) - (3D\_Q(v_8) + 3D\_Q(v_3) + 3D\_Q(v_6) + 3D\_Q(v_1))$. $\tag{2-4}$

Proof: Omitted.

3   The 3D BB-Mat Problem and the 3D BB-Mat Algorithm

In Section 3.1 we state the problem of 3D block based medial axis transform (3D BB-MAT). We then develop the 3D BB-MAT algorithm, which is based on the basic operations stated in Section 2.2, in Section 3.2.

3.1 The 3D BB-Mat Problem

Given a 3D $N \times N \times N$ binary image V, where $V = \{v(i, j, k) \in \{0,1\}, 0 \le i, j, k \le N\text{-}1\}$. Let $D_1 = \{d_1(i, j, k) \mid v(i, j, k) = 1 \text{ of } V\}$ be a set of all black voxels of V, and $D_0 = \{d_0(i, j, k) \mid v(i, j, k) = 0 \text{ of } V\}$ be a set of all white voxels of V. According to Eq. (1-2), we define the 3D BB-MAT of an image V as follows:

$$3D\ BB\text{-}MAT(v(i,j,k)) = \begin{cases} \begin{array}{ll} \text{the height of the largest cube} \\ \text{in the lower - right -back direction} , & \text{if } v(i,j,k) \in D_1; \\ \\ 0, & \text{if } v(i,j,k) \in D_0 \end{array} \end{cases}$$

In order to develop our algorithm, we can define the 3D BB-MAT problem by array $3DBBMAT(v(i, j, k))$ of size N^3 as follows.

Definition 4. $3DBBMAT(v(i,j,k)) =$
$$\begin{cases} \max\{\Phi \mid v(i+\lambda, j+\lambda, k+\lambda) = 1, \text{ for } 0 \le \lambda \le \Phi\text{-}1, \\ \text{and } i+\lambda, j+\lambda, k+\lambda \le N\text{-}1.\}, & \text{if } v(i,j,k)=1; \\ 0, & \text{otherwise} \end{cases}$$
$$(3\text{-}1)$$

Φ is the side length of the maximal cube of 1-voxels for each voxel $v(i, j, k)$, and λ is the subset of Φ, where $0 \le \lambda \le \Phi$ -1. The maximal Φ is stored in array $3DBBMAT(v(i, j, k))$.

The number of voxels $3D\_Q(v)$ dominated by voxel v is based on Eq.(2-3) as stated in Section 2.2. Let $3D\_Q^{-1}(v)$ represent the *reverse-dominated* voxels of $3D\_Q(v)$. To solve the 3D BB-MAT problem, we redefine the 3D dominance relation in the following.

Definition 5. In a 3D binary image, voxel v_1 is *reverse-dominated* by voxel v_2 (denoted by $v_2 \succ v_1$) if $i_{v2} \ge i_{v1}, j_{v2} \ge j_{v1}$ and $k_{v2} \ge k_{v1}$, where (i_{v1}, j_{v1}, k_{v1}) and (i_{v2}, j_{v2}, k_{v2}) are the coordinates of voxels v_1 and v_2, respectively.

Based on Definition 5, the number of voxels $3D\_Q^{-1}(v)$ *reverse-dominated* by voxel v can be computed by Eq.(3-2).

$$3D\_Q^{-1}(v) = \tag{3-2}$$
$$\sum_{k=k_v}^{N-1} \sum_{j=j_v}^{N-1} \sum_{i=i_v}^{N-1} d_1(i,j,k)$$

Like $3D\_Q^{-1}(v)$, we can compute $3D\_Q^{-1}(x)$ in a similar way. The $3D\_Q^{-1}(x)$ of all voxels (i_x, j_x, k_x), where $0 \le i_v \le i_x \le N\text{-}1$, $0 \le j_v \le j_x \le N\text{-}1$, and $0 \le k_v \le k_x \le N\text{-}1$, can be computed by Eq.(3-3).

$$3D\_Q^{-1}(x) = \sum_{k=k_x}^{N-1} \sum_{j=j_x}^{N-1} \sum_{i=i_x}^{N-1} d_1(i,j,k), \text{ where } 0 \le i_v \le i_x \le N\text{-}1, 0 \le j_v \le j_x \le N\text{-}1,$$

and $0 \le k_v \le k_x \le N\text{-}1$.
$$(3\text{-}3)$$

Lemma 3. The 3D dominance counting for the number $H^{-1}(v_1, v_2, v_3, v_4, v_5, v_6, v_7, v_8)$ of voxels contained in a 3D rectangular parallelepiped (or cube) $v_1\ v_2\ v_3\ v_4\ v_5\ v_6\ v_7\ v_8$ is given by $H^{-1}(v_1, v_2, v_3, v_4, v_5, v_6, v_7, v_8) = (3D\_Q^{-1}(v_8) + 3D\_Q^{-1}(v_3) + 3D\_Q^{-1}(v_6) + 3D\_Q^{-1}(v_1)) - (3D\_Q^{-1}(v_7) + 3D\_Q^{-1}(v_4) + 3D\_Q^{-1}(v_5) + 3D\_Q^{-1}(v_2))$.   (3-4)

Proof: Omitted

Lemma 4. Given a 3D $N \times N \times N$ binary image V, and a black voxel $v(i, j, k)$, $0 \le i, j, k \le N\text{-}1$, the 3D block-based medial axis transform at $v(i, j, k)$ is φ and is stored in array 3DBBMAT($v(i, j, k)$), where $\varphi = \max\{\ \Phi\ |\ v(i + \lambda, j + \lambda, k + \lambda) = 1$, for $0 \le \lambda \le \Phi\text{-}1$, and $i + \lambda, j + \lambda, k + \lambda \le N\text{-}1\}$ if and only if

$H^{-1}(v(i, j, k), v(i + \Phi, j, k), v(i + \Phi, j + \Phi, k), v(i, j + \Phi, k), v(i, j, k + \Phi), v(i + \Phi, j, k + \Phi), v(i + \Phi, j + \Phi, k + \Phi), v(i, j + \Phi, k + \Phi)) = \Phi^3$.   (3-5)

Proof: Omitted

3.2 The 3D BB-Mat Algorithm

The 3D block-based medial axis transform of an image algorithm (**Algorithm 3DBBMAT**) consists of three major steps. First, for each voxel $v(i, j, k)$, $0 \le i, j, k \le N\text{-}1$, compute the dominance number $3D\_Q^{-1}(v(i, j, k))$ of the image V by Eq.(3-3). Then, for each black voxel $v(i, j, k)$, $0 \le i, j, k \le N\text{-}1$, compute the 1-voxels possible cube whose side length is Φ, $0 \le \Phi \le N\text{-}1$, by Eq.(3-5). To identify whether a cube of size Φ^3 is obtained by Eq.(3-5), we use a binary search technique to find the maximal value Φ_m from Φ, $0 \le \Phi \le N\text{-}1$. As we can see, if there is a cube of size σ^3 covering voxel $v(i, j, k)$, then it is always covered by a cube of size ρ^3, $0 \le \rho \le \sigma$. This property provides a method to find the maximal value Φ_m from Φ, $0 \le \Phi \le N\text{-}1$, by using the binary search over $\log N$ iterations. Finally, if $3D\_Q^{-1}(v(0, 0, 0)) = N^3$ then 3DBBMAT($v(0, 0, 0)$) = N; otherwise, the 3D block-based medial axis transform is computed by the following equation.

$$3\text{DBBMAT}(v(i, j, k)) = \begin{cases} \Phi_m(i, j, k), & \text{if } v(i, j, k) = 1, 0 \le i, j, k \le N\text{-}1; \\ 0, & \text{otherwise.} \end{cases}$$

The 3D block-based medial axis transform algorithm (**Algorithm 3DBBMAT**) is given below.

Algorithm 3DBBMAT
Input: A 3D $N \times N \times N$ binary image V with $v(i, j, k) \in \{0,1\}$, $0 \le i, j, k \le N\text{-}1$, where each voxel is loaded in processor PE(i, j, k).
Output: 3DBBMAT($v(i, j, k)$), $0 \le i, j, k \le N\text{-}1$.
Step1: Compute the dominance number $3D\_Q^{-1}(v(i, j, k))$, $0 \le i, j, k \le N\text{-}1$, of the image V.

1.1 For each pair of specified indices j and k, processors PE(i, j, k), $0 \le i \le N\text{-}1$, compute the postfix sum of $v(i, j, k)$ by Corollary 1 and store the result in the local variable POS(i, j, k).

1.2 Then for each pair of specified indices i and k, processors PE(i, j, k), $0 \le j \le N\text{-}1$, compute the postfix sum of POS(i, j, k) by Corollary 1 and store the result back to the local variable POS(i, j, k).

1.3 Finally, for each pair of specified indices i and j, processors PE(i, j, k), $0 \le k \le N\text{-}1$, compute the postfix sum of POS(i, j, k) by Corollary 1 and store the final result to the local variable 3D_Q$^{-1}(v(i, j, k))$.

Step2: Compute the maximal cube for the voxel located at $v(i, j, k)$. Each processor PE(i, j, k) with a black voxel $v(i, j, k)$, $0 \le i, j, k \le N\text{-}1$, performs a binary search procedure to find the maximal value Φ_m from Φ, $0 \le \Phi \le N\text{-}1$. Let left, right and middle be the integer variables.

For (left = 0, right = N-1) to left < right pardo

2.1 Let Φ_t = middle = $\lceil (\text{left} + \text{right})/2 \rceil$.

2.2 Read eight dominance numbers from shared memory that are 3D_Q$^{-1}(v(i, j, k))$, 3D_Q$^{-1}(v(i + \Phi_t, j, k))$, 3D_Q$^{-1}(v(i + \Phi_t, j + \Phi_t, k))$, 3D_Q$^{-1}(v(i, j + \Phi_t, k))$, 3D_Q$^{-1}(v(i, j, k + \Phi_t))$, 3D_Q$^{-1}(v(i + \Phi_t, j, k + \Phi_t))$, 3D_Q$^{-1}(v(i + \Phi_t, j + \Phi_t, k + \Phi_t))$, and 3D_Q$^{-1}(v(i, j + \Phi_t, k + \Phi_t))$, respectively.

2.3 Based on the eight dominance numbers obtained in Step 2.2, compute the 3D dominance counting for the number H$^{-1}(v(i, j, k), v(i + \Phi_t, j, k), v(i + \Phi_t, j + \Phi_t, k), v(i, j + \Phi_t, k), v(i, j, k + \Phi_t), v(i + \Phi_t, j, k + \Phi_t), v(i + \Phi_t, j + \Phi_t, k + \Phi_t), v(i, j + \Phi_t, k + \Phi_t))$ by Eq.(3-5).

2.4 If H$^{-1} = (\Phi_t)^3$ then set left = middle and $\Phi_m(i, j, k) = \Phi_t$; else right = middle -1.

End for;

Step3: For each **processor** PE(i, j, k), $0 \le i, j, k \le N\text{-}1$, set 3DBBMAT$(v(i, j, k)) = \Phi_m(i, j, k)$, if $v(i, j, k) = 1$; 3DBBMAT$(v(i, j, k)) = 0$, if $v(i, j, k) = 0$.

Theorem 1. Let $v(i, j, k)$, $0 \le i, j, k \le N\text{-}1$, be a 3D $N \times N \times N$ binary image. Initially, each image voxel $v(i, j, k)$ is loaded in processor PE(i, j, k), respectively. The 3D block-based medial axis transform can be executed in $O(\log N)$ time on the CREW PRAM model using $N \times N \times N$ processors.

Proof: Omitted.

4   The 3D CDT Problem and the 3D CDT Algorithm

Section 4.1 defines the 3D CDT problem from the 2D CDT problem. Section 4.2 establishes the relationship between the 3D CDT problem and the 3D BB-MAT problem. In Section 4.3, **Algorithm 3DCDT** is presented.

4.1 The 3D CDT Problem

Assume a 3D $N \times N \times N$ binary image V, with $v(i, j, k) \in \{0,1\}$, $0 \le i, j, k \le N$-1, where 1 denotes a foreground voxel, 0 denotes a background voxel, and the voxel $v(0, 0, 0)$ is located at the top-left-front corner of the 3D binary image V. Let $D_1 = \{d_1(i, j, k) \mid v(i, j, k) = 1$ of $V\}$ be the set of all foreground voxels of V. According to Eq. (1-1) as stated in Section 1, the 3D chessboard distance transform (3D CDT) of image V is to find an array

$$3DCDT(v(i, j, k)) = \min_{(x,y,z) \in D_1} \{\max(|i - x|, |j - y|, |k - z|)\}, \text{ for } 0 \le i, j, k \le N\text{-}1. \quad (4\text{-}1)$$

4.2 Compute the 3D CDT Problem By the 3D BB-Mat Problem

From the 3DBBMAT($v(i, j, k)$) of an image V, we say that it is a dense 3D BB-MAT or sparse 3D BB-MAT if the voxels of the outside region of an image V are all background voxels or foreground voxels, respectively. The definition of the dense 3D BB-MAT is the one we presented in Section 3.1. In the following, we extend the definition of 3D BB-MAT and 3D CDT problems in eight different directions, the lower-right-back (LRB), the lower-right-front (LRF), the lower-left-back (LLB), the lower-left-front (LLF), the upper-right-back (URB), the upper-right-front (URF), the upper-left-back (ULB), and the upper-left-front (ULF), respectively. For any image V, we use an array LRB_MAT($v(i, j, k)$) to denote the side length of the maximal cube of the lower-right-back direction of $v(i, j, k)$. The definition of the LRB_MAT($v(i, j, k)$) is the same as that of the MAT presented in Section 3.1. Similarly, the MAT in the lower-right-front, the lower-left-back, the lower-left-front, the upper-right-back, the upper-right-front, the upper-left-back, and the upper-left-front directions can be also defined by LRF_MAT($v(i, j, k)$), LLB_MAT($v(i, j, k)$), LLF_MAT($v(i, j, k)$), URB_MAT($v(i, j, k)$), URF_MAT($v(i, j, k)$), ULB_MAT($v(i, j, k)$), and ULF_MAT($v(i, j, k)$), correspondingly. We now define LRB_CDT($v(i, j, k)$), LRF_CDT($v(i, j, k)$), LLB_CDT($v(i, j, k)$), LLF_CDT($v(i, j, k)$), URB_CDT($v(i, j, k)$), URF_CDT($v(i, j, k)$), ULB_CDT($v(i, j, k)$), and ULF_CDT($v(i, j, k)$) to denote the CDT for a 3D image V in eight different directions as the same for those directions of the MAT described above. It is easy to observe that 3DCDT($v(i, j, k)$) is the minimum of these eight components. That is,

$3DCDT(v(i, j, k)) = \min\{LRB\_CDT(v(i, j, k)), LRF\_CDT(v(i, j, k)), LLB\_CDT(v(i, j, k)), LLF\_CDT(v(i, j, k)), URB\_CDT(v(i, j, k)), URF\_CDT(v(i, j, k)), ULB\_CDT(v(i, j, k)), ULF\_CDT(v(i, j, k))\}$, for $0 \le i, j, k \le N$-1, where, (4-2)

$$LRB\_CDT(v(i, j, k)) = \min_{(x,y,z) \in D_1, i \le x \le N-1, j \le y \le N-1, k \le z \le N-1} \{\max(|i - x|, |j - y|, |k - z|)\},$$

$$LRF\_CDT(v(i, j, k)) = \min_{(x,y,z) \in D_1, i \le x \le N-1, j \le y \le N-1, 0 \le z \le k} \{\max(|i - x|, |j - y|, |k - z|)\},$$

$$LLB\_CDT(v(i, j, k)) = \min_{(x,y,z) \in D_1, i \le x \le N-1, 0 \le y \le j, k \le z \le N-1} \{\max(|i - x|, |j - y|, |k - z|)\},$$

$$LLF\_CDT(v(i, j, k)) = \min_{(x,y,z) \in D_1, i \le x \le N-1, 0 \le y \le j, 0 \le z \le k} \{\max(|i - x|, |j - y|, |k - z|)\},$$

$$\text{URB\_CDT}(v(i, j, k)) = \min_{(x,y,z)\in D_1, 0\le x\le i,\, j\le y\le N\text{-}1, k\le z\le N\text{-}1} \{\max(|i - x|, |j - y|, |k - z|)\},$$

$$\text{URF\_CDT}(v(i, j, k)) = \min_{(x,y,z)\in D_1, 0\le x\le i,\, j\le y\le N\text{-}1, 0\le z\le k} \{\max(|i - x|, |j - y|, |k - z|)\},$$

$$\text{ULB\_CDT}(v(i, j, k)) = \min_{(x,y,z)\in D_1, 0\le x\le i, 0\le y\le j, k\le z\le N\text{-}1} \{\max(|i - x|, |j - y|, |k - z|)\},$$

$$\text{ULF\_CDT}(v(i, j, k)) = \min_{(x,y,z)\in D_1, 0\le x\le i, 0\le y\le j, 0\le z\le k} \{\max(|i - x|, |j - y|, |k - z|)\}.$$

Theorem 2. Given a 3D $N\times N\times N$ binary image V, with $v(i, j, k)\in \{0,1\}$, $0\le i, j$, $k\le N\text{-}1$, the 3D chessboard distance transform of image V denoted as $3DCDT(v(i, j, k))$ can be computed as follows.

$3DCDT(v(i, j, k)) = \min\{\text{LRB\_CDT}(v(i, j, k)),$ $\text{LRF\_CDT}(v(i, j, k)),$ $\text{LLB\_CDT}(v(i, j,$ $k)),$ $\text{LLF\_CDT}(v(i, j, k)),$ $\text{URB\_CDT}(v(i, j, k)),$ $\text{URF\_CDT}(v(i, j, k)),$ $\text{ULB\_CDT}(v(i, j,$ $k)),$ $\text{ULF\_CDT}(v(i, j, k))\},$
   $= \min\{\text{LRB\_MAT}(v'(i,\ j,\ k)),$ $\text{LRF\_MAT}(v'(i,\ j,\ k)),$ $\text{LLB\_MAT}(v'(i,\ j,\ k)),$ $\text{LLF\_MAT}(v'(i, j, k)),$ $\text{URB\_MAT}(v'(i, j, k)),$ $\text{URF\_MAT}(v'(i, j, k)),$ $\text{ULB\_MAT}(v'(i, j,$ $k)),$ $\text{ULF\_MAT}(v'(i, j, k))\},$ for $0\le i, j, k\le N\text{-}1$.   (4-3)

Proof: Omitted.

4.3 The 3D CDT Algorithm

We assume that the voxels of the outside region of image V are all background voxels. Clearly, those of the outside region of image V' are all foreground voxels. The correctness of the following algorithm is based on Theorem 2.

Algorithm 3DCDT
Input: A 3D $N\times N\times N$ binary image V with $v(i, j, k)\in \{0,1\}$, $0\le i, j, k\le N\text{-}1$.
Output: $3DCDT(v(i, j, k))$, $0\le i, j, k\le N\text{-}1$.
Step1: Invert the binary image V from $v(i, j, k)$ to $v'(i, j, k)$ of V', where

$$v'(i, j, k) = \begin{cases} 0 & \text{if } v(i, j, k) = 1; \\ 1 & \text{otherwise.} \end{cases}$$

Step2: Assume that the outside region of image V is all background voxels. The outside region of image V' is then all foreground voxels. Then, apply **Algorithm 3DBBMAT** to binary image V' to compute $\text{LRB\_MAT}(v'(i,\ j,\ k))$, $\text{LRF\_MAT}(v'(i,\ j,\ k))$, $\text{LLB\_MAT}(v'(i, j, k))$, $\text{LLF\_MAT}(v'(i, j, k))$, $\text{URB\_MAT}(v'(i, j, k))$, $\text{URF\_MAT}(v'(i, j, k))$, $\text{ULB\_MAT}(v'(i, j, k))$, and $\text{ULF\_MAT}(v'(i, j, k))$, respectively.
Step3: Compute $3DCDT(v(i, j, k))$, by Eq.(4-3).

Theorem 3. Let $v(i, j, k)$, $0\le i, j, k\le N\text{-}1$, be a 3D $N\times N\times N$ binary image. Initially, each image voxel $v(i, j, k)$ is loaded in processor $PE(i, j, k)$. The 3D chessboard distance transform can be computed in $O(\log N)$ time on the CREW PRAM model using $N\times N\times N$ processors.

Proof: Omitted.

5   The Experimental Results of the 3D CDT Problem

Since the PRAM model is not available in the real world, we have implemented an MPI
program to verify the 3D CDT parallel algorithm on an AMD Opteron Model 270 (2.0
GHz/1M L2) cluster system with computing power 0.92 teraflops located at National
Taiwan University of Science and Technology (http://www.ntust.edu.tw/). The running
time and CPUs used for the problem of size 32×32×32 are shown in Fig. 2. Also, note
that the upper curve of 32×32×32 represents the experimental result of the cluster
system, while the lower curve of   Optimal 32×32×32   represents the theoretical
optimal curve of the PRAM model. A theoretical optimal is the optimal that is the same
value from one processor to more processors for the product of the running time and
CPUs. Hence, the communication time can be almost ignored for the   Optimal
32×32×32 . Based on the experimental result of the cluster system, the computation
time for the problem size of 32×32×32 cannot be further reduced when the number
of processors used is more than four. This is due to the fact that AMD Opteron Model
270 is not the shared-memory architecture (PRAM model). With a larger number of
processors, the communication time will worsen due to data exchanging. In fact, the
MPI code is very communication intensive when the problem size is not big enough
and the number of processors used is increased. In Fig. 3, the experimental result shows
that the running time for the problem of size 16×16×16 will increase when the
number of processors used is more than one. n parallel algorithms, the speedup is

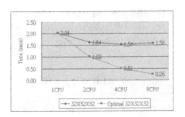

Fig. 2. The time and CPUs used for the CDT of size 32×32×32.

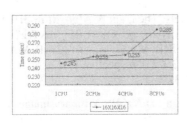

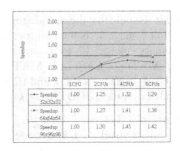

Fig. 3. The time and CPUs used for the CDT of size
16×16×16

Fig. 4. The comparison for the
speedup for the CDT of size
32×32×32, 64×64×64, and 96×96×96,
respectively

usually used to compare the relative performance of the parallel computations. Let P be a given computational problem and let n be its input size. Denote the sequential complexity of P by $T^*(n)$. Let A be a parallel algorithm that solves P in time $T_p(n)$ on a parallel computer with p processors. The definition of speedup [16] achieved by A is $S_p(n) = T^*(n) / T_p(n)$. The speedup curves for the three different problem sizes, $32 \times 32 \times 32$, $64 \times 64 \times 64$, and $96 \times 96 \times 96$ are shown in Fig. 4, respectively. As we can see, for each problem size, the speedup is saturated when the number of processors used is more than four. On the other hand, the speedup is slightly increased with the problem size linearly increases in each dimension.

6 Concluding Remarks

In this paper, we first present an $O(\log N)$ time parallel algorithm for solving the three dimensional block-based medial axis transform problem using N^3 processors on the CREW PRAM model. The relationship between 3D BB-MAT and 3D CDT is then derived. Based on the relationship derived in this paper, the 3D CDT can be also computed in $O(\log N)$ time using N^3 processors on the CREW PRAM model. To the best of our knowledge, the presented results are the first 3D CDT algorithm known. In addition, we have implemented an MPI program to verify the proposed CDT parallel algorithm. The experimental results gave evidence that the speedup saturated when the number of processors used was more than four, regardless of the problem size. Furthermore, the speedup is slightly increased when the problem size linearly increases in each dimension; this implies that the parallel computer (i.e., cluster system) is more suitable for solving problems with bigger size. On the contrary, when more processors are used for a problem whose size is not big enough, the running time for the problem with a small size could be increased due to communication overhead. In the future study, if one can solve the 3D CDT problem in less than $O(\log N)$ time complexity, then the 3D BB-MAT problem can also be solved with the same time complexity.

References

1. Rosenfeld, A., Pfalz, J.L.: Sequential operations in digital picture processing. Journal of the ACM, 471.494 (1966)
2. Blum, H.: Models for the perception of speech and visual form, vol. 11, pp. 362.380. MIT Press (1967)
3. Schwarzkopf, O.: Parallel computation of distance transforms. Algorithmica, 685.697 (1991)
4. Montanvert, A.: Medial line: graph representation and shape description. In: Proc. of the 8th International Conference on Pattern Recognition, pp. 430.432 (1986)
5. Chandran, S., Kim, S.K., Mount, D.M.: Parallel computational geometry of rectangles. Algorithmica, 25.49 (1992)
6. Jenq, J.F., Sahni, S.: Serial and parallel algorithms for the medial axis transform. IEEE Trans. on Pattern Analysis and Machine Intelligence, 1218..1224 (1992)

7. Ramanathan, M., Gurumoorthy, B.: Constructing medial axis transform of extruded and revolved 3D objects with free-form boundaries. Computer-Aided Design, 1370..1387 (2005)

8. Morrison, P., Zou, J.J.: An effective skeletonization method based on adaptive selection of contour points. In: Proc. of the 3th International Conference on Information Technology and Applications, pp. 644..649 (2005)

9. Remy, E., Thiel, E.: Medial axis for chamfer distances: computing look-up tables and neighbourhoods in 2D or 3D. Pattern Recognition Letters, 649..661 (2002)

10. Remy, E., Thiel, E.: Look-Up tables for medial axis on squared Euclidean distance transform. In: Proc. of the 11th Discrete Geometry for Computer Image, pp. 224..235 (2003)

11. Wang, Y.R., Horng, S.J.: An O(1) time algorithm for the 3D Euclidean distance transform on the CRCW PRAM Model. IEEE Trans. on Parallel and Distributed Systems, 973..982 (2003)

12. Wang, Y.R., Horng, S.J.: Parallel algorithms for arbitrary dimensional Euclidean distance transforms with applications on arrays with reconfigurable optical buses. IEEE Trans. on System, Man, and Cybernetics   Part B: Cybernetics, 517..532 (2004)

13. Wang, Y.R.: Fast algorithms for block-based medial axis transform on the LARPBS. In: Proc. of the IEEE International Conference on Systems, Man, and Cybernetics (2005)

14. Lin, S.Y., Horng, S.J., Kao, T.W., Wang, Y.R.: An O(1) time parallel algorithm for the dominance counting and 3D block-based medial axis transform on AROB. In: Proc. of the 6th International Conference on Parallel and Distributed Computing Applications and Technologies, pp. 603..609 (2005)

15. Lee, Y.H., Horng, S.J.: Chessboard distance transform and the medial axis transform are interchangeable. In: Proc. of the IEEE Symposium on Parallel and Distributed Processing, pp. 424..428 (1996)

16. JáJá, J.: An introduction to parallel algorithms. Addison-Wesley, Reading (1992)

17. Preparata, F.P., Shamos, M.I.: Computational geometry an introduction. Springer, Heidelberg (1985)

A General Approach to Predict the Performance Order of TSP Family Problems*

P. Fritzsche, D. Rexachs, and E. Luque

Computer Architecture and Operating Systems Department
University Autonoma of Barcelona. Spain

Abstract. Parallel computers provide an efficient and economical way to solve large-scale and/or time-constrained scientific, engineering, and industry problems. Consequently, there is a need to predict the performance order of both deterministic and non-deterministic parallel algorithms.

The performance prediction of the traveling salesman problem (TSP) is a challenging problem because similar input data sets may cause significant variability in execution times. Parallel performance of data-dependent algorithms depends on the problem size, the number of processors, and other parameters. Discovering the main other parameters is the real key to obtain a good estimation of performance order.

This paper presents a novel methodology to the problem of predicting the performance of a parallel algorithm for solving the TSP. The entire process explores data in search of patterns and/or relationships detecting the main parameters that affect performance. Then, it uses the measured values for this limited number of inputs to produce a multiple-linear-regression model. Finally, the regression equation allows for predicting how the algorithm will respond when given new input data sets. The preliminary experimental results are quite promising.

Keywords: Performance prediction, TSP, Data-dependent algorithms, Parallel computing.

1 Introduction

Parallel computers provide an efficient and economical way to solve large-scale and/or time-constrained scientific, engineering, and industry problems. Consequently, there is a need to predict the performance order of both deterministic and non-deterministic parallel algorithms. Computer designers, professional engineers, and scientists are interested in obtaining realistic figures for the expected performance.

The parallel performance prediction of data-dependent algorithms is an extremely challenging problem because similar input data sets may cause significant variability in execution times. One of the nice features of this kind of algorithms

---

* This work was supported by the CICYT-Spain under contracts TIN 2004-03388 and TIN 2007-64974.

A. Bourgeois and S.Q. Zheng (Eds.): ICA3PP 2008, LNCS 5022, pp. 97–108, 2008.

is that its performance does not depend only on the problem size and on the number of processors. Other parameters must to be taken into account, the values of which are data-dependent. Discovering the main other parameters is the real key to obtain a good estimation of performance order. Good examples of this class of programs are the sorting algorithms, the searching algorithms, the graph partition [1], the knapsack problem, the bin packing [2], the motion planning [3], and the traveling salesman problem (TSP) [4]. Also there are many practical problems that can be formulated as TSP problems [5, 6].

This paper presents a novel methodology to the problem of predicting the performance of a parallel algorithm for solving the TSP. This arises out of the need to give an answer to a great number of problems that are normally set aside. Any minimum contribution in the non-deterministic area represents a great advance due to the lack of general knowledge. Not only it is important to think in the problem that is solved but also in the involved benefit for its family.

The general methodology begins by collecting execution-time data for a considerable number of TSP instances. A well-designed experiment guides the experimenters in choosing what experiments actually need to be performed. This is a complex task and the experiments should provide a representative sample. Then, a data-mining process explores these collected data in search of patterns and/or relationships detecting the main parameters that affect performance. These patterns and/or relationships are modelled numerically in order to generate an analytical formulation of the execution time. As the methodology is based on a black-box approach, the measured values for this representative sample of inputs are used to produce a multiple-linear-regression model. Finally, the regression equation allows for predicting how the algorithm will perform when given new input data sets.

A parallel Euclidean TSP implementation, called **global pruning algorithm**, has been developed and studied. It is used to analyze the influence of indeterminism in performance prediction, and also to show the usefulness of the methodology. It follows the Master-Worker programming paradigm. It is a branch-and-bound algorithm which recursively searches all possible paths and prunes large parts of the search space by maintaining a global variable containing the length of the shortest path found so far. If the length of a partial path is bigger than the current minimal length, this path is not expanded further and a part of the search space is pruned. Its execution time depends on the number of cities (C), the number of processors (P), and other parameters. As a result of our investigation, right now the sum of the distances from one city to the other cities (SD) and the mean deviation of SDs values $(MDSD)$ are the numerical parameters characterizing the different input data beyond the number of cities.

The preliminary experimental results of predictions are quite promising. An important fact has been reached beyond was originally sought. By looking each combination of SD_j and $MDSD$ values coming from C cities, it is also possible to choose the best starting city for the TSP problem. This means invests less time in order to obtain the minimal path.

The rest of the paper is organized as follows. The next section presents a novel methodology to the problem of predicting the performance of a parallel algorithm for solving the traveling salesman problem. Section 3 describes the TSP problem. Also, in this section, a parallel TSP algorithm implementation is discussed. Section 4 focus on of discovering process carried out to find the significant input parameters. Finally, Section 5 summarizes and draws the main conclusions of this work.

2 Methodology

The novel methodology attempts to estimate the performance order of a parallel algorithm that solves the TSP problem. The defined methodology consists of two main phases: the extraction of knowledge and the prediction, see Fig. 1. The hypotheses formulation, the design and composition of experiments, the TSP execution for the selected input data, the knowledge discovery in databases (KDD) process, the understanding of the model, and the quality analysis are stages of the extraction of knowledge phase.

2.1 Extraction of Knowledge

Hypotheses formulation: The hypotheses formulation consists of defining the key parameters that can affect the execution time of the studied application. First of all, it is important to understand the application domain and the relevant prior knowledge, and to analyze their behavior step by step, in

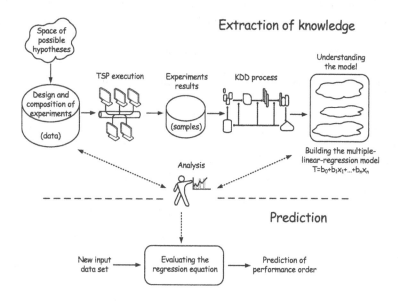

Fig. 1. The novel methodology

a deep way. It is an arduous job that requires specialists to manually or automatically identify the relevant issues. Finding the correct hypotheses (the main parameters) is the basis to obtain a good capacity of prediction. Including too many parameters may lead to an accurate but too complicated or even unsolvable model. Hence, great care should be taken in selecting parameters and a reasonable trade-off should be made. At the end, it is a try-and-error method in the way to identify some of the relevant parameters.

Design and composition of experiments: Defining an experiment involves articulating a goal, choosing an output that characterizes an aspect of that goal and specifying the data that will be used in the study. A well-designed experiment guides the experimenters in choosing what experiments actually need to be performed. The experiments should provide a representative sample.

TSP execution: The TSP algorithm implementation reads an experiment and obtains their results. This action is done by each experiment coming from a representative sample.

KDD process: A KDD process analyzes execution times results from different perspectives and summarizes these into useful information. A brief summarization of this process involves reading the data and constructing a model. Obtaining a good model that is really useful to the problem requires many careful considerations and much objective hard work.

Understanding a data-mining model: Once a data set has been mined, the process of understanding a data-mining model created from the results involves many different aspects. Mainly, the model summary shows the conjunctions that are important to describing the goal.

Data-mining quality analysis: The validation of hypotheses involves comparing the results to known suppositions. Also the quality analysis has to include utility, newness, and interest measurements. This stage can implicate a backward motion to previous steps in order to obtain extra or more precise information.

Building a regression model: Once the main parameters that affect performance have been obtained, their measured values are used to produce a multiple-linear-regression model (MLR model). It allows including the effects of several input variables that are all linearly related to a single output variable ($T = b_0 + b_1 x_1 + \ldots + b_n x_n$). Hence, great care should be taken in analyzing this first approximation because it is difficult to know the degree of complexity of the relationship between the parameters and execution time.

Quality analysis after developing a regression model: From the scientific point of view is essential to find confidence intervals for the regression parameters to provide some indication of how well they model the measured values. Taking this as a basis, it could determine the number of elements in the sample.

2.2   Prediction

The regression equation is used to predict how the analyzed algorithm implementation will perform when given a new input data set. The $b_0, b_1, , b_n$ values are the estimated regression parameters. Replacing $x_1, x_2, , x_n$ with real values in the equation, it is possible to predict the time required.

3   Traveling Salesman Problem

The traveling salesman problem (TSP) is one of the most famous problems (and the best one perhaps studied) in the field of the combinatorial optimization. In spite of the apparent simplicity of their formulation, the TSP is a complex solving problem and the complexity of its solution has been a continue challenge to the mathematicians for centuries.

3.1   Problem Statement

The TSP for C cities is the problem of finding a tour visiting all the cities exactly once and returning to the starting city such that the sum of the distances between consecutive cities is minimized. The requirement of returning to the starting city does not change the computational complexity of the problem.

3.2   TSP Algorithm Implementation

An Euclidean TSP[1] algorithm implementation, called **global pruning algorithm**, to obtain the exact TSP solution in a parallel machine is presented. It is used to analyze the influence of indeterminism in performance prediction, and also to show the usefulness of the methodology. It is a branch-and-bound algorithm which recursively searches all possible paths and prunes large parts of the search space by maintaining a global variable containing the length of the shortest path found so far. It follows the Master-Worker (MW) programming paradigm [5].

Each city is represented by two coordinates in the Euclidean plane then, for each city pair exists a symmetrical distance. Considering C different cities, the Master defines a certain level L to divide the tasks. Tasks are the possible permutations of $C - 1$ cities in L elements. The granularity G of a task is the number of cities that defines the task sub-tree: $G = C - L$. At the start-up execution, the Master sends tasks with a variable containing the length of the shortest path found so far.

A diagram of the possible permutations for 5 cities, considering the salesman starts and ends his trip at the city 1, can be seen in Fig. 2. The Master can divide this problem into 1 task of level 0 or 4 tasks of level 1 or 12 tasks of level 2 for example. The tasks of the first level would be represented by the cities 1 and 2 for the first task, 1 and 3 for the second, followed by 1 and 4 and 1 and 5.

---

[1] For simplicity of implementation, it were considered cities in R^2 instead of R^n. The most straightforward way of computing distances between cities in a two-dimensional space is to compute Euclidean distances. Anyway, the election of distance measure (Euclidean, Manhattan, Chebychev, ...) is irrelevant. The ideas of this paper can be generalized to more general settings.

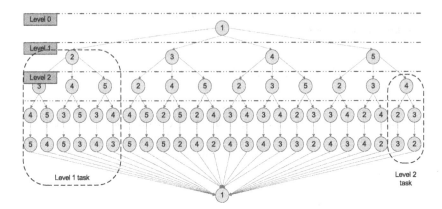

Fig. 2. Possible paths for the salesman considering 5 cities

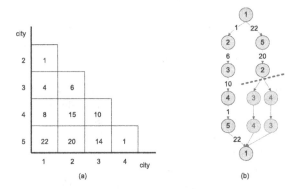

Fig. 3. (a) Matrix of distances (b) Pruning process in the TSP algorithm implementation

Workers are responsible for calculating the distance of the permutations left in the task and sending to the Master the minimum path and distance of these permutations. One of the characteristics of a pruning TSP implementation is that if the length of a partial path is bigger than the current minimal length, this path is not expanded further and a part of the search space is pruned. Consequently, each estimate depends on several factors.

Fig. 3(a) shows a strictly lower triangular matrix of distances, meanwhile Fig. 3(b) exhibits the pruning process for the TSP algorithm implementation where each arrow has the distance between the two cities it connects. Analyzing Fig. 3(b), the total distance for the first followed path (in the left) is of 40 units. The distance between 1 and 2 on the second path (in the right) is already of 42 units. It is then not necessary for the algorithm to keep calculating distances from the city 2 on because it is impossible to reach a better distance for this branch.

4   Discovering the Significant Input Parameters

The execution time for the global pruning algorithm (GP-TSP) depends on the number of cities (C), the number of processors (P), and other parameters. As a result of the investigation, right now the sum of the distances from one city to the other cities (SD) and the mean deviation of SDs values ($MDSD$) are the numerical parameters characterizing the different input data beyond the number of cities (C). But how these final parameters have been obtained? Next, it is described the followed way to discover the above mentioned dependencies (SD and $MDSD$).

Specification of the parallel machine: The execution were reached with a 32 node homogeneous PC Cluster (Pentium IV 3.0GHz., 1Gb DDR-DSRAM 400Mhz., Gigabit Ethernet) at the Computer Architecture and Operating Systems Department, University Autonoma of Barcelona. All the communications have been accomplished using a switched network with a mean distance between two communication end-points of two hops. The switches enable dynamic routes in order to overlap communication.

4.1   First Hypothesis: Location of the Cities (Geographical Pattern)

For simplicity, only a training data set will be analyzed along this section. It consists of 5 different geographical patterns of 15 cities each one (named $G1$ to $G5$). Fig. 4 shows the five patterns handled for the 15 cities.

The GP-TSP algorithm receives the number of cities and their coordinates, and the level. It proceeds recursively searching all possible paths using the pruning strategy and, finally, generating the minimal path and the time spent.

Table 1 shows the obtained execution times (in sec.) by pattern and starting city for the GP-TSP (columns $G1$ to $G5$) executed in 8 nodes of the parallel machine.

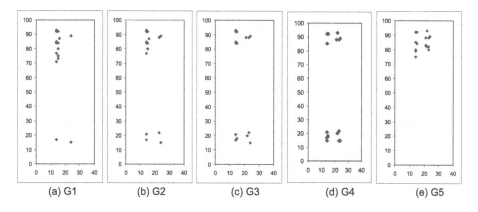

Fig. 4. Five patterns for 15 cities

Table 1. Execution times (in sec.) and assigned cluster for the *GP-TSP*

Starting city	Pattern									
	G1	CL1	G2	CL2	G3	CL3	G4	CL4	G5	CL5
1	216.17	1	36.50	3	15.34	2	10.51	4	8.03	5
2	214.44	1	36.82	3	15.19	2	9.98	4	8.14	5
3	77.25	1	18.16	2	10.31	4	9.95	4	8.02	5
4	72.64	1	18.03	2	10.34	4	10.41	4	7.83	5
5	70.94	1	18.54	2	10.24	4	10.30	4	7.91	5
6	74.21	1	17.83	2	15.24	2	9.88	4	7.98	5
7	75.59	1	38.09	3	15.57	2	9.88	4	8.22	5
8	73.72	1	37.29	3	15.02	2	10.02	4	7.71	5
9	69.47	1	17.79	2	10.27	4	10.49	4	7.82	5
10	74.96	1	17.48	2	10.23	4	9.85	4	8.04	5
11	75.89	1	17.07	2	15.84	2	9.87	4	8.12	5
12	70.17	1	17.39	2	10.28	4	9.97	4	7.78	5
13	73.73	1	18.10	2	10.36	4	10.24	4	7.71	5
14	70.87	1	17.37	2	10.17	4	10.36	4	7.93	5
15	73.30	1	18.00	2	10.32	4	10.26	4	7.87	5
Mean	92.23		22.97		12.32		10.14		7.94	

To discover the internal information of these values, it was decided to apply data mining techniques. In particular, the data mining technique called 'clustering' was chosen to partition the data set into distinctive 'data clusters', so that the data in each cluster share some common trait (similar execution time). This work was done using a k-means algorithm [7] included in a dynamic and open environment of clustering called Cluster-Frame [5]. In order to find 5 clusters, k was fixed in 5. The idea was to obtain quite similar groups with respect to the groups (patterns) used at the beginning. The initial centroids were randomly selected by the clustering application. The chosen objective function was the squared error function, Eq. 1

$$\sum_{j=1}^{k}\sum_{i=1}^{n}|x_i^{(j)} - c_j|^2 \tag{1}$$

where $|x_i^{(j)} - c_j|^2$ is a chosen distance measure between a data point $x_i^{(j)}$ and the cluster centroid c_j, the entire function is an indicator of the distance of the n data points from their respective cluster centroids.

Columns $CL1, .., CL5$ in Table 1 show the assigned cluster for each sample. For the clusters 1 to 5, the centroids values were 92.22 sec., 16.94 sec., 37.17 sec., 10.19 sec., and 7.94 sec., respectively.

The quality evaluation involves the validation of the above mentioned hypothesis. For each sample, the assigned cluster was confronted with the defined graphic pattern previously. The percentage of hits expresses the capacity of prediction. A simple observation is that the run times were clustered in a similar way to patterns fixed at starting, the capacity of prediction was of 75% for the

GP-TSP. This means that there was a close relationship between the patterns and the run times.

Conclusions: The initial hypothesis for the *GP-TSP* was corroborated; the capacity of prediction was greater than 75% for the full range of experiments worked. This value gave evidence of the existence of other significant parameters. Therefore, a deep analysis of results revealed an open issue remained for discussion and resolution, the singular execution times by pattern. Another major hypothesis was formulated. At this stage, the asymptotic time complexity was defined as *O(C, P, pattern)*.

4.2 Second Hypothesis: Location of the Cities and Starting City (C_1)

The analyzed training data set is the same used previously. Comparing Fig. 4 with Table 1, it is easy to infer some important facts. The two far cities in Fig. 4(a) correspond with the two higher time values of Table 1(G1). The four far cities in Fig. 4(b) correspond with the four higher execution time values of Table 1(G2). The six far cities in Fig. 4(c) correspond with the six higher time values of Table 1(G3). The cities in Fig. 4(d) are distributed among two zones so, the times turn out to be enough similar, see Table 1(G4). Finally, the cities in Fig. 4(e) are enough closed so, the times are quite similar, see Table 1(G5).

Another important observation is that the mean of execution times by group decreases as the cities approach.

Conclusions: Without doubt, the location of the cities and the starting city (C_1) play an important role in run times; the hypothesis was corroborated. Anyway, an open issue remained for discussion and resolution, how to relate a pattern (in general) with the numerical value of the execution time. This relationship would be able to establish a numerical characterization of patterns. On this basis, an original hypothesis was formulated. At this point, the asymptotic time complexity for the *GP-TSP* was redefined as $O(C, P, pattern, C_1)$.

4.3 Third Hypothesis: Sum of Distances and Mean Deviation of Sum of Distances

What parameters could be used to quantitatively characterize different geographical patterns in the distribution of cities? Right now for each pattern, the sum of the distances from one city to the other cities (SD_j, as shown on Eq. 2) and the mean deviation of SDs values ($MDSD$) are the worked inputs.

$$\forall j : 1 \leq j \leq C \quad SD_j = \sum_{i=1}^{C} \sqrt{(x_j - x_i)^2 + (y_j - y_i)^2} \tag{2}$$

If a particular city j is very remote of the others, its SD_j will be considerably greater to the rest and consequently the execution time G will grow also. This can be observed in Table 2.

Table 2. Execution times (in sec.) and sum of the distances for the *GP-TSP*

Starting city	Pattern									
	G1	SD1	G2	SD2	G3	SD3	G4	SD4	G5	SD5
1	216.17	853.94	36.50	746.10	15.34	664.60	10.51	643.75	8.03	148.74
2	214.44	887.44	36.82	740.49	15.19	649.14	9.98	574.23	8.14	123.19
3	77.25	315.51	18.16	369.56	10.31	467.99	9.95	574.97	8.02	124.96
4	72.64	230.11	18.03	383.38	10.34	490.55	10.41	611.45	7.83	111.79
5	70.94	226.88	18.54	345.83	10.24	477.42	10.30	599.99	7.91	103.35
6	74.21	244.56	17.83	330.76	15.24	638.04	9.88	530.72	7.98	109.78
7	75.59	276.09	38.09	820.63	15.57	707.70	9.88	578.78	8.22	172.52
8	73.72	294.62	37.29	789.80	15.02	678.07	10.02	555.70	7.71	141.15
9	69.47	233.53	17.79	370.10	10.27	491.52	10.49	635.54	7.82	104.16
10	74.96	234.84	17.48	323.12	10.23	446.48	9.85	544.61	8.04	124.64
11	75.89	259.19	17.07	332.87	15.84	643.65	9.87	534.91	8.12	131.68
12	70.17	234.22	17.39	325.19	10.28	449.03	9.97	534.36	7.78	96.29
13	73.73	306.99	18.10	383.11	10.36	504.79	10.24	595.58	7.71	102.81
14	70.87	239.19	17.37	327.02	10.17	451.21	10.36	592.68	7.93	111.28
15	73.30	295.27	18.00	372.00	10.32	494.09	10.26	639.61	7.87	147.14
MDSD		140.94		165.47		90.60		31.56		16.78

Why is it need to consider *MDSD* in addition to *SD* as a significant parameter? Quite similar *SD* values from the same experiment (same column) of Table 2 imply similar execution times. The *SD1* values for starting city 4 and 10 are 230.11 and 234.84, respectively. Their execution times (*G1*) are similar 72.64 and 74.96. Instead, this relation is not true considering similar *SD* values from different experiments (different columns). The *SD1* value for starting city 3 and the SD2 value for starting city 10 are similar (315.51 and 323.12, respectively) but the execution times are completely dissimilar. The different values of *MDSD* for *SD1* and *SD2* explains the different execution times for similar *SD* values.

Conclusions: The asymptotic time complexity for the global pruning algorithm should be defined as $O(C, P, SD, MDSD)$.

Another important fact has been reached beyond what was originally sought. By looking each combination of SD_j and $MDSD$ values coming from C cities, it is also possible to choose the best starting city for the TSP problem. This means invests less time in order to obtain the minimal path.

4.4   Building a Multiple-Linear-Regression Model

The *GP-TSP* algorithm has been executed for a great amount of training patterns in order to take enough experimental data to validate this experimental approach. Then, as the methodology is based on the black-box approach, these experimental results have been used to create a multiple-linear-regression model.

There are four independent input variables $(C, P, SD, MDSD)$ and the basis form of the four-dimensional regression model for the execution time (T) is

$$T = b_0 + b_1 C + b_2 P + b_3 SD + b_4 MDSD \qquad (3)$$

where b_0, b_1, b_2, b_3, and b_4 are the regression parameters to estimate. There exist m measurements of the output T for various combinations of the inputs C, P, SD, and $MDSD$. Each measurement can be expressed as

$$T_i = b_0 + b_1 C_i + b_2 P_i + b_3 SD_i + b_4 MDSD_i + e_i \qquad (4)$$

where e_i is the residual for the data $(C_i, P_i, SD_i, MDSD_i, T_i)$.

To find the regression parameters b_0, b_1, b_2, b_3, and b_4, it is necessary to minimize the sum of squares of these residuals, denoted SSE.

$$SSE = \sum_{i=1}^{m} e_i^2 = \sum_{i=1}^{m} (T_i - b_0 - b_1 C_i - b_2 P_i - b_3 SD_i - b_4 MDSD_i)^2 \qquad (5)$$

The Eq. 5 takes on its minimum value when the partial derivatives of SSE with respect to b_0, b_1, b_2, b_3, and b_4 are all set to zero. This procedure then leads to a system of equations. The solution could be found by using any of the standard methods for solving systems of equations or using any available software package designed for this purpose [8].

4.5   Evaluating the Regression Equation

Finally, the regression equation is used to predict how the *GP-TSP* algorithm will perform when given new input data sets. Replacing C, P, SD, and $MDSM$ with real values in Eq. 3, it is possible to estimate the time required to find the minimal path for this master-worker global pruning TSP algorithm.

5   Conclusions

This paper introduces a novel methodology to estimate the execution time order of a hard data-dependent parallel algorithm that solves the TSP problem. It is important to understand that the parallel performance achieved depends on several factors, including the application, the multiprocessor architecture, the data distribution, and also the methods used for partitioning the application and mapping its components onto the architecture.

The general methodology begins by collecting execution-time data for a considerable number of TSP instances. A well-designed experiment guides the experimenters in choosing what experiments actually need to be performed. This is a complex task and the experiments should provide a representative sample. Then, a data-mining process explores these collected data in search of patterns and/or relationships detecting the main parameters that affect performance. These patterns and/or relationships are modelled numerically in order to generate an analytical formulation of the execution time. As the methodology is based on a black-box approach, the measured values for this representative sample of inputs are used to produce a multiple-linear-regression model. Finally, the regression equation allows for predicting how the algorithm will perform when given new input data sets.

A *GP-TSP* algorithm has been studied. It is used to analyze the influence of indeterminism in performance prediction and also to show the usefulness and the profits of the methodology. The execution time for the global pruning algorithm depends on the number of cities (C), the number of processors (P), and other parameters. As a result of the investigation, right now the sum of the distances from one city to the other cities (SD) and the mean deviation of SDs values $(MDSD)$ are the numerical parameters characterizing the different input data beyond the number of cities (C). The followed way to discover these final parameters has been exhaustively described. Finally, their asymptotic time complexity has been defined $O(C, P, SD, MDSD)$.

Building a multiple-linear-regression model with the four independent input variables $(C, P, SD, MDSD)$ and, then, using the regression equation, a prediction of performance order for a new data set it is possible to give.

Another important fact has been reached beyond what was originally sought. It is possible to take advantage of the relationship between SD_j and $MDSD$ values coming from C cities to invests less time obtaining the minimal path.

References

[1] Skiena, S.: The algorithm design manual. Springer, New York (1998)
[2] Martello, S., Toth, P.: Knapsack problems: algorithms and computer implementations. John Wiley & Sons, Inc., New York (1990)
[3] Geraerts, R., Overmars, M.H.: Reachability analysis of sampling based planners. In: IEEE International Conference on Robotics and Automation, pp. 406–412 (2005)
[4] TSP page (2008), http://www.tsp.gatech.edu/history/
[5] Fritzsche, P.: Podemos predecir en algoritmos paralelos no-deterministas? PhD Thesis, University Autonoma of Barcelona, Computer Architecture and Operating Systems Department, Spain (2007), http://caos.uab.es/
[6] Fritzsche, P.C., Rexachs, D., Luque, E.: Extracting knowledge to predict tsp asymptotic time complexity. In: ICDMW 2007: Proceedings of the Seventh IEEE International Conference on Data Mining Workshops, Washington, DC, USA, pp. 309–318. IEEE Computer Society, Los Alamitos (2007)
[7] MacQueen, J.B.: Some methods for classification and analysis of multivariate observations. In: Le Cam, L.M., Neyman, J. (eds.) Proc. of the fifth Berkeley Symposium on Mathematical Statistics and Probability, vol. 1, pp. 281–297. University of California Press (1967)
[8] Lilja, D.: Measuring computer performance: a practitioner's guide. Cambridge University Press, New York (2000)

Examining the Feasibility of Reconfigurable Models for Molecular Dynamics Simulation

Eunjung Cho[1,*], Anu G. Bourgeois[1], and José Alberto Fernández-Zepeda[2]

[1] Computer Science Department of Georgia State University
echo@student.gsu.edu, anu@cs.gsu.edu
[2] Dept. of Computer Science, CICESE, MEXICO
fernan@cicese.mx

Abstract. A Molecular Dynamics (MD) system is defined by the position and momentum of particles and their interactions. The dynamics of a system can be evaluated by an N-body problem and the simulation is continued until the energy reaches equilibrium. Many applications use MD for biomolecular simulations and the simulations are performed in multiscale of time and length. The simulations of the relevant scales require strong and fast computing power, but it is even beyond the reach of current fastest supercomputers. In this paper, we design R-Mesh Algorithms that require O(N) time complexity for the Direct method for MD simulations and O(r)+O(logM) time complexity for the Multigrid method, where r is N/M and M is the size of R-Mesh. Our work supports the theory that reconfigurable models are a good direction for biological studies which require high computing power.

1 Introduction

Extensive research has been focused on the field of Molecular Dynamics (MD) over the past 20 years [1-3]. In the field of biology, MD simulations is continuously used to investigate biological studies including protein folding, enzyme catalysis, conformational changes associated with biomolecular function and molecular recognition of proteins, DNA, and biological membrane complexes. Many applications use MD for biomolecular simulations and the simulations are performed in multiscale of time and length. The simulations of the relevant scales require strong and fast computing power, but it is even beyond the reach of current fastest supercomputers. [1, 4].

Many approaches have been proposed to improve the performance of MD simulation in terms of the time. These approaches are divided into two categories by focusing on either the software or on the hardware. The software approach involves developing efficient algorithms to calculate the forces. Currently, many algorithms have been introduced and large scale parallel computers are used to achieve reasonable computational time. Among the algorithms, Ewald s method [5] runs in $O(N^{3/2})$ time and Particle Mesh Ewald (PME) [2, 6] method applies discrete fast Fourier

* Research sponsored by Molecular Basis of Disease (MBD) fellowship since 2006.

A. Bourgeois and S.Q. Zheng (Eds.): ICA3PP 2008, LNCS 5022, pp. 109..120, 2008.
© Springer-Verlag Berlin Heidelberg 2008

transforms (FFT) to compute long-range interactions and reduce $O(N^{3/2})$ to $O(N\log N)$ on a general purpose processor. Multi-Grid (MG) [3] method requires $O(N)$ time complexity for a given accuracy on a general purpose processor where N is the number of atoms in a molecular system to be performed.

The hardware approach has focused on running MD simulations on special purpose processors or developing Application-Specific Integrated Circuits (ASIC) to achieve much faster calculation time. Since MD simulations are performed for large number of atoms in a molecular system, many studies exploits supercomputing systems or parallel systems to achieve better performance. Alam *et al.* [1, 4] observe the performance of supercomputing systems for running MD simulation packages (AMBER, NAMD, LAMMPS). NAMD and LAMMPS have been reported to scale to up to a few thousand nodes, while AMBER s PME method does not scale beyond 128 processors [1, 7] due to the communication overheads. They expect that peta-FLOPS-scale computing power in the near future will meet the speed for biological studies [4], but not of the current time. Special purpose processors [8] and application-specific Integrated Circuits (ASIC) for MD simulation [9] require highly cost, complicated processes, and long development spans.

Another research direction to achieve better performance is to adopt *reconfigurable models* to run large scale problems. Reconfigurable models provide the ability to customize circuits to specific problem inputs at run time and the ability to reuse the same logic resources in different configurations from one phase of a computation to the next [10]. These features enable efficient solutions to many problems, including image and video processing, cryptography, object tracking, digital signal processing, and networking. Previous work developed a Field programmable Gate Array(FPGA)-based MD simulator. They achieved faster simulation than the simulation on a general purpose processor [11-13] and FPGA board is much cheaper compared to ASIC and special purpose processor or supercomputing system.

In this paper, we are proposing a project that exploits another reconfigurable model to run MD simulations in a flexible and efficient manner. The Reconfigurable Mesh (R-Mesh) is a simple model to describe and understand since it uses a mesh topology to interconnect processors. Many published results use the R-Mesh (or variations) as the model of computation [14]. We design fast and efficient R-Mesh algorithms for MD simulations and thus bring a new concept to the field of biology. This work demonstrates that the large scale biological studies can be simulated in close to real time.

The R-Mesh algorithms we design highlight the feasibility of R-Mesh to evaluate potentials with faster calculation times. Specifically, we develop R-Mesh algorithms for both the Direct method and Multigrid method. The Direct method evaluates exact potentials and forces by Equation 1 but takes takes $O(N^2)$ calculation time for evaluating electrostatic forces on a general purpose processor. Multigrid (MG) method adopts an interpolation technique to reduce calculation time to $O(N)$ for a given accuracy. Although the MG method achieves $C \cdot N$ calculation time, the constant C is a large number. However, our R-Mesh algorithms provide $O(N)$ time complexity for the Direct method and $O(r)+O(\log M)$ time complexity for the Multigrid method, where r is N/M and M is the size of the R-Mesh.

The contribution of this paper is presenting another approach to solve the intensively time consuming and large scale problem of molecular dynamics simulations. Although the R-Mesh is a theoretical model, our work supports the theory that reconfigurable models are a good direction for biological studies which require high computing power.

This remainder of the paper contains the following materials. In Section 2, we provide background material for MD simulations and Multigrid algorithm. In Section 3, we describe the R-Mesh and present our proposed R-Mesh algorithms for MD simulation. Section 4 analyzes our algorithms and summarizes our idea. Finally, Section 5 provides concluding remarks

2 Background of Molecular Dynamics Simulation

This section briefly describes the basics of Molecular Dynamics (MD) simulation and algorithms for MD simulation. Since we are focusing on the Multigrid method, we provide some more detail for this algorithm.

2.1 Molecular Dynamics Simulation

In Molecular Dynamics simulation, dynamics are calculated by Newtonian mechanics [6]. MD simulation integrates acceleration to obtain position and velocity changes of atoms in the system. This process is typically continued every 1 femtosecond until the system stabilizes.

There are other approaches to describe forces of an MD system. Newton s equation of motion describes nature conserving the energy, but other approaches modify the forces to achieve equilibrium states satisfying certain specified requirements, such as constant temperature, constant pressure or rigid molecules.

F_i represents i^{th} atom s force and can be described by the potential energy.

$$\vec{F}_i = -\nabla_i U(\vec{x}_1, \vec{x}_2, ..., \vec{x}_N) + \vec{F}_i^{\,extended} \quad ,$$

where U is the potential, N is the number of atoms in the system and $\vec{F}_i^{\,extended}$ is an extended force like velocity-based friction. The *potential U* consists of bonded and non-bonded potentials. It takes $O(N)$ time to calculate the bonded potentials and $O(N^2)$ for non-bonded potentials. So many researchers focus on the non-bonded interactions due to the intensive computational time. Non-bonded interactions can be divided as *electrostatic* potential and *Lennard-Jones* potential. *Electrostatic* potential represents Coulomb potential and *Lennard-Jones* potential represents a van der Waals attraction and a hard-core repulsion. The *Lennard-Jones* potential can be calculated in $O(N)$ time, since the *Lennard-Jones* function decays very fast [2]. *Electrostatic* potential takes $O(N^2)$ time by Equation 1 and many studies try to reduce the time complexity. We also are focusing on long-ranged interactions, especially electrostatic forces due to the intensive computational time.

$$U_{ij}^{electrostatic} = \frac{1}{4\pi\varepsilon_0} \frac{q_i q_j}{\left\| \vec{x}_{ij} \right\|^2} \tag{1}$$

where $U_{ij}^{electrostatic}$ is *electrostatic* potential between atom i and atom j and π and ε_0 are constant numbers and q_i and q_j are the charges of atoms i and j.

2.2 Multigrid Method for Molecular Dynamics Simulation

The Multigrid (MG) method was introduced in the 1960 s to solve partial differential equations (PDE). Recently it has been applied and implemented for *N*-body problems and achieves O(*N*) time complexity for a given accuracy. The basic idea of MG is to hierarchically separate the force potential into a *short range part* plus a *smooth part (slowly varying part of energy)*. MG method uses gridded interpolation for both the charges (source) and the potentials (destination) to represent its smooth (coarse) part [3]. The splitting and coarsening are applied recursively and define a grid hierarchy (Refer to Figure 1). MG method is faster for a given error rate at given accuracy than other methods such as Ewald s method [5] and Multipole method [15].

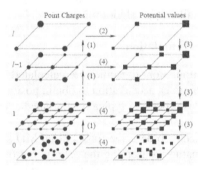

Fig. 1. The multilevel scheme of Multigrid method [3]. (1) Aggregate to coarser grids (2) Compute potential induced by the coarsest grid(3) Interpolate potential values from coarser grids (4) Local corrections.

Although there are many methods for evaluating potentials and forces, we propose R-Mesh algorithms implementing MG method and the Direct method. The Direct method is a basic and exact method for electrostatic potentials. The reason we choose the MG method is that it provides faster calculation time than other methods and we can easily map the gridded interpolation of MG method to the mesh topology of an R-Mesh. By doing this, we are able to achieve O(*r*)+O(log*M*) time complexity on the R-Mesh.

3   Reconfigurable Mesh and Proposed Algorithm

In this section, we provide the basic concepts of the Reconfigurable Mesh (R-Mesh) and present our R-Mesh algorithms for both the Direct method and Multigrid (MG) method of MD simulations.

3.1   Reconfigurable Mesh

An R × C Reconfigurable Mesh (R-Mesh) is a two-dimensional array of processors connected in an R × C grid. Each processor in the R-Mesh has direct external connections   to adjacent processors through a set of four input/output ports. A processor

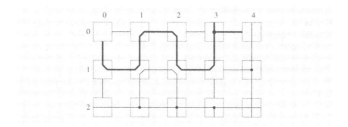

Fig. 2. Internal connections of an R-Mesh

can internally partition its set of ports so that ports in the same block of a partition are fused. These partitions, along with external connections between processors, define a global bus structure that connects the ports of processors. All ports that are part of the same bus are said to be in the same component of the R-Mesh. Any data written from one of these ports can be read by all connected ports in a single step. Figure 2 shows a 3 × 5 R-Mesh depicting the fifteen possible port partitions of a processor. The R-Mesh is a synchronous model that may change its bus configurations at each step. It also assumes negligible delay on buses. In this paper, we assume the concurrent read and exclusive write (CREW) model.

3.2   Proposed R-Mesh Algorithms

MD simulation repeatively evaluates forces until the energy reaches equilibrium. If the function for evaluating forces requires $O(N^2)$ time complexity such as the Direct method, the entire time complexity is $K \cdot O(N^2)$, where K is the number of iterations and is usually a large number. Therefore it is very important to reduce the time for evaluating forces. In this section, we develop several algorithms for the R-Mesh that require much less calculation time.

3.2.1   Algorithms for Direct Method
The Direct method uses Equation 1 to evaluate electrostatic potential and takes $O(N^2)$ time on a general purpose processor where N is the number of atoms in a molecular system. We develop R-Mesh algorithms for the Direct method. Algorithm 1 is the main module of the MD simulation. Algorithm 1 requires $K \cdot O(N)$ time complexity on an N processor reconfigurable linear mesh. In Algorithm 1, $p(i)$ and $q(i)$ are local data for the position and charge of atoms. *DirectComputeForce( )* evaluates forces of each atom and is described in Algorithm 1-1. *doOneAtomPair(i, j)* in Algorithm 1-1 evaluates the potential energy between atom i and atom j. *UpdateVelocity()* and *Up-datePosition()* updates the velocity and position of atoms and takes $O(1)$ time.

Algorithm 1. (MD simulation with Direct method)
1. Model : N processors (N is # of atoms) 1-dimensional R-Mesh
2. Input: proc(i) store p(i)={p_0, p_1, f , p_{N-1}} and q(i)={q_0, q_1, f , q_{N-1}}
3. Output : proc(i) store force(i)={$force_0$, $force_1$, f $force_{N-1}$} and updated p={p_0, p_1, f , p_{N-1}} and proc(0) store total energy in E

begin   // K×O(N) (K is the number of iteration)
MDSimulation_Direct ( )
      while E is not changed do
          DirectComputeFoce(p, q) // O(N)
          UpdateVelocity(pos, force, E)
          UpdatePostion(pos, force, E)
          proc(i) broadcast updated position of atom *i* and force to all process // O(N)
      end_while
end

Algorithm 1-1. (DirectComputeForce)
1. Model : N processors (N is # of atoms) 1-dimensional R-Mesh
2. Input: proc(i) store p(i)={p_0, p_1, f , p_{N-1}} and q(i)={ q_0, q_1, f , q_{N-1}}
3. Output : proc(i) store force(i)={f_0, f_1, f , f_{N-1}} and Proc(0) store total energy in E

begin   // O(N)
DirectComputeForce( )
      each proc(i)
        for j←1 to N-1 do
           force(i) = force(i) + doOneAtomPair(i, j) // O(1)
        end_for
        e(i) = e(i) + Calculate_Energy(force(i))   // O(1), calculate energy for atom i

      compute E = e(0)+e(1) + f +e(N-1) with N R-mesh and proc(0) store E // O(logN)
end

3.2.2 Algorithms for Multigrid Method

The Multigrid (MG) method takes O(N) time on a general purpose processor, where N is the number of atoms in a molecular system. We developed an R-Mesh algorithm for the MG method that requires O(r)+O(log$M$) time complexity on an $X \times Y \times Z$ 3-dimensional R-Mesh, where r is N/M and $M = X \times Y \times Z$ is the number of finest grid points applied to MG method for a given parameter. The value of M is usually much smaller compared to N unless the molecular system to be simulated is very small. For example, MG method determines finest grid points to (13, 13, 13) for the molecular system with N =309 atoms to achieve 0.0008 relative accuracy [11]. In this case M is 13*13*13 = 2,197. A large molecular system that has N=14,281 atoms determines finest grid points (21, 21, 21) to achieve 0.0005 relative accuracy. In this case M is 21*21*21=9281, which is smaller compared to number of atoms (14281).

Algorithm 2 is the main module of the MD simulation and requires $K \cdot$(O(r)+O(log$M$)) time complexity. The main module is similar to Algorithm 1, but with a preprocessing function (Algorithm 2.1) that distributes atoms to the nearest 64 processors. Those 64 processors correspond to the closest grid points to atoms. This function runs based on the flag (*CheckChangedGrid*) that is assigned by *CheckGrid-Point( )*. This function checks the new position and its grid point. Usually the atoms retain their previous grid points assigned, so the calculation time of *preprocessing( )* is negligible over the entire simulation .

Algorithm 2. (MD simulation with Multigrid method)
1. Model : M processors ($X \times Y \times Z$ R-Mesh, $M = X \times Y \times Z$ is # of finest grid point)
2. Input: proc(i, j, k) hold store p(i,j,k)={ p_{start}, .. , $p_{start+c-1}$} and q(i,j,k)={ q_{start}, .., $q_{start+c-1}$},
      which *start* = i*c +j*X*c+k*X*Y*c and *c* = N/M
3. Output : proc(i, j, k) store force(i,j,k)={f_0, f_1.. f_r}, p(i,j,k)={p_0, p_1.. ,p_r} and proc(0,0,0) hold E,
      r is number of atoms assigned in proc(i, j, k)

begin   // $K \times (O(r) + O(\log M))$ (K is the number of iteration)
MDSimulation_Multigrid ( )
        while energy is not changed do
            if(CheckChangedGrid == true)
                Preprocessing( )   // O(N)
            End_if
                MultigridComputeForce(p(i,j,k), q(i,j,k))
                proc(i, j, k) run UpdateVelocity(p*(i,j,k)*, force*(i,j,k)*, E)
                proc(i, j, k) run UpdatePostion(p*(i,j,k)*, force*(i,j,k)*, E)
                proc(i, j, k) set CheckChangedGrid ← CheckGridpoint(p(i,j,k))
        end_while
end

Algorithm 2-1 describes *preprocessing( )* that distributes information of atoms to nearby processors. proc(*i, j, k*) represents grid point (*i, j, k*) at level 0. *calGridpoint (start+m, $p_{start+m}$)* returns *grid_pos* and atom *start+m* assigned to *grid_pos* to interpolate. *calThetas(grid_pos(i,j,k), $p_{start+m}$)* calculates *thetas* and we use 4th hermite interpolation function to calculate thetas. *Anterpolate( )* module (Algorithm 2-2-1) uses this information to calculate Q_0 (charge of finest grid). This algorithm takes O(*N*) time due to the *N* broadcasting steps required.

Algorithm 2-1. (Preprocessing)
1. Model : M processors
2. Input: proc(i, j, k) hold store p(i,j,k)={ p_{start}, .. , $p_{start+c-1}$} and q(i,j,k)={ q_{start}, .., $q_{start+c-1}$},
      which *start* = i*c +j*X*c+k*X*Y*c and *c* = N/M
3. Output : proc(i, j, k) store D(i,j,k) = {d_0, d_1.. d_r}, which d_m = (index, p, q thetas, grid_pos),
      r is number of atoms assigned in proc(i, j, k)

begin
Preprocessing ( )
        If D(i,j,k) s grid_pos is changed   // O(N)
            for m ← 0 to c-1 do   // *c* = N/M
                grid_pos← calGridpoint (start+m, $p_{start+m}$)
                thetas← calThetas(grid_pos(i,j,k), $p_{start+m}$)
                D(i,j,k).d_m = (start+m, $p_{start+m}$,· $q_{start+m}$ thetas, grid_pos)
            end_for
            send D(i,j,k).d_m to proc(D(i,j,k).d_m.grid_pos) //N broadcasting times
        else   keep previous D(i,j,k)   //O(1)
        end_if
end

MultigridComputeForce() described in Algorithm 2-2 evaluates the forces of each atom. Each processor represents the grid points for the finest grid. It consists of 6 steps. Step 1 is *Anterpolate( )* to interpolate weights for the position of atoms and anterpolate the charge q onto the finest grid (level 0). Step 2 is coarsening that anterpolates the grid charge from the current *level* to *level+1*. correction(i) requires $O($ $Nx(i) \cdot Ny(i) \cdot Nz(i))$, where $Nx(i)$, $Ny(i)$, $Nz(i)$ = grid points at i^{th} level and Level = level of the MD simulation. Step 3 is computing the potential for the top level. Step 4 is interpolating the grid charge from *level* to *level-1*. Step 5 is computing the energy of the top grid level. Step 6 is interpolating the force from grid level 0.

Algorithm 2-2. (Multigrid method for MD simulation with n atoms)
1. Model : M processors ($X \times Y \times Z$ R-Mesh, M=$X \times Y \times Z$ is # of finest grid point)
2. Input: proc(i, j, k) hold $D(i,j,k) = \{d_0, d_1.. d_r\}$, which d_m = (index, p, q thetas, grid_pos), r is number of atoms assigned in proc(i, j, k)
3. Output : proc(i, j, k) store force(i,j,k)=$\{f_0, f_1.. f_r\}$, p(i,j,k)=$\{p_0, p_1.. ,p_r\}$ and proc(0,0,0) hold E, r is number of atoms assigned in proc(i, j, k),

```
begin
MultigridComputeForce(p, q)
        Step 1) Anterpolate( )                        // O(1)
        Step 2) for i ← 0 to Levels-1
                fineToCoarse ( i )          // O(1)
                correction ( i )            // O( Nx(i)· Ny(i)· Nz(i))
             end_for
        Step 3) direct ( )                  // O( Nx(Level)· Ny(Level)· Nz(Level))
        Step 4) for i ← 0 to Level-1
                coarseToFine (i)            // O(1)
        end_for
        Step 5) energy( )        // O(logM)
        Step 6) interpolateForce (  )       // O(r)
end
```

Algorithm 2-2-1 describes *Anterpolate( )* that anterpolates and interpolates weights for the position of atoms and anterpolates the charge onto grid level 0. This algorithm requires O(1) time complexity. Since each atom is interpolated to the nearest grid that are *order×order×order* grid points, broadcasting is performed on an *order×order×order* R-Mesh. The algorithm is designed so that there is no overlapping and processors can broadcast data simultaneously. The actual number of broadcasting steps is *(order-1)^4*, where *order* is the order of interpolation function. After broadcasting data, each processor updates $Q_0(i, j, k)$, which is the grid charges at level 0. Figure 3 shows the broadcasting step with a 2-dimensional R-Mesh.

Algorithm 2-2-1. (Anterpolate)
1. Model : M processors ($X \times Y \times Z$ R-Mesh, M=$X \times Y \times Z$ is # of finest grid point)
2. Input: proc(i, j, k) hold $Q_0(i, j, k)$=0 and hold $D(i,j,k) = \{d_0, d_1.. d_r\}$, which d_m=(index, p, q thetas, grid_pos), r is number of atoms assigned in proc(i, j, k)
3. Output : proc(i, j,k) update $Q_0(i, j, k)$

```
begin
Anterpolate ( )  // O(1)
        Step1) proc(i, j, k) broadcast D(i, j, k,) to the nearest processors
        For rem←0 to order-1 do
          For ix ←0 to order-1 do
            For jx ←0 to order-1
```

```
            For kx←0 to order-1 do
                If (i+ix)%order==rem && (j+jx)%order==rem && (k+kx)%order==rem
                    proc(i,j,k) broadcast D(i,j,k) to proc(i, j, k)
                                        ~proc(i+order, j+order, k+order) //O(1)
                    end_if
                end_for
            end_for
            end_for

        Step2) temp(i,j,k) ← Cal_GridCharge(D(i,j,k))
            //D(i,j,k).d.q* D(i,j,k).d.theta.X* D(i,j,k).d.theta.Y* D(i,j,k).d.theta.Z
        Step3) Q₀(i, j, k) ← Q₀(i, j, k) + temp(i,j,k)
end
```

Step2) $temp(i,j,k) \leftarrow Cal\_GridCharge(D(i,j,k))$
//$D(i,j,k).d.q * D(i,j,k).d.theta.X * D(i,j,k).d.theta.Y * D(i,j,k).d.theta.Z$
Step3) $Q_0(i, j, k) \leftarrow Q_0(i, j, k) + temp(i,j,k)$

Figure 3 shows that processor(i, j) broadcasts data to the nearest 15 processors. Figure 3 (a) shows the first broadcasting step of processor(i, j) where $i\%4 == 0$ and $j\%4 == 0$. Then in the second step, the next group of nodes broadcast their data as shown in Figure 3 (b). These nodes have indices so that $i\%4 == 0$ and $(j-1)\%4 == 0$. This continues for a total of $(order-1)^4$ steps.

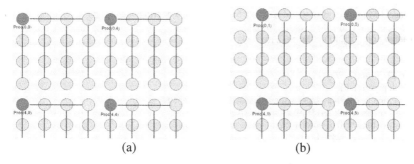

(a)   (b)

Fig. 3. Example of broadcasting in Algorithm 2-2-1 with *order* = 4, Proc(0, 0), Proc(0, 4), proc(4, 0) and proc(4,4) broadcast data simultaneously, Proc(0, 1), proc(0, 5), proc(5, 1) and proc(5,5) broadcast data simultaneously

Algorithm 2-2-2 is the coarsening process. It coarsens grid charges from *level* to *level+1* and requires $O(1)$ time complexity. The actual number of broadcasting steps is $(order-1)^3$. *Coarsening( )* in Algorithm 2-2-2 expands broadcasting to 64 processors similar to Algorithm 2-2-1. Due to the lack of space we omit the algorithm detail.

Algorithm 2-2-2. (FinetoCoarse(L))
1. Model : M processors (X×Y×Z R-Mesh, M=X×Y×Z is # of grid point at level L)
2. Input: proc(i, j, k) hold D(i,j,k) =(Q_L(i, j, k), theta) and L
3. Output : proc(i, j, k) update Q_{L+1}(i, j, k)

begin
FinetoCoarse (L) // O(1)
```
        Step1) proc(i, j, k) broadcast D(i, j, k,) to the nearest processors
            For ix ←0 to order-1 do
                For jx ←0 to order-1
```

```
                For kx←0 to order-1 do
                    If (i+ix)%order==0 && (j+jx)%order==0 && (k+kx)%order==0
                        Coarsening(i,j,k) //O(1)
                    end_if
                end_for
        end_for
            end_for

    Step2) temp(i,j,k) ← Cal_GridCharge(D(i,j,k)) // Q_L(i, j, k)*theta.X*theta.Y*theta.Z

    Step3) Q_{L+1}(i, j, k) ← Q_{L+1} (i,j,k) + temp(i,j,k)
    end_for
end
```

Algorithm 2-2-3 interpolates grid charges from *level* to *level-1*. This algorithm updates $V_{level-1}$ which is the potential at *level-1* and requires O(1) time complexity. Ratio and order are constant numbers and Ratio represents the ratio between Level L and *L-1*.

Algorithm 2-2-3. (CoarseToFine(L))
1. Model : M processors (X×Y×Z R-Mesh, M=X×Y×Z is # of grid point at L)
2. Input: proc(i, j, k) hold V_{level}(i, j, k) and theta ={X, Y, Z}
3. Output : proc(i, j, k) update $V_{level-1}$(i, j, k)

```
begin
CoarseToFine(L)  // O(1)
    Each proc(i, j, k)
        Step 1) calculate temp using coarsened V_level and thetas
            i1←i/Ratio, j1←j/Ratio, k1←k/Ratio
            for i0←0 to order-1 do
                i2← i1+i0
                for j0←0 to order-1 do
                    j2← j1+j0
                    for k0←0 to order-1 do
                        k2← k1+k0
                        temp=temp+V_level(i2,j2,k2)*theta.X[i0]*theta.Y[j0]* theta.Z[k0]
                    end_for
                end_for
        end_for
        Step2) V_level-1(i, j, k) = V_level-1(i, j, k) + temp
end
```

----

4   Results and Analysis

As explained above, Cray XT3 and Blue Gene/L provides scale to up to a few thousands nodes due to the communication overheads [1, 4]. With this limitation, it is not possible to provide accommodating computing speed for biology activity with current computing power. The communication overhead limits the performance and scaling on microprocessors and massively-parallel systems [16]. FPGA-based simulators [11-13] lead that feasibility of exploiting Reconfigurable models on a large scale problems such as the MD simulation. We support the feasibility of reconfigurable models by providing theoretical theorems with R-Mesh algorithm for the MD simulation.

Our results for the Direct method require $O(N)$ time complexity an N R-Mesh. We are able to improve upon the results for the MG method. While we also are able to achieve $O(r)+O(\log M)$ time complexity, the number of processors required are much less. The R-Mesh algorithm requires $M=X \times Y \times Z$ processors corresponding to the number of finest grid points rather than N processors corresponding to the number of atoms in the system. For most systems M is much smaller than N, thus reducing the size of the simulating machine. This improvement is due to the natural mapping of the layout of the MD system in a grid pattern to the three-dimensional structure of the R-Mesh.

Theorem 1. *Molecular Dynamics simulation of a molecular system with N atoms can be performed in $K \cdot O(N)$ time on an N processor reconfigurable linear R-Mesh, when the simulation exploits the Direct method to evaluate electrostatic potential. K is the number of iterations to reach equilibrium. (Algorithm 1)*

Theorem 2. *Molecular Dynamics simulation of a molecular system with N atoms can be performed in $K \cdot (O(r)+O(\log M))$ time on an $X \times Y \times Z$ 3-dimensional R-Mesh, when the simulation exploits the multigrid method to evaluate electrostatic potential. r is N/M. $M= X \times Y \times Z$ is the number of finest grid points applied to Multigrid method at a given parameter. K is the number of iterations to reach equilibrium. (Algorithm 2)*

5 Conclusion

In biology field, MD simulations are used continuously for biological activities. Since MD simulation is a large scale problem and multiscale in length and time, there have been many approaches with solutions to meet the speed required. We support the idea that utilize Reconfigurable models to perform large scale problems such as MD simulations. We design R-Mesh Algorithms and previously have been worked on developing an FPGA-based simulator.

In this paper, we develop R-Mesh algorithms for two Molecular Dynamics simulation methods, Direct method and Multigrid method. The Direct method requires $O(N^2)$ time for evaluating electrostatic forces and provides accurate results if executed sequentially. We develop an R-Mesh algorithm that implements Direct method. It requires $O(N)$ time complexity with an N processor R-Mesh (Theorem 1). We also develop an R-Mesh algorithm that implements the Multigrid method to evaluate electrostatic forces. The Multigrid method takes $O(N)$ calculation time at a given accuracy for a sequential implementation. But our R-Mesh algorithm requires $O(r)+O(\log M)$ time complexity with an $X \times Y \times Z$ R-Mesh (Theorem 2). This algorithm requires M processors, where M is the number of finest grid points $(M=X \times Y \times Z)$. Since M is usually a much smaller number compared to N, this algorithm provides very fast simulation time with a small number of processors. Therefore our R-Mesh algorithm is a feasible choice for developing the Multigrid method for MD simulations and likely other large scale biological problems.

References

1. Alam, S.R., Vetter, J.S., Agarwal, P.K.: Performance characterization of molecular dynamics techniques for biomolecular simulations. In: Proceedings of the eleventh ACM SIGPLAN symposium on Principles and practice of parallel programming, pp. 59..68 (2006)
2. Rapaport, D.C.: The Art of Molecular Dynamics Simulation. Cambridge University Press, Cambridge (2004)
3. Sagui, C., Darden, T.: Multigrid methods for classical molecular dynamics simulations of biomolecules. The Journal of Chemical Physics 114, 6578 (2001)
4. Alam, S.R., Agarwal, P.K.: On the Path to Enable Multi-scale Biomolecular Simulations on PetaFLOPS Supercomputer with Multi-core Processors. In: Sixth IEEE International Workshop on High Performance Computational Biology (HiCOMB) (2007)
5. Toukmaji, A.Y., Board, J.A.: Ewald summation techniques in perspective: a survey. Computer Physics Communications 95(2-3), 73..92 (1996)
6. Skeel, R.D., Tezcan, I., Hardy, D.J.: Multiple grid methods for classical molecular dynamics. Journal of Computational Chemistry, 2002 23(6), 673..684 (2002)
7. Agarwal, P.K., Alam, S.R.: Biomolecular simulations on petascale: promises and challenges. Journal of Physics: Conference Series 46(1), 327..333 (2006)
8. Komeiji, Y., et al.: Fast and accurate molecular dynamics simulation of a protein using a special-purpose computer. Journal of Computational Chemistry, 1997 18(12), 1546..1563 (1997)
9. Toyoda, S., et al.: Development of MD Engine: High-speed accelerator with parallel processor design for molecular dynamics simulations. Journal of Computational Chemistry 20(2), 185..199 (1999)
10. Vaidyanathan, R., Trahan, J.L.: Dynamic Reconfiguration: Architectures and Algorithms. Plenum Pub Corp. (2003)
11. Cho, E., Bourgeois, A.G., Tan, F.: An FPGA Design to Achieve Fast and Accurate Results for Molecular Dynamics Simulations. In: Stojmenovic, I., Thulasiram, R.K., Yang, L.T., Jia, W., Guo, M., de Mello, R.F. (eds.) ISPA 2007. LNCS, vol. 4742, p. 256. Springer, Heidelberg (2007)
12. Azizi, N., et al.: Reconfigurable molecular dynamics simulator. In: Annual IEEE Symposium on Field-Programmable Custom Computing Machines, FCCM 2004, pp. 197..206 (2004)
13. Gu, Y., VanCourt, T., Herbordt, M.C.: Accelerating molecular dynamics simulations with configurable circuits. Computers and Digital Techniques, IEE Proceedings 153(3), 189...195 (2006)
14. Nakano, K.: A Bibliography of Published Papers on Dynamically Reconfigurable Architectures. Parallel Processing Letters 5(1), 111..124 (1995)
15. Rankin, W.T., Board Jr., J.A.: A portable distributed implementation of the parallel multipoletree algorithm. In: Proceedings of the Fourth IEEE International Symposium on High Performance Distributed Computing, 1995, pp. 17..22 (1995)
16. Crowley, M., et al.: Adventures in Improving the Scaling and Accuracy of a Parallel Molecular Dynamics Program. The Journal of Supercomputing 11(3), 255..278 (1997)

Parallel Simulated Annealing for Materialized View Selection in Data Warehousing Environments

Roozbeh Derakhshan[1], Bela Stantic[2], Othmar Korn[2], and Frank Dehne[3]

[1] ETH Zurich, Switzerland
[2] Institute for Integrated and Intelligent Systems
[3] Griffith University, Brisbane, Australia
[4] School of Computer Science, Carleton University, Canada

Abstract. In order to facilitate efficient query processing, the information contained in data warehouses is typically stored as a set of materialized views. Deciding which views to materialize represent a challenge in order to minimize view maintenance and query processing costs. Some existing approaches are applicable only for small problems, which are far from reality. In this paper we introduce a new approach for materialized view selection using Parallel Simulated Annealing (PSA) that selects views from an input Multiple View Processing Plan (MVPP). With PSA, we are able to perform view selection on MVPPs having hundreds of queries and thousands of views. Also, in our experimental study we show that our method provides a significant improvement in the quality of the obtained set of materialized views over existing heuristic and sequential simulated annealing algorithms.

Keywords: Parallel Simulated Annealing, Data Warehousing, Materialized view selection.

1 Introduction

Data warehouses integrate data from multiple heterogeneous databases and other information sources. A data warehouse(DW) is a repository of historical information available for querying and analysis. To avoid accessing the original data sources and increase the efficiency of the warehousing queries, information within a data warehouse is organized as a set of views from different production databases. These views are often referred to as materialized views. The large computation and space required for view materialization implies that it is impractical to materialize all possible views. Hence, there is a need for selecting an appropriate set of views to materialize which increases the query performance, commonly referred to as the *view selection problem* [9].

Because materialized views have to be in synchronization with source data, any change to the source should be reflected to the views as well. Therefore, in the data warehousing view maintenance cost also has to be considered not just the query processing cost. The trade-off between query performance and view

A. Bourgeois and S.Q. Zheng (Eds.): ICA3PP 2008, LNCS 5022, pp. 121–132, 2008.

maintenance cost makes materialized view selection one of the most challenging problems in data warehousing [13]. Based on a set of frequently asked DW queries, the task is to select a set of views to materialize so that the total query processing and view maintenance cost is minimized.

The materialized view selection problem is NP-hard[9]. Several heuristic algorithms have been proposed in the literature to address the view selection problem. We classified them into four major groups according to [1]:

Deterministic algorithms: The classic solution for this problem uses heuristics which usually construct or search a solution in a deterministic manner and apply some kind of heuristics(e.g greedy algorithm) to decrease the solution space [10,9,2]. In [11] an extension is proposed, which improved the quality by using index on the selected views. In [3] a "chunk" based precomputation method was introduced. This method precomputes a subset of chunk aggregates which provide better but not near optimal results over the heuristic approaches.

Genetic algorithms (GA): The above methods are effective when the number of views is relatively small. In order to obtain better solutions for a bigger number of views with respect to view maintenance and query processing costs genetic algorithms have been introduiced [16,4]. The basic idea is to start with a random initial population and generate offspring by random variations (e.g., crossover and mutation). The "fittest" members of the population survive the subsequent selection. The algorithm terminates as soon as there is no further improvement over a period or after a predetermined number of generations. The fittest individual found is the solution. However, the possibility of infeasible solutions creates some problems. In fact, the approach proposed in [4] does not contain a "penalty" method to discourage infeasible solutions. This deficiency has subsequently been addressed in [16].

Randomize algorithms: Algorithms in this class pursue a completely different approach: a set of moves is defined. These moves constitute edges between the different solutions of the solution space; two solutions are connected by an edge if (and only if) they can be transformed into one another by exactly one move. Simulated Annealing(SA) as a type of randomize algorithm performs a random walk along the edges according to a cooling schedule, and terminates as soon as no applicable ones exist or lose all the energy in the system(frozen state). In [19,17], SA has been applied to the view selection problem. [19], showed that by using SA the cost of a selected set of materialized views is up to 70% less than the genetic [4] and heuristic algorithms [15].

Hybrid algorithms: Hybrid algorithms combine the strategies of pure deterministic and pure randomized algorithms. Solutions obtained by deterministic algorithms are used as starting points for randomized algorithms or as initial population members for genetic algorithms. In [5], hybrid approach has been applied for the view selection problem, which combines the power of genetic algorithms in global search with heuristic's ability in fine-grained local search, to find a good set of materialized views.

In [4,15,19,5], GA and SA tries to find the best set of intermediate results (views) in the Multiple View Processing Plan(MVPP) graph [15] so that the cost of query processing and view maintenance is minimized. However, the number of views in the MVPP graph is relatively small(e.g: 60 queries and 250 views). In [16,10] genetic algorithms and heuristics have been proposed to select the best set of views to materialize from an AND/OR view graph [9]. The number of nodes in their AND/OR view graph is not going further than 250 either.

In this paper we introduce a new approach for materialized view selection using Parallel Simulated Annealing (PSA) to select views from an input Multiple View Processing Plan (MVPP). With PSA, we are able to perform view selection on MVPPs having a much larger number of queries and views, which reflects the real data warehousing environment. As solution quality is affected by the number of times that the initial solution is perturbed, by performing simulated annealing with multiple inputs over multiple compute nodes concurrently, PSA is able to increase the quality of obtained sets of materialized views. In experimental study, conducted on real production data with more than 250 queries and thousand of views (intermediate nodes), we showed that our approach using PSA in conjunction with MVPP outperforms heuristic method [15] and sequential SA [19] to the extent of factor five considering the cost of obtained set of views.

The rest of this paper is organized as follows: Section 2 gives an overview on our framework for the materialize view selection problem, followed by our running example and some preliminaries for the Multiple View Processing Plan (MVPP) and its cost model. Section 4 discusses our Parallel Simulated Annealing(PSA) approach and how we apply PSA to solve materialized view selection. Section 5 present and analyse our experimental results. Section 6 concludes the paper.

2 Materialized View Selection

Materialized view selection is an important design decision in data warehouse construction. Here we present our framework to select a set of views to materialize based on the given frequently used set of queries in the data warehouse environment. As figure 1 shows, the input is a list of frequently used queries. This list will then be an input to our XML convertor box, which translates the text queries to XML format. We found that the MVPP builder works better with XML format than with plain text. The out-put from the XML convertor will go to the MVPP builder which creates the MVPP graph. The MVPP graph will be an input to our parallel simulated annealing algorithm. The output from the simulated annealing algorithm would be an appropriate set of nodes to materialize in order to minimize the query processing and view maintenance cost.

2.1 Running Example

In this section, we present an example to motivate the discussion of materialized view selection in data warehouses. Our example is taken from a sample data warehouse application that analyzes trends in sales, and which was used in [14]. We used this running example just for explanation, however the data and query

Fig. 1. A framework for materialized view selection in data warehousing environments

sets which we used for our experiments are explained in section 5. The relations and the attributes of the running example's schema are:

```
Product  (Pid, name, Did)
Division (Did, name, city)
Order (Pid,Cid, quantity, date)
Customer (Cid, name, city)
Part (Tid, name, Pid, supplier)
```

We use Pd, Div, Ord, Cust and Pt to refer to the above relations. Furthermore, we assume that all of these relations are stored at the same site and we do not need to consider data communication costs in our cost calculation. Suppose that we have the four following frequently used queries:

```
Query 1: Select Pd.name          Query 2: Select Pt.name
           From Pd, Div                    From Pd, Pt, Div
           Where Div.city= "LA" and        where ere Div.city="LA"
           Pd.Did=Div.Did                  and Pd.Did=Div.Did
                                           and Pt.Pid=Pd.Pid


Query 3: Select Cust.name,       Query 4: Select Cust.city,date
           Pd.name, quantity              From Ord, Cust
           From Pd, Div, Ord, Cust        Where quantity>100 and
           Where Div.city= "LA" and       Ord.Cid=Cust.Cid
           Pd.Did=Div.Did   and
           Pd.Pid=Ord.Pid and
           Ord.Cid=Cust.Cid and
           Date > 7/1/96
```

In Figure 2 we show a global query access plan for the above four queries. This plan is referred to as the Multiple View Processing Plan (MVPP)[15]. The query access frequencies are indicated above each query node. For simplicity, we assumed that the base relations Pd, Div, Ord, Cust, and Pt are updated once during the process of materialized view selection. There are different options for selection of a set of views to be materialized: (1) materialize all of the nodes in the MVPP; (2) materialize some of the intermediate nodes (e.g. tmp2, tmp3, tmp7, etc.); (3) do not materialize any of the nodes in MVPP. Option (1) and (3) are not realistic because for option (1), we do not have enough time and space to materialize all of the nodes in MVPP. Option (3) implies that we have to execute all queries on the raw data set which will result in excessive query processing times. The best option is to materialize an appropriate subset of views that minimizes view maintenance and query processing costs.

Suppose there are some materialized intermediate nodes in the MVPP. For each query, the cost of query processing is its query frequencies multiplied by the cost of the query accesses to the materialized nodes. The maintenance cost for materialized view is the cost used for construction of the view (here we assume that rebuilding is used whenever an update of an involved base relation occurs) [15]. For example, if tmp2 is materialized, the query processing cost for Q1 is $10 * 35.25$. The view maintenance cost is $2 * (35.25 + 0.25)$. The total cost for an MVPP is the sum of all query processing and view maintenance costs. What follows is a specification and the definition of the cost model for an MVPP.

3   Multiple View Processing Plan (MVPP)

We are using an MVPP [15] together with parallel simulated annealing for selecting the best set of views to materialize. As shown in Figure 2, the MVPP is a directed acyclic graph (DAG) that represents a query processing plan. The leaf nodes in this graph represent the base relations, and the root nodes represent the queries. Analogous to query execution plans there can be more than one MVPP for the same set of views. This depends upon the access characteristics of the applications and physical data warehouse parameters. We choose one of the possible optimal MVPPs. Note that the quality of the selected MVPP can

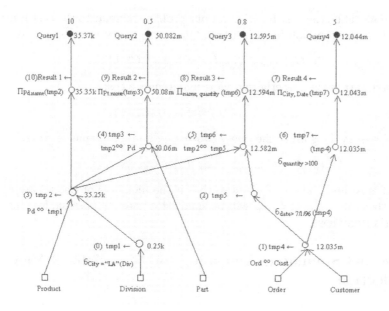

Fig. 2. A MVPP for running example queries

effect on our result. An MVPP is a DAG $M = (V, A, C_q^a, C_m^r, f_q, f_u)$ where V is a set of vertices, A is a set of arcs over V defined as follows:

- For every relational algebra operation in the query tree, for every base relation, and for every distinct query, create a vertex;
- For $v \in V, T(v)$ is the relation generated by the corresponding vertex v. $T(v)$ can be a base relation, intermediate node while processing a query, or the final result for a query;
- For any leaf vertex v, (that is one which has no edges pointing to the vertex), $T(v)$ corresponds to a base relation. Let L be a set of leaf nodes;
- For any root vertex v (that is one which has no edges going out of the vertex), $T(v)$ corresponds to a global query. Let R be a set of root nodes;
- If the base relation or intermediate result relation $T(u)$ corresponding to vertex u is needed for further processing at a node v, introduce an arc $u \longrightarrow v$;
- For every vertex v, let $S(v)$ denote the source nodes which have edges pointed to v; for any $v \in L, S(v) = \phi$, $S^*(v)$ be the set of descendants of v;
- For every vertex v let $D(v)$ denote the destination nodes to which v is is pointed; for any $v \in R$, $D(v) = \phi$;
- For $v \in V, C_q^a$ is the cost of query processing q accessing $T(v)$; $C_m^r(v)$ is the cost of maintaining T (v) based on changes to the base relation $S^*(v) \cap R$, if $T(v)$ is materialized.
- f_q, f_u denote query frequency and base relation maintenance frequency respectively.

3.1   Cost Model

We can now define the cost function for our problem, similar to the cost function in [15]. The cost function has two parts. One is the query processing cost:

$$C_{queryprocessing}(v) = \Sigma_{q \in R} f_q C_a^q(v)$$

the second part is the materialized view maintenance cost:

$$C_{maintenance}(v) = \Sigma_{r \in R} f_u C_m^r(v)$$

the total cost is the sum of the query processing and maintenance costs:

$$C_{total}(v) = C_{queryprocessing}(v) + C_{maintenance}(v)$$

Our goal is to find the set of views so that if the members of the set are materialized then the value of C_{total} will be smallest among all possible feasible sets of materialized views.

4   Parallel Simulated Annealing for Materialized View Selection

The motivation to use a Parallel Simulated Annealing (PSA) algorithm in solving the materialized view selection problem was based on observing that the data warehouse has a huge number of views and queries. Therefore in the view selection problem the solution space has many local minimas. A simple local search algorithm proceeds by choosing a random initial solution and generating a neighbor from that solution. The neighboring solution is accepted if it is a cost decreasing transition. Such a simple algorithm has the drawback of often being trapped to a local minimum. The simulated annealing algorithm, though by itself it is a local search algorithm, avoids getting trapped in a local minimum by also accepting cost increasing neighbors with some probability. In sequential SA according to [20]: first an initial solution is randomly generated, and a neighbor is found and is accepted with a probability of min(1,exp(-δ/T), where δ is is the cost difference and T is the control parameter corresponding to the temperature of the physical analogy and will be called temperature. On the slow reduction of temperature, the algorithm converges to the global minimum, but the time taken increases drastically.

Simulated annealing is inherently sequential and hence very slow for problems with large search space. Therefore, to speed up the computation a parallelization of SA is very desirable. Also, since solution quality in the SA algorithm is affected by the number of times that we perturb an initial random solution, the parallelization of SA with multiple inputs over multiple compute nodes concurrently will lead us to the better quality of solution.

In the following subsections, we describe how to apply PSA to design a solution for the materialized view selection problem. More precisely, we provide a suitable representation of solution space, followed by PSA's parameters and their desirable values.

4.1   Parallel Simulated Annealing Framework

There have been many attempts toward parallelizing simulated annealing. Each of these methods classified parallel simulated annealing differently. Classification in [6][12] distinguished between *single* and *multiple-walks* (Figure 3). This is the first distinguishing criterion: the number of paths which are evaluated in the search space of the optimization problem. In a *single-walk* algorithm only a single path in the search space is traversed, whereas in a *multiple-walk* approach several different paths are evaluated simultaneously. In *single-walk* algorithms after evaluating a part of the neighborhood of the current solution either only one step is traversed (*single-step parallelism*) or a sequence of steps is made from the current solution (*multiple-step parallelism*). In *multiple-walk* algorithms the parallel walks can be independent or may interact according to a communication pattern.

In this paper, we are using the independent walks parallelization which is called the Multiple Independent Runs(MIR) [7]. In this parallelization strategy no communication of moves or solutions is required. Independent runs of sequential SA are executed in each processor and the best found solution is chosen as the end result. Therefore, there is no need to add any communication cost to the total cost of the obtained set of materialized views.

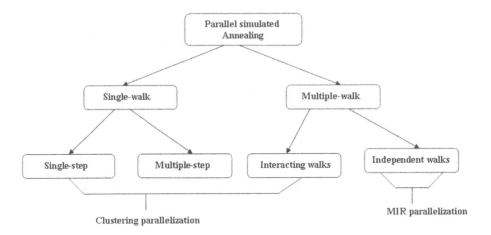

Fig. 3. Classification of parallel approaches for simulated annealing

4.2 Solution Representation

The problem to be solved can be stated as follows: given a MVPP graph (see figure 2) we attempt to find the best set of intermediate nodes (views) that can answer all queries with minimal cost. We do not use an MVPP directly as input into our PSA algorithm. We first convert the set of views to a binary string of 1s and 0s to represent views that will and will not be materialized, respectively. Our mapping strategy differs from [4],[5] and [16]. We number our nodes starting at the base relations moving left to right, and we continue up to the right-most node at the top of the graph. Nodes are numbered 0 to m-1 (where m is the number of intermediate nodes). We use a mapping array of size m-1 where each index in the array corresponds to a graph node. In our mapping array a '1' denotes that the corresponding node in the graph should be materialized and a '0' that the node is not materialized. For example in the binary string (0,0,0,0,1,1,0,0,1,1,0) we will materialize nodes 4,5,8 and 9.

4.3 Parallel Simulated Annealing Parameters

The success and quality of the SA algorithms either sequential or parallel relies on choosing the right parameters. Generally, we can categorize SA parameters into two separate classes: *generic parameters* and *problem specific parameters*. *Generic parameters* such as: initial temperature, cooling schedule and run factor are concerned with parameters of the SA algorithm itself . The *problem specific parameters* such as: initial configuration of our solution space, perturbing the configuration and cost function are dependent on the specific problems.

Here we first explain each of the *generic parameters*:

Initial temperature: The temperature T can affect the number and ratio of acceptance of each move. This value has traditionally been chosen so that nearly all moves are accepted. We set our starting temperature large enough to allow an acceptance value of 90. If the starting temperature is larger, the run length may increase with no improvement in cost. Too low temperature may lead to premature levelling off of the algorithm.

Cooling schedule: The temperature decrement factor for the exponential cooling is set to a constant value of 0.7. This value performed sufficiently well on our problem, although the algorithm is not particularly sensitive to this parameter.

Run factor: In this paper we use MIR which provides a better quality solution than the solution of a sequential run with the same length. We have another important parameter which we call *run factor*. a bigger value of run factor means more iterations for each run and we will gain the better quality solution. However, this increasing run length will increase the time length for each run and the complete annealing process. So we have to choose a run factor big enough to gain the high quality of answer in a reasonable amount of time. In our experiments, we found that the quality of answer is heavily depending on the value of run factor. Thus, we set the appropriate value for run factor after many test runs.

The *problem specific parameters* are:

Initial configuration: In our initial configuration we map array with a randomized set of zeros and ones. We do not employ a penalty function to discourage infeasible solutions, instead we use a simple verification method. We check the feasibility of each initial configuration against the number of queries that the solution can answer. If the solution is not feasible, we simply bypass it. For example the sequence (0,0,0,1,0,0,1,0,0,0,0) is a feasible solution for our sample problem. In figure 2 the materialized node 3 can answer queries 1 to 3 and materialized node 6 can answer the 4th query.

Perturbing the configuration: In the spirit of the physical annealing process, neighboring configurations must be similar in the sense that they represent only a slight perturbation in the system's state[18]. We define the neighborhood of a configuration to contain all configurations that differ from it by giving a 50% chance to each randomly chosen node to be materialized or unmaterialized. For example, for solution (0,0,0,1,1,0,1) we randomly pick node number 4 whose value is 1, then we just simply change the value to 0. So our solution after perturbing would be (0,0,0,0,1,0,1). Our experiments showed that this simple method ensures that our annealing algorithm will not get trapped in local minima in early stages.

Cost function: We use the cost function described in section 3.1. For example, to calculate the overall cost for the solution (0,0,0,1,0,0,1,0,0,0,0) we add C_{total} for nodes 3 and 4.

5   Experimental Evaluation

To show the practical relevance of our approach to materialized views selection problem, we performed an extensive experimental evaluation and compared it with heuristic method [15] and sequential SA because in previous study it was shown that the sequential SA is better than the GA [19]. The experiment involves execution of our PSA application over an optimized MVPP for a set of queries. The PSA application is a C++ program, which uses a robust PSA library (parSA 2.1) implementation [8] with the addition of materialized view selection component. Tests are performed on SUN Microsystems V20z dual AMD Opteron 2.6 GHz with 4GB RAM. The MVPP input is provided by our custom C++ MVPP builder, which creates an optimized MVPP for testing set of SQL queries, their frequency of usage and number of rows in tables as a input. The number of nodes in our MVPP inputs exceeds one thousand. For the testing, we used the real data from production database. This database is used for generation of data warehousing database, which analyzes the trend in using university resources. The source database consist of more than 100 relations. The number of rows in particular tables is up to 10 million. We have chosen 250 frequently used queries and assigned frequency according to usage.

5.1   Results

In Figure 4 we show results for our PSA algorithm (for 4, 8 and 16 compute nodes) against the heuristic and sequential SA algorithms. The heuristic algorithm provides a benchmark for our normalized results. The graph shows that our PSA algorithm approach generates solutions with costs more than 4 times less than the heuristic algorithm. For a smaller number of queries the results for sequential SA and PSA are similar. For a larger number of queries (more than 150) the PSA algorithm outperforms sequential SA, particularly for 16 compute

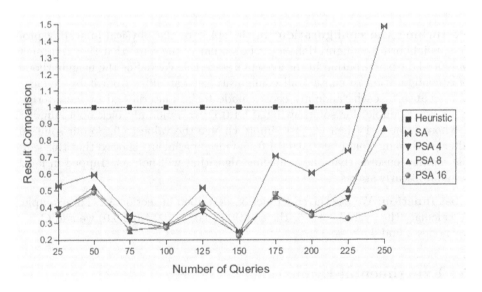

Fig. 4. Comparison of the solution quality (view maintenance and query processing costs) between our PSA, sequential SA algorithm, and heuristic method (normalized to "1")

nodes. The PSA results are consistently better than both the sequential SA and heuristic algorithms.

6   Conclusion and Future Work

In this paper we have described a new approach that is demonstrably better than the existing approaches for materialized view selection based on Parallel Simulated Annealing. In experimental study we show that our approach provides a significant improvement in the quality of the obtained set of materialized views compared to previously used methods for materialized view selection (Heuristic method and sequential SA). Additionally we show that our method can be efficiently applied to the large data warehousing systems, this leads to a significant improvement in query processing time and view maintenance costs. More specifically, in this study, we:

- Classified the existing methods for materialized view selection problem in order to identify their advantages and disadvantages,
- Proposed Parallel simulated annealing (PSA) framework which uses as input Multiple View Processing Plan (MVPP),
- showed that PSA can be efficiently applied to larger number of queries. Larger number of queries is more representative of real data warehousing systems,
- Experimentally evaluated the PSA by comparing its performance with heuristic method and sequential SA, and demonstrated its overall superior performance. The PSA algorithm approach generates solutions with costs up to 4 times less than the heuristic algorithm,
- We showed that PSA scaled with the increasing number of compute nodes.

As a future work we intend to do the testing with larger number of compute nodes and to use a more sophisticated parallel approach to achieve further improvement in the quality of results.

Acknowledgements

This research is partly sponsored by ARC (Australian Research Council) Discovery grant - Coarse Grained Parallel Algorithms, nr. DP0557303.

References

1. Steinbrunn, M., Moerkotte, J., Kemper, A.: Heuristic and Randomized Optimization for the Join Ordering Problem. Very Large Data Base 6, 191–208 (1997)
2. Harinarayan, V., Rajaraman, A., Ullman, J.D.: Implementing Data Cubes Efficiently. In: ACM SIGMOD, pp. 205–216 (1996)
3. Shukla, A., Deshpande, P., Naughton, J.: Materialized View Selection of Multidimensional Datasets. In: Proceeding of the 24th VLDB Conference, pp. 488–499 (1998)

4. Zhang, C., Yang, J.: Genetic Algorithm for Materialized View Selection in Data Warehouse Environments. In: Mohania, M., Tjoa, A.M. (eds.) DaWaK 1999. LNCS, vol. 1676, pp. 116–125. Springer, Heidelberg (1999)
5. Zhang, C., Yao, X., Yang, J.: An Evolutionary Approach to Materialized Views Selection in a Data Warehouse Environment. IEEE Transactions on Systems and Cybernetics Part C: Applications and Reviews 31(3), 282–294 (2001)
6. Aarts, E., Lenstra, K.J.: Local Search in Combinatorial Optimization. John Wiley (1997)
7. Kliewer, G., Tschoke, S.: A General Parallel Simulated Annealing Library and its Application in Airline Industry. In: Proceedings of the 14th International Parallel and Distributed Processing Symposium (IPDPS), pp. 55–61 (2000)
8. Kliewer, G., Tschoke, S.: Parallel Simulated Annealing Library (parSA), University of Paderborn (2007), http://www.uni-paderborn.de/~parsa
9. Gupta, H., Mumick, S.: Selection of Views to Materialize Under a Maintenance Cost Constraint. In: Beeri, C., Bruneman, P. (eds.) ICDT 1999. LNCS, vol. 1540, pp. 453–470. Springer, Heidelberg (1998)
10. Gupta, H., Mumick, S.: Selection of Views to Materialize in a Data Warehouse. IEEE Transactions on Knowledge and Data Engineering 17(11), 24–43 (2005)
11. Gupta, H., Harinarayan, V., Rajaraman, A., Ullman, J.D.: Index Selection for OLAP. In: Proc. Int'l Conf. on Data Engineering, pp. 208–219 (1997)
12. Azencott, I.R.: Simulated Annealing: Parallelization Techniques. Wiley (1992)
13. Widom, J.: Research Problems in Data Warehouse. In: 4th International Conferance on Information, Knowledge and Managment, pp. 25–30 (1995)
14. Yang, J., Karlapalem, K., Li, Q.: A Framework for Designing Materialized Views in Data Warehousing Environment. Technical Report HKUST-CS96-35 (1996)
15. Yang, J., Karlapalem, K., Li, Q.: Algorithm for Materialized View Design in Data Warehousing Environment. In: VLDB 1997, pp. 136–145 (1997)
16. Lee, M., Hammer, J.: Speeding up Materialized View Selection in Data Warehouses Using a Randomized Algorithm. Int. J. Cooperative Inform. Syst. 10, 327–353 (2001)
17. Kalnis, P., Mamoulis, N., Papadias, D.: View Selection Using Randomized Search. Data and Knowledge Engineering 42(1), 89–111 (2002)
18. Davidson, R., Harel, D.: Drawing Graphs Nicely using Simulated Annealing. ACM Transactions on Graphics 15, 301–331 (1996)
19. Derakhshan, R., Dehne, F., Korn, O., Stantic, B.: Simulated Annealing for Materialized View Selection in Data Warehousing Environment. In: Proceedings of the 24th IASTED international conference on Database and applications, pp. 89–94 (2006)
20. Janaki, R., Sreenivas, T.H., Subramaniam, G.K.: Parallel Simulated Annealing Algorithms. Journal of parallel and distributed computing 37, 207–212 (1996)

An Operational Approach to Validate the Path of BGP

Ping Li, Wanlei Zhou, and Ke Li

School of Engineering and Information Technology,
Deakin University, Melbourne, Australia
{pingli,wanlei,ktql}@deakin.edu.au

Abstract. BGP (Border Gateway Protocol) is a fundamental component of the current Internet infrastructure. However, BGP is vulnerable to a variety of attacks, since it cannot ensure the authenticity of the path attributes announced by BGP routers. Despite several solutions have been proposed to address this vulnerability, none of them is operational in real-world due to their immense impact on original BGP. In this paper, we propose a *Deployable Path Validation Authentication* scheme, which can effectively validate the path of BGP. Through analysis and simulation we show that this scheme has little impact on the performance and memory usage for the original BGP, and can be adopted in practice as an operational approach.

Keywords: BGP, security, AS, Internet.

1 Introduction

BGP [1] is the de facto inter-domain routing protocol of the Internet and has been deployed since the commercialization of the Internet. However this protocol implicitly depends on hearsay, since each BGP router believes and repeats what it has heard from other BGP routers. Malicious routers can insert false information into the path attributes, which makes many attacks possible, since path attributes are factors to make route selection decisions. This vulnerability of BGP is considered as lack of *path validation*, which contributes greatly to the increasing number of Internet attacks

Many solutions have been proposed to authenticate path validation. S-BGP (Secure BGP) [2] is one of the earliest security proposals, and probably the most concrete one. It uses cascaded signatures, a method that every BGP speaker along the way digitally signs the data, to secure path attribute. This proposal can provide high security. However it takes time to generate and verify signatures when sending and receiving route every time, so its convergence time is unbearable. Furthermore, signature information makes BGP message larger and increases storage requirement. The immense cost of S-BGP is the main cause of its not being deployed in practice.

soBGP (secure origin BGP) [3] is proposed as an alternative to S-BGP. It uses AS (autonomous systems) topology to validate *aspath*, which is the most important path attribute. Although this method degrades security to some degree compared with S-BGP, it s a good thought by getting tradeoff of security and cost. However it still can t be deployable, since the method of getting AS topology in soBGP counters the

A. Bourgeois and S.Q. Zheng (Eds.): ICA3PP 2008, LNCS 5022, pp. 133..143, 2008.

distributed nature of BGP. And soBGP introduces new messages, which is a challenge for BGP deployment.

In this paper, we propose a Deployable Path Validation Authentication (DPVA) scheme which has two objectives: to be deployable and to have path validation. To be deployable means that the DPVA scheme must have little impact on the original BGP, must be easily compatible with original BGP, and must be deployed incrementally. Path validation means that the DPVA scheme can ensure path validation. In this scheme, we achieved above two objectives by building an *aspath* table which reflects genuine AS topologies of Internet, and then validating paths by checking this *aspath* table. It looks similar with soBGP, but it can be deployable and is more secure than soBGP. Our analysis and simulation show that this scheme has little impact on the performance and memory usage of the original BGP, and can be deployed in the real world.

This scheme is not intended as a replacement for the comprehensive BGP security infrastructures. We don t specifically address origin authentication which is another security issue for BGP, and neither deal with the public key distribution of BGP routers. However it can replace the path authentication part of any such BGP security solutions (e.g., S-BGP, soBGP).

A comprehensive analysis of the security vulnerabilities in BGP is developed by Murphy in [5]. The author points out that BGP has three fundamental vulnerabilities: (1) BGP has no internal mechanism that provides strong protection of the integrity, freshness, and peer entity authenticity of the messages in peer-peer BGP communications. (2) No mechanism has been specified within BGP to validate the authority of an AS to announce NLRI information. (3) No mechanism has been specified within BGP to ensure the authenticity of the path attributes announced by an AS. This paper focuses on the third issue.

2   Design of the Deployable Path Validation Authentication Scheme

In BGP each autonomous system (AS) is assigned a unique integer as its identifier, known as the AS number. An AS manages subnetworks, each one described by an IP *prefix*--a range of IP addresses. A router running the BGP protocol is known as a BGP *speaker*. A BGP speaker communicates with a set of other BGP speakers, known as its *peers*, or *neighbours*. BGP peers constantly exchange the set of prefixes and paths for the prefixes--via *UPDATE* messages. The paths are also called *path attributes* which are a set of attributes of the prefixes in the UPDATE messages. *Aspath* is the most important attribute. It s a vector of ASes that packets must traverse to reach the originating AS. Last AS in the vector is the originator of this route. Each AS advertises the prefixes it is originating to its peers, and forwards the received information to each of their other neighbours. When BGP speaker forwards prefixes to other ASes, it will append it s own AS number to the *aspath*.

The original BGP (i.e. BGP4) just supports the IPv4 route. To support routing for multiple network layer protocols, MP-BGP (Multiple-protocol extension for BGP) [4] was defined. It uses the capability advertisement procedures to determine whether the speaker could use multi-protocol extensions with a particular peer. And it uses two new attributes, MP_REACH_NLRI (Multi-protocol Reachable NLRI) and MP_UNREACH_NLRI (Multi-protocol Unreachable NLRI) to carry the set of reachable and unreachable prefixes for corresponding Network Layer protocols.

In this study, our goal is to provide a Deployable Path Validation Authentication (DPVA) scheme. This scheme can be divided in two steps. The first step is to build an *aspath* table which reflects the genuine AS topologies of Internet. To get good compatibility with original BGP, we introduce a new address family -- AFI_AS, and use MP-BGP to get this *aspath* table. To secure *aspath* information, we introduce the *aspair* declaration which can effectively protect *aspath* from being tampered. The second step is to ensure path validation. When a BGP speaker receives a prefix, it will check if there is a same *aspath* in the *aspath* table with the prefix s *aspath*. A hash searching algorithm is introduced in the checking process, so that the path authentication has little impact on the original BGP performance.

Our design also supports incremental deployment, because immediate deployment and use of any new technique throughout the Internet is not possible. We provide different options for different deployment stages.

We don t deal with the public key distribution in our scheme, and we assume every BGP speaker has owned a Public/private Key or all BGP Speakers in every AS have shared a Public/private Key which depends on the policy. Since lack of security is a norm for Internet routing protocols besides BGP, and we believe uniform key distribute mechanisms will be generated in the near future. The key distribute methods in other BGP security solutions, such as SBGP, soBGP, may be used in our scheme as well.

2.1 Building As-Path Table

BGP is an AS distance-vector protocol: every BGP speaker appends its own AS to the *aspath* of received prefixes, and then forwards these prefixes with the appended *aspath* to its neighbours. So in the original BGP design we can get all *aspath*s reaching other ASes from *aspath*s of received prefixes. Therefore if every AS just sends a BGP update message without actual prefixes, and other ASes forward them following above rules, then we also can get all *aspath*s reaching other ASes from *aspath* of these few update messages. Furthermore, if the *aspath* can t be maliciously modified in the above forwarding processing, then we can get an *aspath* table which reflects the genuine AS topologies of Internet. This is the key idea of our design.

We implement the above idea by using a new address family (AFI_AS) in MP-BGP. Because MP-BGP had been carried out by most of the router manufacturers, it will be effortless to upgrade devices if just to support a new address family. MP-BGP can be well compatible with original BGP. Capability advertisement procedures can determine if neighbours support AFI_AS, so the new format definition will not cause any compatibility problems. And we don t have to introduce new messages by using MP-BGP. In addition, the processing of every address family is independent, so the processing of normal BGP route won t be affected by the AFI_AS address family.

To ensure the AFI_AS *aspath* won t be tampered, we introduce the *aspair* declaration, which is signed by a BGP speaker to authenticate one direction neighbour relationship of a pair of AS. *Aspair* declaration is composed of the sending AS, receiving AS, signer, sequence number and signature. The sending AS (ASs) and receiving AS

(ASr) form one direction neighbour relationship. We use (ASs ASr) to donate this *aspair*. The signer is the identifier of the sending AS. The sequence number indicates the time sequence that signature is issued. For an *aspair*, a more recently issued signature means a larger sequence number. The sending AS encrypts the *aspair* and the sequence number using its private key (Ks) to create the signature. We use (ASs ASr)Ks to donate the *aspair* declaration. The *aspair* declaration is carried in the prefix domain of the MP_REACH_NLRI or MP_UNREACH_NLRI attribute.

When the AFI_AS address family is initiated, an *aspath* table, which holds all the verified *aspath*, and an *aspair* table, which holds all the *aspair* declarations, should be generated. When a new AFI_AS neighbour is established, a BGP speaker will send all the *aspath*s in the *aspath* table, and its local AS to this neighbour.

When a BGP speaker sends an AFI_AS *aspath* to its neighbour, firstly, it will append its local AS number to this *aspath*, and puts all *aspair* declarations along this *aspath*, and the *aspair* declaration that its own AS to receipt AS, to the MP_REACH_NLRI attribute. For example, Suppose AS_k has an *aspath* {AS_{k-1}, AS_{k-2} f AS_0}, AS_0 is the origin AS of the *aspath*. AS_k would forward this *aspath* to AS_{k+1}. Then it should append AS_k to this *aspath*, to get *aspath* s {AS_k, AS_{k-1} f AS_0}, and find all *aspair* declarations $(AS_i\ As_{i+1})K_i$, i=0f k-1, and $(AS_k\ AS_{k+1})K_k$, then put them in the MP_REACH_NLRI attribute which can include many *aspair* declarations. *Aspath_s* is carried in the *aspath* attribute domain.

If a BGP speaker receives AFI_AS update, it should check the following: if it had received all the *aspair* declarations along the *aspath* attribute; if it had received the *aspair* declaration that sending AS to its own AS; if all the *aspair* signatures had been verified; and if the first AS in the *aspath* is the sending AS. If all the checks pass, then the *aspath* is put into the *aspath* table which will be used to authenticate the BGP route, and it is forwarded to other neighbours as well. For the example mentioned above, AS_{k+1} would receive an AFI_AS update, with *aspath* attribute *aspath_s*, and *aspair* declarations $(AS_i\ As_{i+1})K_i$, i=0f k. Lack of any *aspair* declarations would lead to the failure of the *aspath* check.

Fig. 1 shows how the *aspath* and *aspair* signatures are transmitted. We have four ASes numbered as 1, 2, 3, and 4, respectively. AS 1 initiates the process by sending AFI_AS announcement [{1}, S_1], which means it has *aspath* 1. S_1 is the *aspair* declaration, generated by signing (1 2), its AS number first, then the intended recipient, then a sequence number by its private key K_1. When AS 2 receives this announcement, it firstly verifies every *aspair* declaration S_1, then will add it s own AS, and send AFI_AS announcement [{2, 1}, S_1, S_2] to AS3. Other ASes continue this process. If all AS initiate an AFI_AS *aspath*, then every AS can get all *aspath*s to reach other ASes. For example, AS 4 will get *aspath*, {3,2,1},{3,2},{3}.

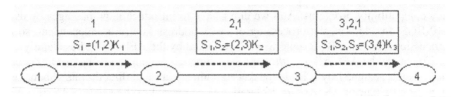

Fig. 1. The process of AFI_AS

Our design also supports withdrawing *aspath*s. When a BGP speaker (AS$_{local}$) detects a BGP neighbour is down (AS$_{shut}$), it will delete all the *aspath*s received from this neighbour, and then send an AFI_AS update to other neighbours with an *aspair* declaration withdrawal. The withdrawing *aspair* is (AS$_{shut}$ AS$_{local}$), and the withdrawing *aspair* declaration (AS$_{shut}$ AS$_{local}$)K$_{local}$ is signed by the AS$_{local}$, not the AS$_{shut}$, which can avoid malicious *aspath* withdrawal, and only the AS whose neighbour relationship is down is entitled to announce the corresponding *aspair* withdrawal. The *aspair* declaration withdrawal is put in MP_UNREACH_NLRI attribute. The receiver of this *aspair* withdrawal will forward it to other neighbours, and delete all the *aspath*s related to this *aspair*. As shown in figure 2, if AS 3 detects that the neighbour AS 2 becomes down, it will delete *aspath* {2,1},{2} from its *aspath* table, then sends *aspair* withdrawal (2,3)K$_3$ to AS 4. AS 4 will delete *aspath* {3,2,1},{3,2} from its *aspath* table.

Aspair declaration can effectively protect *aspath* from being tampered. Suppose AS$_k$ has an *aspath*{AS$_{k-1}$ ƒ AS$_a$ ƒ AS$_b$...AS$_0$}, and ASa is not adjacent with AS$_b$. If AS$_0$ wants to tamper the *aspath*, and sends as AS_AFI *aspath* {AS$_{k-1}$ ƒ AS$_a$ AS$_b$...AS0} to its neighbour, it also needs to send an *aspair* declaration {AS$_b$ AS$_a$}K$_b$. But because only AS$_b$ owns the K$_b$, so AS$_k$ can t generate this declaration, and can t tamper the *aspath* successfully.

Our design also can prevent *aspath* replay attacks, which hasn t been considered in other proposals. When a BGP speaker receives an *aspair* withdrawal, the *aspair* declaration may just be labeled expired. If it later receives this *aspair* declaration again, the BGP speaker would check the sequence number of the new *aspair* declaration. If this sequence number is not larger than the expired one, then the new *aspair* declaration will be ignored.

In addition, we set a limitation for being an AFI_AS neighbour that only BGP speakers connected directly can be AFI_AS neighbours, which can defend colluding adversaries. Suppose AS$_a$ has an as-path {AS$_k$ ƒ AS$_b$...AS$_0$}, then AS$_a$ and AS$_b$ can collude to tamper the *aspath* to {ASb...AS0} by established BGP neighbours in tunnel. However, with this limitation ..ASa and ASb can t be AFI_AS neighbours since they are not connected directly, so colluding attacks is also impossible. Furthermore, because the configuration of different address family can be different, so we don t need to worry about the compatibility with old configurations.

We choose RSA as the cryptographic algorithm. It s well known that the overhead for operating signature and verifying signature is huge. But the overhead is different for different cryptographic algorithm and different processing strategy. Operating signature takes longer in RSA than in DSA. However verifying signature takes an order of magnitude longer in DSA than in RSA. For our scheme, the count to sign is the number of BGP speaker s neighbours. The count to verify signature is the number of *aspair*. The number of *aspair* is far more than the number of BGP neighbours, so we select the RSA as our signature algorithms.

To avoid sending repeated *aspair* declaration and verifying signature repeatedly, if an *aspair* declaration had been sent to a neighbour before, we can choose don t send it again. And when a BGP speaker receives a repeated *aspair* declaration, if the sequence number is not larger than the old one, it may not verify again. This can improved the performance further. AS shown in figure 2, in AS 4, it will have *aspath* {1,2,3},{2,3},{3}, so *aspair* (3,4) will be sent by AS 3 three times.

BGP has two kinds of neighbour, EBGP and IBGP. All above description is for EBGP. There is some difference for IBGP, however. For example, BGP speakers just forward *aspath* to IBGP neighbours, not appending its own AS, and do not initiate its own AS to IBGP neighbours. There is similar difference for withdrawing process as well.

2.2 Checking Path Validation

Now the *aspath* table has been established by AFI_AS address family. When received a BGP normal route, the BGP speaker should check if there is an identical *aspath* in the *aspath* table. To improve the performance of this process, we only store one *aspath* attribute for identical *aspath* attributes of BGP routes and AS_AFI *aspath*, which point to this *aspath*, and we use counters to identify how many routes or AS_AFI use the *aspath*. All these *aspath* are organizied in hash, so that they can be searched quickly. Because many routes have the same *aspath*, so the memory usage of system can be saved as well.

Next, we give the detailed algorithms for receiving a verified AS_AFI *aspath* and for receiving a BGP normal route:

Algorithm: Receiving a verified AS_AFI *aspath*

```
search the aspath attribute hash
if not find one
    create an aspath attribute, add to hash table
    point the AS_AFI aspath to this aspath attrbute
    label this aspath attribute verified
else if find one
    point the AS_AFI aspath to this aspath attrbute
        if this aspath attribute is not verified
            label this aspath attribute verified
            find all the BGP routes which point to this
aspath attribute
            label them from invalid to valid
            (which may invoke sending them to neighbours)
add this AS_AFI aspath to aspath table
(which may invoke send AFI_AS aspath to neighbours)
```

Algorithm: Receiving a BGP normal route

```
search the aspath attribute hash
if not find one
    create an aspath attribute, add to hash table
    point the BGP route to this aspath attrbute
else if find one
    point the BGP route to this aspath attrbute
        if this aspath attribute is verified
            label the route from invalid to valid
add this route to BGP routing table
```

In practice, we recommend that sending AFI_AS *aspath* prior to sending the routes, so that BGP speakers don t have to find all the BGP routes which have the same *aspath* attribute with the AFI_AS *aspath*.

From the above algorithms, we can see that normal BGP route processing is only added a process of judging if the *aspath* has a verified flag. And usually the AS_AFI *aspath* is received prior to BGP routes, so when BGP speaker receives routes, they needn t generate *aspath*. From this point of view, the performance of processing BGP normal routes is improved.

2.3 Incremental Deployment

Our design also provides some options to support increment deployment.

In the early stage of deployment, AFI_AS is only supported by sparse ASes, so we may set the policy that the routes whose *aspath* partly or wholly overlapped with AFI_AS *aspath* have high priority. We even can set a different priority according to the overlap degree. Routes with higher priority would have more chance to be selected.

In the medium stage of deployment, AFI_AS may be supported by areas. These areas may need to change AFI_AS information. Our design can allow two remote BGP speakers to establish AFI_AS neighbour across several ASes. But in this case, they just forward AFI_AS *aspath*, and don t append their own ASes to the *aspath*.

In the later stage of deployment, AFI_AS may be supported by nearly all ASes. So we may set the policy that only the routes whose *aspath* is the same with one of AFI_AS *aspath* are valid.

3 Evaluation

Huge negative performance impact on BGP is one of the main reasons why none of the existing BGP security solutions are deployed in practice. Especially we can t ignore the memory overhead for storing signature, and CPU overhead for operating signature and verifying signature. In this section, we present the memory overhead and CPU overhead of our proposal through statics analysis and actual simulation. And in both analysis and simulation, we use data source from real Internet BGP routes obtained from RIS (Routing Information Service), so that the results can reflect the actual application. RIS is an RIPE NCC project to collect and store Internet routing data. It has some BGP monitoring points which establish BGP connections with some real BGP routers, and accept BGP updates from these routers, but not send back updates.

3.1 Memory Overhead

In our DPVA design, we add two tables: the *aspath* table and the *aspair* table. So we can evaluate the memory overhead by computing how much memory the contents in these two tables consume.

Firstly we extracted BGP routing tables of different AS respectively from the RIS data of Jan.1, 2006. Then we randomly selected several AS s routing table, and calculated their numbers of prefixes, *aspath*s and *aspair*s. From the result shown in table 1, we can know that the numbers of prefixes, *aspath*s and *aspair*s are nearly consistent in every AS. So we can use the average number to compute the memory overheard. For the *aspath* table, since an *aspath* attribute which requires much memory has been existed in the original BGP, so only the memory to organise the *aspath* table is required. Assuming the average size of organising an *aspath* is 64 bytes, 1.8M bytes memory would be required for storing 28,708 *aspath*s. For the *aspair* table, if RSA signature arithmetic is used, 128bytes will be required for one *aspair*, and 3.4M bytes will be required for 26,808 as-pairs. In total, these two tables consume 5.2M bytes of memory. Memory for storing one BGP route is about 0.8Kbytes in cisco s routers, which can be calculated from cisco s data [8]. So 140M bytes memory will be consumed for storing 174852 BGP routes. Therefore we are looking at 5.2M bytes of memory cost, just adding *3.7%* to the original BGP memory usage.

Table 1. Prefix, *aspath*, *aspair* and RA numbers of BGP routes

AS	4608	3741	513	16186	7018	3333	average
Prefix	175094	174189	177570	173756	173408	176454	174 852
Aspath	28586	28757	28627	28254	28845	29600	28708
Aspair	27171	27018	27382	27058	25071	27534	26808
RA	804440	531527	595372	787855	457916	557163	622378

We also evaluated the memory overhead for S-BGP s path authentication. The RA numbers S-BGP requires for these selected ASes is also shown in table 1. Assuming the average size of RA is 128 bytes, the total memory for storing 622378 RAs is about 80M, which is far more than our scheme. Table 2 shows this comparison.

Table 2. Comparison of memory cost

	Original BGP	Our Proposal (DPVA)	S-BGP
Memory usage	140 MB	145.2 MB; 3.7% more	220 MB; 57.1% more

3.2 CPU Overhead

We evaluate the CPU overhead from two aspects: static analysis and actual simulation. Firstly we analyse the cost of signing operation and verifying signature, since cryptography consumes much CPU time. Then we present our simulation results using Opnet.

In our design, the count for signing operation is the number of the BGP neighbour AS. The count for verifying signature is the number of *aspair*. We calculated and obtained these counts in the case of BGP routers rebooting from previous several AS s routing table we had extracted.

We also obtained the count for signing operation and verifying signature in S-BGP. The analysis in [6] showed that the executing time to sign and verify signature using the DSA algorithm is 0.015ms and 31ms respectively in a 200MHz system, and for RSA algorithm is 50ms and 2.5ms respectively. S-BGP uses the DSA algorithm, whereas we use the RSA algorithm. From collected data we can estimate the total time for S-BGP to execute signature when rebooting in a router (200MHz) is more than several hours, but our scheme needs no more than 2 minutes.

However, BGP routers normally are kept stable and must not reboot frequently for keeping the Internet routing steady. So next we evaluated the cryptographic processing impact in normal situation. Since BGP routes daily variation is not obvious, we calculated the BGP routes monthly variation firstly, and then evaluated the processing cost of these monthly variations.

We obtained the RIS data from the first day for several months of 2006, and calculated the stable and added *aspair*s, prefixes and *aspath*s in AS 7018. We found that the number of added *aspair*s every month is about 1800. The cryptographic processing for these *aspair*s is about 5s (2.5ms * 1800), which will not be a burden to normal BGP processing.

We also found that the number of unstable *aspath*s (3000, according to collected data) is only about 15% of unstable prefixes (20000, according to collected data), which means the AS topology keeps relative steady when prefixes vary, and we needn t send AFI_AS *aspath*s frequently when prefixes vary.

Now we have analysed the impact of cryptography. Considering the CPU overheard is affected by many factors besides cryptography, we present our simulation using Opnet further. We set up two routers configured as BGP neighbours with each other, and then one router sends routing data to the other. We use the convergence time of the other router to evaluate the CPU overhead. Convergence time indicates the time to finish receiving and processing all routing update messages. Although the Internet topology is very complex, our simulation can be considered a miniature of whole Internet as our simulation includes a full routing processing: sending routes, receiving routes and processing routes.

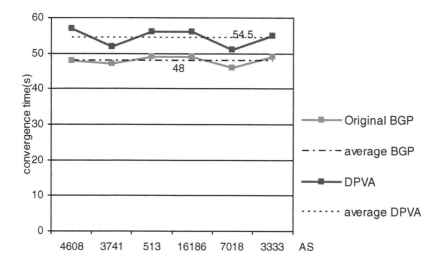

Fig. 2. Convergence time for processing whole routing table

Firstly we use the data of whole routing table from several selected ASes, and simulate the case that router starting, receiving and processing whole routing table from neighbour AS, which has the greatest overheard. Since the whole table simulation time is large, we select one every four routes. As shown in fig. 2, we found that the convergence time in our scheme only increases about 13.5% ((54.5-48)/48) compared with the original BGP when routers starting.

Then we use the data of monthly dynamics, and simulate in the case that router steady, and just processing a small quantity of varied routes. Fig. 3 presents the convergence time for processing monthly dynamic variation of AS7018. We can see that the CPU overhead of our scheme is small when routers are steady.

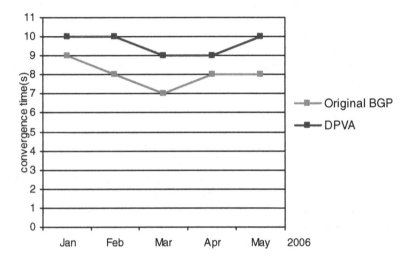

Fig. 3. Convergence time for processing dynamics in AS 7018

3   Conclusion

This paper proposes a Deployable Path Validation Authentication for BGP, which is different from previous BGP security proposal in that it can be really deployed in practice. It doesn t introduce new message, nearly has no change to the normal BGP route processing, and can be easily upgraded by manufactures. Most importantly is that it has little performance and memory impact to the original BGP, and can be deployed incrementally. At the same time, it can effectively protect paths from being tampered. It can defend replay attacks and colluding attacks which were seldom considered in previous proposals.

References

1. Rekhter, Y., Li, T., Hares, S.: A Border Gateway Protocol 4 (BGP-4), RFC4271
2. Lynn, C., Seo, K.: Secure BGP (S-BGP), http://www.ir.bbn.com/sbgp/draft-clynn-s-bgp-protocol-01.txt

3. White, R.: Architecture and Deployment Considerations for Secure Origin BGP (soBGP), http://tools.ietf.org/html/draft-white-sobgp-architecture-01
4. Bates, T., Rekhter, Y., Chandra, R., Katz, D.: Multiprotocol Extensions for BGP-4, RFC 2858
5. Murphy, S.: BGP Security Vulnerabilities Analysis, RFC 4272
6. Nicol, D.M., Smith, S.W., Zhao, M.: Evaluation of Efficient Security for BGP Route Announcements using Parallel Simulation. J. Simulation Practice and Theory 12, 187..216 (2004)
7. Hu, Y.-C., Perrig, A., Sirbu, M.: SPV: Secure Path Vector Routing for Securing BGP. In: SIGCOMM 2004, pp. 179..192. ACM Press (2004)
8. Achieve Optimal Routing and Reduce BGP Memory Consumption, http://www.cisco.com/warp/public/459/41.shtml

1-Persistent Collision-Free CSMA Protocols for Opportunistic Optical Hyperchannels

Jing Chen[1], Jianping Wang[2], Hui Yu[3], Ashwin Gumaste[4], and S.Q. Zheng[5]

[1] Telecommunications Engineering Program, University of Texas at Dallas,
Richardson, TX 75083
jxc030100@utdallas.edu
[2] Department of Computer Science, City University of Hong Kong, Hong Kong
jianwang@cityu.edu.hk
[3] Computer Engineering Program, University of Texas at Dallas,
Richardson, TX 75083
hxy041000@utdallas.edu
[4] School of Information Technology, Indian Institute of Technology,
Powai, Mumbai, India 400076
ashwing@ieee.org
[5] Department of Computer Science, University of Texas at Dallas,
Richardson, TX 75083
sizheng@utdallas.edu

Abstract. Recently, a new WDM optical network infrastructure named SMART [1], which is capable of dynamically setting up, modifying, and tearing down optical connections, was proposed. The performance of SMART is determined by the performance of its hyperchannels, which are essentially optical buses or light-trails. Previously proposed CSMA protocols for unidirectional optical buses can be used as distributed medium access control protocols for hyperchannels. However, these protocols are either unfair, or not work-conserving. In this paper, we propose a class of work-conserving, collision-free, and fair CSMA protocols for opportunistic hyperchannels which are tailored hyperchannels for SMART. We show that the performances of our proposed protocols are much better than that of p_i-persistent CSMA and that of priority-based CSMA protocol in terms of throughput and fairness.

Keywords: Optical network, WDM, CSMA, SMART network, Light-Trail, opportunistic hyperchannel.

1 Introduction

Optical Wavelength Division Multiplexing(WDM) technology has been considered as the basis of the next generation Internet for a while. However, the perfect balance between the utilization of the enormous bandwidth provided by the optical fiber and the satisfaction of ever-changing service requirements using the commodity optical devices has not been well achieved.

Recently, a new optical network infrastructure called *Scalable Multi-Access Reconfigurable Transport* (SMART) hypernetwork has been proposed[1]. Equipped

A. Bourgeois and S.Q. Zheng (Eds.): ICA3PP 2008, LNCS 5022, pp. 144–156, 2008.

with a rich menu of switching techniques (such as circuit switching, pipelined circuit switching, packet switching and burst switching) and connection types (such as dedicated, demand-assignment and elastic connections), SMART is able to manage optimized connections, and enforce individual service qualities and overall network performance using the commodity optical devices.

The underlying physical network of SMART is a *reconfigurable WDM hypernetwork* with reconfigurability distributed over network nodes. Such a reconfigurable WDM hypernetwork consists of multi-access hyperchannels. A hyperchannel, same as *Light-Trail*[2], is essentially a unidirectional optical bus where each node in a hyperchannel is capable of transmitting and receiving data. Thus, a hyperchannel with n nodes can accommodate C_n^2 connections in a time-multiplexing mode without complex optical switching configuration as studied in the optical networks over the past decade. Such an architecture can efficiently utilize bandwidth in subwavelength granularity. For connections with the source node and the destination node residing in separate hyperchannels, a *hyperpath* consisting of multiple hyperchannels with optical-electrical-optical (OEO) junctions connecting two adjacent hyperchannels can be found to accommodate such connections.

Given the inherent bus property of the hyperchannel, one fundamental task is to manage the access contention among the contending nodes in order to improve the efficiency of the hyperchannel. Similar as the traditional Media Access Control (MAC) protocols, the hyperchannel access control also aims to achieve the balance of throughput and fairness.

There are two categories of dynamic multiple access coordination: *centralized dynamic scheduling* (CDS) and *distributed dynamic scheduling* (DDS)[1]. In [3], we introduced a class of CDS protocols and showed that these protocols can emulate output queued scheduling of a multiplexer to ensure QoS under certain conditions. A major disadvantage of these CDS protocols is that a control hyperchannel is required to deliver the transmission schedule.

DDS protocols for unidirectional optical buses have been well investigated in the context of *carrier sense multiple access* (CSMA) protocols. The simplest DDS protocol as proposed in [2] for the unidirectional optical bus is that whenever the downstream nodes sense the data from the upstream nodes, the downstream nodes will interrupt their transmissions and free the bus for the transmission from the upstream nodes. For the simplicity of the presentation, such a DDS protocol is referred to as *priority based* CSMA protocol in this paper. Priority based CSMA protocol can obviously achieve near optimal throughput at the cost of severe unfairness to the downstream nodes. Other CSMA protocols, i.e. [4,5,6,7,8,9], which can be applied to hyperchannels, either suffer from significant overhead (due to expensive optical collision detection) or are unfair (providing some nodes more favorable service than others). Further, these protocols can be applied to either fold bus or dual-bus, but not both. To reduce the overhead and provide fairness, a CSMA protocol called p_i-persistent protocol for slotted fold bus is proposed in [10] and then extended for slotted dual-bus [11]. It was shown

---

[1] In this paper, the term of multi-access control protocol and the term of packet scheduling algorithm are used interchangeably.

that theoretically p_i-persistent protocols provide improved fairness, throughput, and average packet delay, assuming that p_is, which are the parameters used to control packet transmissions, match the traffic pattern and service requirement. Since traffic pattern and service requirement change dynamically, the complex process of collecting traffic and service information, computing new p_is, and notifying all nodes with their new p_is makes p_i-persistent protocols highly non-practical. Furthermore, there is probability that no nodes will transmit the data even if they have data to transmit and the bus is idle in the p_i-persistent protocols, i.e. an idle time slot goes downstream while all nodes don't transmit packets with probability $(1 - p_i)$. Thus, p_i-persistent protocols cannot fully utilize the bus capacity.

The objective of this research is to achieve the high throughput close to the *Priority based* CSMA protocol and the fairness close to p_i-persistent protocols without the overhead involved in p_i-persistence protocols. We propose a class of 1-persistent collision-free CSMA protocols where an intermediate node can persistently transmit its traffic whenever it has the traffic in its queue, so called "1-persistent" CSMA protocol. 1-persistent CSMA protocol can achieve the high throughput and it may also result in the high collision if the traditional unidirectional optical bus is applied. In this paper, the collision-free property is achieved by utilizing the *opportunistic hyperchannel*, which is an innovative unidirectional optical bus architecture introduced in [13]. In an opportunistic hyperchannel as to be explained in detail later, any intermediate node which is about to transmit the data will "cut" the hyperchannel into two segments where the traffic from the upstream nodes will be intercepted at the current node and allow the current node to transmit its data without collision. The current node will re-connect the two segments of the hyperchannel into one once its queue is empty.

The remains of the paper is organized as follows. In Section 2, we introduce p_i-persistent protocols. In Section 3, we introduce the structure of an opportunistic hyperchannel. In Section IV, we describe the features of a class of 1-persistent CSMA/CF protocols. In Section 5, we give the performance analysis of the proposed 1-persistent CSMA/CF protocol. We present our simulations results in Section VI, and conclude the paper in Section VII.

2 p_i-Persistent CSMA Protocol in an Unidirectional Optical Bus

The carrier sense multiple-access (CSMA) is a type of widely used technique in shared-medium packet communication systems. With CSMA, each node that has a packet to transmit attempts to avoid packet collision by listening to the channel, and based on the status of the channel, the node operates according to a particular CSMA scheme running in the system. For example, node N_i in a system running the p_i-persistent CSMA operates as:

(1) If the channel is sensed idle, it transmits the packet with probability p_i;
(2) If the channel is sensed busy, it waits until the channel goes idle (i.e. persisting on transmitting) and then transmits the packet with probability p_i.

By slotting time into segments whose duration is exactly equal to the transmission time of a single packet (assuming fixed-length packets), the channel operates in a synchronized mode. Every node starts to transmit its packets only at the beginning of a slot so that two or more conflicting packets overlap (if any) completely rather than partially, providing an increased channel efficiency. This is referred to as a slotted system. Otherwise, the system is called unslotted.

Unidirectional transmission property of optical buses inherently give some nodes higher priorities than others because of their relative positions on the bus, which may result in unfairness. This kind of unfairness can be solved by giving different p_i for different nodes. Slotted p_i-persistent protocols were analyzed in [10,11,12]. It was shown that, by deriving the steady-state probabilities of all nodes using queuing theory, a set of p_is can be computed to enforce fairness. Theoretical analysis and simulation result of [10,11,12] show that theoretically an unidirectional optical bus can provide fair service using p_i-persistent CSMA protocols.

The drawbacks of p_i-persistent protocols include: (1) Obviously, any p_i-persistent protocol is not work-conserving; i.e. the channel may be idle with waiting packets. (2) In addition, packets transmitting collision cannot be completely avoided, which wastes channel bandwidth. (3) The responsiveness of p_i-persistent protocols is slow. To achieve desired performance, p_is have to be computed beforehand for specific traffic pattern and/or service requirement. Even for a small traffic change in one node, p_is have to be recalculated and nodes have to be notified of new p_is. For dynamic traffic and/or service requirements, this process is not only wasting more channel bandwidth, but also slow in response to changes of network conditions. Thus, the theoretical performance of p_i-persistent protocols is unrealistic in practice.

3 System Model

The proposed work in this paper is based on the opportunistic hyperchannel architecture which was introduced in [13] based on [14]. There are two types of opportunistic hyperchannels, namely, fold connected opportunistic hyperchannel and dual opportunistic hyperchannel. A *fold connected opportunistic hyperchannel* shown in Figure 1(a) has a folded optical bus structure, providing full connectivity. A *dual opportunistic hyperchannel* consists of two independent opportunistic hyperchannels, each being called a *partially connected opportunistic hyperchannel*, in opposite directions in the form of Figure 1(b), providing full connectivity. A partially connected opportunistic hyperchannel is shown in Figure 1(b). For discussion purpose, we restrict our attention to the partially connected opportunistic hyperchannel shown in Figure 1(b). This restriction does not affect the applicability of our protocol to fold and dual hyperchannels. For convenience, and without loss of generality, we simply call a partially connected opportunistic hyperchannel an opportunistic hyperchannel.

In an $(n + 1)$-node opportunistic hyperchannel, as shown in Figure 1(b), the nodes are labeled $N_0, N_1, \cdots, N_n$, with N_0 and N_n as the *starting node* and

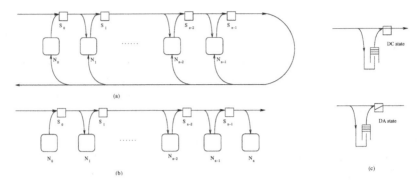

Fig. 1. Opportunistic hyperchannel. (a) A folded opportunistic hyperchannel. (b) A partially connected opportunistic hyperchannel. (c) Two states of the CA switch associated with a node in an opportunistic hyperchannel.

end node, respectively. Node N_0 and N_n can only transmit and receive packets, respectively. Each intermediate node N_k can receive packets from the upstream nodes and transmit packets to the downstream nodes by controlling its *continue-add (CA) switch* S_k to be one of two states, *DC state* or *DA state*, according to its traffic situation. When S_k is set to be in DC state, the signal from the upstream nodes can drops a copy at node N_k and passes S_k simultaneously. When S_k is set to be in DA state, it intercepts the signal from the upstream nodes and transmits packets from local buffers of N_k without collision. The signal from the upstream nodes passes the receiver and goes into the electrical buffer which node N_k would process later.

4   1-Persistent Collision-Free CSMA Protocols

In what follows, we describe a simple 1-persistent collision-free fair CSMA (CSMA/CF) protocol designed for an $(n + 1)$-node opportunistic hyperchannel. In this protocol, each intermediate node N_k, $0 < k < n$, maintains two queues q_k^0 and q_k^k. The packets from the upstream nodes of N_k are always dropped at node N_k, some of which will be added to q_k^0 depending on the state of S_k. The locally generated packets are stored in q_k^k.

If there is no locally generated packet at q_k^k, S_k remains in DC state. The first locally generated packet at N_k will trigger S_k to be changed from DC state to DA state. Whenever $q_k^0 \neq \emptyset$ or $q_k^k \neq \emptyset$, a packet with the lowest timestamp will be scheduled to be transmitted persistently. Thus, S_k remains to be in DA state as long as $q_k^0 \neq \emptyset$ or $q_k^k \neq \emptyset$. S_k goes back to DC state if and only if $q_k^0 = \emptyset$ and $q_k^k = \emptyset$.

Clearly, the opportunistic hyperchannel give rise to a class of collision-free CSMA protocols that utilize the knowledge of packets received by intermediate nodes. To implement such a 1-persistent collision-free CSMA protocol, the following two technical issues have to be addressed:

- The opportunistic hyperchannel architecture introduces the overhead of physically switching a 2:1 optical switch from DC state to DA state or from DA state to DC state. The timing operation of the state change of a CA switch will make a difference on mitigating the effect of this overhead over the packets.
- Since each packet from the upstream nodes will be dropped at N_k, N_k needs to determine which packets should go to q_k^0 to be transmitted to the downstream nodes.

In the remains of this section, we firstly introduce a mechanism for the timing operation of the state change at a CA switch. We then present the procedure for each node to determine whether the packet from a upstream node should be buffered or not, followed by the implementation of 1-persistent collision-free CSMA protocol at each node.

4.1 Timing Operation of the State Change

Suppose that it takes t_g time to switch from one state to the other at a 2:1 optical switch. Let the transmission delay of a packet be T. With the advance of the switching technology, t_g can be expected to be much less than T. We assume the propagation delay is negligible given the high transmission speed of the light.

The timing operation of the state change for a CA switch works as follows. At each node, a t_g time latency, referred to as "guard time", is inserted between the transmission of two consecutive packets. Thus, the period of each time slot will be $T + t_g$. Suppose in a time slot i where the duration of time slot i is $[i(T+t_g), (i+1)(T+t_g))$, a packet from either q_k^0 or q_k^k is transmitted, then the transmission must have been finished by the time of $(i+1)T + i * t_g$. If no more packets in either queue, at the time period of $[(i+1)T + i * t_g, (i+1)(T+t_g))$, S_k will be switched from DA state to DC state. As we can see, a node will be able to transmit a packet and also change its state in one time slot.

This approach divides each time slot into two portions, one portion for packet transmission and one portion for the potential state change. During the time portion of the state change, no data transmission is ongoing, thus it will not cause any incomplete packet, which means less forwarding work is needed at the intermediate nodes. Such an incomplete avoidance makes such an approach very efficient when $t_g \ll T$.

4.2 Queuing Decisions for Received Packets

The packets dropped at N_k include: (i) packets from N_k's upstream nodes that have passed S_k when S_k is in DC state. The destinations of these packets can be the upstream nodes of N_k, N_k itself, or the downstream nodes of N_k. (ii) packets from N_k's upstream nodes that are stored in N_k when S_k is in DA state. For these packets, some of them should be discarded, some of them should enter queue q_k^0 for later transmission, and some of them should be taken if the destination of the packets is N_k.

With respect to a received packet p, at the end of the time slot, N_k will process p according to the following procedure:

- case 1: if S_k is in DC state, discard it; otherwise,
- case 2: if the destination of p is an upstream node of N_k, discard it; otherwise,
- case 3: if the destination of p is N_k, take it; otherwise,
- case 4: put p at the end of q_k^0.

4.3   Implementation of 1-Persistent Collision Free Protocol

In this protocol, we assume that all nodes share the same system clock and each packet is associated with two attributes, $d(p)$ and $t_{stamp}(p)$, which are the destination of p and the system time at which p is generated. Let $p_{i,k}$ be the packet generated at N_k at time slot i.

The CSMA/CF protocol is described by a set of concurrent processes, with $CSMA/CF\_Generate_k$, $CSMA/CF\_Receive_k$ and $CSMA/CF\_Send_k$ residing in N_k, $0 < k < n$; it is assumed that node N_0 transmits a packet whenever it is available and node N_n receives any packet it senses. Procedure $GENERATE_k$ returns a packet p generated at node N_k where a null value is returned if no packet is generated at N_k. Suppose that the current system time can be found out by executing a procedure $TIME()$. Procedure $RECEIVE_k$ returns a packet p if p arrives at N_k; otherwise, a null value is returned. It stores p into q_k^0 only if p needs to be forwarded. Procedure $DEST\_ID_k(p)$, which returns the destination node ID of packet p, is used to determine whether or not p needs to be forwarded. Procedures $ENQUEUE(p, q_k^j)$ is used to store packet p into q_k^j and procedure $DEQUEUE(q_k^j)$ returns a packet from q_k^j. Procedure $TIMES(q_k^j)$ returns the t_{stamp} value of the first packet in q_k^j.

Processes $CSMA/CF\_Generate_k$, $CSMA/CF\_Receive_k$, and $CSMA/CF\_Send_k$ for N_k are given as follows:

```
process CSMA/CF_Generate_k
repeat
    p := GENERATE_k;
    if p ≠ null then
        t_stamp(p) := TIME();
        ENQUEUE(p, q_k^k);
        if S_k is in DC state then
        set S_k to DA state during next packet gap;
end-repeat
```

```
process CSMA/CF_Receive_k
repeat
    p := RECEIVE_k;
    if p ≠ null and DEST_ID_k(p) > k and S_k is in DA state
    then ENQUEUE(p, q_k^0);
end-repeat
```

---

process $CSMA/CF\_Send_k$
repeat
   while $q_k^0 \neq \emptyset$ or $queue_k^k \neq \emptyset$ **do**
     if $q_k^0 \neq \emptyset$ and $queue_k^k \neq \emptyset$ **then**
       $t_k^0 := TIMES(q_k^0);$
       $t_k^k := TIMES(q_k^k);$
       if $t_k^0 \leq t_k^k$ **then** $j := 0$ **else** $j := k;$
     else if $q_k^0 \neq \emptyset$ **then** $j := 0$ **else** $j := k;$
     $p := DEQUEUE(q_k^j);$
     transmit packet $p;$
   end-while
   set S_k to DC state during next packet gap;
end-repeat

As we see, the packets in q_k^k are always inherently sorted according to the increased timestamp. However, the packets in q_k^0 might not be sorted, e.g., the packets with higher timestamp are in front of the packets with lower timestamp in q_k^0. This can be explained as follows. Suppose that a packet $p_{i,k}$ is generated at N_k in time slot i. S_k is changed from DC state to DA state during the time slot i. At the end of the time slot i, q_k^k must be $\{p_{i,k}\}$ and q_k^0 must be $\emptyset$. N_k will send p_{ik} out to the downstream node at time slot $i+1$ even if there are some packets with lower timestamp at the queues of N_k's upstream nodes. p_{ik} might be queued at one of its downstream nodes and the packets with lower timestamp may join the same queue before p_{ik} is sent out.

Given the above property, in order to achieve better fairness, we need to sort the packets in q_k^0 for $1 \leq k \leq n$ in the non-decreasing timestamp order. With the sorted packets in q_k^0, node N_k only needs to compare the timestamp of the two packets at the heads of q_k^0 and q_k^k and transmits the packet with the lower timestamp at each time slot. The packet transmitted at N_k at each time slot must have the lowest timestamp among all packets available at N_k's q_k^0 and q_k^k. A min-heap queue for q_k^0 and first-in-first-out (FIFO) queue for q_k^k can well achieve the fairness property of CSMA/CF. If a min-heap queue is applied to q_k^0, the time complexity of both $CSMA/CF\_Receive_k$ and $CSMA/CF\_Send_k$ is $O(\log m_k)$ where m_k is the number of available packets at q_k^0. The CSMA/CF protocol using the min-heap queue for q_k^0 $(1 \leq k \leq n)$ is referred to as CSMA/CF/1 in this paper. At each time slot, t_g time portion can be used to maintain the min-heap queue. However, if the queue size is too long, it might not be feasible to maintain the min-heap queue within t_g.

In this paper, we also propose an alternative CSMA/CF protocol where both q_k^0 and q_k^k are FIFO queues, referred to as CSMA/CF/2. Though CSMA/CF/2 can not achieve as good fairness as CSMA/CF/1, the time complexity of both $CSMA/CF\_Receive_k$ and $CSMA/CF\_Send_k$ is $O(1)$ per packet. Through the simulation, we can see that fairness that $CSMA/CF/2$ can achieve is quite close to that of CSMA/CF/1.

5   Performance Analysis

In this section, we analyze the performance of CSMA/CF/1 by deriving a worst case upper bound for packet delays in comparison with a fair packet scheduler. We only consider the $(n+1)$-node partially connected opportunistic hyperchannel shown in Figure 1(b), since the delay bound obtained also applies to the n-node fully connected opportunistic hyperchannel of Figure 1(a). The rightmost node N_n is called the *end node* of the bus. We assume that packets have the same size. Packets are transmitted in time slots.

Assume the operation starting time of an $(n + 1)$-node opportunistic hyperchannel to be 0. We say that packet $p_{i',k'} < p_{i,k}$ if and only if $i' < i$ or $i' = i$ and $k' > k$. Clearly, there is a total order on the packets generated in the nodes N_j, $0 \leq j \leq n - 1$, of an $(n + 1)$-node opportunistic hyperchannel. Define a packet scheduling algorithm *General Round Robin* (GRR) which enforces packet $p_{i',k'}$ reaching the end node before packet $p_{i,k}$ if and only if $p_{i',k'} < p_{i,k}$. Conceptually, GRR transmits packets to the end node in rounds, with each round consisting of packets generated at the same time, in the increasing order of packet generating times, and transmits packets in the same round in the decreasing order of node indices. Clearly, *GRR* is a fair algorithm which cannot be implemented distributively without knowing the arriving order of packets. We analyze the performance of CSMA/CF/1 by comparing them with algorithm *GRR*.

Let $t_{GRR}(p)$, $t_{CSMA/CF/1}(p)$ be the time at which packet p reaches the end node in an $(n+1)$-node opportunistic hyperchannel according to the GRR algorithm and CSMA/CF/1 protocol respectively. We assume the signal propagation delay over fiber to be 0. Define the delay of packet p using CSMA/CF/1 with respect to GRR as $D_n^1(p) = t_{CSMA/CF/1}(p) - t_{GRR}(p)$. Note that $D_n^1(p)$ can be negative, when p reaches the end node using CSMA/CF/1 earlier than the time it reaches the end node using GRR. Define

$$D_n^{1*} = \max_{\text{all packets } p} \{D_n^1(p)\},$$

which is the worst case delay upper bound for CSMA/CF/1 protocol compared with the GRR algorithm.

Theorem 1. *For CSMA/CF/1, $D_n^{1*} \leq (n - 1) \cdot (T + t_g)$.*

Proof. Consider a packet $p_{i,k}$ where $1 \leq k \leq n$. Let $A_{i,k}$ be the set of packets that are in the system when $p_{i,k}$ is generated with $p' < p_{i,k}$ for $p' \in A_{i,k}$. Given the work-conserving property of CSMA/CF protocol, there must also be $|A_{i,k}|$ packets in the system when $p_{i,k}$ is generated no matter which scheduling algorithm is applied. Clearly, in the GRR algorithm, packet $p_{i,k}$ will have a delay of $|A_{i,k}|(T + t_g)$.

Suppose that packet $p_{i,k}$ reaches the destination at time slot t under CSMA/CF/1. Because the system will keep busy as long as there are packets in the system, there will be one packet reaching destination at any time period i' for $i' = i+1, \ldots, t$. Among the packets arrived at the destination during the period from time slot $i + 1$ to time slot $t - 1$, if there is a packet $p_{i',k'}$ with higher timestamp than $p_{i,k}$, then we say $p_{i,k}$ has an extra delay caused by $p_{i',k'}$.

Now we claim that the total extra delay incurred to $p_{i,k}$ cannot be more than $n - k$. Such a claim implies that $p_{i,k}$ will not have more delays of $(n - k)(T + t_g)$ in CSMA/CF than it has in GRR.

Since the only packets which may cause extra delay to $p_{i,k}$ are the packets from N_k's downstream nodes, if we can prove that at most one packet with the lower timestamp can be inserted in front of $p_{i,k}$ at each downstream node of N_k during the time period from time slot $i + 1$ to time slot $t - 1$, our claims hold. Consider a node N_j with $j \geq k$, which is a downstream node of N_k.

- Case 1. Suppose node N_j is in DA state at time slot i. Then node N_j cannot be switched to DC state before $p_{i,k}$ passes node N_j because q_j^0 will not be $\emptyset$ as long as there are packets in the queues of N_j's upstream nodes. In such a case, any packet $p_{i',j}$ with $i' \geq i$, i.e., with lower priority than $p_{i,k}$, will be first inserted into the local queue at node N_j. Consequently, $p_{i',j}$ cannot be sent out from node N_j until $p_{i,k}$ passes node N_j. In other words, $p_{i',j}$ will not cause any extra delay to $p_{i,k}$
- Case 2. Suppose that node N_j is in DC state at time slot i. Then it keeps in DC state and does not block any packet until a packet $p_{i',j}$ is generated at time $i' \geq i$.
  - Case 2.1. If $p_{i',j}$ is generated after $p_{i,k}$ passes node N_j, then $p_{i',j}$ will not cause any extra delay to $p_{i,k}$.
  - Case 2.2. If $p_{i',j}$ is generated before $p_{i,k}$ passes node N_j, then $p_{i',j}$ causes node N_j to be switched from DC state to DA state, and may reach destination earlier than $p_{i,k}$. In such a case, $p_{i',j}$ causes one extra delay to $p_{j,k}$. After this, node N_j cannot be switched to DC state before $p_{i,k}$ passes node j, an analysis similar to Case 1 as we have conducted.

Summarizing the above cases, we know that at most one extra delay will be caused to $p_{i,k}$ at any node N_j for $j \geq k$. Thus, any packet generated at N_k will experience at most $(n - k)(T + t_g)$ more delay in CSMA/CF/1 protocol than in GRR algorithm. The packets generated at N_1 may experience $(n - 1)(T + t_g)$ more delay in CSMA/CF/1 protocol than in GRR algorithm. This completes the proof of Theorem 1.

6   Simulation

We conducted simulations to compare the performance of 1-persistent CSMA/CF protocols running on an opportunistic hyperchannel with p_i-persistent CSMA/CD protocol and priority-based CSMA protocol running on a traditional unidirectional optical bus.

The hyperchannel architecture we simulated is the partially connected hyperchannel shown in Figure 1(b) with 11 nodes. The destinations of all packets are uniformly distributed on all its downstream nodes. For example, the destinations of packets generated at node N_k is uniformly distributed in $[k + 1, n - 1]$. Such a

setting is based on the consideration of constructing the practice-case scenarios
of the 11-node architecture of Figure 1(b).

The packet arrival process (i.e. packet generating process) at node N_k is assumed to be a Poisson process with parameter λ_k, and system load is uniformly
distributed among all nodes, which means $\lambda_k = \lambda_j$, $0 \leq j, k < n$. Then, system
load can be identified by $\lambda = \sum_{i=0}^{n-1} \lambda_i$. We assume fixed packet length in the simulation. We compare the following three performance metrics: (1) throughput,
(2) global average delay, and (3)average delay at each node. A higher throughput
or a lower global average delay indicates that the system is more work-conserving.
The average delay at each node can be used as the measurements of fairness.

6.1   Throughput and Global Average Delay

In the opportunistic hyperchannel, a packet will be dropped at the first downstream node which is in DA state after it passes its destination instead of occupy-
ing the whole optical bus. Thus, the connections without any overlap can transmit their packets simultaneously without confliction. Therefore, the throughput
achieved in the opportunistic hyperchannel with 1-persistent collision free protocol can be larger than the bandwidth of a wavelength. Since the medium is occupied with waiting packets in the system while priority-based CSMA protocol is
the scheduler, the throughput is equal to the bandwidth of a wavelength, which is
100% showed as Figure 2(a). p_i-persistent achieve lower throughput than that of
priority-based CSMA protocol for non-work conserving property. Figure 2(a) verifies this property. The global average delay of 1-persistent CSMA/CF protocols
is the minimum as shown in Figure 2(b), which is consistent with the throughput.

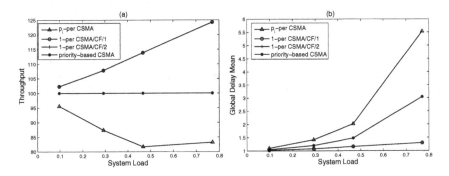

Fig. 2. (a)throughput vs. system load; (b) global average delay vs. system load

Figures 2(a) and 2(b) also show that the curves of 1-persistent CSMA/CF/1
and CSMA/CF/2 protocols almost completely overlap. This indicates that, for
practical purpose, CSMA/CF/2 is a better choice than CSMA/CF/1 because of
its $O(1)$ time complexity.

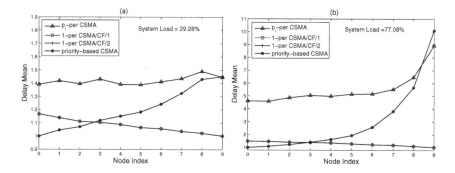

Fig. 3. (a) Average delay vs. node index when system load=29.28%; (b) average delay vs. node index and system load=77.08%

6.2   Average Packet Delay

For the priority-based CSMA protocol, the upstream nodes have higher priority, thus the average delay at the upstream nodes is lower than that of the downstream nodes. As a result, the average delay curve in Figure 3 for priority-based CSMA protocol is a increasing curve.

For p_i-persistent CSMA/CD protocol, the average delay at each node is similar if p_i is correctly calculated, which means if the real traffic demand matches the estimated traffic demand. As shown in Figure 3(a), when the system load is low, the curve of the average delay for p_i-persistent CSMA/CD protocol is quite flat. However, when the system load is high, as shown in Figure 3(b), the difference of the average delay among nodes can be dramatic, which means that the fairness of p_i-persistent protocol is hard to achieve if the real traffic demand does not match the estimated traffic demand.

For 1-persistent CSMA/CF protocols, the downstream nodes intend to have lower average delay since they can block the packets from the upstream nodes and transmit their locally generated packets each time when they switch from DC state to DA state. Thus, the curves of the average delay for 1-persistent CSMA/CF protocols are decreasing curves.

In general, the average delay at each node in 1-persistent CSMA/CF protocols is much less than that in p_i-persistent CSMA/CD protocol.

7   Conclusion

We introduced 1-persistent CSMA/CF protocols for opportunistic hyperchannel in this paper. 1-persistent CSMA/CF protocols can achieve both fair service and efficiency compared with the p_i-persistent CSMA protocol and priority-based CSMA protocol running on a traditional unidirectional optical bus. We believe that the features of opportunistic hyperchannels can be used to design more high-performance medium access control protocols.

References

1. Zheng, S.Q., Gumaste, A.: SMART: an Optical Infrastructure for Future Internet. In: Proceedings of the 3rd International Conference on Broadband Communications, Networks, and Systems (Broadnets 2006) (2006)
2. Gumaste, A., Chlamtac, I.: Light-Trails: a Novel Conceptual Framework for Conducting Optical Communications. In: Proc. of IEEE Workshop on High Performance Switching and Routing (HPSR) (June 2003)
3. Chen, J., Zheng, S.Q., Gumaste, A.: QoS Assuring Access Control Protocols for Hyperchannels in SMART Network. In: The 18th IASTED International Conference on PDCS (November 2006)
4. Tobagi, F., Borgonovo, F., Fratta, L.: Expressnet: a High-Performance Integrated-Services Local Area Network. IEEE Journal on Selected Areas in Communications 1, 898–913 (1983)
5. Tobagi, F., Fine, M.: Performance of Unidirectional Broadcast Local Area Networks: Expressnet and Fasnet. IEEE Journal on Selected Areas in Communications 1, 913–926 (1983)
6. Tseng, C.-W., Chen, B.-U.: D-Net, a New Scheme for High Data Rate Optical Local Area Networks. IEEE Journal on Selected Areas in Communications 1, 493–499 (1983)
7. Abeysundara, B.W., Kamal, A.E.: Z-Net: a Dual Bus Fiber-Optic LAN Using Active and Passive Switchers. INFOCOM 1, 19–27 (1989)
8. Kamal, A.E., Abeysundara, B.W.: X-Net: a Dual Bus Fiber-Optic LAN Using Active Switches. ACM SIGCOMM Computer Communication Review 19, 72–82 (1989)
9. Maxemchuk, N.F.: Twelve Random Access Strategies for Fiber Optic Networks. IEEE Trans. Commun. COM-36, 942–950 (1988)
10. Mukherjee, B., Meditch, J.S.: The p_i-persistent Protocol for Unidirectional Broadcast Bus Networks. IEEE Trans. Commun. COM-36, 1277–1286 (1988)
11. Mukherjee, B.: Performance of a Dual-Bus Unidirectional Broadcast Network Operating under Probabilistic Scheduling Strategy. In: Proceedings of SIGMETRICS 1989, vol. 17(1) (1989)
12. Mukherjee, B.: On the Infinite Buffer Model and the Implementation Aspects of the p_i-persistent Protocol for Unidirectional Broadcast Bus Networks. In: IEEE International Conference on Commun., June 1988, vol. 1, pp. 273–277 (1988)
13. Chen, J., Yu, H., Wang, J., Zheng, S.Q.: Opportunistic Optical Hyperchannel and Its Distributed QoS Assuring Access Control, Technical Report UTDCS-29-07 (August 2007), Submitted to Journal Publication
14. Gumaste, A., Zheng, S.Q.: Light-Frames - Pragmatic Framework for Optical Packet Transport: Extending Ethernet LANs to Optical Networks. IEEE/OSA Journal of Lightwave Technology 24(10), 3598–3615 (2006)

An Optimization of Context Sharing for Self-adaptive Mobile Applications

Nearchos Paspallis and George A. Papadopoulos

Department of Computer Science, University of Cyprus
P.O. Box 20537, Postal Code 1678 Nicosia, Cyprus
{nearchos,george}@cs.ucy.ac.cy

Abstract. Because of the high potential of mobile and pervasive computing systems, there is an ongoing trend in developing applications exhibiting context awareness and adaptive behavior. While context awareness guarantees that the applications are aware of both their context and their own state, dynamic adaptivity enables them to react on their knowledge about it and optimize their offered services. However, because in pervasive computing environments there is also a need for enabling arbitrary synergies, such a behavior also requires appropriate algorithms implementing the adaptation logic required to reason on the sensed context and dynamically decide on the most appropriate adaptations. This paper discusses how utility function-based approaches can use context-awareness for that and, additionally, it shows how the decision-making process is improved with respect to both performance and resource consumption by using a more intelligent approach.

Keywords: Self-adaptive, Context-aware, Optimization, Mobile computing.

1 Introduction

Today, one can observe an ever increasing trend in the use of mobile systems and applications which are used to assist us with our everyday tasks. As these applications become more ubiquitous, developers are faced with both opportunity and challenge. Adaptive, mobile applications are designed to constantly adapt to the contextual conditions in an autonomous way, with the aim of optimizing the quality of their service. The complexity of self-adaptive software though, renders their development significantly more difficult. As Paul Horn has quoted in IBM s manifesto of autonomic computing [1], tackling the development complexity, which is inherent in modern autonomic systems, is the next grand challenge for the IT industry.

When aiming complicated, autonomous and adaptive software, one of the most important hurdles is to provide suitable software engineering methods, models and tools, to ease the development effort. Current approaches aim to achieve this by using architectural [2] and modeling tools [3]. Other approaches propose development methodologies such as the separation of the functional from the extra-functional concerns in the design and development of adaptive, mobile applications [4].

A. Bourgeois and S.Q. Zheng (Eds.): ICA3PP 2008, LNCS 5022, pp. 157..168, 2008.
© Springer-Verlag Berlin Heidelberg 2008

Abstracting adaptive, mobile applications with compositions of individual and reusable components [5] offers many benefits, including the opportunity to delegate part of the adaptation responsibility to a different layer (middleware). This paper discusses the proactive and reactive approaches for sharing context information with the purpose of achieving distributed adaptation reasoning. Furthermore, it proposes an optimization which is shown to significantly improve distributed context-awareness in terms of number of needed message exchanges.

The rest of this paper is organized as follows: Section 2 introduces the basic terms of context-awareness and adaptation reasoning. Then, Section 3 presents a basic approach to adaptation reasoning and proposes an optimization, aiming at minimizing the number of context change messages to be communicated. Then, Section 4 describes a case study scenario and validates some of the approaches proposed in the previous section, and Section 5 discusses related work. Finally, the paper concludes with Section 6 which presents the conclusions and points to our plans for future work.

2   Adaptation Enabling Middleware

Often, applications featuring context-awareness and adaptivity, exhibit a common pattern: context changes are monitored and evaluated against the possible adaptation options so that the optimal choice is dynamically selected. This pattern naturally leads to the attempt of encapsulating and automating much of these tasks, in the form of appropriate middleware tools. The *Mobility and Adaptation-enabling Middleware* (MADAM) project [6] has aimed at providing software developers with reusable models and tools, assisting them in the design and implementation of adaptive, mobile applications. To facilitate the reusability of adaptation strategies, a middleware layer was proposed which can be used to encapsulate context monitoring, adaptation reasoning logic and reconfiguration tasks. Building on MADAM s legacy, the *Self-Adapting Applications for Mobile Users in Ubiquitous Computing Environments* (MUSIC) project [7] envisions to improve the results of MADAM and also to extend the application domain from mobile to ubiquitous computing.

As illustrated in Fig. 1, the middleware layer can serve by automating three basic functions: First, it monitors the context for changes and notifies the adaptation logic module when a relevant change occurs. Second, it reasons on the context changes and makes decisions about which application variant should be selected (different application variants refer to different component compositions providing the same functionality with different extra-functional properties). This step typically includes the dynamic formation of all possible application variants, as they are defined by corresponding component metadata. Finally, when an adaptation is decided, the configuration management instructs the underlying component framework to apply it (i.e. it reconfigures the application by setting adjustable parameters and by binding or unbinding the involved components and services).

The adaptation reasoning refers to the process where a set of possible variants are first formulated, based on the composition plans provided by the application [2], and then evaluated with the aim of selecting the adaptation which optimizes the utility for the given context. This process is triggered by changes to the context, which in this case includes the user context (preferences, activities, state, mood, etc), the computing

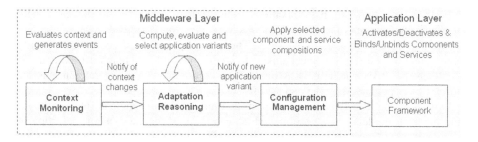

Fig. 1. High-level structure of a typical context-aware, adaptation-enabling middleware

context (devices, networks, UI options and capabilities, available composition plans and services, etc) and the environment (location, weather, light and noise, etc).

The adaptations are performed at the application layer, where different components and services can be interchangeably replaced (or [re]connect to each other in different configurations) in order to form different variants of the application. Although these variants are assumed to be characterized by different extra-functional properties, they are nevertheless assumed to offer the same functional service. This results in different application variants, which can offer different levels of *Quality of Service* (QoS) depending on their contextual conditions. To enable self-adaptation, these variants are then evaluated (e.g. using utility functions) and the optimal one is selected (for an example see [8]).

Assuming a centralized system, the decisions are taken locally (i.e. no networking interactions are required), and the decided application variants are limited to non-distributed ones. However, while the lack of networking requirements improves the system s robustness, it also prevents it from exploiting the opportunities arising when distributed compositions are available. More particularly it misses the opportunity of supporting distributed compositions, which allow hosts to better exploit resources and services offered by other hosts. This is particularly important in mobile and pervasive computing environments where frequent context changes and scarce resources render the exploitation of distributed resources extremely useful. For instance, a mobile device is enabled to delegate processor-intensive tasks (such as text-to-speech) to appropriate server nodes, thus better utilizing the globally available resources.

This paper discusses a basic approach which allows for distributed decision-making and distributed compositions (i.e. applications comprising of components residing on distributed nodes). The approach builds on the basic architectural-based model for runtime adaptability, as it is described by Floch *et al* [2].

2.1 Problem Description and Requirements

In its simplest form, a centralized architecture can be designed so that it supports the adaptation of a single, non-distributed application. The composition plans specify a set of possible variants, which are all evaluated whenever a relevant context change is sensed. A natural evolution of this approach is the support of composition plans where some of the components are allowed to be distributed. This implies the definition and use of distributed composition plans, i.e. plans defining compositions where some of the components are possibly deployed on distributed nodes.

Furthermore, an additional relaxation of the original form refers to the case where the distributed variants are formed and decided on a single central node or they are formed and decided in a distributed way. The latter approach is of course significantly more complex as it requires mechanisms to enable the nodes to reach trusted and fair agreements. For the latter, it is assumed that the common point of reference is the *utility*, as it is perceived by the end user [8].

In this context, the dynamic adaptation reasoning problem can be defined as the requirement for models and algorithms which can be used for the dynamic selection of the most suitable variant. In this case, the suitability of a variant refers to its fitness to the user needs, as it is measured by the *utility* offered to the end user. The next section discusses a straightforward approach for enabling adaptation reasoning and an optimization which minimizes the number of messages required to be communicated for distributed context sharing.

3   Adaptation Reasoning

We consider the case where adaptive, component-based applications are defined as collections of software components which can be configured to derive a number of variants according to a set of composition plans. These components are defined as self-containing modules of code, which can communicate with each other through a set of ports. In practice, many systems use computational reflection to reason and possibly alter their own behavior, as well as component-orientation to *allow independent deployment, and composition by third parties* [5].

The composition plans are defined at design time and they are used to dynamically construct different variants of the application. Individual variants are designed so that they offer an advantage (such as better resource utilization) compared to the others in varying context. Naturally, each variant is designed with the aim of maximizing the utility of the application for at least a subset of the context space.

In autonomic systems, the possible approaches for making adaptation reasoning are classified to *action-based*, *goal-based* and *utility function-based* [10]. In this work we consider the use of utility functions for two reasons: First they facilitate scalability and, second, they support dynamically available, arbitrary components.

Utility functions are simple computational artifacts which are used to compute the utility of an application variant: i.e. a quantifiable scalar value, reflecting the *utility* perceived by the end user. In this respect, the overall objective of the middleware can be defined as the continuous evaluation of all possible variants with the aim of always selecting the one which maximizes the utility offered to the end user .

Assuming there is only a single application which is managed by the middleware the utility function can be implemented as a function which maps application variants, context conditions and user preferences to scalar values, as depicted in the following:

$$(p,c): (p_1, p_2, f\ , p_N) \cdot (c_1, f\ , c_M) \rightarrow [0,1] \tag{1}$$

In this formula, the $p_1, \quad , p_N$ values correspond to the available variants, and the $c_1, \quad , c_M$ values correspond to the possible points in the context space (this includes the user preferences, as part of the user context). In other words, the utility function is used to map each combination of a composition plan and context condition to a scalar number (typically in the range of [0, 1]). As this definition indicates, all the parameter types are subject to change. Thus, the aim is to always select a composition which maximizes the utility. The evaluation process is triggered whenever any of the arguments (i.e. context and available variants) changes.

Although it is assumed that the computed scalar utility reflects the benefit as that is perceived by the user, there are currently no general methods which can guarantee the precision of such an assignment. Rather, approaches such as the one used in the MADAM project [6] simply encourage the assignment of utilities to components and composition plans in an empirical manner (i.e. using the developers intuition). When the application is sufficiently complex, there is no straight-forward method or approach which can guarantee that there is a perfect (or even close) match between the computed utility value and the actual user desires. Nevertheless, it is argued that constructing utility functions in an empirical manner, in combination with experimental evaluation, can result in reasonable solutions with moderate effort.

Finally, as it is evident from the definition of the utility functions, the performance of the selection process is inversely proportional to the number of possible variants. Naturally, the adaptation reasoning becomes less efficient as the number of composition plans increases. This becomes more evident with larger, distributed applications featuring large numbers of possible variants, especially as this number typically increases exponentially with the number of used components.

3.1 Developing Applications with Compositional Plans

In order to be able to define applications in a dynamic, compositional way, a recursive approach is defined as follows: The primary modeling artifacts defined, are the *component types* and the *component implementations*. A component type can be realized by either a component implementation, or by a well-defined composition of additional component types (i.e. a composite component type). The latter enables the dynamic formation of alternative compositions in a recursive manner (in this case the recursion ends when all the component types have been assigned to either a composite component type or to an actual component implementation). The application is defined by an application type, which is itself a component type.

Additionally, the composition plans are predefined (i.e. at development time rather than at runtime). For instance, the model which is defined in [3] specifies how to construct different composition plans (and thus variants) for an application, and thus it aims at the developers rather than the runtime system. The latter uses the composition plans to dynamically compose the possible variants during the evaluation phase.

The applications are also defined in a recursive manner: for each step, of which a new layer is defined, specifying how the abstract component type is implemented. Always, the first layer is a layer with a single composite component type, abstracting the whole application. Depending on whether the application interacts with other applications or not, the first layer includes a composition plan with possibly some input (dependency) and some output (offered) services (or ports in component-orientation terminology). Subsequent layers expose further details of the composition plan by specifying additional component implementations and component types. The recursion ends when a layer is reached where all component types are fully resolved with component implementations.

Evidently, variability is enabled by allowing the use of various alternatives for particular component types. Each such alternative adds to the total number of possible variants. During the adaptation process, all possible variants are computed with the purpose of being evaluated.

3.2 Adaptation Reasoning

A centralized adaptation reasoning approach implies that the decisions are taken locally, and that no negotiation with other peers is required [11]. On the other hand, a distributed approach allows coordination between the collaborating peers, thus allowing the proposition and agreement of mutually accepted decisions.

A typical centralized implementation, triggered by context changes, is expressed by the following pseudo-code:

```
1. Detect a relevant context change

2. For all application variants (including distributed
   ones), compute the utility value for the new context

3. If the optimal variant is different from the current
   one, then adapt (reconfigure the application)
```

First, the adaptation reasoning is triggered by a relevant context change event. In this case, the relevance is computed by analyzing the utility functions of the deployed applications and extracting the context types which affect their outcome. The next step simply iterates through all possible variants and computes their utility value. The last step evaluates the computed values and selects the variant which maximizes the utility. If that variant is different from the one already selected, then an adaptation occurs by applying the new, optimal variant. Although not shown in this algorithm, another optimization would be to evaluate *how much* does the newly selected variant improves on the current one. If the margin is too small, then it is usually better to skip the adaptation, as it typically incurs additional overhead cost (i.e. for reconfiguration). Ideally, the exact cost of each prospective adaptation should be taken into account when selecting on the reaction to a context change. However, when distributed context sharing is considered, the context change events can be distributed, which implies a higher cost for each message in terms of resources.

We assume an approach where the adaptation managers directly consult their corresponding context managers (instead of their remote adaptation manager peers), which subsequently provide them with access to the information that is required to assess all the possible application variants, including the distributed ones. In this way, the best variant can be efficiently selected and applied. In [16], two main strategies were discussed for optimizing the communication between the distributed devices: First, a *proactive* strategy which aims at communicating as much information as soon as it is available. In practice, with this strategy the nodes are always aware of as much context information as possible, which as a result minimizes the response time at the cost of increased messages communications carrying the required context updates. Alternatively, a *reactive* strategy aims at minimizing the number of communicated messages at the cost of slower reaction time. This strategy activates the adaptation reasoning process only when a context change is sensed, which subsequently triggers the exchange of all relevant context changes from the participating peers. This results in less message communications of context events at the cost of increased response time. Hybrid approaches are also possible, one of which is presented in this paper with the purpose of achieving both minimal communication of messages and quick response times.

3.3 Optimizing the Adaptation Reasoning through Context Management

As it was argued in the previous subsections, adaptation reasoning can be solely based on offering component types and assigning a utility value to them (which on the client side appears as cost). Thus, practically, the distributed aspect of adaptation reasoning can be implemented exclusively through the use of appropriate context distribution mechanisms, facilitating the exchange of needed context data among the collaborating nodes. This subsection discusses an approach for optimizing distributed adaptation reasoning in the form of minimizing the number of messages required to be exchanged as a result of context change events.

Typically, the context management systems inform their peers about the subset of context data they are interested in, which as a result triggers a distributed context change event whenever a relevant change is detected. For example, if node A is interested in context elements c_1, , c_P , which are not locally available but are offered by a peer node B, then node A can simply register for it. For example, this would occur if node A had no local sensors available for that particular context type, while some of its applications depend on it [9].

Naturally, the straight-forward approach includes node A sending an update message to node B every time *any* context change occurs to the registered context elements. However, this would be unnecessary, as not all context changes have a potential of causing an adaptation. Assuming that the two nodes share a copy of the relevant utility functions, then a natural optimization would be for node A to ask node B to further process context changes, and filter out any context change messages that are unlikely to cause an adaptation, before communicating them to A.

Of course, this also implies that node B will go through the same evaluation process for all possible variants as node A would, which as described earlier can be a quite heavy process, especially for a mobile device. However, it is argued that this process can still offer significant benefits with regards to resource usage. Assuming that the serving node is sufficiently powerful, it is expected that the gain of minimizing the communicated context messages dominates the cost of processing and filtering context change events.

4   Case Study Example and Experimental Evaluation

As a means of better illustrating the use of the optimization approach described in Section 3.3, this section describes a case study example and also provides an evaluation which arguably validates its potential. The gathered results are based on simulations and aim at identifying and measuring the improvements that could result from the application of the proposed approaches. Further details such as the actual overhead incurred when making a decision is not discussed, but nevertheless the primary

objective of this evaluation is to illustrate that performance can be improved by showing that the number of required context coordination messages is reduced.

In this respect, we have revisited the scenario discussed in [11], which describes an
application used by onsite workers for assisting them into performing their everyday
tasks. This application offers three primary modes of operation: Visual UI interaction,
Audio UI interaction with local Text-to-Speech (TTS) and Audio UI interaction with
remote TTS (illustrated in Fig. 2). Each of these modes is optimized for offering the
best quality to the user under different context conditions. For the purposes of evaluating the context and selecting the optimal mode, the following property predictors
and utility function have also been defined, as illustrated in Fig. 3.

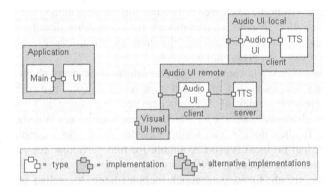

Fig. 2. The compositional architecture of the case study scenario

The composition of different variants is achieved through the exploitation of the
offered component types and component implementations, as shown in Fig. 2 and
discussed in Section 3.1 and Section 3.2. This figure illustrates the composition of a
simple application. At the highest abstraction layer, an application consists of a single
component type, which in this case is named *Application*. This component type is
composite, and thus describes its architectural composition as the simple binding of
two component types: *Main* and *UI*. The first is assumed to be an atomic component
implementing the main application s logic, while the latter is assumed to be a component providing UI functionality. Although not depicted in this figure, the main component type is provided by a component implementation. The UI component type,
however, is further decomposed in three possible variants: The first one is provided
by a single atomic implementation, namely the *Visual UI*. The second and third are
equivalent in terms of architecture (an *Audio UI* component type bound to a Text-to-
Speech or *TTS* component type), but differ in their deployment plan as in one case the
TTS component type is deployed *locally*, while in the other case *remotely*. Subsequent
layers specify that the *Audio UI* and the *TTS* component types are provided as single,
atomic component implementations (not shown in Fig. 2).

Given this composition plan, a utility function was also defined, along with a set of
property predictors, which are used to dynamically evaluate the utility value for each
possible variant, and for specific context values. In this case, we consider three simple
context types only: *bandwidth* which refers to the available network bandwidth (as a

percentage), *response* which corresponds to the user s need for quick response, and *hands-free* which corresponds to the user s need for hands-free operation. The bandwidth and response context properties are constrained to numeric values in the range [0, 100], and the hands-free property is constrained to false or true values only. The exact configuration of the property values and the property predictors for each of the three variants is depicted in Fig. 3.

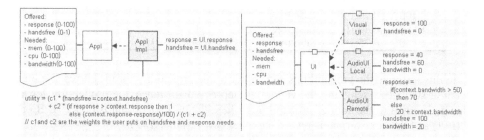

Fig. 3. The left side illustrates the application s dependence on the *response* and *hands-free* properties. It also describes the definition of the *utility function*. The right side, illustrates the three possibilities for implementing the UI role, which comprise the three primary modes of operation for the application. The utility of the latter is defined using a *property predictor*.

Given these metadata, and a set of context property values, one can compute the utility of any variant. However, not all context changes can affect the selected variant, i.e. a transition in the value of a context property does not imply that an adaptation will be triggered. It is exactly this fact that it is exploited in the optimization approach defined in Section 3.3. In order to validate its usefulness, we used this example and computed the ratio of context changes that could potentially trigger an adaptation.

Table 1 shows the results of our evaluation, which was performed as follows: First, different domains for the values of each of the three context properties were defined: the *bandwidth*, the *response* and the *hands-free*. In this case, the bandwidth value-set of (0:10:40) implies that the bandwidth is simulated with all values between 0 and 40 with a step of 10. Next, for each of these context combinations, we computed the number of different context settings that favor the use of each of the three possible variants. Then, the adaptation probability is computed as follows: It is assumed that each context setting corresponds to a different node in a fully connected graph. Furthermore, each of the graph nodes is colored with one of three colors, based on the variant which optimizes the utility for that context setting. Finally, the probability is computed by assuming that any context change can occur with the same probability, and by counting the number of node-transitions that cause an adaptation (i.e. connect nodes of different colors).

Equivalently, the probability for switching across different variants can be computed using the following probability formula:

$$p= p(A_1){\cdot}(p(B_2)+p(C_2))+p(B_1){\cdot}(p(A_2)+p(C_2))+p(C_1){\cdot}(p(A_2)+p(B_2)) \qquad (2)$$

Table 1. Adaptation evaluation outcomes as a result of different context settings; the last column depicts the probability that a context change can potentially trigger an adaptation

Bandwidth	Response	Hands-free	iVisual UI	Audio UI Loc	Audio UI Rem	Adaptation Probability
0:10:40	0:25:100	false:true	20	18	12	65%
0:10:40	0:20:100	false:true	30	18	12	62%
0:20:100	0:25:100	false:true	24	28	8	60%
0:20:100	0:20:100	false:true	36	28	8	58%
40:10:80	0:20:100	false:true	30	30	0	50%
40:10:80	0:25:100	false:true	20	30	0	48%

In this formula, the probabilities $p(A_i)$ refer to the probability for the corresponding event at step i (i.e. selecting the variant at step i). For instance, the probability for a change is equal to the sum of probabilities where the current variant is either A, B or C ($i=1$) and the next variant is one of the other two variants ($i=2$).

As it is shown in Table 1, a context change does not always imply an adaptation. Actually, the probability for an adaptation ranges from 65% down to 48% for the given scenario. The columns of the three variants illustrate the number of configurations for which that variant is *optimal*. The main lesson from this evaluation process is that when the distributed nodes coordinate at the context sharing level, the number of messages required for coordination can be significantly reduced (in this example by more than 50%). Notably, this experiment has assumed that the context properties were identical in both nodes (i.e. both devices refer to the same notion of bandwidth, response and hands-free requirements). Finally, the constants of the utility function were tuned to $C_1=80$ and $C_2=20$ respectively (see utility function in Fig. 3).

5 Related Work

There is a substantial amount of literature on adaptive, mobile systems. A very good description of composite adaptive software is provided by *McKinley et al* in [13]. This paper studies many basic concepts of adaptation, such as how, when and where to compose. One statement in this work is that the main technologies which are required for supporting compositional adaptations are Middleware, Separation of Concerns (SoC), Computational reflection and Component-based design. This is in agreement with the spirit of this paper. Applications are expressed in components, and SoC is achieved by defining utility functions which express the adaptivity properties of the compositions. Architectural reflection is used for enabling the actual reconfigurations required for adaptivity and a middleware is assumed in the background, collecting the distributed context management and distributed adaptation reasoning functionalities.

Another approach for enabling adaptivity from the coordination community is LIME, which enables coordination by means of logical mobility as it is described in [14]. In this case, the mobile hosts are assumed to communicate exclusively via transiently shared tuple spaces. LIME offers decoupling both in space and time and allows adaptations through reactive programming, i.e. by supporting the ability to react to events.

The Aura project [15], which built on the legacy of the Odyssey and Coda projects, also describes a relevant approach. Aura targets primarily pervasive applications. For this reason it introduced auras (which correspond to user tasks) as first class entities. To this direction, the same project categorizes the techniques which support user mobility into: use of mobile devices, remote access, standard applications (ported and installed at multiple locations) and finally use of standard virtual platforms to enable mobile code to follow the user as needed.

Unlike the existing literature, the approach which is described in this paper aims for self-adaptive applications which are constructed and dynamically adapted using architectural models. Additionally, this approach builds on previous work which described two alternative strategies for distributed adaptation reasoning: *proactive* and *reactive* approach [16]. Both of these offered significant advantages, depending on the deployment environment. However, the hybrid strategy proposed in this paper enables distributed adaptation reasoning merely through distributed context management. Furthermore, it combines benefits from both the reactive and proactive strategies, to achieve better results in terms of required communicated messages and response time, something that is illustrated and validated through the description and the examination of a case study example.

6 Conclusions

In this paper we have examined the problem of distributed context management and adaptation reasoning, and we proposed an approach for overcoming it. Building on two previous approaches, namely proactive and reactive adaptation reasoning, we proposed a hybrid approach which aims at optimizing the number and timing of communicated context change messages. This approach was illustrated and validated through a case study example, which highlights its potential.

In the future, we plan to investigate further approaches which can enable agile and efficient adaptation reasoning for distributed computing environments. Furthermore, we aim at further studying the relationship between distributed context-awareness and distributed adaptation reasoning, and propose approaches which further challenge it.

Acknowledgments. The authors would like to thank their partners in the MUSIC-IST project, and acknowledge the partial financial support provided to this research by the European Union (6th Framework Programme, contract number 035166).

References

1. Horn, P.: Autonomic Computing: IBM s Perspective on the State of Information Technology, IBM Corporation (2001), http://www.research.ibm.com
2. Floch, J., Hallsteinsen, S., Stav, E., Eliassen, F., Lund, K., Gjorven, E.: Using Architecture Models for Runtime Adaptability. IEEE Software 23(2), 62..70 (2006)
3. Geihs, K., Khan, M.U., Reichle, R., Solberg, A., Hallsteinsen, S., Merral, S.: Modeling of Component-Based Adaptive Distributed Applications. In: 21st ACM Symposium on Applied Computing (SAC), Dijon, France, April 23-27, 2006, pp. 718..722 (2006)

4. Paspallis, N., Papadopoulos, G.A.: An Approach for Developing Adaptive, Mobile Applications with Separation of Concerns. In: 30th Annual International Computer Software and Applications Conference (COMPSAC), Chicago, IL, USA, September 17-21, 2006, pp. 299..306. IEEE Computer Society Press, Los Alamitos (2006)
5. Szyperski, C.: Component software: beyond object-oriented programming. ACM Press / Addison-Wesley Publishing Co (1998)
6. The MADAM Consortium: Mobility and Adaptation Enabling Middleware (MADAM), http://www.ist-madam.org
7. The MUSIC Consortium: Self-Adapting Applications for Mobile Users in Ubiquitous Computing Environments (MUSIC), http://www.ist-music.eu
8. Alia, M., Eide, V.S.W., Paspallis, N., Eliassen, F., Hallsteinsen, S., Papadopoulos, G.A.: A Utility-based Adaptivity Model for Mobile Applications. In: 21st International Conference on Advanced Information Networking and Applications Workshops (AINAW), Niagara Falls, Ontario, Canada, May 21-23, 2007, pp. 556..563. IEEE Computer Society Press, Los Alamitos (2007)
9. Paspallis, N., Chimaris, A., Papadopoulos, G.A.: Experiences from Developing a Context Management System for an Adaptation-enabling Middleware. In: 7th IFIP International Conference on Distributed Applications and Interoperable Systems (DAIS), Paphos, Cyprus, June 5-8, 2007, pp. 225..238. Springer Verlag, Heidelberg (2007)
10. Walsh, W.E., Tesauro, G., Kephart, J.O., Das, R.: Utility Functions in Autonomic Systems. In: International Conference on Autonomic Computing (ICAC), New York, NY, USA, May 17-18, 2004, pp. 70..77. IEEE Press, Los Alamitos (2004)
11. Alia, M., Hallsteinsen, S., Paspallis, N., Eliassen, F.: Managing Distributed Adaptation of Mobile Applications. In: 7th IFIP International Conference on Distributed Applications and Interoperable Systems (DAIS), Paphos, Cyprus, June 5-8, 2007, pp. 104..118. Springer Verlag, Heidelberg (2007)
12. Chen, G., Kotz, D.: A Survey of Context-aware Mobile Computing Research, Technical Report: TR2000-381, Dartmouth College, Hanover, NH, USA (2000)
13. McKinley, P.K., Sadjadi, S.M., Kasten, E.P., Cheng, B.H.: Composing Adaptive Software. IEEE Computer 37(7), 56..64 (July 2004)
14. Murphy, A.L., Picco, G.P., Roman, G.-C.: LIME: A Middleware for Physical and Logical Mobility. In: 21st IEEE International Conference on Distributed Computing Systems (ICDCS), Phoenix (Mesa), Arizona, USA, April 16-19, 2001, p. 524. IEEE Computer Society, Los Alamitos (2001)
15. Sousa, J.P., Garlan, D.: Aura: an Architectural Framework for User Mobility in Ubiquitous Computing Environments. In: 3rd Working IEEE/IFIP Conference on Software Architecture, Montreal, Canada, August 25-31, 2002, pp. 29..43. Kluwer Academic Publishers, Dordrecht (2002)
16. Paspallis, N., Papadopoulos, G.A.: Distributed Adaptation Reasoning for a Mobility and Adaptation Enabling Middleware. In: 8th International Symposium on Distributed Objects and Applications (DOA). LNCS, vol. 4277, pp. 17..18. Springer, Heidelberg (2006)

A Network Service for DSP Multicomputers

Juan A. Rico-Gallego[1], Jesús M. Álvarez-Llorente[1], Juan C. Díaz-Martín[2], and Francisco J. Perogil-Duque[2]

[1] Department of Engineering of Computer Systems and Telematics,
[2] Department of Computer and Communication Technology
University of Extremadura, Avda. Universidad s/n, 10071, Cáceres, Spain
{jarico,llorente,juancarl,fperduq}@unex.es

Abstract. Programmers of embedded digital signal processors often have to deal with the devices of the platform or with low level hardware abstraction layers in order to reach the better performance from a given algorithm. This complexity increases when the application is distributed on multicomputers such as those by Sundance' , Hunt Engineering' , etc. These machines are loosely coupled networks based on carrier boards hosting modules of digital signal processors and FPGAs. This paper describes the design and implementation of a network layer library for these platforms. We show how, without a significative lost of performance, it improves the portability of target applications by avoiding the hardware communication complexities. More important yet, it broadens the spectrum of network applications and middlewares that these powerful platforms can support.

Keywords: Digital signal processing, distributed embedded systems, DSP multicomputers.

1 Introduction and Related Work

Advanced digital signal processing applications, like vision and high-frequency radio communications, usually overcome the processing capacity of a digital signal processor (DSP), and have to be distributed among the set of processors provided by DSP multicomputers like those by Sundance' , Hunt Engineering' , etc. Programmers usually have to deal with the hardware when building high-performance DSP applications. Communication devices of the multicomputer raise this complexity. We have designed and developed a network library whose interface hides the communication hardware of the platform. Its implementation, in turn, follows the design principle of portability and it achieves performance enough to serve as a building block for more complex communication facilities and middlewares. The library has been constructed and tested in PCI and CompactPCI DSP multicomputer boards from Sundance' ([1]). A Sundance SMT310Q carrier board can host up to four Texas Instruments standard Modules (TIM). Each TIM usually integrates one or two Texas Instruments TMS320C6416 processors running up to 1 GHz, with 1 MByte of fast internal SRAM memory and 32 or more Mbytes of external SDRAM memory. Texas instruments DSPs are broadly used in high performance real time signal processing applications.

A. Bourgeois and S.Q. Zheng (Eds.): ICA3PP 2008, LNCS 5022, pp. 169..172, 2008.

They natively run DSP/BIOS, a proprietary small RTOS for task management and synchronization in a single processor.

Diamond ([2]) is a distributed RTOS for Sundance machines. It is currently the only system software in the market for Sundance boards. A Sundance board without Diamond is in practice unusable. Diamond puts our Network Service in perspective. Under Diamond, a distributed application is an immutable graph of tasks (nodes) and data streams (arrows) statically configured. Every task has a vector of input ports and a vector of output ports that connect tasks by name. These vectors are passed to the *main* routine of the task. A program called the *configurer* running in the host PC combines task image files to form the executable that it later loads on each processor. A user-supplied textual configuration file drives the configurer. It specifies the hardware (available processors and physical links connecting them), the software (tasks and how they are connected), and how tasks are assigned to processors. A task sends a message msg by invoking

```
chan_out_message(size, msg, out_ports[0]);
```

Note that no addressing is involved, what makes a communication independent of the rank of the receiver or its specific location. As a result, the source code of a task is independent of the graph it is in. Static configuration ensures the real-time application will keep enough processing power and communication bandwidth during its life time, but prohibits something as simple and useful as forking new applications at run-time. Another severe limitation is that it is not possible a sporadic communication between two unconnected tasks.

The Network Service is a small contribution in that address. In contrast with Diamond, it is not a closed solution for mapping a distributed algorithm to a multi-DSP, but an open *library* upon the local RTOS, whatever it is, that enables the deployment of advanced communication middlewares, as the Internet Communication Engine (ICE) or the Message Passing Interface (MPI) on this kind of platforms.

2   Design Issues and Performance

The layout of the whole design is shown in figure 1. The OSI (Operating System Interface) layer provides a partial POSIX 1003.1c (Pthreads) interface. It implements the well known Pthreads mutexes and condition variables on top of DSP/BIOS counting semaphores in an efficient way. This allows porting the library to another RTOS in a direct way. For instance, OSI runs also on top of Xilkernel, a small RTOS for Virtex-II FPGA soft processors as PowerPC 405 and MicroBlaze. A typical Sundance TIM module provides up to four Sundance Digital Bus (SDB) communication ports. SDB can operate at a frequency of 120 MHz and transmit 16-bit in each cycle, reaching a maximum physical rate of 240 MByte/s. SHB is a faster version which can transmit 32-bits in each cycle with a 100 MHz clock, reaching 400 MByte/s. SDB ports can be connected by physical wires following a design criterion. This allows combining the processors in any topology.

LNK layer is the link level. It manages the point to point streams of bytes between two TIMs physically connected by a SDB wire. LNK performs the fragmentation of large messages and hides the SDB programming. Its main data structure is the so named *cyclic buffer*. This buffer stores the incoming frames arrived from the SDB device via the on-chip EDMA device. Its size is configurable, and it is always loaded in fast internal memory. One of the DMA channels is programmed at initialization time to take a SDB as source and the cyclic buffer as destination in an endless loop. This overlapping of communication and computation makes LNK quite efficient. The EDMA raises an interrupt when a whole frame has been completed in the cyclic buffer. This interrupt just awakes a sporadic internal task. This task extracts the payload, which passes to NET by invoking an upcall procedure.

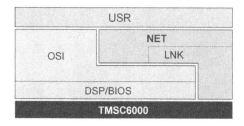

Fig. 1. Context and internal design of the Network Service (NET)

This procedure makes the decision of routing the packet or delivers it to the user destination protocol (in USR). In this last case NET, in turn, extracts the payload and invokes the upcall procedure installed by the user protocol. In addition to a reliable connectionless point to point communication, NET provides a broadcast service and routing, all this hiding the communication hardware. NET is intended to support more advanced communication libraries. For instance, eMPI ([3]) is an ongoing implementation of the Message Passing Interface standard for embedded platforms. The most important NET primitives are given next:

```
int  NET_init      (NET_topology *tpl);
void NET_finalize  (void);
int  NET_install   (int (*upcall)());
int  NET_send      (iovec *iov, int cnt, int dstMch, int prot);
int  NET_broadcast (iovec *iov, int count);
```

NET is complemented with a multicomputer loader. It greatly simplifies the process of loading the applications on the board and provides NET with the configuration of the platform it is running on. This configuration can also be passed by USR to NET as a parameter of NET_init. The bootloader is really a worm that explores the multicomputer and stores the obtained information.

Figure 2 gives performance figures. A task in a SMT395 TIM A sends messages to a task in a SMT395 TIM B connected by a 32-bit SDB bus. NET provides a bandwidth of around 275 Mbyte/s. The same test has been carried out on Diamond (version 3.3). Diamond shows a peak in performance of up to 400 MBytes/s when one of the available SDBs is dedicated to communicate of two given tasks. If the link is shared by more than two tasks (*virtual* link), the performance decreases below NET.

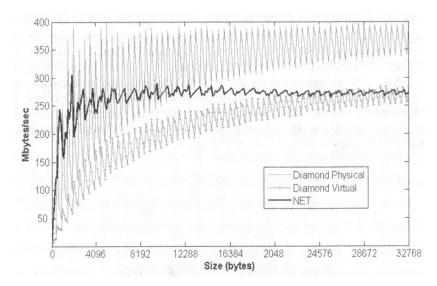

Fig. 2. Diamond and NET bandwidth test for increasing message sizes. Diamond only over-comes our library when it reserves the physical SDB link for the communicating tasks.

3 Conclusions

Today demanding signal processing applications, mainly coming from the vision and radio-communications fields, are supported by DSP multicomputer platforms, such are those by Sundance. Current system software for these platforms, however, only supports a single application in a dedicated way. In our view, the main contribution of this paper is the finding that an abstract network layer can be built on these state of the art machines without a serious performance penalty. This fact, first, allows that these expensive systems can be shared by two or more applications and, second, enables the deployment of communication middlewares, such as MPI.

Acknowledgments. This work has been supported by CDTI under program Ingenio 2010 (project CENIT-2005 HESPERIA) and the II Plan de Desarrollo Tecnológico de la Junta de Extremadura (project 2PR03A042).

References

1. http://www.sundance.com
2. http://www.31.com/Diamond/Diamond.htm
3. Rico-Gallego, J.A., Díaz-Martín,, Álvarez Llorente, J.C., Jesús, M.: An MPI Implementation for Distributed Signal Processing. In: Di Martino, B., Kranzlmüller, D., Dongarra, J. (eds.) EuroPVM/MPI 2005. LNCS, vol. 3666, pp. 475.482. Springer, Heidelberg (2005)

A Non-blocking Multithreaded Architecture with Support for Speculative Threads

Krishna Kavi[1], Wentong Li[1], and Ali Hurson[2]

[1] University of North Texas
{kavi,wl}@cse.unt.edu
[2] Missouri University of Science and Technology
hurson@mst.edu

Abstract. In this paper we provide both a qualitative and a quantitative evaluation of a decoupled multithreaded architecture that uses non-blocking threads. Our architecture is based on simple in-order pipelines and complete decoupling of memory accesses from execution pipelines. We extend the architecture to support thread level speculation using snooping cache coherency protocols. We evaluate the performance gains from speculations by varying the number of load/store instructions compared to computational instructions, miss speculation rates and the degree of thread level speculation. Our architecture presents a viable alternative to complex superscalar and super-speculative CPUs.

Keywords: Multithreaded Architectures, Cache Coherency, Thread Level Speculation, Decoupled Architecture.

1 Introduction

Superscalar and VLIW architectures are the main architectural models used in commercial processors. These models allow for more than one instruction to be issued on every cycle. Modern processors expend large amounts of silicon area and transistor budgets to achieve higher levels of performance with techniques such as out-of-order execution, branch and value prediction and speculative instruction execution. It has been shown that these techniques are approaching diminishing returns in terms of further improving single processor performance [1]. This has led to an increased interest in architectures that support concurrent processing, and multicore or chip multiprocessors (CMP) systems. The complexity of the underlying superscalar architecture makes it harder to scale the clock frequency for these designs.

It appears that the dataflow computing paradigm is back in vogue, as an alternative to superscalar models, as can be seen from recent architectural proposals including TRIPS [3, 4] and Wavescalar [5]. However, implementing dataflow model at instruction level (such as token driven models) requires complex hardware for communicating operands among instructions. In contrast, our architecture uses dataflow like synchronization at the thread-level, while using control flow semantics within a thread. This approach minimizes instruction level communication, but permits for scalable implementations. Our architecture should be also be contrasted with Wavescalar [5] that uses a complex memory-ordering scheme that involves tagging each memory transaction with a

A. Bourgeois and S.Q. Zheng (Eds.): ICA3PP 2008, LNCS 5022, pp. 173..184, 2008.
© Springer-Verlag Berlin Heidelberg 2008

predecessor and successor memory access. We use epoch numbers with threads and extend cache coherency protocols to achieve proper memory ordering.

Our architecture differs from other multithreaded architectures in two ways: i) our threads are based on dataflow paradigm, and ii) we completely decouple all memory accesses from execution pipeline. The underlying non-blocking thread model permits for clean separation of memory accesses from execution (which is very difficult to coordinate in other programming models). Data is pre-loaded into an enabled thread's register context prior to its scheduling on the execution pipeline. After a thread completes execution, the results are post-stored from its registers into memory. The execution engine relies on control-flow like sequencing of instructions, but our architecture performs no (dynamic) out-of-order execution and thus eliminates the need for complex instruction issue and retiring hardware. These hardware savings may be utilized to include either more processing units on a chip or more register sets to increase the degree of multithreading. Moreover, it was stated that a significant power is expended by instruction issue logic, and the power consumption increases quadratically with the size of the instruction issue width [6], and thus our architecture should be more energy efficient since we perform in-order instruction issue.

We are able to perform some quantitative evaluation of our architecture using hand-coded programs. Our goal here is to provide both a quantitative (albeit limited in scope) and a qualitative evaluation of our innovative architecture. In this paper we extend our architecture to support speculative execution of threads using epoch numbers and provide some preliminary quantitative analysis.

1.1 Related Research

Compilers extract parallelism by spawning multiple loop iterations concurrently, and with hardware support for thread-level speculation (TLS) that enforces dynamic data and control dependency checks, compilers can more aggressively exploit thread level concurrency. Marcuello et. al., [7] proposed a multithread micro-architecture that supports speculative thread execution within a single processor. This architecture contains multiple instruction queues, register sets, and a very complicated multi-value cache to support speculative execution of threads. Zhang et. al., [8] proposed a scheme that supports speculative thread execution in large scale distributed shared memory (DSM) systems relying on cache coherence protocols. Steffan et. al., [9] proposed an architecture that supports TLS execution both within a CMP core and large scale DSMs. This design is based on conventional architecture, but needs very extensive support from the operating system. The design is based on cache coherence protocols, but the published literature does not provide details on the implementation. Our design needs a small amount of extra hardware to implement speculation in the context of SDF architecture.

2 Scheduled Dataflow Architecture

A processing element in our scheduled dataflow architecture (SDF) is composed of three components: Synchronization Processor (SP), Execution Processor (EP) and thread schedule unit. Each thread is uniquely represented by a continuation <FP, IP,

RS, SC>, where FP is the Frame Pointer (where thread input values are stored), IP is the Instruction Pointer (which points to the thread code), RS is a register set (a dynamically allocated register context), and SC is the synchronization count (the number of inputs needed to enable the thread). The synchronization count is decremented when a thread receives its inputs, and the thread is scheduled on SP when the count becomes zero. SP is responsible for pre-loading data needed by the thread into its context (i.e., registers), and post-storing results from a completed thread into memory or *frames* of destination threads. The EP performs thread computations, including integer and floating point arithmetic operations, and spawns new threads. A more general implementation can include multiple EPs and SPs to execute threads from either a single task or independent tasks. Multiple SPs and EPs can be configured into multiple clusters. Inter-cluster communications will be achieved through shared memory.

An Example. To understand the decoupled, scheduled dataflow concept, consider one iteration of the innermost loop of matrix multiplication: c[i,j] = c[i,j] + a[i,k]*b[k,j]. Our SDF code is shown in Figure 1. In this example we assume that all necessary base addresses and indexes for the arrays are stored in the thread s frame. The thread is enabled after it receives all inputs in its frame, and a register context is allocated.

Preload :	LOAD	RFP|2, R2	# base of a into R2	body:	MULTD	R8,R9 R11	#a[i,k]*b[k,j] in R11
	LOAD	RFP|3, R3	# index a[i,k] into R3		ADDD	R10,R11, R10	# c[i,j] + a[i,k]*b[k,j] in R10
	LOAD	RFP|4, R4	# base of b into R4		FORKSP	poststore	#transfer to SP
	LOAD	RFP|5, R5	# index b[k,j] into R5		STOP		
	LOAD	RFP|6, R6	# base of c into R6				
	LOAD	RFP|7, R7	# index c[i,j] into R7				
	IFETCH	R2, R3, R8	# fetch a[i,k] to R8	poststore:	ISTORE	R6,R7, R10	#save c[i,j]
	IFETCH	R4, R5, R9	# fetch b[k,j] to R9		STOP		
	IFETCH	R6, R7, R10	# fetch c[i,j] to R10				
	FORKEP	body	# transfer to EP				
	STOP						

Fig. 1. A SDF Code Example

SP executes the *preload* portion of the code to transfer data into the registers allocated for the thread. The *body* portion of the code is executed by the EP performing necessary computations while the *poststore* portion is completed by the SP to store results into either the frames of other threads (and possibly enabling them) or the I-structure [10]. I-structure access instructions (IFETCH and ISTORE) need a base and an index into the array and these values are contained in a pair of registers. Note that only SP accesses data caches (frame cache and I-structure cache) while EP only accesses thread registers. A thread can move between EP and SP as needed to fetch or store data from/to registers (FORKSP and FORKEP serve this purpose and they take 4 cycles). Although not shown in this example, SP can perform index and address computations since each SP is provided with an integer arithmetic unit. Unlike token driven models, our instructions (for example MULTD) are provided with a pair of store locations (in our example R8 and R9) for input operands so that the instructions need not be executed immediately when the second operand arrives (as is the case in token driven models). Our instructions are *scheduled* like control flow architectures using program counters. Our instruction driven approach eliminates the need for complex communications to exchange tokens among processing elements. We simplified this example to illustrate the general structure of SDF code. In general, techniques such as loop unrolling can be used to increase the size of the loop body, and multiple threads can be created to execute loop iterations in parallel.

3 Thread-Level Speculation Schema for the SDF Architecture

For the non-speculative SDF architecture, if there is an ambiguous RAW (true dependence) that cannot be resolved at compile time, the compiler generates sequential threads to guarantee correct execution using I-structure [10] semantics. This will reduce the performance of programs. However, with hardware support for speculative execution of threads and committing results only when the speculation is verified, a complier can more aggressively create concurrent threads.

3.1 SDF Architecture Supported by the Schema

Our TLS schema not only supports speculative execution within a single SDF cluster consisting of multiple EPs and SPs, but also supports speculation among SDF clusters using distributed shared memory (DSM). Our design is derived from a variation of the invalidation based MESI protocol [13]. By applying the MESI protocol, we can enforce coherence of data caches on different nodes in a DSM system. We add extra hardware in each node to maintain intra-node coherence.

3.2 States in Our Design

In our schema, an invalidate message will be generated by a node to acquire exclusive ownership of data stored in a cache line before updating the cache. In addition to the 3 states of MESI protocol (Excusive (E), Shared (S), and Invalid (I)), we add two more states: speculative read of an exclusive data (SpREx) and speculative read of a shared data (SpR.Sh)[1]. We can distinguish the states easily by adding an extra S (Speculative read) bit to each cache line. Table 1 shows the encoding of the states.

Table 1. Encoding of Cache Line States

	SpRead	Valid	Dirty(Exclusive)
I	X	0	X
E/M	0	1	1
S	0	1	0
SpR.Ex	1	1	1
SpR.Sh	1	1	0

---

[1] We do not permit speculative writes.

3.3 Hardware Design of Our Schema

In the new architecture, a (speculative) thread is defined by a new continuation -- <FP, IP, RS, SC, EPN, RIP, ABI >. The first four elements are the same as the original continuations in SDF (see Section 2). The added elements are the epoch number (EPN), retry instruction pointer (RIP) and an address-buffer ID (ABI). For any TLS schema, an execution order of threads must be defined based on the program order. We use epoch numbers (EPN) for this purpose. Speculative threads must commit[2] in the order of their epoch numbers. RIP defines the instruction at which a failed speculative thread must start its retry. ABI defines the buffer ID that is used to store the addresses of speculatively-read data. For the non-speculative thread, the three new fields will all be set to zero. We add a separate queue for speculative threads to control the order of their commits. Figure 2 shows the overall design of our new architecture .

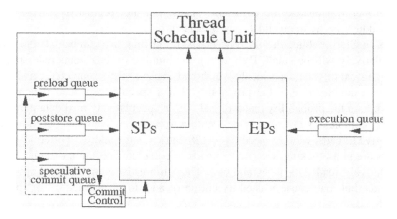

Fig. 2. Overall Design

For the controller (Thread Schedule Unit) to distinguish between speculative and non-speculative threads, it only needs to test the epoch field of the continuation to see if it is equal zero (as stated previously, a non-speculative thread s EPN is set to zero and any continuation that has a non-zero epoch number is a speculative thread). The commit control maintains the epoch number of the next thread that can commit based on the program order and will test the epoch number of a continuation that is ready for commit. If these numbers are the same and no data access violations are found in the reorder buffer associated with the thread, the commit controller will schedule the thread for commit (i.e, schedule the thread on SP for post-store). If there is a violation, the commit controller sets the IP of that continuation to RIP and places it back in the preload queue for re-execution. At this time, the thread becomes non- speculative.

We use a few small fully-associative buffers to record the addresses of data that are speculatively accessed by speculative threads. Data addresses are used as indices into these buffers. The small fully associative buffers can be implemented using an

---

[2] In our architecture, a thread commits its results to memory by executing the post-store part of its code.

associative cache where the number of sets represents the maximum number of speculative threads and the associativity represents the maximum number of speculative data that can be read by a thread. For example, a 64 set 4-way associative cache can support 64 speculative threads, with 4 speculative address entries per thread. The address buffer ID (ABI) is assigned when a new continuation for a speculative thread is created. When a speculative read request is issued by a thread, the address of the data being read is stored in the address buffer assigned to the thread and the entry is set to valid. When a speculatively read data is subsequently written by a non-speculative thread, the corresponding entries in the address buffers are invalidated, preventing speculative threads from committing. The block diagram of address buffer for a 4-SP node is shown in Figure 2. This design allows invaliding a speculatively-read data in all threads simultaneously. It also allows different threads to add different addresses into their buffers. When an invalidate request comes from the bus or a write request comes from inside the node, the data cache controller will change the cache line states, and the speculative controller will search the address buffer to invalidate appropriate entries.

Threads in SDF architecture are fine-grained and thus the number of data items read speculatively will be small. By limiting the number of data items read speculatively, the probability that a speculative thread successfully completes can be improved. For example, if p is the probability that a speculatively read data will be invalidated, then the probability that a thread with n speculatively read data items will successfully complete is given by $(1-p)^n$. With 4 to 8 speculative reads per thread and 16 speculative threads, we only need 64 to 128 entries in the address buffers. Because our threads are non-blocking, we allow threads to complete execution even if some of the speculatively read data is invalidated. This eliminates complex mechanisms to abort threads, but may cause wasted execution of additional instructions of speculative threads.

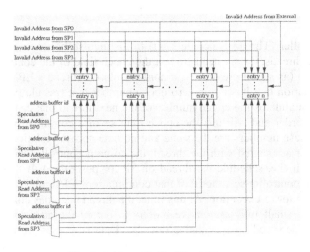

Fig. 3. Address Buffer Block Diagram

3.4   States Transition Diagram

A speculative thread cannot write any results to data cache. The results of a thread (during post-store) are not committed unless all speculative reads remain valid at the time the thread is ready for commit (in the order of epoch numbers). An invalid speculation will force the thread to retry using RIP pointer.

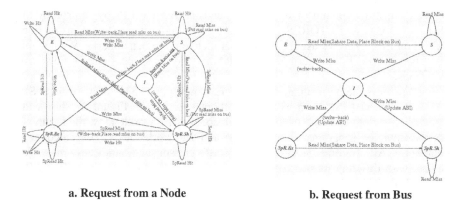

a. Request from a Node   **b. Request from Bus**

Fig. 4. State Transition Diagrams

Figure 3 shows the state transition diagrams for tracking data reads and writes by speculative and non-speculative threads. Figure 3a shows the cache line state transitions due to requests from a node within a cluster (i.e., intra-node). The key idea is that every speculative read will change the cache line state to speculative and also allocates an entry in the corresponding ABI buffer and every (non-speculative) write will invalidate the entries in the ABI buffer. Figure 3b shows the cache line state transitions due to bus activities (i.e., inter-node transactions). The write miss message from the bus will invalidate cache line and corresponding ABI entries. Due to the page limits, we will not explain these diagrams in detail, but they are similar to MESI type cache coherency protocols.

3.5   Instruction Set Architecture Extension

We added three new instructions to SDF instruction set for thread-level speculation support. The first instruction is for speculatively spawning a thread. This instruction will request the system to assign an epoch number and an ABI for the new continuation. The second instruction is for speculatively reading data, which will cause the addition of an entry into the address buffer associated with that continuation. It should be noted that not all reads of a speculative thread are speculative reads. A compiler can resolve most data dependencies and use speculative reads only when static analyses cannot determine memory ordering. It should also be noted that when a speculative thread is invalidated, the retry needs only to re-read speculatively-read data. The third instruction is for committing a speculative thread. This instruction places the speculative thread continuation into the speculative thread commit queue.

3.6 Experiment and Results

We extend our SDF simulator with this speculative thread execution schema. This simulator performs cycle-by-cycle functional simulation of SDF instructions.

3.6.1 Synthetic Benchmark Results[3]

We created benchmarks that execute a loop containing variable number of instructions. We control the amount time a thread spends at SPs and EPs by controlling the number of LOADS and STORES (workload on SP) and computational instructions (workload on EP). Then we use the TLS to parallelize these benchmarks. We test this group of benchmarks both in term of the scalability and the success rate of the speculative threads.

Figure 4a shows the performance of a program that spends 33% of the time at SPs and 67% of time at EPs, when executed without speculation. Figure 4b shows the performance for programs with 67% SP workload, 33% EP workload, while Figure 4c shows the data for programs with 50% SP and EP workloads (if executed non-speculatively). All programs are tested using different speculation success rates. We show data with different number of functional units: 8SPs-8EPs, 6SPs-6EPs, 4SPs-4EPs, and 2SPs-2EPs.

Since our SDF performs well when the SPs and EPs have balanced load (and achieve optimal overlap of threads executing at EPs and SPs), we would expect best performance for the case shown in Figure 4c and when the success of speculation is very high (closer to 100%). However, even if we started with a balanced load, as the speculation success drops (and is closer to zero), the load on EPs increase because failed threads will have to re-execute their computations. As stated previously, a failed thread only needs to re-read the data items that were read speculatively and data from a thread are post-stored only when the thread speculation is validated. Thus a failed speculation will disproportionately add to EP workload. For the case shown in Figure 4b, with a smaller EP workload, we obtain higher speed-ups (compared Figures 4a or 4c) even at lower success rates of speculation, since EPs are not heavily utilized in this workload. For the 33%-66% SP-EP workload in Figure 4a, even a very high success rates will not lead to high performance gains on SDF, because EP is overloaded to start with, and the mis-speculative will add to the load of EPs.

From this group of experiments, we can draw the following conclusions. Speculative thread execution can lead to performance gains over a wide range of speculation success probabilities. We can obtain at least 2-fold performance gain when the success of speculation is greater than 50%. If the success rate drops below 50%, one should turn off speculative execution to avoid excessive retries that can overload EPs. When the EP workload is less than the SP workload, we can tolerate higher rates of mis-speculation. Finally, when the success rates are below 50%, the performance does not scale well with added SPs and EPs (8SPs-8EPs, 6SPs-6EPs, and 4SPs-4EsP all show similar performance). This suggests that the success of speculation can be used to decide on the number of SPs and EPs needed to achieve optimal performance.

---

[3] These are actual programs written for SDF and run on our simulator. We controlled the number of Load/Store instructions, and controlled which speculative threads successfully commit (post-store) their results.

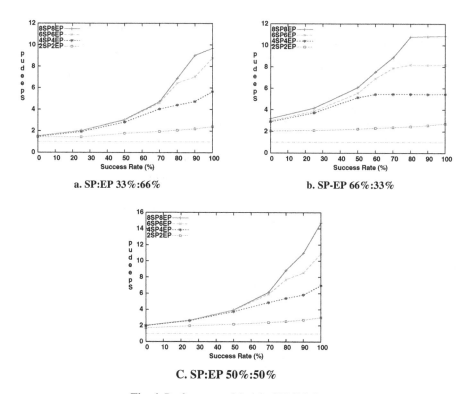

a. SP:EP 33%:66%

b. SP-EP 66%:33%

C. SP:EP 50%:50%

Fig. 4. Performances Model of TLS Schema

3.6.2 Real Benchmarks

To further test our design, we selected a set of real benchmarks. We hand-coded these benchmarks using SDF assembly language. This group of benchmarks includes: Livermore loops 2 and 3; two major functions from compress() and decompress() (from 129.compress) and four loops chosen from 132.ijpeg. Table 2 shows the detailed description of the benchmarks. We code these benchmarks in two forms: one without speculation, where all the threads are executed linearly, and the other with speculation. In the speculative execution, earlier iterations (or threads with lower epoch numbers) generate speculative threads for later iterations (or threads with higher epoch numbers).

Table 2. Selected Benchmarks

Suite	Application	Selected Loops
Livermore		Loop2
Loops		Loop3
SPEC 95	129.Compress95	Compress.c:480 while loop
		Compress.c:706 while loop
	132.ijpeg	Jccolor.c:138 for loop
		Jcdectmgr.c:214 for loop
		Jidctint.c:171 for loop
		Jidctint.c:276 for loop

We evaluated performance gains using different number of SPs and EPs and the results are shown in Figure 5. The speculative execution does achieve higher speed-ups - between 30% and 158% for 2SP-2EP configuration and between 60% and 200% speedup for 4SP4EP configuration. To compare our results with those of [9], we use the parallel coverage parameter defined in [9]. Using 4SP4EP configuration to compare with their 4 tightly coupled, single threaded superscalar pipeline processors, for compress95 we achieve a speedup of 1.94 compared to 1.27 achieved by [9]; and a speedup of 2.98 for ijpeg compared to 1.94 achieved by [9].

Another finding from Figure 5 is that our performance does not scale well after 4SP4EP configuration. This is because of the way we generated threads ...we generate very limited number of speculative threads, since each iteration only generates one new speculative thread. However with an optimizing compiler, it will be possible to generate as many speculative threads as needed to fully utilize available processing and functional units.

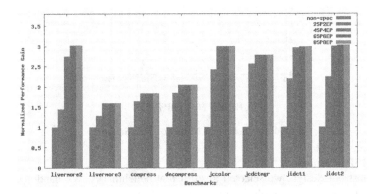

Fig. 5. Performance gains normalized to non-speculative implementation

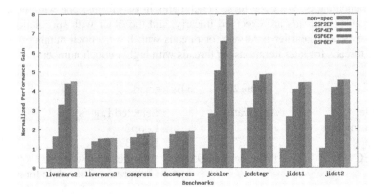

Fig. 6. Performance gains normalized to non-speculative implementation

We repeated our experiments with the same benchmarks but using a control thread that spawning multiple speculative threads at a time. For livermore loops, the control thread spawns 10 iterations a time, and for the compress95 and the jpeg, the control thread spawns 8 iterations a time. The results are shown in Figure 6. For most cases, this approach does show better scalability with added functional units. Livermore loop 3 and compress are the exceptions. For these applications, the mis-speculation is very high and since on mis-speculation all threads become non-speculative (executing sequentially) the available concurrency is reduced. It should be noted, however, our approach does lead to higher speedups than those reported in [9].

4 Summary and Conclusions

Our goal here is to provide a qualitative and a quantitative evaluation of an innovative non-blocking multithreaded architecture that decouples all memory access from execution pipeline. Our quantitative evaluations are limited to hand-coded benchmarks. At this time, we do not have a compiler, but we hope that we will be able find support to design and implement an optimizing compiler for our architecture. An optimizing compiler is needed to take full advantage of SDF features.

In previous sections we have shown that SDF can achieve scalable performance that is comparable or better than Simplescalar, VLIW and SMT architectural paradigms. We also have shown that thread level speculation on SDF can lead to speedups that are better than or comparable to other speculative execution models. In addition, SDF offers several qualitative advantages over existing architectural paradigms.

Separating PEs into SPs and EPs has distinct advantages. One can tailor the number of SP and EP units included in a single computation cluster to maximize performance of experimentally determined computation needs. The number and types of functional units (viz., integer and floating point arithmetic units) within these processing elements can also be varied. The EPs and SPs can easily be run at different clock speeds, providing power savings. Such control is easier to implement in our system than proposed globally asynchronous, locally synchronous (GALS) designs that contain multiple clock domains (MCD s) ([15], [16]). And by keeping the EP and SP pipelines extremely simple with no out-of-order instruction execution, we can address power constraints, provide additional computing power by including multiple simple SP and EP clusters on a chip, or more register sets.

SDF uses non-blocking threads, leading to non-preemptive scheduling of threads. Although real-time systems often use pre-emptive scheduling to meet required reactive times, non-preemptive scheduling is more efficient, particularly for soft real-time applications and applications designed for multithreaded systems, since the non-preemptive model reduces the overhead needed for switching among tasks (or threads) [17]. The decoupled memory of SDF implies that each thread goes through at least 3 scheduling points: *preload* when the thread s inputs (and I-structure data) are transferred to its registers at an SP, *execute* when the thread performs its computation at an EP, and *poststore* when the thread transfers results from its registers to memory or other threads at an SP. Each of these scheduling points allows us to determine which thread should be scheduled. Such fine-grained real-time scheduling is not possible with other thread models. The non-preemptive execution is applicable even to speculative threads, thus simplifying the management of thread-level speculation. All threads are allowed to complete but only those threads that can commit are allowed to complete post-store portions of their code.

References

[1] Agarwal, V., Hrishikesh, M.S., Keckler, S.W., Burger, D.: Clock Rate Versus IPC: The End of the Road for Conventional Microarchitectures. In: 27th International Symposium on Computer Architecture (ISCA), June 2000, pp. 248..259 (2000)

[2] Tullsen, D.M., Eggers, S.J., Levy, H.M., Lo, J.L.: Simultaneous multithreading: Maximizing on-chip parallelism. In: International. Symposium on Computer Architecture (ISCA), June 1995, pp. 392..403 (1995)

[3] Sankaralingam, K., Nagarajan, R., Liu, H., Huh, J., Kim, C.K., Burger, D., Keckler, S.W., Moore, C.R.: Exploiting ILP, TLP, and DLP Using Polymorphism in the TRIPS Architecture. In: 30th International Symposium on Computer Architecture (ISCA), June 2003, pp. 422..433 (2003)

[4] Burger, D., et al.: Scaling to the end of silicon with EDGE architectures. IEEE Computer, 44..55 (July 2004)

[5] Swanson, S., Michelson, K., Schwerin, A., Oskin, M.: WaveScalar. In: Proceedings of the 36th International Symposium on Microarchitecture(MICRO), December 2003, pp. 291... 302 (2003)

[6] Onder, S., Gupta, R.: Superscalar execution with direct data forwarding. In: Proc of the International Conference on Parallel Architectures and Compiler Technologies, Paris, October 1998, pp. 130..135 (1998)

[7] Marcuello, P., Gonzalez, A., Tubella, J.: Speculative Multithreaded Processors. In: Proceeding of the International Conference on Supercomputing, July 1998, pp. 77..84 (1998)

[8] Zhang, Y., Rauchwerger, L., Torrelas, J.: Hardware for Speculative Parallelization of Partially-Parallel Loops in DSM Multiprocessors. In: 5th International Symposium on High-Performance Computer Architecture (HPCA), January 1999, pp. 135..141 (1999)

[9] Steffan, J.G., Colohan, C.B., Zhai, A., Mowry, T.C.: A Scalable Approach to Thread-Level Speculation. In: 27th International Symposium on Computer Architecture (ISCA), June 2000, pp. 1..12 (2000)

[10] Arvind, Nikhil, R.S., Pingali, K.K.: Istructures: Data-structures for parallel computing. ACM Transactions on Programming Languages and Systems 4(11), 598..632 (1989)

[11] Burger, D., Austin, T.M.: The SimpleScalar Tool Set Version 2.0, Tech Rept. #1342, Department of Computer Science, University of Wisconsin, Madison, WI

[12] Terada, H., Miyata, S., Iwata, M.: DDMP s: Self-timed Super-pipelined Data-driven Multimedia Processor. Proceedings of the IEEE, 282..296 (February 1999)

[13] Hennessy, J.L., Patterson, D.A.: Computer Architecture: A Quantitative Approach, 3rd edn. (2003)

[14] Hurson, A.R., Lim, J.T., Kavi, K.M., Lee, B.: Parallelization of DOALL and DOACROSS Loops ..A Survey. Advances in Computers 45, 53..103 (1997)

[15] Magklis, G., et al.: Dynamic Frequency and Voltage Scaling for a Multiple Clock Domain Microprocessor. IEEE Micro, 62..69 (November/December 2003)

[16] Semeraro, G., et al.: Dynamic frequency and voltage control for multiple clock domain microarchitecture. In: Proc. of International symposium on microarchitecture (MICRO-35), pp. 356..370 (2002)

[17] Jain, R., Hughes, C.J., Adve, S.V.: Soft Real-Time Scheduling on Simultaneous Multithreaded Processors. In: Proceedings of the 23rd IEEE International Real-Time Systems Symposium (December 2002)

Finding Synchronization-Free Parallelism Represented with Trees of Dependent Operations

Wlodzimierz Bielecki[2], Anna Beletska[1], Marek Palkowski[2], and Pierluigi San Pietro[1]

[1] Dipartimento di Elettronica e Informazione, Politecnico di Milano,
20122 via Ponzio 34/5, Milano, Italy
{beletska,sanpietr}@elet.polimi.it
[2] Faculty of Computer Science, Technical University of Szczecin,
70210 Zolnierska 49, Szczecin, Poland
{wbielecki,mpalkowski}@wi.ps.pl

Abstract. Algorithms are presented for extracting synchronization-free parallelism available in arbitrarily nested parameterized loops. The parallelism is represented with synchronization-free trees of dependent operations. Sets representing trees can be described with non-linear expressions. The main idea is to firstly extract sources of synchronization-free trees and next to generate parallel code based on a while loop. Experimental results are presented exposing speed-up and efficiency of parallel programs written in the OpenMP standard on the basis of code generated by the algorithms proposed.

1 Introduction

Finding coarse-grained parallelism in loops is of great importance to get scalable performance for parallel and distributed computing. Its purpose, however, is not limited to this, since it may also increase program performance on a uniprocessor system by enhancing data locality.

Different techniques have been developed to extract coarse-grained parallelism that is represented with synchronization-free slices of computations available in loops, for example, those presented in papers [1,2,3,4,5]. Unfortunately, there does not exist any technique allowing us to extract slices represented with sets described with non-linear expressions. Hence, potential parallelism is left unexploited in some cases.

In this paper, we demonstrate how to extract synchronization-free trees of transitively dependent operations when well-known techniques do fail to extract such trees. We show how to generate code scanning slices even when they are represented with sets described with non-linear forms. Proposed algorithms are applicable to the arbitrarily nested parameterized loop.

2 Background

A nested loop is called *perfectly nested* if all its statements are comprised within the innermost nest. Otherwise, the loop is called *imperfectly nested*. An *arbitrarily nested*

A. Bourgeois and S.Q. Zheng (Eds.): ICA3PP 2008, LNCS 5022, pp. 185..195, 2008.
© Springer-Verlag Berlin Heidelberg 2008

loop can be both perfectly and imperfectly nested. An *operation* is a particular execution of a statement of the loop body for a given iteration.

Two operations I and J are *dependent* if both access the same memory location and if at least one access is a write. I and J are called the *source* and *destination* of a dependence, respectively, provided that I is lexicographically smaller than J (I $\prec$ J, i.e., I is always executed before J).

In this paper, we deal with *affine loop nests* where i) for given loop indices, lower and upper bounds as well as array subscripts and conditionals are affine functions of surrounding loop indices and possibly of structure parameters (i.e., parameterized loop bounds), and ii) the loop steps are known positive constants.

Our approach requires an exact representation of loop-carried dependences and consequently an exact dependence analysis which detects a dependence if and only if it actually exists. To describe and implement our algorithms, we choose the dependence analysis proposed by Pugh and Wonnacott [6] where dependences are represented by dependence relations.

A dependence relation is a tuple relation of the form {[*input_list*] $\rightarrow$ [*output_list*]: *formula*}, where *input_list* and *output_list* are lists of variables and/or expressions used to describe input and output tuples and *formula* describes the constraints imposed upon *input_list* and *output_list* and it is a Presburger formula built of constraints represented with algebraic expressions and using logical and existential operators.

We distinguish between a single dependence (a pair of operations: dependence source and destination) and a dependence relation representing multiple dependences.

We distinguish between a dependence graph representing all the dependences among loop operations and a reduced dependence graph being composed by vertices for each statement s_i, $1 \le i \le r$, of the loop and edges joining vertices according to dependence relations $R_{i,j}$, where $i,j \in [1,r]$, being exposed by an exact dependence analysis, r is the number of statements within the loop body.

Definition 1. An *ultimate dependence source* is a source that is not the destination of another dependence.

Program slicing is a viable method to restrict the focus of a task to specific subcomponents of a program. Program slicing was first introduced by Mark Weiser [7], with a notion of slice based on the deletion of statements: a slice is an executable subset of program statements that preserves the original behavior of the program with respect to a subset of variables of interest and at a given program point [8].

Iteration space slicing [9] takes dependence information as input to find all statement instances of a given loop nest, which must be executed to produce the correct values for the specified array elements.

In this paper, we use the following definition of a slice.

Definition 2. Given a dependence graph, D, defined by a set of dependence relations, S, a *slice* is a weakly connected component of graph D, i.e., a maximal subgraph of D such that for each pair of vertices in the subgraph there exists a directed or undirected path.

If there exist two or more slices in D, then taking in the account the above definition, we may conclude that all slices are *synchronization-free*, i.e., there is no dependence between them.

Definition 3. The *source(s) of a slice* is the ultimate dependence source(s) that this slice comprises.

In this paper, we present algorithms to extract synchronization-free slices whose topology is a tree. Each tree is represented by a set of operations transitively dependent on a *single* dependence source such that there does not exist an operation being a dependence destination corresponding to two or more different dependence sources.

We use standard operations on relations and sets, such as intersection ($\cap$), union ($\cup$), difference ($-$), domain R, range R, relation application ($S' = R(S)$: $e' \in S'$ iff $\exists e$ s.t. $e \rightarrow e' \in R$, $e \in S$). In detail, the description of these operations is presented in [6,10,11].

The algorithm presented in this paper deals with strongly connected components (SCCs). An SCC is a maximal subset of vertices and edges of a reduced dependence graph [5] where for every pair of vertices there exists a directed path.

3 Motivating Example

To demonstrate that the well-known affine transformation framework (ATF) does fail to extract synchronization-free slices for particular loops, let us consider the following perfectly-nested loop

Example 1

```
for (i=1; i<=n; i++)
    for (j=1; j<=n; j++)
s1:    a[i,j]=(j==1?a[2*i][j]:a[i][j+1]);
```

Dependences originated by this loop (see Fig. 1) can be represented by the following dependence relations

$$R^1_{s1,s1} := \{[i,1] \rightarrow [2i,1]: 1 \leq i \ \& \ 2i \leq n\},$$

$$R^2_{s1,s1} := \{[i,j] \rightarrow [i,j+1] : 1 \leq i \leq n \ \& \ 1 \leq j < n \ \}.$$

In order to extract synchronization-free parallelism by means of ATF, we use the relations above to construct the following system of equations

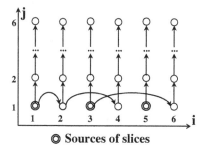

Fig. 1. Dependences for motivating example for n=6

$$\begin{cases} C_{11}*i+C_{12}+c_1 = C_{11}*2i+C_{12}+c_1; \\ C_{11}*i+C_{12}*j+c_1 = C_{11}*i+C_{12}*j+C_{12}+c_1. \end{cases}$$

The solution to this system is $\begin{bmatrix} C_{11} & C_{12} & c_1 \end{bmatrix} = \begin{bmatrix} 0 & 0 & \text{arbitary value} \end{bmatrix}$. Such a solution means that ATF fails to extract two or more slices for this example. We are unaware of any other technique allowing us to extract synchronization-free parallelism available in this loop.

4 Extracting Synchronization-Free Trees

In order to extract synchronization-free trees of dependent operations described by dependence relations, first of all we need to preprocess those relations so that we are able to perform further calculations on them. Provided that each lower bound of loop indices is non-negative, the algorithm of the preprocessing is the following.

Algorithm 1. Dependence relation preprocessing

Input: set $S\_IN := \{R_{i,j} \mid i, j \in [1,q] \}$ of dependence relations representing an SCC, where values of i, j represent the statement identifiers and are increased in the order in which statements appear in the source code; each $R_{i,j}$ denotes the union of all the relations describing dependences between statements i and j, q is the number of vertices in the SCC; the number of loop indices, n.

Output: set of preprocessed dependence relations, S_OUT.

Method:
  $S\_OUT := S\_IN;$
  foreach relation $R_{i,j} \in S\_OUT$ do
1. **if** the number of input and/or output tuple elements of a relation is fewer than n
    then transform relation $R_{i,j}$ so that each its input and output tuple has exactly n elements, by inserting the value -1 at the rightmost positions of the tuples, i.e., the tuple of the form $[e] := [e_1 \ e_2 \ f \ e_{n-k}]$, $k \geq 1$, substitute for the tuple $[e_1 e_2 ... e_{n-k} \ \underbrace{-1 \ -1 \ .... \ -1}_{k}]$;

2. insert at the rightmost position of each input and output tuples of $R_{i,j}$ values of i and j, respectively, i.e., transform $R_{i,j} := \{[e] \rightarrow [e']\}$ into $R_{i,j} := \{[e,i] \rightarrow [e',j]\}$.

Let us note that if the loop body contains a single statement, then it is not necessary to preprocess dependence relations because all of them describe self-dependences between instances of the same statement and the size of input and output tuples of each relation is the same.

The idea of the algorithm extracting trees is the following. First, using set S comprising all the preprocessed dependence relations extracted for a given loop, we calculate a relation, R, being the union of all the dependence relations included in set S. Next, we check whether R describes any common dependence destination, i.e., an operation that is a destination of two or more dependences. If this is not the case, we can conclude that all slices are represented with trees. Then, we calculate set, Sources, composed of all the ultimate dependence sources represented with R, and finally generate code scanning synchronization-free trees preserving all the dependences available in an original loop.

Algorithm 2. Extracting synchronization-free trees of dependent operations

Input: set $S := \{ R_1, R_2, ..., R_n \}$, $n \geq 1$, of preprocessed dependence relations describing an SCC.

Output: code scanning synchronization-free trees preserving all the dependences in an original loop.

Method:
1. Calculate $R := R_1 \cup R_2 \cup ... \cup R_n$.
2. Check whether R describes any common dependence destination as follows
   2.1. find set CDD := $\{[e] : e = R(e') = R(e'') \ \& \ e',e'' \in$ domain(R) $\& \ e' \neq e''\}$;
   2.2. if set CDD is empty, then R does not describe any common dependence destination, go to step 3. Otherwise the algorithm fails to extract synchronization-free trees for the given set of dependence relations, the end.
3. Compute a set, Sources, including all ultimate dependence sources as the difference between the sets representing dependence sources and destinations, respectively
   Sources := domain R .. range R.
4. Generate code scanning synchronization-free trees preserving all dependences of an original loop of the form
   genOuterLoops (in: Sources; out: OuterLoops, L_I);
           foreach I in L_I **do**
                   genWhile (in: OuterLoops, I; out: WhileLoop);

where:
- The function *genOuterLoops*(in: *OperSet*; out: *Loops, VectorList*) generates a set of outer loop nests, Loops, to scan operations comprised in set *OperSet*, and returns a list of parameterized iteration vectors *VectorList*, one vector I from list *VectorList* corresponds to one outer nest of loops generated, i.e., the number of elements in list *VectorList* is equal to the number of nests generated. Let us note that in the general case, set *Sources* is a union of parameterized polyhedra whose constraints are affine because the constraints of the result of the difference operation on affine sets is also affine. Hence, any well-known technique can be applied to implement the function *genOuterLoops,* e.g., those published in [12-16]. All outer loops *OuterLoops* can be executed in parallel because they scan independent sources of synchronization-free slices.

- **foreach** I in L_I **do** means for each outer nest of loops generated by the function *genLoops* and being associated with vector I from list L_I .
- the function *genWhile* (in: *OuterLoops*, I; out: *WhileLoop*)

1. generates code named *WhileLoop* of the form:

```
S' := I;
while (S' ≠ Ø); {
    S_tmp := Ø;
        (par)foreach I∈ S' do  /* par  means that all elements of S' can be
                                executed in parallel because there are no dependences
                                among them*/
            stₖ(I'); /* statement k of an original loop (k is defined  by the
                        rightmost value of I) to be executed in the  iteration given
                        by vector I' (I' is represented by the first n-1 values of I) */
        foreach i, i=1,2,..,n do
            if Rᵢ(I') ∈ domain Rᵢ then
                        J := Rᵢ(I);    /* calculate a set of operations to be
                                        executed in the next iteration */
                    Add J into S_tmp;
            end
        end
    end
    S' := S_tmp; }
```

2. Inerts code *WhileLoop* in the corresponding nest of loops *OuterLoops*.

Note that each while loop iteration executes all the operations whose operands have already been calculated and prepares a set of operations to be executed at the next iteration. That is, operations are executed as soon as their operands are available, preserving in such a way all dependences exposed for an original loop. Such a schedule (assigning a time of execution to each operation of the loop) is known to be *free-schedule* [5].

5 Extracting Synchronization-Free Trees for the Motivating Example

Analyzing Figure 1 representing dependences available in the loop of the motivating example, we can see all synchronization-free slices are trees or chains (a chain is the particular case of a tree). Because the body of the loop contains a single statement, the preprocessing of dependence relations by means of Algorithm 1 is not necessary and we omit this procedure. We apply Algorithm 2 and extract synchronization-free slices as follows.

1. $R := R^1_{s1,s1} \cup R^2_{s1,s1} = \{[i,1] \to [2i,1]: 1 \le i \ \& \ 2i \le n\} \cup \{[i,j] \to [i,j+1]: 1 \le i \le n \ \& 1 \le j < n\};$

2. Set CDD is empty, we go to Step 3.

3. Sources := {[i,1]: Exists (alpha : 2alpha = 1+i && 1 <= i <= n, 2n-3)}.

4. Code generated can be represented by means of the following pseudocode

```
parfor(t=1; t<=min(n,2*n-3); t+=2)  /* outer loop is generated by
                                        the Omega Calculator*/
```

```
{    I=[t,1];
     Add I to S';      /* I is the source of a tree */
     while(S'!= Ø) {
     S_tmp=Ø;
     (par)foreach(vector I=[i,j] in S') {
          s1(I) ;  /* the original loop statement to be executed at iteration I */
          if(j==1 && 1<=i && 2*i<=n) {/* if R₁(I) ∈domain R₁*/
               ip = 2*i;   jp = 1;      /* J= [ip,jp]=R₁(I) */
               add J=[ip,jp] to S_tmp;  }
          if(1<=i && i<=n && 1<=j&&j<n) { /*if R₂(I)∈ domain R₂ */
               ip = i;   jp = 1+j;      /* J=[ip,jp]= R₂(I) */
               add J=[ip,jp] to S_tmp;  }
     }
     S'=S_tmp;
     }
}
```

6   Another Example

Let us consider another example, an imperfectly nested loop borrowed from [17] for which well-known techniques fail to extract synchronization-free slices.

Example 2

```
for  (i=0;i<=n;i++)
      for (j=0;j<=n;j++)
s1:        x[i,j]=(i%2 ==0 ? x[i,j-1]: y[i-1,j])
      for j=n downto 0
s2:        y[i,j]=(i%2 ==0 ? x[i,j]: y[i,j+1])
```

Dependences (see Fig. 2) originated by this loop can be represented by the following set of preprocessed relations

$R_{s1,s1} := \{[i,j,1] \rightarrow [i,j+1,1]: \text{exists } (k: 2*k=i \,\&\, k\geq 0 \,\&\, 0\leq i\leq n \,\&\, 0\leq j\leq n-1)\};$
$R_{s1,s2} := \{[i,j,1] \rightarrow [i,j,2]: \text{exists } (k: 2*k=i \,\&\, k\geq 0 \,\&\, 0\leq i\leq n \,\&\, 0\leq j\leq n)\};$
$R_{s2,s1} := \{[i,j,2] \rightarrow [i+1,j,1]: \text{exists } (k: 2*k=i \,\&\, k\geq 0 \,\&\, 0\leq i\leq n-1 \,\&\, 0\leq j\leq n)\};$
$R_{s2,s2} := \{[i,j,2] \rightarrow [i,j-1,2]: \text{exists } (k: 2*k+1=i \,\&\, k\geq 0 \,\&\, 0\leq i\leq n \,\&\, 1\leq j\leq n)\}.$

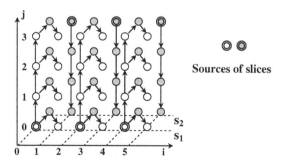

Fig. 2. Dependences for Example 2

Applying Algorithm 2, we get the following pseudocode

```
parfor(t=0; t<=n; t++)
{      if (intMod(t,2) == 0){
              I=[t,0,1]; /* I is a source of a tree */
              Add I to S';
              Exec(S'); }          /* call function Exec() */
       if (intMod(t+1,2) == 0){
              I=[t,n,2]; /* I is a source of a tree */
              Add I to S';
              Exec(S'); }}         /* call function Exec() */
void Exec (S'){
  while((S'!= ∅)) {
       S_tmp= ∅;
       (par)foreach(I=[i,j,k] in S') {
       if(k==1) /* execute the 1st statement of the orginal loop */
              x[i][j] = ((i%2) ==0) ? x[i][j-1] : y[i-1][j];
       else if(k==2) /* execute the 2nd statement of the original loop */
              y[i][j] = ((i%2) ==0) ? x[i][j]   : y[i][j+1];
       /* calculating vector J= (ip,jp,kp]) */
       if(k>=1&&k<=1&& i%2==0&&0<=i&&i<=n&&0<=j&&j<n) {
              /* if (R1,1(I) ∉domain R1,1) then do */
              ip = i; jp = 1+j;  kp = k;   /* J= R1,1(I) */
              Add J to S_tmp; }
       if(k<=1&&k>=1&&i%2==0&&0<=i&&i<=n&&0<=j&&j<= n) {
              /* if (R1,2(I) ∉ domain R1,2) then do */
              ip = i; jp = j; kp = 1+k;    /* J= R1,2(I) */
              Add J to S_tmp; }
       if(k<=1&&k>=1&&i%2==0&&0<=i&&i<=n&&0<=j&&j<= n) {
              /* if (R2,1(I) ∉domain R2,1) then do */
              jp = j; ip = i+1; kp = k-1; /* J=R2,1(I) */
              Add J to S_tmp; }
       if(k<=1&&k>=1&&i%2==0&&0<=i&&i<=n&&0<=j&&j<= n)   {
              /* if (R2,2(I) ∉ domain R2,2) then do */
              ip = i;  jp = j-1; kp = k; /* J= R2,2(I) */
              Add J to S_tmp;} }
       S' = S_tmp;}   }
```

7 Experiments

To evaluate the performance of code generated by the proposed approach, we have developed a tool that implements the algorithms presented in this paper using the Omega Project Software (Petit − for exposing dependence relations and the Omega calculator − for the calculations envisaged by our algorithm). Applying this tool, we have generated code for the loops of Example 1 (Section 3) and Example 2 (Section 6). Using the OpenMP API [18] to describe parallelism available in loops, we inserted appropriate pragmas and clauses into the code generated. For these loops, we have carried experiments on the machine Intel Xeon 1.6 Ghz, 8 processors (2 x 4-core CPU, cache 4 MB), 2 GB RAM, Ubuntu Linux. Table 1 presents the results where the column *for* presents the execution time of an original loop (in seconds), the column *while* presents the execution time of a while loop generated(in seconds), S and E denote speed-up and efficiency, respectively. Let us recall that if T(P) is the time required to complete the task on P processors, the speedup is the ratio S=T(1)/T(P). Efficiency, on the other hand, is a measure of how much of available processing power is being used: E = S/P = T(1) / (P * T(P)). Under our experiments, T(1) is the time of the execution of a corresponding source *for* loop, while T(P) is the time of the parallel execution of a corresponding *while* loop being produced by our approach.

Table 1.

Loop	n	1 CPU		2 CPU		4 CPU		8 CPU	
		for	while	S	E	S	E	S	E
Ex. 1	250	0,014	0,016	1,273	0,636	1,167	0,292	1,077	0,135
	500	0,056	0,064	1,436	0,718	2,074	0,519	2,667	0,333
	1000	0,224	0,257	1,659	0,830	3,027	0,757	4,148	0,519
	1500	0,504	0,573	1,732	0,866	3,170	0,792	5,538	0,692
	2000	0,922	1,006	1,787	0,893	3,453	0,863	6,188	0,773
Ex. 2	500	0,011	0,017	1,000	0,500	1,100	0,275	1,100	0,138
	1000	0,045	0,063	1,216	0,608	1,607	0,402	1,731	0,216
	2000	0,179	0,268	1,398	0,699	1,989	0,497	2,887	0,361
	4000	0,717	0,964	1,428	0,714	2,464	0,616	4,006	0,501
	8000	2,856	3,834	1,453	0,727	2,589	0,647	4,916	0,614

From the results obtained, it may be deduced that on one CPU, there is no considerable difference between the execution times of a source *for* loop and a corresponding *while* loop generated by means of Algorithm 2. The performance of code generated by Algorithm 2 depends considerably on the volume of calculations executed by a slice (the product of the volume of calculations represented by the loop statements and the number of the loop iterations). If this volume of calculations results in the time of calculations that is greater than time overhead (incurred by a while loop generated by Algorithm 2 and threads management in a multiprocessor environment), we get positive speed-up (S>1) at running a generated parallel loop on a multiprocessor with shared memory.

8 Related Work

Unimodular loop transformations [2], permitting the outermost loop in a nest of loops to be parallelized, find synchronization-free parallelism. But unimodular transformations can be applied only to perfectly-nested loops and do not allow such transformations as loop fission, fusion, scaling, reindexing, or reordering [1].

The affine transformation framework (polyhedral approach), considered in many papers, for example, in papers [3,4,5,19,20,21] unifies a large number of previously proposed loop transformations. However, it possesses a number of limitations preventing the extraction of all synchronization-free trees described with affine forms (Example 2 in this paper) as well as it fails to extract synchronization-free trees described with non-linear forms (Example 1 in this paper).

Paper [22] presents an approach to build free-schedules for extracting fine-grained parallelism only, it does not concern extracting synchronization-free slices.

Our contribution consists in demonstrating how we can extract synchronization-free slices of the tree topology and how to generate parallel code to scan operations of a tree being described with non-linear forms.

9 Conclusion and Future Work

We introduced algorithms to extract coarse-grained parallelism being represented with synchronization-free trees of dependent operations described with non-linear forms. Such trees can be extracted for arbitrarily nested parameterized loops. Our experiments demonstrate that we can reach positive speed-up of parallel code generated according to the presented algorithms on a multiprocessor with shared memory when the time of the execution of computations represented by a slice is greater than time overhead incurred by a while loop generated and treads management in a multiprocessor environment. Our future research direction is to derive techniques for extracting slices being represented not only by trees, but also by graphs of an arbitrary topology.

References

1. Allen, R., Kennedy, K.: Optimizing Compilers for Modern Architectures, p. 790. Morgan Kaufmann, San Francisco (2001)
2. Banerjee, U.: Unimodular transformations of double loops. In: Proceedings of the Third Workshop on Languages and Compilers for Parallel Computing, pp. 192.219 (1990)
3. Feautrier, P.: Toward automatic distribution. Journal of Parallel Processing Letters 4, 233...244 (1994)
4. Lim, W., Cheong, G.I., Lam, M.S.: An affine partitioning algorithm to maximize parallelism and minimize communication. In: Proceedings of the 13th ACM SIGARCH International Conference on Supercomputing (1999)
5. Darte, A., Robert, Y., Vivien, F.: Scheduling and Automatic Parallelization, Birkhäuser Boston (2000)
6. Pugh, W., Wonnacott, D.: Constraint-based array dependence analysis. ACM Trans. on Programming Languages and Systems (1998)
7. Weiser, M.: Program slices: formal, psychological, and practical investigations of an automatic program abstraction method, PhD thesis, University of Michigan, Ann Arbor, MI (1979)
8. Weiser, M.: Program Slicing. IEEE Transactions on Software Engineering SE-10(7), 352...357 (1984)
9. Pugh, W., Rosser, E.: Iteration Space Slicing and Its Application to Communication Optimization. In: Proceedings of the International Conference on Supercomputing, pp. 221...228 (1997)

10. Kelly, W., Pugh, W., Rosser, E., Shpeisman, T.: Transitive Closure of Infinite Graphs and its Applications. International Journal of Parallel Programming 24(6), 579.598 (1996)
11. Kelly, W., Maslov, V., Pugh, W., Rosser, E., Shpeisman, T., Wonnacott, D.: The omega library interface guide, Technical Report CS-TR-3445, University of Maryland (1995)
12. Ancourt, C., Irigoin, F.: Scanning polyhedra with do loops. In: Proceedings of the Third ACM/SIGPLAN Symposium on Principles and Practice of Parallel Programming, pp. 39... 50. ACM Press, New York (1991)
13. Bastoul, C.: Code Generation in the Polyhedral Model Is Easier Than You Think. In: Proceedings of the PACT 13 IEEE International Conference on Parallel Architecture and Compilation Techniques, Juan-les-Pins, pp. 7..16 (2004)
14. Boulet, P., Darte, A., Silber, G.A., Vivien, F.: Loop parallelization algorithms: from parallelism extraction to code generation. Parallel Computing 24, 421.444 (1998)
15. Quillere, F., Rajopadhye, S., Wilde, D.: Generation of efficient nested loops from polyhedra. International Journal of Parallel Programming 28 (2000)
16. Vasilache, N., Bastoul, C., Cohen, A.: Polyhedral code generation in the real world. In: Proceedings of the International Conference on Compiler Construction (ETAPS CC 2006). LNCS, pp. 185.201. Springer, Vienna, Austria (2006)
17. Gupta, G., DaeGon, Kim, Sanjay, Rajopadhye, V.: Scheduling in the Z-Polyhedral Model. In: Proceedings of IPDPS 2007 (2007)
18. http://www.openmp.org
19. Lim, W., Lam, M.S.: Communication-free parallelization via affine transformations. In: Proceedings of the Seventh workshop on languages and compilers for parallel computing, pp. 92..106 (1994)
20. Feautrier, P.: Some efficient solutions to the affine scheduling problem, part i, one dimensional time. International Journal of Parallel Programming 21, 313.348 (1992)
21. Feautrier, P.: Some efficient solutions to the affine scheduling problem, part ii, multidimensional time. International Journal of Parallel Programming 21, 389.420 (1992)
22. Beletskyy, V., Siedlecki, K.: Finding Free Schedules for Non-uniform Loops. In: Kosch, H., Böszörményi, L., Hellwagner, H. (eds.) Euro-Par 2003. LNCS, vol. 2790, pp. 297... 302. Springer, Heidelberg (2003)

Lee-TM: A Non-trivial Benchmark Suite for Transactional Memory

Mohammad Ansari, Christos Kotselidis, Ian Watson,
Chris Kirkham, Mikel Luján, and Kim Jarvis

School of Computer Science, University of Manchester
{ansari,kotselidis,watson,kirkham,lujan,jarvis}@cs.manchester.ac.uk

Abstract. Transactional Memory (TM) is a concurrent programming paradigm that aims to make concurrent programming easier than fine-grain locking, whilst providing similar performance and scalability. Several TM systems have been made available for research purposes. However, there is a lack of a wide range of non-trivial benchmarks with which to thoroughly evaluate these TM systems.

This paper introduces Lee-TM, a non-trivial and realistic TM benchmark suite based on Lee's routing algorithm. The benchmark suite provides sequential, lock-based, and transactional implementations to enable direct performance comparison. Lee's routing algorithm has several of the desirable properties of a non-trivial TM benchmark, such as large amounts of parallelism, complex contention characteristics, and a wide range of transaction durations and lengths. A sample evaluation shows unfavourable transactional performance and scalability compared to lock-based execution, in contrast to much of the published TM evaluations, and highlights the need for non-trivial TM benchmarks.

1 Introduction

Concurrent programming is a complex discipline known for its difficulty even to obtain correct programs. Orchestrating lock acquisition and release between multiple threads to ensure functionally correct execution is challenging and time-consuming. Transactional Memory [1,2] (TM) is an alternative concurrent programming paradigm that promises to abstract away the difficulties of managing access to shared resources, but still maintain good scalability and performance. With the growing need for widespread concurrent programming to take advantage of multi-core processors [3], TM research has surged.

Following from database theory, TM guarantees atomicity, consistency, and isolation among threads accessing shared structures, but abstracts away the details of how these guarantees are achieved. Programmers simply have to annotate those parts of their code that access shared structures as *transactions*, and the TM system automatically detects and manages access conflicts.

Recently, several Software TM (STM) systems have been proposed in the literature that provide sufficient performance for use as research platforms such as DSTM2 [4], McRT-STM [5], RSTM [6], tinySTM [7], and TL2 [8]. However,

A. Bourgeois and S.Q. Zheng (Eds.): ICA3PP 2008, LNCS 5022, pp. 196–207, 2008.

there is a lack of non-trivial benchmarks with which to evaluate them, and with which to evaluate novel TM ideas.

Lee-TM is a new non-trivial benchmark suite for TM systems based on the well known Lee's routing algorithm [9] used in circuit routing. Lee's routing algorithm has many of the desirable properties of a non-trivial TM benchmark such as large amounts of parallelism, complex contention characteristics, and a wide range of transaction durations and lengths. Lee-TM provides the following implementations of Lee's routing algorithm: sequential, coarse-grain and medium-grain locking, and transactional and optimized transactional. Lock-based implementations are provided to enable direct performance comparison with transactional versions, and meaningfully measure the benefit of using TM.

The rest of this paper is organized as follows. Section 2 gives an overview of TM and the desirable properties of non-trivial benchmarks. Section 3 describes Lee's routing algorithm, and Section 4 describes the implementations provided by the Lee-TM benchmark suite. Section 5 presents a sample evaluation using a state-of-the-art TM system. Section 6 describes related work, and Section 7 concludes this paper.

2   TM and Non-trivial Benchmarks

TM is a concurrent programming paradigm that aims to make parallel programming as straightforward as programming with coarse-grain locks, but provide the performance and scalability of fine-grain locks. TM requires a programmer to annotate those parts of their code that access shared structures as *transactions*, and an underlying TM run-time automatically detects and manages *access conflicts*. A transaction performs writes on shadow memory as the run-time maintains a *read set* of accessed data, and *write set* of modified data. Access conflicts between concurrently executing transactions occur as read/write or write/write conflicts to shared data, and are detected by the TM run-time by comparing the read and write sets of all transactions. This *validation* of sets can be lazy (at the end of a transaction's execution its sets are compared against all others), or eager (each read or write request is compared as it happens). When a conflict is detected, it is necessary to *abort* (and restart) one of the conflicting transactions. *Contention management* is invoked to make this decision, and there are several contention management policies in the literature [10,11,12]. Only when a transaction completes execution (i.e. *commits*), are the values in its write set made visible to the rest of the program.

However, there is a lack of complex TM benchmarks with which to evaluate TM systems, and it has been argued [13] that non-trivial, or realistic, benchmarks are needed to further TM research (by studying their execution), and to present the 'real' benefits of TM. Informally, the desirable features of a non-trivial TM benchmark are:

- large amounts of potential parallelism
- difficult to fine-grain parallelize using locks (making TM attractive),

- based on a real-world application (giving confidence in TM),
- several types of transactions (several annotated code blocks),
- complex contention (amount of contention varies widely during execution),
- transactions with a wide range of durations (length), and
- transactions with a wide range of numbers of data accesses (size).

Recently, non-trivial TM benchmarks have become an active research area, and a few non-trivial benchmarks have appeared in the literature [13,14] that meet many of the characteristics mentioned above, and they are compared with Lee's routing algorithm in the related work (Section 6). Lee's algorithm is presented in the next section.

3   Lee's Routing Algorithm

Circuit routing is the process of automatically producing an interconnection between electronic components. Lee's routing algorithm is attractive for parallelization as realistic circuits consist of thousands of routes, and each one can potentially be concurrently routed. Table 1 presents key terminology used in this paper. Lee's routing algorithm connects a source grid cell to a target grid cell in two phases: *expansion* and *backtracking* (Figure 1). Expansion performs a breadth-first search from the source grid cell until the target grid cell is located, or all cells have been visited. During the search each grid cell is checked that it is not occupied, and then numbered by its distance from the source grid cell. Occupied cells cannot be crossed directly, and routing must divert around them.

Table 1. Circuit routing terminology

Grid — represents abstractly the final printed circuit board on which all components and routes will be placed. The grid can be multi-layered, permitting a 3D grid
Grid cell — a grid consists of indivisible grid cells.
Grid block — contiguous grid cells can be grouped into grid blocks.
Route — a list of grid cells that connects a source grid cell to a target grid cell.
Obstruction — a predefined grid block inaccessible for routing. Examples are electronic components, mounting holes, servicing areas, etc.

Backtracking executes if expansion locates the target grid cell. Backtracking starts at the target grid cell and iteratively finds a neighboring grid cell with a lower number than its own and occupies it, until it reaches the source grid cell.

It is usual to perform routing in ascending order of length, i.e. shortest routes first. This ensures that longer routes, which naturally have more alternatives, do not displace shorter ones from their natural positions. This also minimizes the number of unroutable routes; a desirable property for performance comparisons.

In addition, to achieve successful and realistic routing of the example circuits, a certain amount of refinement in both the expansion and backtracking phases of the algorithm have been added. These are concerned with constraining the

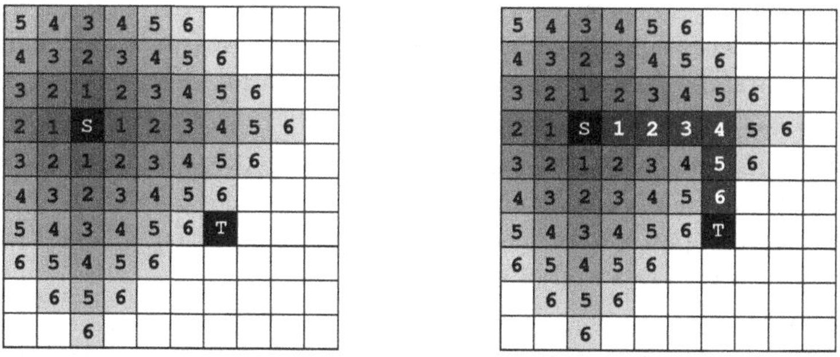

Expansion phase from source grid cell S to target grid cell T.

Backtrack phase connecting target grid cell T to source grid cell S.

Fig. 1. Illustration of expansion and backtracking in Lee's routing algorithm

routes in certain ways so that the routing does not generate a 'spaghetti' layout, and their detail is omitted in this paper.

4   Lee-TM

Lee-TM is a benchmark suite that has five implementations of Lee's routing algorithm: sequential, coarse-grain and medium-grain lock-based, and transactional and optimized transactional. They are named Lee-TM-seq, Lee-TM-cg, Lee-TM-mg, Lee-TM-t, and Lee-TM-ter, respectively, and are described below.

4.1   Sequential (Lee-TM-seq)

First, the source and target grid cell coordinates of each route, and coordinates for each obstruction, are read from a file. The obstructions are marked on the grid immediately, whilst the source-target pairs are added to a work queue. The work queue is then sorted in ascending route length order, as motivated in Section 3.

The main program loop gets a route from the work queue by calling the function getNextRoute(), and then performs expansion and backtracking with layNextRoute(). Expansion is performed by reading from a *main grid* and writing the expansion values on a private *temporary grid*. If the expansion is successful, the values in the temporary grid are used in backtracking, which writes to the main grid. The program finishes when the work queue is empty.

4.2   Concurrent Implementations

Minimal changes are required to make Lee-TM-seq multi-threaded. Each thread needs its own temporary grid, and the work queue needs to be synchronized to ensure multiple threads do not get the same route. The single work queue could become a bottleneck, but the experiments have not yet shown contention in its access. Nonetheless, a future version of the benchmark will decentralize the work queue. Finally, access to the main grid needs to be kept consistent, and this is explained separately for each concurrent implementation below.

Coarse-Grain Lock-Based (Lee-TM-cg). Lee-TM-cg is simple: all threads serialize on access to `layNextRoute()`. This prevents the main grid from being read by a thread (expansion) while another thread is modifying it (backtracking), which could lead to a race condition.

Medium-Grain Lock-Based (Lee-TM-mg). Lee-TM-mg splits the main grid into as many equal-sized grid blocks as there are threads and associates a lock with each grid block. For each route, if the source and target coordinates are located in the same grid block, then the associated lock is requested, and routing is performed. If the source and target coordinates are in different grid blocks, then multiple alternatives are available.

A complex alternative for routes that span multiple grid blocks is to acquire locks for all the necessary grid blocks. A priori, it is impossible to know which grid blocks may be needed, thus requiring progressive lock acquisition. Without a careful lock acquisition/release protocol in place, threads will deadlock. This approach is applicable to fine-grain locking, and quickly shows how challenging that would be to implement (consequently making TM attractive).

Instead, Lee-TM-mg adopts a simpler alternative where routes that do not fit in a single grid block are added to a *deferred work queue*. Once the main work queue is exhausted, the grid blocks are re-sized such that there are half as many as before, and the deferred work queue is swapped with the main queue. As grid blocks double in size at each swap of work queues, more routes can be laid. This reduction of grid blocks continues until there is only one grid block for the whole grid, at which point any existing route will definitely be routed or discarded (as unroutable), albeit serially.

Transactional (Lee-TM-t). There is something naturally transactional about circuit routing. Each route can be treated as an independent transaction. Each routing transaction can perform its own expansion, backtrack, and then try to commit the route it has found. If any of the grid cells used by the route have concurrently been occupied and committed by another route, then the transaction must be abandoned and restarted. However, it is important to realize that now the detection of interference, abandonment and restarting are fundamental functionality provided by TM. There is no need to program safe access to the main grid explicitly as is required with the previous lock-based implementations.

Lee-TM-t is implemented in DSTM2 [4], a state-of-the-art Java STM implementation. DSTM2 transactional semantics require concurrently accessed data to be annotated as transactional data. Since DSTM2 offers object-level conflict detection the main grid was changed from a three dimensional primitive array into a three dimensional transactional object array. This was the only change needed to provide the equivalent of fine-grain locking, but using transactions.

Optimized Transactional (Lee-TM-ter). Lee-TM-ter extends Lee-TM-t. Watson *et al.* [15] studied Lee's routing algorithm in an abstracted TM environment. Their key insight was understanding that the expansion phase adds unnecessary data to the read set, and that a transaction that generates a complete route between a source point and a destination point simply needs in its read set those grid cells that identify the complete route; no more, no less. They suggested that using early release [16], which removes data from the read set before any validation occurs, would optimize the read set and lead to dramatically more exploitable parallelism. The optimized transactional implementation provided by Lee-TM implements this approach.

4.3   Verifier

Lee-TM includes a verifier to check that all successful routes exist on the grid when routing is complete. A verification error suggests either an error in the code (if it has been changed) or in the TM system if executing transactional implementations. This feature is useful when evaluating novel TM ideas, as subtle errors in the TM system can be difficult to recognize from the, often large, execution output of a non-trivial benchmark that has no verifier.

5   Workload Characterization

A sample evaluation using a state-of-the-art TM system, called DSTM2 [4], is presented to highlight the value of Lee-TM. A discussion of the performance results is presented, followed by an investigation of the transactional characteristics of Lee-TM's transactional implementations to explain the observed performance.

5.1   Experimental Environment

The lock-based and transactional implementations provided by Lee-TM are compared using one synthetic and two real circuit boards (Figure 2) — each circuit is of size 600×600, and two layers. The workload characterization is performed on a shared memory 8-core (i.e. 4 dual core) Opteron 2.4GHz machine running openSUSE 10.1 64-bit and Sun JDK 1.6 64-bit with flags -Xms1024m -Xmx4096m, with 2, 4, or 8 threads. The transactional implementations are executed using all contention management policies [10,11,12] provided with DSTM2, but results are only shown for the Priority contention manager, as it had the best performance overall. The Priority manager aborts younger transactions, i.e. those with the most recent start time. Experiments are run three times and the best results reported.

5.2   Sample Performance Evaluation

The first experiment employs a trivial synthetic circuit layout, shown in Figure 2a. It contains 841 sparsely spaced short routes with no overlaps, i.e. 841 transactions to commit, with no possible contention. The aim of this experiment is to present baseline performance and scalability that can be achieved by lock-based and transactional implementations.

Figure 2b shows the execution time to route the circuit *simple*. For Lee-TM-cg there is no speedup regardless of the number of threads used. This occurs since the the coarse-grain lock on the whole main grid effectively leads to serial execution. Lee-TM-mg shows poor results initially, but has a speedup of 2.5 from 2 to 8 threads, and surpasses coarse-grain performance at 8 threads. Lee-TM-mg shows poorer than expected results because the routes, all having identical length, are ordered top-left to bottom-right, thus all threads are usually attempting to acquire the same grid block lock. The transactional implementations perform best in all cases except at two threads, and scale well with a 3.4 fold speedup from 2 to 8 threads.

Figures 2c and 2e show two complex circuit called *main* and *mem*, respectively. Both are microcode microprocessor layouts consisting of 1506 and 3101 routes, i.e. transactions to commit, respectively, and were used in routing algorithm research. The layouts contain a rich variety of route lengths and overlaps. Their execution times are shown in Figures 2d and 2f, respectively.

Lee-TM-cg again shows no scalability regardless of the number of threads. Lee-TM-mg has better initial performance than with the circuit *simple* because it is less prone to the problem of route ordering, but shows worse scalability with a speedup of only 1.2 from 2 to 8 threads. However, the most significant outcome is that of the transactional implementations.

Lee-TM-t is consistently worse than both lock-based implementations by a large margin. Even in the best case (at 2 threads) it is 3.8 times slower than Lee-TM-mg, and the scalability is far worse than seen with the circuit *simple*, with a speedup of only 1.16 from 2 to 8 threads. Lee-TM-ter performs 2-3 times better than Lee-TM-t, and has a speedup of 2.15 from 2 to 8 threads, but is only on par with Lee-TM-cg performance at 8 threads.

It is obvious that transactional performance and scalability seen in the circuit *simple* has not been realized with the two more complex circuits. To better understand the losses in performance, the next section analyzes profiled data to characterize the transactional behavior of Lee's routing algorithm.

5.3   Analysis of the Transactional Profile

Figure 3a shows the ratio of aborts to commits for each experiment. The experiment with the circuit *simple* has no aborts by design, but the other two complex circuits have an increasing ratio of aborts as the number of threads rises. The benefit of early release is obvious as the ratio of aborts to commits falls dramatically for both *main* and *mem*, re-emphasizing the benefit of early release as concluded by Watson et al. [15].

Figure 3b shows the percentage of time spent executing wasted work (aborted transactions). Both *main* and *mem* show increasing amounts of wasted work as the number of threads rises, but the wasted work for Lee-TM-t increases by greater amounts. This helps explain difference in execution time between the two

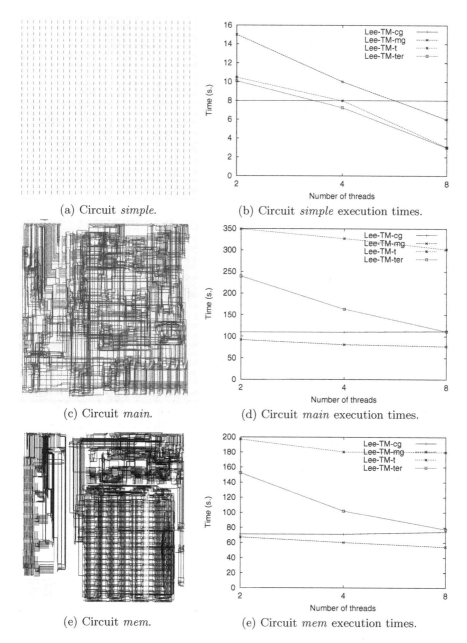

(a) Circuit *simple.*

(b) Circuit *simple* execution times.

(c) Circuit *main.*

(d) Circuit *main* execution times.

(e) Circuit *mem.*

(e) Circuit *mem* execution times.

Fig. 2. Circuits used in the sample evaluation, and their execution times using lock-based and transactional implementations

implementations: Lee-TM-t spends more time executing aborted transactions. Since the ratios in Figure 3a correlate to those in Figure 3b, there may be benefit

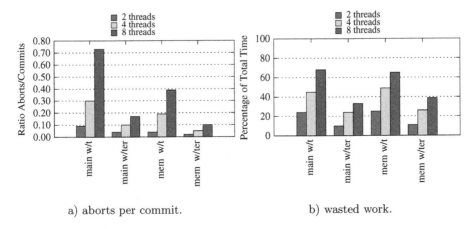

a) aborts per commit.   b) wasted work.

Fig. 3. Transactional profiling data: a) shows the ratio of aborted transactions to committed transactions, b) shows the percentage of total execution time spent executing aborted transactions (wasted work). Circuit *simple* is not shown as it has no aborts or wasted work. Note: Lee-TM-t results have 'w/t' suffix, and Lee-TM-ter results have 'w/ter' suffix.

in attempting to detect doomed (to abort) transactions sooner, and abort them early to reduce the amount of wasted work, and improve execution time.

Figure 4 shows the abort histograms for the circuits *main* and *mem* (the histograms for the circuit *simple* have been omitted as it has no aborts). These graphs show the count of routes aborted by a given number before finally committing, and present perhaps the most interesting results because the histogram for Lee-TM-t indicates that a few routes take tens of aborted attempts before committing. For circuit *main* at 8 threads, Lee-TM-ter commits all routes within nine aborts each, while Lee-TM-t commits 26 routes with more than nine aborts each (the abort profile of the circuit *mem* shows similar statistics). Although this represents 1.7% of the routes (i.e. workload), it is almost solely responsible for a 35% difference in wasted work between Lee-TM-t and Lee-TM-ter for the circuit *main* at 8 threads. The large amount of aborts experienced by a small number of transactions is another sign that the contention manager could be enhanced to make better decisions, and thus may be an avenue to explore in future work to reduce the amount of wasted work.

Finally, Table 2 shows the ratio of the average committed transaction read set size in Lee-TM-t to Lee-TM-ter. The benefit of early release is significant in

Table 2. Ratio of avg committed transaction read set size in Lee-TM-t to Lee-TM-ter

	simple	main	mem
2 threads	41	453	288
4 threads	41	342	226
8 threads	41	267	190

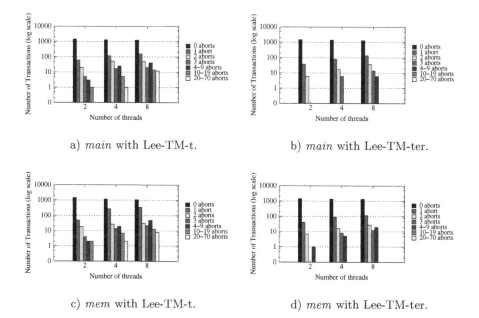

a) *main* with Lee-TM-t.   b) *main* with Lee-TM-ter.

c) *mem* with Lee-TM-t.   d) *mem* with Lee-TM-ter.

Fig. 4. Abort histograms of routes in complex circuits *main* and *mem*. Circuit *simple* is not shown as it has no aborts.

the execution of all three circuits, resulting in Lee-TM-ter's read set shrinking by at least 41 times over Lee-TM-t's read set. Reducing the read set results in faster execution time as it reduces cache thrashing.

6 Related Work

The lack of complex benchmarks for studying TM is a known issue. The majority of benchmarks used in the evaluation of TM systems fit into the following categories:

- micro-benchmarks, such as linked lists, and concurrent hash tables;
- benchmarks whose parallelism is already explicit and optimized, such as JavaGrande, and SPECjbb; and
- benchmarks with limited concurrency, such as SPEC JVM98.

Apart from Lee-TM, few other benchmarks provide complex transactional behavior. Those seen in the literature are STMBench7 [13], and the STAMP benchmark suite [14]. STMBench7 is adapted from OO7, a database benchmark, and has over 5000 lines of code. It simulates real-world scenarios by performing dynamic and complex modifications and traversals on a non-trivial shared data structure. STMBench7 provides a coarse-grain and medium-grain locking implementation for comparison with the transactional one. The STAMP benchmark suite consists of three benchmarks: genome (gene sequencing), kmeans (k-clustering), and vacation (travel booking system). Each of these is over 1000 lines of code, and is supplied with a transactional and a sequential implementation, but no lock-based solution. Lee-TM has a smaller code base (<800 lines), yet provides complex transactional behavior through the complex circuits employed for routing. Lee-TM has sequential, coarse-grain and medium-grain locking, transactional, and optimized transactional (using early release) implementations.

Both STMBench7 and STAMP benchmarks (except for genome), due to the nature of their computation, lack a verifier as there is no simple way to validate the final data structure. Lee-TM comes with a verifier since it is easy to use the original circuit layout data set and follow, for each route, from the source grid cell to the target grid cell.

7   Summary

Lee-TM is a new benchmark suite based on Lee's routing algorithm with sequential, lock-based, and transactional implementations. Lee's routing algorithm provides many of the desirable properties of a non-trivial TM benchmark through complex circuit layouts, such as large amounts of parallelism, complex contention behavior, and large variety of transaction durations and sizes.

A sample performance evaluation using complex circuits, which had potential parallelism in the thousands, showed optimized transactional performance only reaching par with coarse-grain locking at 8 threads, and never reaching the performance of medium-grain locking. Unoptimized transactional execution was, in the best case, four times slower than medium-grain locking. This result highlights the need for complex benchmarks to stress TM systems.

The analysis of the transactional characteristics of Lee-TM's transactional implementations showered there is much work wasted in executing doomed (to abort) transactions. At 8 threads, less than 2% of the transactions, due to being aborted tens of times, resulted in unoptimized transactional execution having 35% more wasted work than the optimized transactional execution, and consequently 2.7x slower execution time. The analysis identified contention management as a target of future research to make better decisions that result in less wasted work, and thus better performance.

References

1. Shavit, N., Touitou, D.: Software transactional memory. In: PODC 1995: Proceedings of the 14th Annual ACM Symposium on Principles of Distributed Computing, pp. 204–213. ACM Press (1995)
2. Herlihy, M., Eliot, J., Moss, B.: Transactional memory: Architectural support for lock-free data structures. In: ISCA 1993: Proceedings of the 20th Annual International Symposium on Computer Architecture, pp. 289–300. ACM Press (1993)
3. Olukotun, K., Hammond, L.: The future of microprocessors. ACM Queue 3(7), 26–29 (2005)

4. Herlihy, M., Luchangco, V., Moir, M.: A flexible framework for implementing software transactional memory. In: OOPSLA 2006: Proceedings of the 21st Annual Conference on Object-Oriented Programming Systems, Languages, and Applications, pp. 253–262. ACM Press (2006)

5. Saha, B., Ali-Reza Adl-Tabatabai, Hudson, R.L., Minh, C.C., Hertzberg, B.: McRT-STM: a high performance software transactional memory system for a multi-core runtime. In: PPoPP 2006: Proceedings of the 11th ACM SIGPLAN Symposium on Principles and Practice of Parallel Programming, pp. 187–197. ACM Press, New York (2006)

6. Marathe, V., Spear, M., Herio, C., Acharya, A., Eisenstat, D., Scherer III, W., Scott, M.: Lowering the overhead of software transactional memory. In: TRANSACT 2006: First ACM SIGPLAN Workshop on Transactional Computing (June 2006)

7. Riegel, T., Felber, P., Fetzer, C.: A lazy snapshot algorithm with eager validation. In: Dolev, S. (ed.) DISC 2006. LNCS, vol. 4167, pp. 284–298. Springer, Heidelberg (2006)

8. Dice, D., Shalev, O., Shavit, N.: Transactional locking II. In: Dolev, S. (ed.) DISC 2006. LNCS, vol. 4167, pp. 194–208. Springer, Heidelberg (2006)

9. Rubin, F.: The Lee path connection algorithm. IEEE Transactions on Computers C-23(9), 907–914 (1974)

10. Scherer III, W., Scott, M.: Contention management in dynamic software transactional memory. In: CSJP 2004: Workshop on Concurrency and Synchronization in Java Programs (July 2004)

11. Scherer III, W., Scott, M.: Advanced contention management for dynamic software transactional memory. In: PODC 2005: Proceedings of the 24th Annual Symposium on Principles of Distributed Computing, pp. 240–248. ACM Press (2005)

12. Guerraoui, R., Herlihy, M., Pochon, B.: Toward a theory of transactional contention managers. In: PODC 2005: Proceedings of the 24th Annual Symposium on Principles of Distributed Computing, pp. 258–264. ACM Press (2005)

13. Guerraoui, R., Kapałka, M., Vitek, J.: STMBench7: A benchmark for software transactional memory. In: EuroSys 2007: Proceedings of the 2nd European Systems Conference, pp. 315–324. ACM Press (2007)

14. Minh, C.C., Trautmann, M., Chung, J.W., McDonald, A., Bronson, N., Casper, J., Kozyrakis, C., Olukotun, K.: An effective hybrid transactional memory system with strong isolation guarantees. In: ISCA 2007: Proceedings of the 34th Annual International Symposium on Computer Architecture, pp. 69–80. ACM Press, New York (2007)

15. Watson, I., Kirkham, C., Luján, M.: A study of a transactional parallel routing algorithm. In: PACT 2007: Proceedings of the 16th International Conference on Parallel Architectures and Compilation Techniques, pp. 388–400. IEEE Computer Society Press (2007)

16. Herlihy, M., Luchangco, V., Moir, M., Scherer III, W.N.: Software transactional memory for dynamic-sized data structures. In: PODC 2003: Proceedings of the 22nd Annual Symposium on Principles of Distributed Computing, pp. 92–101. ACM Press (2003)

Performance of OpenMP Benchmarks on Multicore Processors

Ami Marowka

Shenkar College of Engineering and Design
12 Anna Frank, Ramat-Gan, 52526, Israel
amimar2@yahoo.com

Abstract. The appearance of Multicore processors brings high performance computing to the desktop and opens the doors of mainstream computing for parallel computing. This paradigm shift leads the integration of parallel programming standards for high-end shard-memory machine architectures into desktop programming environments. In this paper we present a performance study of these new systems. We evaluate the performance of an OpenMP shared-memory programming model that is integrated into Microsoft Visual Studio C++ 2005 and Intel C++ compilers on a multicore processor. We benchmarked using the NAS OpenMP high-level applications benchmarks and the EPCC OpenMP low-level benchmarks. We report the basic timings, scalability, and run-time profiles of each benchmark and analyze the running results.

1 Introduction

For many years parallel computers have been used only by an exclusive scientific niche. Only universities and research institutions backed by government budgets or funded by multi-billion-dollar companies could afford to purchase state-of-the-art parallel machines. Multiprocessor machines are very expensive and demand expertise in system administration and programming skills. Parallel computing therefore remains a specialized field of an exclusive community.

Now, two complementary technologies bring parallel computing to the desktop. On the hardware side is the multicore processor for desktop computers [1], and on the software side is the integration of the OpenMP parallel programming model into Microsoft Visual C++ 2005. These technologies promise massive exposure to parallel computing that nobody can ignore, thus making a technology shift unavoidable. Unfortunately, writing a parallel code is more complex than writing a serial code [2]. Parallel programming is extremely difficult. This is where the OpenMP programming model comes into the picture [3]. OpenMP helps developers to create multithreaded applications more easily while retaining the look and feel of serial programming.

The extra development effort and code complexity of parallel programming give rise to an obvious question Is it worthwhile? The best way to answer this question is by benchmarking. This paper presents a performance study of OpenMP shared-memory programming model [3] that was integrated into

A. Bourgeois and S.Q. Zheng (Eds.): ICA3PP 2008, LNCS 5022, pp. 208–219, 2008.

Microsoft Visual Studio C++ 2005 and Intel C++ compilers on a multicore processor. The benchmarking was conducted using the NAS OpenMP parallel benchmark suite [4] with different sizes of input classes, and the EPCC OpenMP directives benchmarks [7,12]. We report the basic timings, scalability, and run-time profiles of each benchmark and analyze the running results.

The rest of this paper is organized as follows. In Sections 2, 3, and 4 we provide brief overviews of the OpenMP, NPB benchmarks, and EPCC micro-benchmarks respectively. Section 5 is an in-depth analysis of the benchmarks results and Section 6 presents our conclusions.

2   OpenMP Programming Model

OpenMP is a tool for writing multi-threaded applications in a shared memory environment [3]. It consists of a set of compiler directives and library routines. The compiler generates a multi-threaded code based on the specified directives. OpenMP is essentially a comparatively recent standardization SMP (Symmetric Multi-Processor) development and practice. By using OpenMP, it is relatively easy to create parallel applications in FORTRAN, C, and C++. Compiler and third party applications support is becoming more common.

An OpenMP program begins with a single thread of execution called the master thread. The master thread spawns teams of threads in response to OpenMP directives, which perform work in parallel. Parallelism is thus added incrementally: the serial program evolves into a parallel one. OpenMP directives are inserted at key locations in the source code. These directives take the form of comments in FOR-TRAN and pragmas in C and C++. The compiler interprets the directives and creates the necessary code to parallelize the indicated tasks/regions. The parallel region is the basic construct that creates a team of threads and initiates parallel execution. Most OpenMP directives apply to structured blocks, which are blocks of code with one entry point at the top and one exit point at the bottom. The number of threads created when entering parallel regions is controlled by the value of the environment variable OMP_NUM_THREADS. The number of threads can also be set by a function call from within the program, which takes precedence over the environment variable.

3   NAS Parallel Benchmark

We used the NPB OpenMP-C benchmark suite to evaluate the OpenMP perfor-mance on our dual-core computer. The NPB OpenMP version is based on NPB 2.3-serial version and was developed as part of the Omni project [6]. The NAS Parallel Benchmarks (NPB) [4,5] was devised by the Numerical Aerodynamic Simulation Program of NASA for the performance analysis of highly parallel computers. The NPB are valuable since they are rigorous and close to real-life needed applications. The NPB consist of five kernels and three simulated appli-cations. They all compute or simulate different algorithmic and computational aspects of aerodynamic applications. For most of the kernels it is possible to select the problem size. Sometimes the problem sizes are called: Class S or T (12x12x12), Class W (24x24x24), and Class A 64x64x64). The following is a brief description of the five kernels and the three applications we used in our work.

Kernel EP. In the embarrassing parallel benchmark, two-dimensional statistics are accumulated from a large number of Gaussian pseudo-random numbers, which are generated according to a particular scheme that is well suited for parallel computation.

Kernel MG. The MG (Multi-grid) benchmark is a simplified multi-grid kernel, which solves a 3-D Poisson PDE. The Class W problem uses the same size grid as Class S but has a greater number of inner loop iterations.

Kernel CG. In the CG (Conjugate Gradient) benchmark, a conjugate gradient method is used to compute an approximation to the smallest eigen value of a large, sparse, symmetric positive definite matrix. This kernel is typical of unstructured grid computations applications.

Kernel FT. In the FT (3-D FFT PDE) benchmark, a 3-D partial differential equation is solved using FFTs. This kernel performs the essence of many spectral methods. This benchmark is somewhat unique in that computational library routines may be legally employed.

Kernel IS. The IS (Integer Sort) benchmark tests a sorting operation that is important in particle method codes. This type of application is similar to particle-in-cell applications of physics, wherein particles are assigned to cells and may drift out. The sorting operation is used to reassign particles to the appropriate cells.

BT is a simulated CFD application that uses an implicit algorithm to solve 3-dimensional (3-D) compressible Navier-Stokes equations. The finite differences solution to the problem is based on an Alternating Direction Implicit (ADI) approximate factorization that decouples the x, y, and z dimensions. The resulting systems are Block-Tridiagonal of 5X5 blocks and are solved sequentially along each dimension.

SP is a simulated CFD application that has a similar structure to BT. The finite differences solution to the problem is based on a Beam-Warming approximate factorization that decouples the x, y, and z dimensions. The resulting system has Scalar Pentadiagonal bands of linear equations that are solved sequentially along each dimension.

LU is a simulated CFD application that uses the symmetric successive over-relaxation (SSOR) method to solve a seven-block-diagonal system resulting from finite-difference discretization of the Navier-Stokes equations in 3-D by splitting it into block Lower and Upper triangular systems.

4   EPCC Microbenchmarks

The EPCC micro-benchmark suit is a set of benchmarks that measure the overhead incurred by OpenMP compiler directives of a specific OpenMP implementation [7,12]. Three classes of overhead can be measured by the EPCC micro-benchmark suit: synchronization, loop scheduling, and array operations. The current release supports the OpenMP 2.0 standard. The overhead cost incurred by a specific compiler directive is measured by comparing the sequential execution time of a section code containing the compiler directive, and the parallel execution time of the same code. The measurements are repeated a few times for statistical stability. By using the EPCC micro-benchmark, the developer is able to compare the relative efficiency of different implementations of OpenMP running on the same platform; choose the more efficient construct of two semantically equivalent; and predict the overall performance of an application. Although there are other tools in the market that were developed for similar purposes as EPCC, such as ompP [10] and Sphinx [13], EPCC software is considered the de-facto standard of its kind.

5   Experimental Results

We tested the performance of the EPCC micro-benchmarks and the NAS OpenMP kernels and applications on dual-core computers based on Intel Pentium D 820 2.80 GHz with 2 X 1MB L2 cache, 2 X 16KB L1 cache and 512MB main memory, and Intel Core 2 Duo processor 1.86Ghz E6300, 4MB shared L2 cache, 2 X 32KB L1 cache and 1GB main memory. On the software side we used the OpenMP version 2.0 of Intel C++ OpenMP compiler 9.1 under the XP operating system. All the benchmarks were also compiled by Microsoft Visual Studio C++ 2005 and evaluated on the above dual-core machines. However, the differences between the results obtained by using the Microsoft and Intel compilers are negligible, so they are not shown here. Only the results obtained by Intel compiler are shown here.

First, we measured the overhead cost of the OpenMP directives by using the EPCC micro-benchmarks. In general, it is an important practice to start parallel application benchmarks by examining on the testbed machine the overhead incurred by the primitive functions used by the programming model for parallelism. This way the programmer has a priori knowledge of the effects of various possible overhead sources on the total performance of the applications. Figures 1, 2, 3, and 4 show results measured on the Intel Pentium D and Intel Core 2 Duo machines while running EPCC micro-benchmarks compiled by Intel C++ compiler 9.1.

Figure 1 depicts the OpenMP synchronization overheads measured by running the EPCC micro- benchmarks with two threads. First, it can be observed that the overhead cost is less than 20 microseconds in all cases. This low overhead has a negligible effect on the NAS applications performance that will be discussed later. Second, the OpenMP directive overheads on Intel Core 2 Duo are up to 50% less than the overheads incurred by the directives on Intel Pentium D. This improvement is mainly due to the L2 cache memory architecture of the Core 2 Duo processor. We will elaborate on this architecture later. Third, we also mesuared the directive overhrads by running the EPCC benchmarks with one and four threads (the results are not shown here). we found that the overhead of

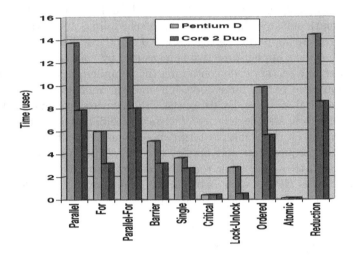

Fig. 1. OpenMP Synchronization overheads of two threads on Intel Pentium D and Intel Core 2 Duo machines

a single core is relatively high. Thus, it is better for single threaded applications to be compiled with the OpenMP option set to off. Moreover, the overhead in the case of a single thread is usually the same as in two threads, while in the case of four threads the overhead usually increases dramatically due to the competition of two threads on a single core.

Further analysis of the results leads to the following conclusions: the combined directive Parallel-For is more efficiently used than the Parallel and For directives, which are used separately; it costs less to use the Critical directive than to use the Lock-Unlock pair directives; the Barrier and Single directives have a relatively low overhead; the Order and Reduction clauses have a relatively high cost, as can be expected; and, finally, the overhead of Atomic directive is negligible and thus is recommended for use, where possible, instead of the Critical or Lock-Unlock directives. We omit the discussion on scalability with respect to the number of cores because it is useless to do such an analysis when the machines have only two cores.

Figure 2 depicts the Array (or privatization) overheads of four clauses: Private, Firstprivate, CopyPrivate, and Copyin for 2 threads on Intel Pentium D and Core 2 Duo machines. First, it can be observed again that Intel Core 2 Duo processor presents lower overheads than Pentium D processor. Moreover, the results show that the Private, Firstprivate, and Copyin clauses are incurred similar and acceptable overhead cost (15 μs and 8 used for Pentium D and Core 2 Duo respectively) for the array allocation process. The CopyPrivate demonstrates excellent performance and a negligible overhead cost that enables super-efficient inter-threads communication.

Figures 3 and 4 describe the OpenMP loop scheduling overheads of the Static, Dynamic, and Guided clauses for chunk sizes of 1 to 128 when running with two

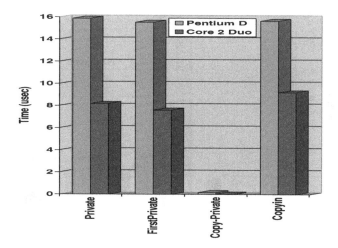

Fig. 2. OpenMP Array Scheduling (privatization) overheads of two threads on Intel Pentium D and Intel Core 2 Duo machines

threads, for Core 2 Duo and Pentium D machines respectively. It can be observed that each clause has a different pattern. In the case of Pentium D, the block cyclic scheduling (Static) presents similar overhead (~ 5.8 μs) for all chunk sizes. The Dynamic scheduling is decreases rapidly from the maximum point at a chunk size of one (32.21 μs) to the minimum at a chunk size of 128 (6.80 μs). The Guided scheduling has a similar pattern but with a more moderate decreasing curve. The maximum point is at a chunk size of one (9.51 μs) and the minimum point is at a chunk size of 128(3.18 μs). The conclusion is that by increasing the chunk size the loop scheduling overhead is minimized.

In the case of Core 2 Duo, the loop scheduling overheads present similar pattern compare to Pentium D, but the overheads are up to 50% lower than those of Pentium D. The block cyclic scheduling (Static) is reach its optimal overhead at a chunk size of eight (2.47 μs). The Dynamic scheduling is decreases rapidly from the maximum point at a chunk size of one (20.21 μs) to the minimum at a chunk size of 64 (3.32 μs). The Guided scheduling has a similar pattern but with a more moderate decreasing curve. The maximum point is at a chunk size of one (4.59 μs) and the minimum point is at a chunk size of 128(3.35 μs).

The bottom line of the EPCC micro-benchmarks results is that the overhead incurred by the OpenMP directives and clauses are low and will not harm the performance of the NBP application benchmarks.

The NPB benchmarks were conducted with three different input sizes: S, W, and A for two threads. The total running time of each benchmark was measured by wall-clock time. The speedup, efficiency, and the overhead of each run were calculated as follows:

$Speedup = T_1/T_{p,k}$. Where T_1 is the time measured for running with single core and $T_{p,k}$ the time measured with p cores and k threads.

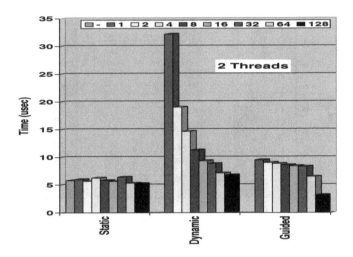

Fig. 3. OpenMP Loop Scheduling overheads of two threads on Intel Pentium D machine

Efficiency $= T_1/(p \cdot T_p)$. Where T_1 is the time measured for running with single core and T_p the time measured with p cores.

Overhead $= T_{p,k} - T_1/p$. Where T_1 is the time measured for running with single core and $T_{p,k}$ the time measured with p cores and k threads.

We ran the original benchmarks that appear in [6] without any modification. Due to space limitations, we present here only the running results where 2 cores were used, with 2 threads and input class W (24x24x24). However, the behavior of the benchmarks results for input classes S and A are similar to input class W. The results of the IS kernel are omitted due to a problem known to the developers of the benchmarks suit, which they will fix in the next release.

Table 1 presents the NPB efficiency as calculated from the total execution time and the overhead time (in seconds) when running on top of Pentium D machine for the class W of the seven different benchmarks in the NAS OpenMP suite. The results obtained with Core 2 Duo machine are very similar and are not shown here.

Figure 5 plots the calculated speedup of the NPB benchmarks, for the case of 2 threads, on Pentium D and Core 2 Duo machines. Figure 6 is a bar graph that depicts the percentage of the computation time and the overhead time as part of the total execution time, in the case of Pentium D machine.

Analysis of these results leads to the following findings:

The EP Kernel falls into the category of applications termed "embarrassingly parallel" based on the trivial partition ability of the problem, while incurring no data or functional dependencies, and requiring little or no communication between processors. It is included in the NPB suite to establish the reference point for peak performance on a given platform. Therefore, it is not surprising that EP achieved perfect speedup and efficiency (2.05 and 1.03 respectively) in the case of Pentium D.

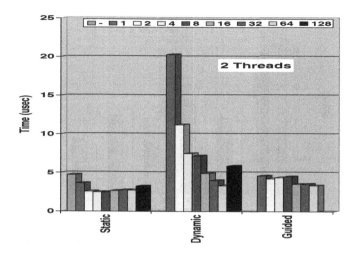

Fig. 4. OpenMP Loop Scheduling overheads of two threads on Intel Core 2 Duo machine

As can be observed from Figure 5, the speedups of Pentium D and Core 2 Duo machines are similar, and thus the following discussion is true for the case of Core 2 Duo although the numbers are of Pentium D case. The LU decomposition application shows good speedup and efficiency for two cores, 1.88 and 0.94 respectively, but in the case of 4 threads the speedup drops drastically to 0.17. The MG Kernel rigorously exercises both short and long distance communication, although the communication patterns are highly structured. The MG kernel shows more modest speedup (1.45) and efficiency (0.73) for 2 threads while for 4 threads the speedup drops to 0.87.

The rest of the benchmarks (FT, MG, CG, BT, and SP) show poor speedups and efficiencies. These results can be explained by the logical structure of the application, which does not match the underlying architecture of the dual-core processor. For example, the FT kernel uses FFT on a complex array to solve a three-dimensional partial differential equation. Communication patterns in this kernel are structured and long distance in nature and this benchmark represents the essence of many "spectral" codes or eddy turbulence simulations. The CG kernel is used in conjugate gradient methods to approximate the smallest eigenvalue of a symmetric, positive definite, sparse matrix with a random pattern of non-zeros. The communication patterns in this kernel are long- distance and unstructured.

These observations reveal the following conclusions. First, all the benchmarks, except EP, achieve very poor efficiency when the number of threads (4) is greater than the number of cores (2). It happens because the overhead caused by context-switch operations of the competing threads on the CPU resources is high. Moreover, two threads sharing a single core lead to cache conflicts that decrease the hit rate and thus degrade the performance.

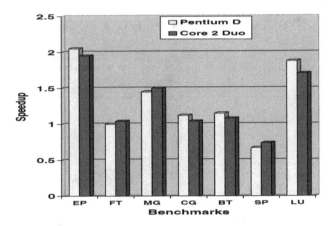

Fig. 5. NPB speedup results of EP, FT, MG, CG, BT, SP, and LU benchmarks for 2 cores; 2 threads; problem class W; on Pentium D and Core 2 Duo machines

The above poor performance of the NPB applications brought us, on the one hand, to extend our study further and to look for possible solutions to improve the performance but without restructuring the application programs, and on the other hand, to extend our understanding of how the underlying hardware works.

The Intel Pentium D processor has a different cache-memory architecture than Intel Core 2 Duo processors [8,9]. The Pentium D 820 processor is a "distributed" cache-memory with two separately L1 caches of 16KB each and two separately L2 caches of 1MB each. One the other side, The Core 2 Duo E6300 is a "shared" cache-memory with two separate L1 caches of 32KB each and a shared L2 cache of 4MB. To understand the implications of these two different architectures on the performance, lets look at the following example.

Let A[100] be a shared array used by two threads running on two different cores. The threads are writing the array at the same time. One thread accesses the first part of the array, A[0-49], and the second one accesses the second half of the array, A[50-99]. In the case of the Pentium D, array A will be copied into the L1 and L2 caches of each core. Now, each time one of the threads completes a write operation, there is a need to update the copy of array A in the neighboring

Table 1. NPB efficiency and overhead time of EP, FT, MG, CG, BT, SP, and LU benchmarks for 2 cores, 2 threads, and problem class W

	EP	FT	MG	CG	BT	SP	LU
Run Time(s)	12.26	0.90	0.61	0.78	15.10	52.31	13.26
Overhead(s)	0.02	0.45	0.16	0.34	4.46	34.67	0.78
Efficiency(s)	0.99	0.5	0.73	0.56	0.7	0.66	0.94

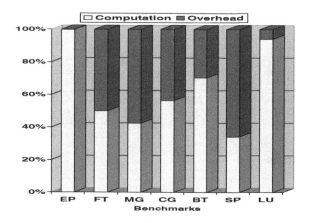

Fig. 6. NPB computation time vs. overhead time of EP, FT, MG, CG, BT, SP, and LU benchmarks for 2 cores, 2 threads and class W on Pentium D machine

core in order to maintain the caches consistency. This update is costly in terms of CPU cycles, as can be seen in Table 2. However, we expected an improvement in the case of Core 2 Duo processor because the L2 cache is shared, but we were disappointed to discover that NBP benchmarks showed only ∼ 4% improvment (in the case of FT. MG and SP) and ∼ 4% worsening (in the case of CG, BT and LU).

So, we continued to explore further and we found another obstacle that we were not aware of: the shared L2 cache of the Core 2 Duo is not banked. The L2 cache serves only one core at any given clock cycle, so a banked organization will not help. A round robin scheme is used to allocate L2 cache services to the cores for scenarios when both cores request L2 service. The false sharing penalty of the Core 2 Duo is depicted in Table 2 and was taken from [9].

We looked further for optimization possibilities for improving the performance of the applications but without need to rewritten the programs.

First, we used a thread affinity option to tie a thread to its data to improve data locality [11]. Since OpenMP does not support thread affinity capabilities we used the Windows operating systems SetThreadAffinityMask option. Monitoring the threads scheduling by the Intel VTune performance analyzer confirmed that each thread was tied to one core during the program execution. Unfortunately, we did not observe any improvement in the performance of the applications. Second, we changed the loop iterations scheduling by using the OpenMP schedule clause. The fact that most of the parallelism of the NPB applications is done by for work-sharing, encouraged us to find the optimal scheduling. We tried the Static, Dynamic, and Guided options with 1, 4, 8, 16, 32, 64, and 128 chunk sizes. Unfortunately, we cannot report any significant improvement in applications performance.

Table 2. False sharing penalties

Case	Data Location	Latency(cycles/nsec)
L1 to L1 Cache	L1 Cache	14 core cycles + 5.5 bus cycles
Through L2 Cache	L2 Cache	14 core cycles
Through Memory	Main Memory	14 core cycles + 5.5 bus cycles + 40-80 nsec

6 Conclusions

Multicore processors will dominate scientific computing, and commercial computing as well, in the near future. Understanding their performance characteristics is essential for design scalable and efficient applications. In this paper, we presented the scalability and efficiency of applications from NPB OpenMP-C suite and the overhead measurements of OpenMP directives and clauses running on Intel Pentium D, and Core 2 Duo machines using MS Visual studio C++ 2005 and Intel C++ compilers.

The benchmarking results show that most of the applications do not scale well, not because of the overhead incurred by the OpenMP directives, but because the NPB applications induced computation and communication patterns which are not cache friendly and result in a lot of false sharing situations. The diversified cache architectures of multicore processors call for new parallel programming languages and compilers that can use the hierarchy of cache memory systems in an efficient manner.

References

1. Geer, D.: Chip makers turn to multicore processors. IEEE Computer (May 2005)
2. Marowka, A.: Parallel Computing on Any Desktop. Communication of ACM 50(9), 74–78 (2007)
3. OpenMP Application Program Interface, http://www.openmp.org
4. Bailey, D.H., Harsis, T., Saphir, W., der Wijngaart, R.V., Woo, A., Yarrow, M.: The NAS Parallel Benchmarks 2.0. Report NAS-95-020, Nasa Ames Research Center (December 1995)
5. Jin, H., Frumkin, M., Yan, J.: The OpenMP Implementation of NAS Parallel Benchmarks and Its Performance. Report NAS-99-011, Nasa Ames Research Center (October 1999)
6. The Omni Project, http://phase.hpcc.jp/Omni/home.html
7. Mark Bull, J.: Measuring Synchronisation and Scheduling Overheads in OpenMP. In: Proceeding of First European Workshop on OpenMP (EWOMP 1999), Lund, Sweden (October 1999)
8. Doweck, J.: Inside Intel Core Micro architecture and Smart Memory Access. A White Paper, Intel (2006)
9. Mendelson, A., Mandelblat, J., Gochman, S., Shemer, A., Chabukswar, R., Niemeyer, E., Kumar, A.: ICMP Implementation in Systems Based on the Intel Core Duo Processor. Intel Technology Journal 10(02) (May 15, 2006)

10. Furlinger, K., Gerndt, M., Dongarra, J.: Scalability Analysis of the SPEC OpenMP Benchmarks on Large-Scale Shared Memory Multiprocessors. In: Proceeding of ICCS 2007 (2007)
11. Tian, T.: Tips for effective usage of the shared cache in multicore architectures. Embedded.com, Jaunyary 23 (2007),
    http://embedded.com/showArticle.jhtml?articleID=196902691
12. Bull, J.M., O'Neill, D.: Microbenchmark Suite for OpenMP 2.0. In: Proceedings of the Third European Workshop on OpenMP (EWOMP 2001), Barcelona, Spain, pp. 41–48 (September 2001)
13. Sphinx Micro-benchmark Suite,
    http://www.llnl.gov/CASC/RTS_Report/sphinx.html

Adaptive Loop Tiling for a Multi-cluster CMP

Jisheng Zhao, Matthew Horsnell, Mikel Luján, Ian Rogers,
Chris Kirkham, and Ian Watson

University of Manchester, UK
{jishengz,horsnell,mikel,irogers,chris,watson}@cs.man.ac.uk

Abstract. Loop tiling is a fundamental optimization for improving data
locality. Selecting the right tile size combined with the parallelization of
loops can provide additional performance increases in the modern of Chip
MultiProcessor (CMP) architectures. This paper presents a runtime optimization system which automatically parallelizes loops and searches
empirically for the best tile sizes on a scalable multi-cluster CMP. The
system is built on top of a virtual machine and targets the runtime parallelization and optimization of Java programs. Experimental results show
that runtime parallelization and tile size searching are capable of improving performance for two BLAS kernels and one Lattice-Boltzmann
simulation, despite overheads.

Keywords: Multi-Cluster CMP, Automatic Parallelization, Loop Tiling,
Feedback-Directed Optimization.

1 Introduction

The tiling of loop iteration spaces is among the most popular and most extensvely
studied automatic program optimization for improving data locality and cache
performance [17,6]. Selecting a suitable tile size is a critical step for improving
performance. Some approaches have been proposed to calculate an optimal tile
size for single processor architectures[7,13].

In the context of CMPs [9,12] and automatic parallelization, selecting the
tile size not only affects cache performance but also the load balance among
processors. For example, consider a 2-dimensional perfectly nested loop with a
square $N \times N$ iteration space for which the optimal tile size is $\frac{N}{3} \times \frac{N}{3}$ for a given
CMP using only one processor. When 4 processors are used in that CMP, load
imbalance will occur using the same tile size; 9 tiles divided among 4 processors
results in one processor receiving one extra tile.

Runtime optimization systems have the advantage of being able to observe
the behavior of an executing application, whereas static compilers rely on predicting that behavior. Due to the limited amount of information available to a
static compiler, optimizing parallel loop tiling for large CMP architectures can
only become more and more complex. Performing runtime empirical searches,
however, provide an alternative approach to improve the parallel execution of a
program on different configurations of a CMP architecture.

A. Bourgeois and S.Q. Zheng (Eds.): ICA3PP 2008, LNCS 5022, pp. 220–232, 2008.
© Springer-Verlag Berlin Heidelberg 2008

Based on our previous research [19], at runtime it is feasible to automatically parallelize loops and also empirically search for adequate loop tiling sizes in CMP architectures with acceptable overheads. In this paper we concentrate on *multi-cluster CMPs* and whether adequate loop tiling sizes can be found at runtime for the automatically parallelized loops. As explained in further details in Section 2, processors are grouped together into clusters and the cache hierarchy is split into multiple levels which either connect the processors within a cluster or connect sets of clusters. The JAMAICA multi-cluster CMP [10] (see Figure 1) contains private L1 and multiple shared L2 caches. The L2 cache is unified containing both data and instructions, further complicating predictions as to how much space is available to data alone.For a multi-cluster CMP system which connects all the clusters by the L2 cache bus, the data locality in each L2 cache determines significantly the runtime performance. This paper investigates optimizations that search for multiple tile sizes to best utilize two levels of on-chip caching in a multi-cluster CMP, using runtime information to drive the search algorithm, in conjunction with an Online Tuning Framework (OTF) [19]. To exploit the cache hierarchy and the cluster structure two tile sizes need to be determined. The runtime tuning mechanism applies loop tiling recursively to target both clusters and cache levels.

The remainder of the paper is organized as follows. Section 2 gives a brief overview of the JAMAICA multi-cluster CMP architecture used in this paper. Section 3 describes the OTF and proposes the runtime tuning mechanism for optimizing the multiple tile sizes. Section 4 describes the experimental methodology. Section 5 presents and discusses the results from experimental evaluation. Section 6 presents related work, while a summary of the paper is presented in Section 7.

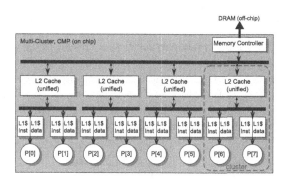

Fig. 1. JAMAICA: a multi-cluster CMP architecture

2 JAMAICA Multi-cluster CMP Architecture

To increase the ability of the JAMAICA architecture [2] to scale with the addition of more processings the single shared bus architecture is replaced by a scalable multi-level cache hierarchy [10] (shown in Figure 1).

The multi-level hierarchy is constructed by dividing the total number of processors into *clusters*. Each cluster contains a number of processing cores connected to a shared L2 cache. Each shared L2 cache is connected to a global on-chip memory network. This hierarchical approach can allow many more cores to be integrated onto a single chip, whilst maintaining shared memory, limiting the span of each interconnect to reduce the effects of cross-chip wire-delay, and with minimal design complexity.

Each intra-cluster network is independently arbitrated and accessed concurrently allowing the cores within each cluster to access the larger *cluster-shared* cache with less contention. The scalability comes at the expense of maintaining cache inclusion and the additional latency of sharing data between clusters. Such a hierarchy may be used to exploit an ever increasing transistor budget and as such is a feasible approach for future architectures.

3   Online Tuning Framework

The Online Tuning Framework (OTF) infrastructure, initially developed for CMP loop optimizations [19], performs automatic parallelization and enables runtime empirical search. It consists of three distinct elements: the Loop Parallelizing Compiler (LPC), the adaptive optimization component (see Section 3.1), and the runtime profiler (see Section 3.2).

The OTF is embedded within the adaptive optimization system (AOS) of the Jikes Research Virtual Machine (RVM) [4]. The Jikes RVM captures runtime information by instrumenting the running code at the method-level. Once the instrumentation indicates that a given method is hot (i.e. the number of times the method is executed is above a threshold), the AOS makes a decision whether to compile it using an optimizing compiler [5]. The OTF hijacks this decision, so that hot methods are also considered for parallelization by the LPC. The parallelized loop is reconstructed as a thread body which will be dispatched by a thread dispatcher method, as shown in Figure 2 (a). The procedure `loadConfiguration` loads the runtime configuration parameters (e.g. the loop tile size) from an AOS database. The `forkThreads` and `joinThreads` method calls create and synchronize those threads executing in parallel the loop body. The `aosProcess` is used to perform runtime tuning (see Figure 2 (b)).

```
void threadDispatcher(......) {        void threadDispatcherWithProfile(......) {
    loadConfiguration()                    long startCycle = getTimeBase();
    forkThreads()                          loadConfiguration();
    ......                                 forkThreads()
    joinThreads()                          ......
}                                          joinThreads()
                                           long executionCycle = getTimeBase() - startCycle;
                                           // Searching and Reconfiguration
                                           aosProcess(executionCycle, numIterations);
                                       }
             (a)                                        (b)
```

Fig. 2. Runtime profiling mechanism

3.1   Adaptive Optimization Component

The Adaptive Optimization Component (AOC) applies one or more optimizations deemed to improve a loop identified by the LPC. Presently, the AOC supports several adaptive optimizations for parallelizable code, although only adaptive tiling is described in this paper.

Adaptive tiling is applied when a perfectly nested loop is identified by the LPC. In the current implementation, 2-dimensional loop traversals of the iteration space are divided into tiles which are then distributed among automatically generated parallel threads. We extend the basic empirical search algorithm [19] to vary the number of loop iterations inside each tile for the clusters and levels of the memory hierarchy. These parameters directly impact the balance between costs associated with thread management, the cache efficiency, and system load. As illustrated in Figure 3, the runtime reconfigurable parameters $L1Tile\_x$, $L1Tile\_y$, $L2Tile\_x$ and $L2Tile\_y$ are tuned using runtime empirical search. Note the parameters $cluster\_x$ and $cluster\_y$ in the two most outer loops. These divide the iteration space among processor clusters. However, these are not part of the search directly as they are determined indirectly by $L2Tile\_x$ and $L2Tile\_y$. The JAMAICA multi-cluster CMP architecture provides a cluster affinity mechanism to create parallel threads either on the local cluster or on remote clusters, which can be viewed as a potential extension to the pthread affinity in Linux/Unix. By splitting the loop iteration space, each cluster has its own thread creator that distributes the tiles to the processors.

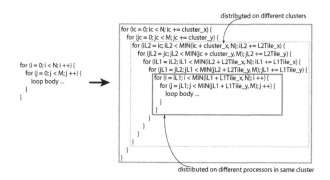

Fig. 3. Tiling transformation for runtime tuning

Each tile has a corresponding divisor pair. Given a divisor pair (D_i, D_j), D_i is the divisor corresponding to the outer loop iterator and D_j corresponds to the inner loop iterator. Adaptive tiling uses a simple hill-climbing algorithm that starts from a divisor pair (D_{i0}, D_{j0}). The initial divisor pair is calculated such that $D_{i0} \times D_{j0} = P_n$, where P_n is the total number of processors. This partition, hereafter referred to as a naïve scheme, simply distributes the tiles evenly among the processing cores. Algorithm 1, included as an appendix, further describes how to calculate D_{i0} and D_{j0}.

The adaptive optimization component of the OTF, increases D_i and D_j iteratively to determine whether smaller tile sizes provide smaller execution times. When no performance improvement is observed, the OTF stops the search. Any divisor pair (D_i, D_j) calculated during iteration is composed such that $D_i \times D_j = k \times P_n$ where k is a positive integer value $(k > 0)$ and P_n is the total number of processors. Algorithm 2, also included as an appendix, presents the search algorithm used to determine the divisor pairs. The search space is a rectangular space which corresponds to the iteration space of a two-level nested loop. Each searching step shrinks the area of the tile by half or changes the shape of the tile.

For the specific multi-cluster CMP architecture considered, two tile sizes (for the L1 and L2 cache) are considered. The adaptive search begins by finding an optimal tile size for the L1 cache, which is a subset of the data within the L2 cache. When an optimal L1 tile size is determined, the OTF searches for a L2 cache tile size using the same searching algorithm but using different initial divisor pairs. Algorithm 3 describes the combined searching mechanism to optimize loop division for a multi-cluster CMP architecture. Recall the example loop shown in Figure 3, the search process for the L1 cache tile considers any rectangle which is contained within a rectangle with sides $cluster_x$ and $cluster_y$. The search space for the L2 cache tile is based on the L1 tile size. Given the optimal divisor pair for L1 tile, (D_x, D_y), the search process for the L2 tile is any rectangle with sides multiples of $\frac{cluster_x}{D_x}$ and $\frac{cluster_y}{D_y}$, respectively, and contained within the rectangle with sides $cluster_x$ and $cluster_y$.

3.2   Runtime Profiling and Overhead

To evaluate the performance of the applied optimizations is predicated upon access to runtime execution profile data. For adaptive tiling, this is achieved by using a profiling thread dispatcher, shown in Figure 2 (b). Two additional statements are inserted at the start and end of the parallelized loops. The first statement extracts from the architecture the cycle count[1] prior to the loops execution and the second statement extracts the cycle count after the loop has executed. The method `aosProcess` is responsible for reporting back to the AOS the total cycle count and the number of loop iterations per thread. The OTF is then able to calculate the execution time per iteration of each invocation of the loop and can make decisions about the comparative performance with other invocations of the same loop under different optimizations and configurations.

How representative are the measured execution times is a major factor for the success of the runtime empirical search, and there are two issues that affect it. The first one is that not all loops are of static length or duration. It is possible that both the number of iterations and the loop contents will vary from invocation to invocation. The second issue is that the execution timings are affected by system noise; for example, cold caches and other unrelated thread

---

[1] Although this mechanism is machine specific; instructions exist in the main architectures: RDTSC (x86), mftb (PPC), TICK register (SPARC).

activity. To overcome these issues, the execution time for a given optimization on a parallelized loop is calculated, as an arithmetic mean of the cycles per iteration for three invocations of that loop. Loops that exhibit large profile deviations, defined as having a *coefficient of variation* (CV) [2] greater than a configurable threshold, for this work set at 0.1, are deemed unstable. When instability is detected the profiling code is switched off and the current best optimization is used.

For each run of the parallelized loop, the profiling mechanism records and evaluates the timing data to progress or stop the search. The average overhead for each searching step is less than 300 cycles, thus the profiling overhead is nearly constant, although the accumulated overhead grows linearly with the number of searching steps. As tile size tuning is based on runtime modification of a set of parameters, there is no additional overhead for recompilation.

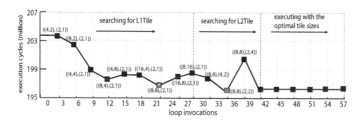

Fig. 4. Searching profile using DGEMM

Figure 4 shows the OTF searching for an optimal divisor during the execution of the DGEMM benchmark. The problem iteration size is 256×256, the hardware is configured as a 2-cluster CMP architecture with each cluster containing 4 processing cores, from now on we refer to such a configuration using the notation: 2c/4p. The L1 cache size is 16KB, and 128KB for each L2 cache, again we will use the notation: 16KB/128KB. The searching algorithm starts from a naïve tile divisor: for the L1 tile $(4, 2)$, and for the L2 tile $(2, 1)$. By the $21st$ invocation of the parallelized loop a local optimal L1 tile size has been found, and a local optimal L2 tile size is found at the $18th$ invocation. Three invocations of the loop are used to assess timing stability. In this experiment the deviation did not exceed the threshold (0.1). The optimal L1 and L2 tile sizes are applied at the $36th$ invocation finishing the search phase. Note that by the very nature of the hill-climbing algorithms used, the adaptive searching finishes after finding locally-optimal solutions.

Once optimal divisors are found for loop tiling, the AOS switches off the runtime profiler and runs any subsequent executions of the loop using the best optimization found. The thread dispatcher, is switched to a version that does not contain the timing instrumentation, so that future execution of the code runs without the cost of the profiling phase; see Figure 5. A runtime code patch mechanism is employed to redirect the execution path to the normal thread

---

[2] Coefficient of variation is the ratio of the standard deviation to the arithmetic mean.

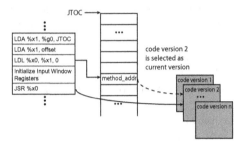

Fig. 5. Code version switching

scheduler. A global data structure, JTOC [5], records references to both versions of the code. Each time the compiled code calls a routine, it is required to first load the method address from the JTOC (see the instructions LDA and LDL), and then jump to the loaded method address (see the instruction JSR), making such code switches possible.

4 Experimental Methodology

The experiments are performed on the multi-cluster CMP JAMAICA architecture [18], using the OTF as part of the adaptive optimization system of the Jikes RVM. The Jikes RVM has been ported to the JAMAICA architecture and runs directly on top of the hardware. The JAMAICA architecture is implemented within a highly configurable cycle-level processor and memory simulation platform. The simulation platform allows the evaluation of the OTF on a wide range of hardware configurations all using the same instruction set. The caches simulated are 4-way set associative.

```
for (int i = 0; i < mLength; i ++) {
  for (int j = 0; j < nLength; j ++) {
    double temp = 0.0;
    for (int k = 0; k < nLength; k ++) {
      temp += alpha * matrixA[i][k] * matrixB[k][j] + beta * matrixC[i][j];
    }
    matrixC[i][j] = temp;
  }
}
              (a) DGEMM
```

```
for (int i = 0; i < length; i ++) {
  for (int j = 0; j < length; j ++) {
    double temp = 0.0;
    for (int k = i; k < length; k ++) {
      temp += matrixA[i][k] * matrixB[k][j];
    }
    matrixC[i][j] = temp;
  }
}
              (b) DTRMM
```

Fig. 6. Level 3 BLAS kernels

Two well known level 3 BLAS [3] kernels (DGEMM and DTRMM) and a 2D Java Lattice-Boltzamann (JLB) simulation (9 variables for each element) [1] are used in the performance evaluation. The kernels for DGEMM and DTRMM appear in Figure 6. Each kernel is executed to completion and validation on each simulated architectural configuration. The configurations assess the performance of the same optimizations in the presence of varying cache sizes, number of clusters and number of processors per cluster.

5   Results and Discussion

Different problem sizes (64×64, 128×128, 256×256 and 352×352 matrix) and different hardware configurations (clusters/processors: 2c/4p, 4c/2p and 4c/4p, and L1/L2 cache sizes: 8KB/128KB, 8KB/256KB, 16KB/128KB and 16KB/256KB) are used in the each experiment. For example, 4c/2p with 16KB/128KB refers to a multi-cluster CMP configured with 4 clusters each with 2 processors (total number of processors 8), and cache of sizes 16KB and 128KB for L1 and L2 cache, respectively.

The graph in Figure 7 presents the speedup attained using the optimal tile sizes compared with that attained using naïve tile sizes. The naïve tile size is defined as the square root of the number of processors. For example, a system with 16 processors has naïve L1 cache tile divisors $(4, 4)$. The divisors are restricted to integer values, thus in a system with 8 processors, the L1 cache tile could either be $(4, 2)$ or $(2, 4)$ (see Algorithm 2). The naïve scheme is in used by static optimizers as it achieves reasonable load balance and data locality. The results of this paper show that the performance can be further improved by performing a runtime empirical search.

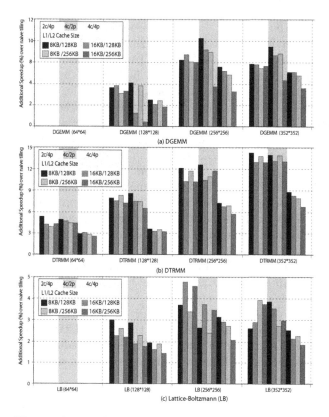

Fig. 7. The speedup compared with a naïve tiling scheme

	2c/4p				4c/2p				4c/4p			
Naïve Divisor	(4,2)(2,1)				(4,2)(2,2)				(4,4)(2,2)			
L1/L2 Cache Size	8KB,128KB	16KB,128KB	8KB,256KB	16KB,256KB	8KB,128KB	16KB,128KB	8KB,256KB	16KB,256KB	8KB,128KB	16KB,128KB	8KB,256KB	16KB,256KB
64*64	(4,2)(2,1)	(4,2)(2,1)	(4,2)(2,1)	(4,2)(2,1)	(4,2)(2,2)	(4,2)(2,2)	(4,2)(2,2)	(4,2)(2,2)	(4,4)(2,2)	(4,4)(2,2)	(4,4)(2,2)	(4,4)(2,2)
128*128	(4,4)(2,1)	(4,2)(2,1)	(4,4)(2,1)	(4,2)(2,1)	(4,4)(2,2)	(4,2)(2,2)	(4,4)(2,2)	(4,2)(2,2)	(4,4)(2,2)	(4,2)(2,2)	(4,4)(2,2)	(4,2)(2,2)
256*256	(8,8)(2,2)	(4,4)(2,2)	(8,4)(2,2)	(4,4)(2,2)	(8,4)(2,2)	(4,4)(2,2)	(8,4)(2,2)	(4,2)(2,2)	(8,4)(2,2)	(4,4)(2,2)	(8,4)(2,2)	(4,2)(2,2)
352*352	(8,16)(4,4)	(8,16)(4,4)	(8,16)(4,2)	(4,4)(4,2)	(8,16)(4,4)	(8,8)(4,2)	(8,16)(4,2)	(8,4)(4,2)	(8,16)(4,2)	(8,4)(4,2)	(8,16)(4,2)	(4,4)(4,2)

(a) DGEMM

	2c/4p				4c/2p				4c/4p			
Naïve Divisor	(4,2)(2,1)				(4,2)(2,2)				(4,4)(2,2)			
L1/L2 Cache Size	8KB,128KB	16KB,128KB	8KB,256KB	16KB,256KB	8KB,128KB	16KB,128KB	8KB,256KB	16KB,256KB	8KB,128KB	16KB,128KB	8KB,256KB	16KB,256KB
64*64	(1,8)(1,2)	(1,8)(1,2)	(1,8)(1,2)	(1,8)(1,2)	(1,8)(1,4)	(1,8)(1,4)	(1,8)(1,4)	(1,8)(1,4)	(1,16)(1,4)	(1,16)(1,4)	(1,16)(1,4)	(1,16)(1,4)
128*128	(4,8)(1,2)	(2,8)(1,2)	(2,8)(1,2)	(2,8)(1,2)	(2,8)(1,4)	(2,8)(1,4)	(2,8)(1,4)	(2,8)(1,4)	(1,16)(1,4)	(1,16)(1,4)	(1,16)(1,4)	(1,16)(1,4)
256*256	(4,8)(2,2)	(4,8)(2,2)	(4,8)(1,2)	(4,8)(1,2)	(4,8)(1,4)	(4,8)(1,4)	(4,8)(1,4)	(4,8)(1,4)	(2,16)(1,4)	(2,16)(1,4)	(2,16)(1,4)	(1,16)(1,4)
352*352	(8,8)(4,2)	(4,8)(4,2)	(8,8)(2,2)	(4,8)(2,2)	(8,8)(2,4)	(4,8)(2,4)	(8,8)(1,4)	(4,8)(1,4)	(2,16)(2,4)	(2,16)(2,4)	(2,16)(1,4)	(2,16)(1,4)

(b) DTRMM

	2c/4p				4c/2p				4c/4p			
Naïve Divisor	(4,2)(2,1)				(4,2)(2,2)				(4,4)(2,2)			
L1/L2 Cache Size	8KB,128KB	16KB,128KB	8KB,256KB	16KB,256KB	8KB,128KB	16KB,128KB	8KB,256KB	16KB,256KB	8KB,128KB	16KB,128KB	8KB,256KB	16KB,256KB
64*64	(4,4)(2,1)	(4,2)(2,1)	(4,2)(2,1)	(4,2)(2,1)	(4,2)(2,2)	(4,2)(2,2)	(4,2)(2,2)	(4,2)(2,2)	(4,4)(2,2)	(4,4)(2,2)	(4,4)(2,2)	(4,4)(2,2)
128*128	(4,8)(2,2)	(4,8)(2,2)	(4,8)(2,1)	(4,8)(2,1)	(4,8)(2,2)	(2,4)(2,2)	(2,4)(2,2)	(4,8)(2,2)	(4,8)(2,2)	(2,4)(2,2)	(4,8)(2,2)	(2,4)(2,2)
256*256	(4,8)(2,2)	(8,16)(4,2)	(8,8)(4,2)	(8,16)(4,2)	(8,16)(4,2)	(4,8)(4,2)	(8,8)(2,2)	(4,8)(2,2)	(8,8)(2,2)	(4,8)(2,2)	(8,8)(2,2)	(4,8)(2,2)
352*352	(8,8)(4,2)	(8,16)(4,4)	(8,8)(4,4)	(8,16)(4,2)	(8,16)(4,2)	(4,8)(4,2)	(8,16)(2,2)	(4,8)(2,2)	(8,8)(2,2)	(4,8)(2,2)	(8,8)(2,2)	(4,8)(2,2)

(c) Lattice-Boltzmann (LB)

Fig. 8. Optimal divisor pairs for different problem sizes and hardware configurations

Figure 8 shows the resulting optimal divisors for all of the evaluated benchmarks. The naïve divisors for DGEMM are: 2c/4p and 4c/2p with L1 tile divisor $(4, 2)$ and L2 tile divisor $(2, 1)$, 4c/4p with L1 tile divisor $(4, 4)$ and L2 divisor $(2, 2)$. The speedup for DGEMM is shown in Figure 7(a). For small problem sizes (e.g. 64×64 matrix), there is no obvious benefit for those configurations with larger L1 cache sizes when compared to the naïve scheme. For larger problem sizes, however, larger divisors produce performance increases. The optimal L2 tile sizes are related to the number of clusters. For example, the best L2 tile divisors for 64×64 matrix are $(2, 1)$ for the 2c/4p configuration and $(2, 2)$ for the 4c/2p and 4c/4p configurations. By increasing the L2 cache size, the L2 cache tile has less effect and its value is near the naïve configuration. This is why the 256KB L2 cache configurations used have lower speedup than the 128KB L2 cache configurations for the same problem size and L1 cache size.

The DTRMM nested loop is intrinsically load imbalanced, because the number of iterations in the inner most loop (k-loop) depends on the iteration of the i-loop, refer to Figure 6 (b). The optimal divisors are shown in Figure 8(b). For configurations 2c/4p and 4c/2p, most of the best divisors for the j-loop L1 tile sizes are 8, which is an even distribution of 8 parallel tasks to the 8 processing cores. Similarly, most of the best divisors for the j-loop L1 tile sizes are 16 for 4c/4p. By increasing the problem size, both the L1 and L2 divisors are increased to gain additional benefits from data locality. The speedups, shown in Figure 7(b), are more pronounced than for DGEMM, however, most of the benefit is attained through better load balancing.

Finally the optimal divisors for JLB, which uses a stencil computation model, are compared to the naïve tile sizes, which are the same as for DGEMM. The speedups are shown in Figure 7(c). Compared with DGEMM, JLB has less cache cross-interference and as a consequence the optimization produces smaller speedups.

6 Related Work

Kisuki, O'Boyle and Knijnebury [11] investigated iterative compilation for loop tiling and loop unrolling. Their proposed compilation system achieved high speedups, outperforming static techniques. The system shows that high levels of optimization can be achieved in a limited number of iterations by applying a hill-climbing like searching algorithm.

The ATLAS project [16,15] applies an automatic tuning mechanism to the BLAS (basic linear algebra software library). Given a BLAS operation, ATLAS uses empirical off-line searches relying on actual execution times to choose the best implementation on a specific architecture. ATLAS typically uses code generators which generate multiple code versions, and has sophisticated search scripts to find the best choice. Despite being an off-line system, ATLAS guides the search using runtime profiling information.

Voss and Eigenmann [14] established an adaptive optimization framework named ADAPT which performs dynamic optimization on hot spots through empirical search. ADAPT uses dynamic recompilation to evaluate different optimizations and a domain-specific language to drive a search on the optimization space for a specific optimization. For example in loop unrolling, each level of unrolling is compiled, executed and timed, and the fastest version is kept and used for subsequent executions of the hot spot. The compiler used for recompilation is run on a separate parallel processor which reduces the recompilation overhead at runtime.

Fursin et al. [8] explored online empirical searches for scientific benchmarks. To reduce runtime code generation overheads, a set of optimized versions of code are created prior to the execution of a program. These versions are then evaluated at runtime with the best performing version chosen for subsequent execution. They employ predictive phase detection to identify the periods of stable repetitive behavior of a program and use these phases to improve the evaluation of alternative optimized versions.

In contrast with the above work, this paper combines a loop-level parallelizing compiler and an adaptive optimization framework, within a virtual machine, that targets a chip multi-cluster CMP architecture which has a multiple level cache hierarchy. The runtime optimization can leverage some strengths of iterative optimization to make JIT more suitable for CMP architectures.

7 Conclusion

Loop tiling is a fundamental optimization for improving data locality. As the use of CMPs increases, selecting the right tile size combined with the parallelization of loops within a virtual machine may be one way of increasing performance. This paper presents a runtime optimization mechanism which automatically parallelizes loops and tunes them for the best tile sizes on a scalable multi-cluster CMP, a feasible next generation multi/many core architecture.

By optimizing the tile sizes for both L1 and L2 caches, a memory intensive application can increase performance. The system is built on top of a virtual machine and targets the runtime parallelization and optimization of Java programs. Experimental results show performance speedups, up to 14.1% for two level 3 BLAS kernels (rectangular and triangular iteration spaces) and a 2D Lattice-Boltzmann simulation (stencil computation with 9 variables per grid point). The speedup is over a traditional parallelization and tiling scheme and also includes the initial overheads involved with profiling.

References

1. Lattice boltzmann method, http://www.latticeboltzmann.com/
2. The Jamaica Project (May 2005),
   http://www.cs.manchester.ac.uk/apt/projects/jamaica
3. Anderson, E., Bai, Z., Bischof, C., Blackford, L.S., Demmel, J., Dongarra, J.J., Du Croz, J., Hammarling, S., Greenbaum, A., McKenney, A., Sorensen, D.: LAPACK Users' guide, 3rd edn. Society for Industrial and Applied Mathematics, Philadelphia (1999)
4. Arnold, M., Fink, S.J., Grove, D., Hind, M., Sweeney, P.F.: Adaptive optimization in the Jalapeño JVM. In: ACM SIGPLAN International Conference on Object-Oriented Programming, Systems, Languages, and Applications, pp. 47–65 (2000)
5. Burke, M., Choi, J., Fink, S., Grove, D., Hind, M., Sarkar, V., Serrano, M., Sreedhar, V., Srinivasan, H., Whaley, J.: The Jalapeño dynamic optimizing compiler for Java. In: Proceedings ACM 1999 Java Grande Conference, San Francisco, CA, United States, June 1999, pp. 129–141. ACM (1999)
6. Carr, S., Kennedy, K.: Compiler blockability of numerical algorithms. Supercomputing, 114–124 (1992)
7. Coleman, S., McKinley, K.S.: Tile size selection using cache organization and data layout. In: SIGPLAN Conference on Programming Language Design and Implementation, pp. 279–290. ACM Press, New York (1995)
8. Fursin, G., Cohen, A., O'Boyle, M., Temam, O.: Quick and practical run-time evaluation of multiple program optimizations. Transactions on High-Performance Embedded Architectures and Compilers 1(1), 13–31 (2006)
9. Hammond, L., Hubbard, B.A., Siu, M., Prabhu, M.K., Chen, M., Olukotun, K.: The Stanford Hydra CMP. IEEE Micro, 71–84 (March–April 2000)
10. Horsnell, M.J.: A chip multi-cluster architecture with locality aware task distribution. PhD thesis, The University of Manchester (2007)
11. Kisuki, T., Knijnenburg, P.M.W., O'Boyle, M.F.P.: Combined selection of tile sizes and unroll factors using iterative compilation. In: International Conference on Parallel Architectures and Compilation Techniques, pp. 237–246 (2000)
12. Kongetira, P., Aingaran, K., Olukotun, K.: Niagara: A 32-way multithreaded sparc processor. IEEE Micro 25(2), 21–29 (2005)
13. Lam, M.S., Rothberg, E.E., Wolf, M.E.: The cache performance and optimizations of blocked algorithms. In: International Conference on Architectural Support for Programming Languages and Operating Systems, pp. 63–74 (1991)

14. Voss, M., Eigenmann, R.: High-level adaptive program optimization with ADAPT. In: ACM SIGPLAN Symposium on Principles and Practice of Parallel Programming, pp. 93–102 (2001)
15. Whaley, R.C., Petitet, A.: Minimizing development and maintenance costs in supporting persistently optimized BLAS. Software: Practice and Experience 35(2), 101–121 (2005)
16. Whaley, R.C., Petitet, A., Dongarra, J.J.: Automated empirical optimizations of software and the ATLAS project. Parallel Computing 27(1–2), 3–35 (2001)
17. Wolfe, M.J.: High performance compilers for parallel computing. Addison-Wesley, Redwood City (1996)
18. Wright, G.: A single-chip multiprocessor architecture with hardware thread support. PhD thesis, The University of Manchester (2001)
19. Zhao, J., Horsnell, M., Rogers, I., Dinn, A., Kirkham, C.C., Watson, I.: Optimizing chip multiprocessor work distribution using dynamic compilation. In: Kermarrec, A.-M., Bougé, L., Priol, T. (eds.) Euro-Par 2007. LNCS, vol. 4641, pp. 258–267. Springer, Heidelberg (2007)

Appendix - Adaptive Tiling Algorithms

Algorithm 1. init_tile_rect (initialize tile size for rectangle iteration space).

Input: Num, number of processors (or clusters).
Output: a initial divisor pair
Implementation:
step 1: $t \Leftarrow \lfloor sqrt(t) \rfloor$;
step 2:
while $(Num\%t)! = 0$ **do**
   $t \Leftarrow t - 1$
end while
step 3: return $(\frac{Num}{t}, t)$

Algorithm 2. tile_search_rect (search tile size for rectangle iteration space).

Input: Num, number of processors or clusters
Output: optimal divisor pair
Implementation:
step 1: $(D_{i0}, D_{j0}) \Leftarrow init\_tile\_rect(P_n)$;
Evaluate the runtime performance by initial tile size (D_{i0}, D_{j0}), get execution cycles E_0
step 2: $(D_i, D_j) \Leftarrow (D_{i0}, D_{j0})$
step 3: $(D_{il}, D_{jl}) \Leftarrow (D_i \times 2, D_j)$; $(D_{ir}, D_{jr}) \Leftarrow (D_i, D_j \times 2)$;
Evaluate the runtime performance by two tile sizes: (D_{il}, D_{jl}) and (D_{ir}, D_{jr}), get execution cycles
E_l and E_r
if $E_0 \leq E_l$ and $E_0 \leq E_r$ **then**
   goto step 4
end if
if $E_r \leq E_l$ **then**
   $(D_i, D_j) \Leftarrow (D_{ir}, D_{jr})$
else
   $(D_i, D_j) \Leftarrow (D_{il}, D_{jl})$
end if
goto step 3
step 4:
if $(D_i, D_j) = (D_{i0}, D_{j0})$ **then**
   goto step 5
else
   return (D_i, D_j)
end if
step 5: $(D_i, D_j) \Leftarrow (D_{i0}, D_{j0})$; $i \Leftarrow 2$
step 6: $(D_{il}, D_{jl}) \Leftarrow (\lfloor \frac{D_i}{i} \rfloor, D_j \times i)$; $(D_{ir}, D_{jr}) \Leftarrow (D_i \times i, \lfloor \frac{D_j}{i} \rfloor)$;
Evaluate the runtime performance by two tile sizes: (D_{il}, D_{jl}) and (D_{ir}, D_{jr}), get execution cycles
E_l and E_r
if $E_0 \leq E_l$ and $E_0 \leq E_r$ **then**
   return (D_i, D_j)
end if
if $E_r \leq E_l$ **then**
   $(D_i, D_j) \Leftarrow (D_{ir}, D_{jr})$; $E_0 \Leftarrow E_r$;
else
   $(D_i, D_j) \Leftarrow (D_{il}, D_{jl})$; $E_0 \Leftarrow E_l$;
end if
$i \Leftarrow i + 1$
goto step 6

Algorithm 3. Multiple levels search.

Input: P_n, number of processors; C_n number of clusters.
Output: optimal divisor pairs for L1 and L2 tile
Implementation:
step1: Search for L1 cache tile size
$L1Tile \Leftarrow tile\_search\_rect(P_n)$, $L1Tile$ is the optimal divisor pair for L1 tile
step2: Search for L2 cache tile size
$L2Tile \Leftarrow tile\_search\_rect(C_n)$, $L2Tile$ is the optimal divisor pair for L2 tile

Quasi-opportunistic Supercomputing in Grid Environments

Valentin Kravtsov[1], David Carmeli[1], Werner Dubitzky[2], Ariel Orda[1],
Assaf Schuster[1], Mark Silberstein[1], and Benny Yoshpa[1]

[1] Technion - Israel Institute of Technology, Haifa, Israel
svali_ds@cs.technion.ac.il
[2] University of Ulster, Coleraine, Northern Ireland

Abstract. The ultimate vision of grid computing are virtual supercomputers of unprecedented power, through utilization of geographically dispersed distributively owned resources. Despite the overwhelming success of grids there still exist many demanding applications considered the exclusive prerogative of real supercomputers (i.e. tightly coupled parallel applications like complex systems simulations). These rely on a static execution environment with predictable performance, provided through efficient co-allocation of a large number of reliable interconnected resources. In this paper, we describe a novel *quasi-opportunistic supercomputer* system that enables execution of demanding parallel applications in grids through identification and implementation of the set of key technologies required to realize the vision of grids as (virtual) supercomputers. These technologies include an incentive-based framework basic on ideas from economics; a co-allocation subsystem that is enhanced by communication topology-aware allocation mechanisms; a fault tolerant message passing library that hides the failures of the underlying resources; and data pre-staging orchestration.

1 Introduction

The total capacity (processing elements, primary and secondary memory) of modern grids (e.g. EGEE [2] and SETI@HOME [1]) often exceed that of an advanced *supercomputer* like IBM's BlueGene. This suggests that such grid computing environments could one day complement the expensive supercomputers. To eat into the predominance of supercomputers, grids will need to improve in their ability to execute tightly coupled parallel applications. Several characteristics of such applications – in addition to their massive computational demands – make their execution on grids particularly challenging.

The co-allocation of a large number of participating CPUs – required prior to computation – is followed by the **synchronous invocation** of subcomputations. In supercomputers, where all CPUs are exclusively controlled by a centralized resource management system, such co-allocation and co-invocation have always been available. In grid systems, however, inherently distributed management coupled with the non-dedicated nature of the computational resources make

A. Bourgeois and S.Q. Zheng (Eds.): ICA3PP 2008, LNCS 5022, pp. 233–244, 2008.

such co-allocation very hard to accomplish in practice. Previous research has focused on co-allocation in grids of supercomputers and dedicated clusters [3], but we are not aware of any co-allocation system for non-dedicated environments.

Synchronous communications typically form a specific communication topology pattern (e.g. *stencil exchange* and local structures in complex systems). This is satisfied by supercomputers via a special-purpose, low-latency, high-throughput interconnects as well as optimized allocation by the resource management system to ensure that the underlying networking topology matches the application's communication pattern [4]. In grids, however, synchronous communications over a WAN are prohibitively slow, and topology-aware allocation is typically not available despite the existing support of communication libraries.

Allocation of resources does not change during runtime. While always true in supercomputers, this requirement is difficult to satisfy in grids, where low reliability of resources and WANs, as well as uncoordinated management of different parts of the grid contribute to extreme fluctuations in the number of available resources.

In a massive synchronous computation, the **high sensitivity of individual processes to failures** usually leads to termination of the whole parallel run. Such failures, while rare in supercomputers because of their reliable hardware, are very common in grid systems.

Co-allocation and fault tolerance are particularly challenging in grids. Clearly, it is impossible to achieve these in a loosely coordinated environment where erratic behavior of resources is allowed. Thus, a realistic but more restricted grid model should be adopted. In this model a grid comprises a set of independently managed clusters which are contributed by different collaborating organizations, each of which is shared by the local organization's users as well as external grid users. In practice, however, even this restricted model would not facilitate co-allocation and fault tolerance. This is because the resources are not dedicated to the execution of grid parallel jobs and can be reallocated in favor of local submissions at any time. Furthermore, local cluster administrators are likely to increase the priorities of local users, possibly disabling remote jobs completely and, thus, effectively 'decomposing' the grid back into individual clusters.

In this article we propose the novel concept of *quasi-opportunistic* grid environments. In such environments, agreements between economic entities (i.e. administrative domains) are enforced through an economic framework that instruments the resource management system with incentives to contribute to the global computational effort. That is why such environments cannot be considered truly opportunistic – hence the notion 'quasi-opportunistic'. The economic framework serves as a basis for the co-allocation subsystem to establish and maintain grid-wide simultaneous allocations of multiple resources, taking into account the communication topology requirements of the applications and utilizing the capabilities of the internal cluster interconnects. Finally, since hardware and network failures in large scale environments are inevitable, a fault-tolerant message passing library is being designed to provide distributed checkpoint restart mechanisms. Integration of all these components is expected to make a quasi-opportunistic grid an alternative to a real supercomputer. This alternative is currently being pursued by the European Commission funded project QosCos-Grid (www.QosCosGrid.com).

2   The Challenges of Supercomputing over a Grid

Non-dedicated resources. Real-world grids comprise many distributively owned clusters of resources, each serving a community of local users while executing externally requested grid jobs. In such a setup, local users are typically prioritized. This policy results in unpredictable performance degradation of the jobs originating from the grid. The fluctuations in resource availability could be prevented by mechanisms that *negotiate* and *enforce* suitable global resource sharing policies (e.g. advance reservation) and provide adequate incentives for the resource providers to maintain these policies. Note that such incentives, if introduced, should be taken into account during scheduling [5].

Frequent failures. Even in the presence of dedicated resources, the inherently distributed nature of grids implies unpredictable and frequent failures. While easily handled with 'embarrassingly parallel' workloads, such failures are devastating for complex parallel computations. Therefore, a grid infrastructure must provide fault tolerance for all its sub-components during run-time [6].

Network heterogeneity. The network topology of a typical grid can be presented as a graph with multiple *cliques* (clusters), with high-capacity links within cliques and low-capacity links among them. High performance cannot be attained unless the grid middleware can expose this topology to the application and apply topology-aware resource allocation algorithms that satisfy the topology requirements of a given application [7].

Data pre-staging orchestration. The system must ensure the availability of input data at all remote resources prior to execution [8].

3   The Principles of Quasi-opportunistic Grids

3.1   Infrastructure

Supercomputing-like capabilities are realized through sharing of resources within a *collaborative grid*. A collaborative grid consists of several organizations that agree to share certain resources within a *virtual organization* (*VO*). Each member of a VO must adhere to two principles. First, it must be in control of its *administrative domain* (*AD*) in terms of resource allocation and sharing policies, as well as their enforcement within this domain. Second, it must contribute some of its resources to the pool of resources shared by the VO. In return it will be granted access to a possibly very large resource pool. The VO members agree to connect their resource pools to a trusted 'grid-level' middleware which in turn is responsible for ensuring optimal resource utilization. This middleware serves as a mediating agent between the clients requiring the resources and the resource providers. Usually, organizations participate in a collaborative grid because the resource requirements of their applications are too demanding to be satisfied by the organization's own resources. It is assumed that each VO participant (which is simultaneously a resource provider and consumer) tries to maximize the benefit from participating in the VO by prioritizing its own resource users. Since such behavior may not be optimal from a global perspective, suitable economics-based models attempt to balance coordinated resource sharing by enticing resource providers to share their resources in exchange for the long-term benefit of having access to the large and powerful VO pool. The mediator controls and maintains central VO-wide scheduling policies. It has a well-defined global utility function, which the mediator tries to maximize in order to achieve a global optimum that benefits all VO participants. Different utility functions result in different resource scheduling and allocation plans. A scheduling policy could be viewed as a pluggable component that defines a scheme for global 'welfare'. Most existing collaborative grid systems employ simple opportunistic approaches to sharing and using resources, e.g. allocate resources when they become available [9]. In our case, such an approach is impractical, as a huge number of tightly coupled tasks need to be executed in parallel. Hence, a scheme ensuring certain levels of quality of service must be introduced and enforced.

3.2   Quality of Service

In service-centric systems, *quality of service* (*QoS*) is defined as the ability of a service to provide a guarantee of a certain quality of the service to the application. Such a guarantee may relate to both quantitative and qualitative properties of a resource. Qualitative properties usually refer to service reliability and user satisfaction, while quantitative characteristics include elements such as networks, CPUs, and storage. Usually, applications specify two QoS requirements: the characteristics of the resource and the period for which the resource is required. Reservation involves giving the application an assurance that the resource allocation will succeed with the required level of QoS. The reservation may be immediate or in advance, and the duration of the reservation may be definite (for a defined period of time) or indefinite (for a specified start time and unlimited duration). However, providing guarantees for resource availability in large-scale grid systems is not a trivial task. The resources must be reserved and co-allocated on many geographically distributed sites.

3.3   Co-allocation of Large Numbers of Resources

Quasi-opportunistic grid systems are envisaged to be used mainly by applications composed of multiple *agents*. These agents are arranged in a dynamic topology with different levels of communication. This scenario implies that if resource co-allocation is to be efficient and effective, the co-allocation system must consider the hierarchical structure of resource requests and offers. We represent this hierarchy by graphs in which vertices represent computational elements and edges represent communication links. Efficient matching between the resource requests and resource offers could be viewed as a graph-matching problem. Once the targeted resources are identified, they should be reserved and made available to run the parallel tasks of the requesting application. We are implementing a co-allocation mechanism that uses advance reservation of resources. This requires that the co-allocation systems of local clusters support advance reservation features. We believe that for large-scale, purely opportunistic grid environments with no resource availability guarantees, it is virtually impossible to solve the co-allocation problem. Such guarantees seem only realistic if resource providers have an incentive to give them.

3.4   Economics-Based Resource Allocation

The complex, parallel grid applications require guaranteed allocation of resources, such as computing elements, network bandwidth, memory, disk storage, databases/datasets, and other specialized resources. One of the main obstacles in providing such guarantees is to make different parts of the grid (AD owners) cooperate so as to enhance the social 'welfare' of the entire system. We cannot rely upon their altruism and need to deal with the problem of 'free-riders' (individual users who have no incentive for sharing their own resources). The free-riding problem does not belong solely to grid systems. Thus, in successful peer-to-peer systems, such as Kazaa or E-Mule, there is a mechanism that offers the user incentives to share. In order to resolve the free-riding issue, we establish a link between the past behavior of the AD and its future utilization of the system, preferring ADs that have a better resource contribution record in the scheduling process. We studied several incentive schemes. The **tit-for-tat** strategy is not suitable for our system for two reasons: (a) it cannot handle heterogeneous requests (a general problem with bartering), and (b) it cannot hold a global view of the players' behavior. For example, if A gave its resources to B and C (and has a positive 'balance' with them) but not to D, why should D prefer A over someone who did share its resources? The **reputation** system has the problem of linking players' reputation ratings with their tasks' valuation. For instance, suppose that A is above B in the reputation system, and B needs C's resources desperately while A can wait, who should get the resources? Finally, in the **virtual payment** method [11], the resource description includes pricing information in both the job description and the resource offer. The scheduler considers this information during the resource allocation process. In this manner, the past behavior of a strategic player can be linked with its future utilization of the system. While posing several implementation-related challenges (e.g. transaction management, non-trivial accounting systems). This scheme does not suffer from the drawbacks of the tit-for-tat and reputation strategies.

In our system we chose to follow the ideas of the virtual payments approach, as it satisfies our requirements to reward well-behaved players. In grid terms, the more resources are shared by the AD, and the more it complies with the signed agreements, the more it will be able to utilize the system. We demonstrate that the virtual payments approach indeed realizes these ideas in Section 5.

Based on the virtual payments technique, we have designed an economics-based resource allocation system. One of its cornerstones is a *round-based* scheme. In each round, an AD, which represents both users of this domain and resources that belong to it, sends *resource bids* and *offers*. A resource bid, which represents a job submission, consists of the resource description and the price a user is willing to pay for the job's execution. A resource offer represents the AD's willingness to share its resources along with a reserved price for each resource offered. In other words, the domain is not ready to share this resource for less than the stated price. Each AD of a VO starts with a predefined budget, divided among the users of the domain. Each AD tries to maximize its budget in order that future requests for resources can be fulfilled. In each round, the system calculates a feasible allocation that maximizes the social welfare according to the bids and offers received from the ADs. At the end of the round, payments are transferred to the related ADs according to the allocation.

3.5 Fault Tolerance

Several techniques are being developed to provide fault tolerance to applications to be run on the quasi-opportunistic grid system. The most important are a distributed checkpoints-and-restart protocol (C/R) and a fault-tolerant MPI protocol [12]. The C/R protocol is intended to partially or completely stop applications if failures occur and migrate them according the scheduling policy. In our system, reliable communication will be achieved by means of a new cross-domain fault-tolerant MPI communication protocol. The majority of the current fault-tolerant MPI implementations provide transparent fault tolerance mechanisms for clusters. However, to provide a reliable connection within a grid computing environment, a fault-tolerant and grid-middleware-aware communication library based on the MPI2 specification will be evaluated for possible implementation.

4 Initial Design

Conceptually, the QosCosGrid system is composed of three main entities: the *end users*, the *administrative domains*, and the *grid level*.

4.1 End User Level

Typical end users of quasi-opportunistic grid systems include physicists, biologists, social scientists and engineers, none of whom is generally very familiar with the intricate technological details of grid technology. Such users are keen to run their applications and are mainly concerned with whether there are enough resources to run them. Whether the resources are sufficient to execute an application depends on two factors: (1) on the number of suitable resources present in the system, and (2) on whether the user's AD is willing to pay for the required resources. To enable application-oriented users to submit and monitor jobs, it is mandatory that the system provide a sophisticated user interface which hides the details of the grid level from the user. Such user interfaces should include a resource planner as well as a budget planner. As each user belongs to one or more ADs, the resource and budget planner needs to negotiate with the appropriate AD level components and services.

4.2   Administrative Domain Level

The responsibility of the ADs is twofold. First, an AD needs to provide reliable grid resources. Second, it needs to serve as a gateway for the end users who belong to it. To support end users, an AD includes a job submission manager component, which is responsible for interaction with the end user components. ADs share the earned virtual money among their users according to a predefined policy, with the ability to prioritize applications and users that are considered important. ADs are the only system entities that can receive or spend its *virtual money*. To manage its economic subsystem efficiently, an AD must include a component which defines and enforces the economic policies inside the AD. Such policies may vary from one AD to another. An additional component on the AD level, the resource manager component, is responsible for ensuring the efficient utilization of the AD's computing, storage and network resources. The resource manager is in charge of advance reservation of resources, resource topology analysis, and publishing. Whenever a job is assigned to be executed on the resources of an AD, the job is handled by the execution manager component. The responsibilities of the execution manager are to allocate resources for job execution, to orchestrate the stage-in and stage-out of data, and to initiate the actual execution of jobs. The execution manager is also responsible for performing corrective actions in case of system failures. It is alerted to such failures by the monitoring subsystem, which constantly polls the quantitative properties of the computational, network, and storage elements in the system and propagates the information to the subscribed services in the AD or grid levels. One of the services requiring such information is the topology-building service, located in the AD level. The topology-building service is responsible for transforming the raw quantitative resource properties into the resource topology graph. Resource topology graphs are used to describe the resource structure in many parts of the system, e.g. resource offers, resource requests, service-level agreements, and more.

4.3   Grid Level

The grid level represents a commonly trusted entity responsible for maximizing the global 'social welfare' within a VO. All services at the grid level are considered *logical singletons*. Clearly, the implementation of such a service could be distributed to achieve high availability. The grid level does not provide or request any resources and thus is not considered an active economic entity; that is, it cannot spend or earn virtual money. However, the grid level serves as a 'virtual bank', which keeps track of the accounts of ADs within a VO and is responsible for all the payment transfers in the system. The grid level also includes a global information system, which provides information regarding the available resources, future reservations, and all the agreements signed among the participants. One of the most important and sophisticated services located at the grid level of the system is the meta-scheduler service. This service acts as a mediator between the resource providers and consumers, and it performs scheduling and co-allocation of resource requests (grid jobs). Using a configurable *utility function* or *objective function*, the meta-scheduler attempts to maximize the 'global welfare' of the system participants by means of advanced scheduling and allocation algorithms. Such an objective function might be defined, for example, to optimize resource utilization, resource providers' revenue, and so on. Resource consumers whose jobs are allocated for execution on one or more ADs other than their own are required to sign an agreement with all ADs in which the terms of resource provision are defined. All signed agreements are stored at the grid level by means of an agreement service. Fulfillment of the agreements is monitored by the monitoring service, which is also located at the grid level. The monitoring service facilitates real-time monitoring and implementation of signed agreements; it also initiates corrective procedures when failures occur. The monitoring services also initiates money transfers between resource providers and consumers when agreements are fulfilled or breached.

4.4   Resource Description Model

When dealing with highly complex parallel applications, a correct and efficient description of the resource offers and resource requests is essential. In the grid community, the most widely accepted and used resource description model is the GLUE schema [13]. It is used to describe the properties of grid resources, such as computational clusters or storage nodes, and includes a very basic description of network interconnections. Although the GLUE schema can describe most of the simple resource infrastructures, it is inadequate for the efficient description of resource topologies which is required for complex parallel applications. Such applications cannot be executed efficiently in a grid environment if all-to-all communication is needed. Efficient execution of the tightly coupled parallel applications relies heavily on precise definitions of execution node topology and interconnection bounds. Such a topology is usually recursive and hierarchical, in contrast to the GLUE schema, which describes the grid as a 'cluster of clusters'. There exists a hierarchical model which contains quantitative properties of both computational and network nodes [14]. Highly sophisticated topology structures can be comprehensively described with this model. We find it to be very flexible and efficient, and thus have chosen to adopt it for the description of resource offers and requests in the QosCosGrid project.

4.5   Life Cycle

To illustrate the functionality of the QosCosGrid system, we describe and analyze the complete life cycle of a job defined by a user. Before a job can be processed by the QosCosGrid system, it must be defined by a user with appropriate authorization and authentication credentials. The job description includes all the standard job properties such as executable, data inputs and outputs, operating system, memory and CPU constraints, valid parameters for each task, and so on. In the job description phase, the user employs the job planner to specify his or her preferences regarding the number of execution nodes, the desired interconnectivity level between bundles of nodes, the required storage space, and so on. All these properties are described in terms of parameters and their minimum, maximum, and default (preference) values. Given this information and the rates or costs of the available resources, the budget planner determines if the funds are sufficient to process the job in the system. After the job is successfully described and planned, its description is transferred from the user level to the user's AD for further processing. The meta-scheduler negotiates with other ADs regarding the necessary resources and the execution start time. If the negotiation is successful, agreements are signed between the user's AD, which is willing to pay for user's job, and all the other ADs, which are ready to share their resources in return for the agreed price. Before the scheduled execution, the job description and all the required executables, libraries and data input files are staged to the execution machines. Upon arrival of the agreed execution time, the execution is started on all sites and is monitored by the monitoring service until the execution is terminated (successfully or with an exception) or a breach of the agreement is detected. If the execution completes successfully, the job execution results are staged out to the predefined storage location.

5   Preliminary Results

All the components of the presented quasi-opportunistic computing system are being actively developed. While the system is still immature and is incapable of performing real computations, we here demonstrate the performance of the economic-based allocation subsystem, as it is clearly a dominant factor in the feasibility of the quasi-opportunistic computing concept as a whole.

We have developed a simulation environment to test our economic model. This environment allows us to describe the model, which includes many ADs trying to submit jobs to the system, the description of those jobs, and the submission processes themselves. Resource allocation by the centralized entity is also simulated, and the service-level agreements are created according to a predefined social welfare function.

We define a system's *utilization index* as the percentage of submitted resource requests in which the user actually received the requested resources in the next allocation round. *Sharing frequency* is defined as the probability that the AD will share its resources in each allocation round. Our experiments were carried out on a fixed number of ADs ($n=10$), each of which starts with the same number of resources and the same amount of money.

Our results indicate that there is always a strong correlation between the revenues that the AD receives and its utilization index. Thus, each AD is motivated to increase its revenues. In addition, we have found that ADs that share their resources more frequently and generously accumulate higher revenues in the long-run. However, an AD that has many frequent users tends to have a lower utilization index. This result conforms to our intuition, since ADs with a constant number of credits to share among a large number of users tend to have fewer credits per user. These results confirm the validity of our system: sharing resources is a preferable strategy for each AD. Therefore, we can expect that the rational behavior of each AD will conform to the system architects' intentions.

Testing the influence of stated reserved prices on the expected long-term revenues, we discovered that any given domain could maximize its revenues by finding its optimal reserved price subject to reserved prices stated by all other domains throughout the system's history. We also developed an approximate algorithm for the calculation of an optimal reserved price.

Another important insight we gained suggests that the initial budget distribution has no effect in the long-run. Although an AD's initial credit affects the allocation in the first few rounds, its future utilization of the system depends only on its own behavior. This is based on the assumption that all the players have valuable resources, i.e. there are domains willing to pay for resources of any of the ADs within the grid. This assumption is legitimate in the context of quasi-opportunistic grids

6   Related Work

The majority of state-of-the-art production and academic grid systems do not address the complete bundle of features discussed in this paper. EGEE [2] has developed a complete grid system that facilitates the execution of scientific applications requiring large computational and data-intensive capabilities within a production-level grid environment. EGEE spans more than 150 sites with more than 30 000 available CPUs. The current version of EGEE's grid middleware, gLite, does not currently support advance reservation. Due to the support of various low-level cluster management systems such as Condor, LSF, PBS, gLite does not support checkpoint and restart protocols, and cannot guarantee the desired level of QoS for very long executions.

HPC4U (www.hpc4u.org) is arguably closest to the objectives of QosCosGrid. Its objective is to expand the potential of the grid approach to complex problem solving. This would be done through the development of software components for dependable and reliable grid environments, combined with service level agreements and commodity-based clusters providing quality of service. The QosCosGrid project differs from HPC4U mainly in its 'grid orientation'. QosCosGrid assumes multi-domain, parallel executions (in contrast to within-cluster parallel execution) and applies different MPI and checkpoint/restart protocols that are grid-oriented and highly scalable.

TeraGrid (www.teragrid.org) is a US national project offering extremely high computational and data capacities. Its objectives are different to those of the QosCosGrid project, as the TeraGrid already offers considerable supercomputing abilities. Hence, since each site contains reliable and robust nodes, the need to provide QoS through software is eliminated. TeraGrid does not seem to support advance reservation and automated job co-allocation.

7   Summary and Conclusions

Computer-based simulations of complex natural phenomena and man-made arti-facts are increasingly employed in a wide variety of sectors. Typically, such sim-ulations require computing environments which meet very high specifications in terms of processing units, primary and secondary storage, communication, and reliability. Supercomputers are the de facto technology for delivering the required specifications. Acquiring, operating and maintaining supercomputers carry considerable costs which many organizations cannot afford. The work-ing assumption of the QosCosGrid project is that a grid could be enhanced by suitable middleware to provide features and performance characteristics that re-semble those of a supercomputer. We refer to such a grid as quasi-opportunistic supercomputer. We have argued that in order to realize a quasi-opportunistic supercomputer in a collaborative grid, we must implement a resource alloca-tion mechanism that goes beyond the opportunistic approaches of current grid systems. In particular, the co-allocation of a large number of resources requires advance reservation features and non-trivial QoS guarantees. Moreover, to es-tablish a successful collaborative grid, ADs and users need incentives so that their resource provision and consumption behavior will yield long-term mutual benefit. We investigated some economics-based concepts for resource allocation which could foster 'global welfare' and address issues such as 'free riding'. We showed that service-level agreement concepts are likely to play an important role in the enforcement of an economics-based scheduling and allocation system. The volatile nature of grid resources necessitates sophisticated fault-tolerance features in the QosCosGrid system. Developments are underway for a fault-tolerant and grid-middleware-aware communication library based on the MPI2. The initial design of the QosCosGrid revolves around three main elements: end users, ADs, and the grid level. Critical to application-oriented end users are user interfaces that hide intricate grid details from the end user. To real-ize some of the requisite features of the QosCosGrid system, we identified the basic system components and their required roles at the AD level. These in-clude a job submission, resource, and execution manager. Ultimately, the grid level is responsible for ensuring the satisfaction of all participants (ADs, end users) of the VO. In particular, the grid level is designed to provide a meta-scheduler service which acts as a mediator between the resource providers and resource consumers and performs scheduling and co-allocation of resource re-quests (grid jobs). The grid level also serves as a 'virtual bank' which han-dles the exchange of the money used to implement the economics model of the system. A grid-level monitoring service oversees the fulfillment of signed agreements.

Acknowledgments

This work is supported by the European Commission FP6 grant QosCosGrid, contract no.: 033883.

References

1. University of California: SETI@Home. The Search for Extra-Terrestrial Inteligence (SETI) (2007), `http://setiathome.ssl.berkeley.edu`
2. Gagliardiand, F., Jones, B., Grey, F., Bgin, M.-E., Heikkurinen, M.: Building an infrastructure for scientific grid computing: Status and goals of the EGEE project. Philosophical Transactions A of the Royal Society: Mathematical, Physical and Engineering Sciences 363(833), 1729–1742 (2005)
3. Kuo, D., Mckeown, M.: Advance reservation and co-Allocation protocol for grid computing. In: 1st Int'l Conference e-Science and Grid Computing, p. 8 (2005)
4. Aridor, Y., Domany, T., Goldshmidt, O., Moreira, J.W., Shmueli, E.: Resource Allocation and Utilization in the Blue GeneL Supercomputer. IBM Journal of Research and Development 49(2-3), 425–436 (2005)
5. Buyya, R., Abramson, D., Giddy, J., Stockinger, H.: Economic models for resource management and scheduling in grid computing. Concurrency and Computation: Practice and Experience 14, 1507–1542 (2002)
6. Reed, A.D., Lu, C.-d., Mendes, C.L.: Reliability challenges in large systems. Future Generation Computer Systems 22(3), 293–302 (2006)
7. Karonis, N.T., Toonen, B., Foster, I.: MPICH-G2: A Grid-enabled implementation of the Message Passing Interface. Journal of Parallel and Distributed Computing 63(5), 551–563 (2003)
8. Dail, H., Berman, F., Casanova, H.: A decoupled scheduling approach for grid application development environments. Journal of Parallel and Distributed Computing 63(5), 505–524 (2003)
9. Venugopal, S., Buyya, R., Winton, L.: A grid service broker for scheduling e-science applications on global data grids. Journal of Concurrency and Computation: Practice and Experience 18(6), 685–699 (2005)
10. Raman, R., Livny, M., Solomon, M.: Policy driven heterogeneous resource co-allocation with gangmatching. In: Proc. of the 12th IEEE Int'l Symposium on High Performance Distributed Computing (HPDC-12), pp. 80–89 (2002)
11. Irwin, I., Chase, J., Grit, L., Yumerefendi, A.: Self-recharging virtual currency. In: Proc. of the 2005 ACM SIGCOMM Workshop on Economics of Peer-to-Peer System, pp. 93–98 (2005)
12. Snir, M., Otto, S., Huss-Lederman, S., Walker, D., Dongarra, J.: MPI: The Complete Reference. MIT Press, Cambridge (1996)
13. Andreozzi, S., Sgaravatto, M., Vistoli, C.: Sharing a conceptual model of gridresources and services. Computing in High Energy and Nuclear Physics, 24–28 (2003)
14. Lacour, S., Perez, C., Priol, T.: A network topology description model for grid application deployment. In: Proc. 5th IEEE/ACM Int'l Workshop on Grid Computing, pp. 61–68 (2004)

Explicit Control of Service Execution to Support QoS-Based Grid Scheduling

Claudia Di Napoli and Maurizio Giordano

Istituto di Cibernetica "E. Caianiello" - C.N.R.
Via Campi Flegrei 34, 80078 Pozzuoli, Naples - Italy
{c.dinapoli,m.giordano}@cib.na.cnr.it

Abstract. Grid scheduling is shifting from a system-centric approach towards a user-centric one, i.e. service provision is driven by both user and provider-dependent Quality-of-Service (QoS) requirements. In this scenario, the possibility to explicitly control the execution of services allows providers to make different decisions on the QoS they provide their services with according to the requirements of new service requests. In the present work an infrastructure that allows providers to dynamically adapt the execution of services according to both the changing conditions of the environment where they operate in, and the requirements of service users is presented. The infrastructure is based on program *continuations* to provide service schedulers with application-level primitives to handle suspension and resuming of service execution. The same primitives are also accessible as web service operations by consumer programs so allowing to change QoS parameters of requested services at run-time. This approach makes the proposed infrastructure a flexible and easily programmable middleware to experiment with different scheduling policies in service-oriented scenarios. As a case of study, we show that on top of a time-sharing low-level scheduling, a provider can adopt a high-level scheduling policy using service suspension and resuming primitives so that consumer priority requirements can be met at run-time.

1   Introduction

Computational grids represent the new research challenge in the area of distributed computing. They aim to provide a unified computational infrastructure composed of geographically distributed heterogeneous resources cooperating with each other through middleware software to enable usage of the collection of these resources in an easy and effective manner.

In the present work a service-oriented approach is adopted as described in [1], where grid resources are abstracted as *grid services*, i.e. computational capabilities exposed to the network through a set of well-defined interfaces and standard protocols used to invoke the services from those interfaces, and they have to be identified, published, allocated, and scheduled. Services are not subject to centralized control (i.e. they live within different control domains and they do not rely on a central management system), they use standard, open,

A. Bourgeois and S.Q. Zheng (Eds.): ICA3PP 2008, LNCS 5022, pp. 245–256, 2008.

general-purpose protocols and interfaces (i.e. not application-specific), and they can be combined in order to deliver added value functionalities so that the utility of the resulting system is significantly greater than the sum of its parts. In order to provide such a computational infrastructure, grid technologies should support shared and coordinated use of diverse resources in a dynamic environment [1].

A service is provided by the *body* responsible for offering it, we refer to as *service provider*, for consumption by others, we refer to as *service consumers*, under particular conditions. In this view, service providers (that can be individuals, organizations, groups, government, and so on) are independent and autonomous entities representing the interface between a service consumer and a required functionality, i.e. a grid service. Users will be able to access and share these computational capabilities on demand over the Internet, relying on an infrastructure that is expected to be resilient, self-managing, and always available, and above all that is perceived as a unified framework by end users.

A service request is fulfilled when the consumer requirements can be met by the service provider that received the request, i.e. when consumers Quality-of-Service requirements can be met by providers Quality-of-Service capabilities [2]. The term Quality-of-Service is used in a general sense referring to a very wide range of non-functional service characteristics. It is beyond the scope of the present work to study how complex the quality of a service can be, and how to characterize it, i.e. how many parameters should be considered and how it can be represented. This is mainly a domain-specific problem.

In this approach, service providers architectures must include mechanisms for the provision of known quality levels and for the possibility to change quality levels when necessary. So, providers need to have control on the execution of their services in order to accommodate for the changing conditions under which a service could be supplied. In such a way providers are able to decide at run-time "how" to fulfil a service request, i.e. what Quality-of-Service they can supply.

In this work we present an infrastructure to model service providers to control the execution of services at application level, by allowing for service suspension and resuming in a way similar to process preemption in traditional operating system design. The infrastructure relies on *continuation* programming paradigm [3] to support service execution state saving and restoring: by managing program continuations service providers can change at run-time parameters affecting service provision either driven by consumer or system requirements.

In order to test the flexibility of the infrastructure, a cost-based time-sharing scheduling algorithm has been implemented and tested to show how different scheduling behaviours can be obtained at application level without relying on operating system facilities.

The rest of the paper is so organized: section 2 describes the service provider architecture that provides service execution control by means of user-level preemption mechanisms; section 3 discusses the cost-based resource sharing scheduling policy implemented in a service application scenario; section 4 reports the results obtained experimenting with the implemented scheduling policy; finally section 5 reports some concluding remarks.

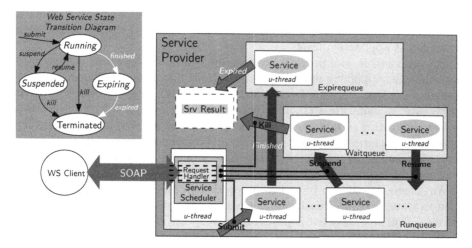

Fig. 1. Services provider architecture and service state transition

2   Service Provider Architecture

In order to be able to provide services that meet Quality-of-Service requirements of both service consumers (e.g. cost, response time) and service providers (e.g. throughput, profit, CPU utilization), it is crucial to be able to control the execution of services in accordance with new events occurring in the environment since these requirements cannot be statically determined.

Service preemption mechanisms are a way to provide full control of service execution and they can be implemented (or simulated) using several approaches, both at application and operating system level. For example, at application level the Java language provides (deprecated) thread suspension/resuming support. Other approaches as [4] use signals (SIGSTOP/SIGCONT) available in most operating systems.

The main objective of the proposed service provider architecture is to provide application-level preemption of services in order to support the development of dynamic policies for service execution at programming level. Service preemption is provided at application-level by using program *continuations*.

A continuation relative to a point in a program represents the *remainder of the computation* from that point [3], so a continuation is a representation of the program current execution state. Continuation capturing allows to package the whole state of a computation up to a given point. Continuation invocation allows to restore the previously captured state restarting the computation from that point. Although any programming system maintains the current continuation of each program instruction it evaluates, these continuations are generally not accessible to the programmer. Some programming languages provide *first-class continuations*, i.e. data objects that may be named by variables, passed as arguments to procedures, returned as results of procedures, and included in data structures [5]. The possibility to handle continuations as first-class objects together with constructs to capture and resume continuations allow to build in a hosting programming environment lightweight user-level threads that can be scheduled at application level.

The proposed service provider architecture can be implemented using a hosting language supporting first-class continuations management. The current implementation is in Stackless Python [6] that supports user-level threads based on continuations, named *tasklets*. The Python scripting language offers a fast prototyping and testing programming environment for the proposed SOA framework, with minor performance penalties compared to other languages like C. Furthermore, Python is one of the languages that provides a satisfactory support of libraries and tools for the development of web services.

We designed a service provider equipped with mechanisms to process, from time to time, arrival of notification messages in order to suspend and resume the execution of a service it is providing by respectively capturing and restoring its continuation. The control of service execution can be driven both by the service provider itself and by any client program. Service preemption, driven or not by client requests, is carried out by the provider storing at the preemption points the execution state (the continuation) of the specified service. A client program may represent either a service consumer that requires a service result, or a metascheduler or a service broker trying to adapt local service execution policies so that resources can be shared in a reliable and efficient way in a heterogeneous and dynamically changing environment like the grid.

The architecture, depicted in figure 1, is represented by a *service container* consisting of a pool of lightweight user-level threads, named *u-threads* whose implementation supports thread suspension and resuming at application level. U-threads are the wrapping execution contexts of web service *operations*, so u-threads suspension and resuming methods are means to control web service executions. Web service operations are supplied as parameters to u-threads and executed within their context. Thus the wrapping guarantees the required functionalities to suspend and resume web service operations. In the rest of the paper the term *service instance* refers to the execution of a web service operation.

A u-thread and the enveloped service instance can be in the following states:

- *running:* the service instance is executing or ready to be scheduled for execution; all running services are kept in the *Runqueue* and by default executed in time-sharing mode by assigning to each u-thread a *time quantum.*
- *suspended:* the service instance is not terminated yet, but cannot be scheduled for execution; all suspended services are maintained in the *Waitqueue;*
- *expiring:* the service instance terminated, but the descriptor of the wrapping u-thread is still alive to make the service result available for successive requests; all expiring services are kept in the *Expirequeue;*
- *terminated:* the service instance terminated and the descriptor of the wrapping u-thread is freed and no longer available (in the *Expirequeue*) because either a specified expiration time elapsed, or the client requested and obtained the service result before the expiration time. The expiration time

is not necessarily a system parameter, and it could be specified as a QoS parameter at the service submitting phase.

The main u-thread, named *Service Scheduler*, represents the execution context of the service provider and it is always in the *running* state. It interleaves service scheduling activities with processing of incoming requests from clients performed by the *Request Handler*, the module responsible for probing incoming SOAP messages. A client may request the invocation of a service (service submission) or force the state transition of an already invoked service (suspending, resuming or killing the service).

In order to provide clients with full control of service execution we defined and implemented a web service exposing the following WSDL operations: submit, suspend, resume and kill. They represent *meta-operations* because they are invoked by clients to control and monitor web service executions.

When the client invoke one of these operations an asynchronous request/ response interaction with polling [7] takes place. Asynchronicity allows the client to proceed the computation concurrently with the web service execution until the operation result is required. At this point the client needs to synchronize with the provider and it establishes a new communication to retrieve the result: this is carried out by the probe request.

The Request Handler processes each client request by executing the corresponding system-internal primitive available at the Service Scheduler level to control service execution. The primitives are: *submit, suspend, resume, kill* (black arrows in the state transition diagram of figure 1).

While service submission and killing are always carried out upon requests from clients, service suspension and resuming can be also invoked by the Service Scheduler to implement a particular scheduling policy that uses service preemption at programming level.

The *submit* primitive creates a new u-thread wrapping up a specified service operation and puts it in the *running* state.

The Service Scheduler maintains three queues to manage u-threads, together with the corresponding wrapped service instances, in different states:

- *Runqueue* contains all service instances running or ready to be scheduled for execution. Services in this queue are by default executed in time-sharing mode by assigning to each u-thread a *time quantum*.
- *Waitqueue* contains all service instances suspended and thus removed from the Runqueue. The provider may decide to suspend or resume service execution according to its own scheduling policy, and upon receiving specific SOAP requests from an external application, e.g. a metascheduler.
- *Expirequeue* contains all u-threads descriptors wrapping up terminated service instances whose results are not requested yet by clients via SOAP messages. U-threads are maintained in an inactive state in this queue to temporarily store unused service results until a certain *expiration time* is elapsed. The expiration time is not necessarily a system specific parameter, and it could be specified as a QoS parameter at the service submitting phase.

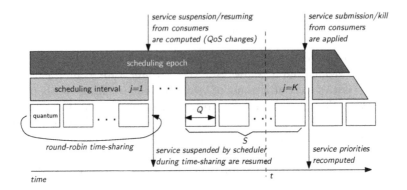

Fig. 2. Two-level scheduling policy

3   QoS-Based Service Scheduling

In order to reach the full potential of grid computing, it is well-recognized that the grid needs to shift towards production-oriented scenarios in which service providers are motivated to make available the resources they provide.

A computational economy approach can be used to provide the possibility of buying and selling computational resources in the same way as goods and services are bought and sold in the real world economy [8]. Adopting a computational economy-based view [9] where services are provided at a given cost constitutes *per se* a mechanism for encouraging resource owners to contribute their resource(s) for the construction of the grid, and compensate them based on the resource usage, i.e. on the value of the work done. So, the ultimate success of computational grids as a production-oriented commercial platform for solving problems is critically dependent on the support of economy-based mechanisms to resource management. In such "commercial" computational grids, resource owners act as service providers that make a profit by selling their services to users that act as buyers of computational resources for solving their problems.

Economic-based grids represent the reference application scenario of the present work, so that QoS parameters include a *cost* of the service to be provided. In our framework it is possible to associate to a service request a `qos` parameter taking into account the cost of the service so both the client and the provider may use its value to drive service execution scheduling.

3.1   A Two-Level Scheduling Policy

The scheduling algorithm presented here is a variant of the one proposed in [4].

In our application scenario each service execution request is submitted with a *cost* parameter. The service cost c_i is a positive floating number greater than 0.1. The value 0.1 is assumed as the default value the provider assigns to services with no cost specification. The consumer may request services with associated costs greater than 0.1. The service provider agrees with the consumer to execute the required service with a priority given by the following expression (once its state becomes runnable):

$$p_i = \frac{c_i}{\sum_{j=0}^{N} c_j} \qquad (1)$$

where N is the total number of "alive" services at a certain execution time: a service is said to be "alive" if it is either in the *suspended* or in the *running* state, as defined in section 2. Thus, by definition, p_i is in the interval $(0, 1]$.

The scheduling algorithm is described in figure 2. It consists of a two levels scheduling, named *scheduling epochs* and *scheduling intervals*.

Scheduling epochs. A scheduling epoch consists of a fixed-sized sequence of *scheduling intervals* of time. The number of scheduling intervals is a parameter of the scheduler.

In each interval a time-sharing policy is adopted to allocate a set of time quanta to services in the *Runqueue*.

Priorities are recomputed just before the beginning of each epoch. At that time the client requests, arrived during the previous epoch, are processed; thus new service submission and deletion messages sent by clients may change priorities of all service running in the system. By the priority definition given in (1) service suspension and resuming requests do not change the priority values of all "alive" services. Service submission and deletion requests respectively adds and subtracts an "alive" service thus changing the priority of services.

With this assumption processing suspension and resuming requests can take place within scheduling intervals without requiring priority recomputation. Submission and deletion requests are processed only just before the beginning of a new epoch. At that time, new services are added to the *Runqueue* and priorities are updated accordingly before new service instances may start. To implement this strategy we used a *Readyqueue* to buffer service submissions occurring during the current epoch, to move them in the *Runqueue* before the beginning of the next epoch to start new service executions.

Within an epoch service priorities are assumed to be constant although the number of running services may change due to service termination. This is a minimal inaccuracy in priority estimation compared to the extra overhead produced by frequent priority updates.

Scheduling intervals. In a scheduling interval the available time quanta are allocated to services in the *Runqueue*. During a scheduling interval incoming client messages are not processed because they are served at the next scheduling interval (or the next epoch).

All scheduling intervals have the same number of equal-sized quanta: the number of quanta (S) for each interval and the quantum size (Q) are scheduling parameters that are fixed once the service container object is instantiated.

Let t be the time relative to an epoch, where $t = 0$ at the beginning of each epoch. Let $j = 1, \ldots, K$ be the index of the current interval in the epoch. For any t within an epoch $n_i(t)$ is the number of quanta used by a service instance i

starting from the beginning of the epoch. So, $n_i(t)Q$ is a measure of the *cpu time* spent during the epoch by the service at the time t. A measure of the service *utilization time* $u_i(t)$, referred to one epoch, at time t is given by the expression:

$$u_i(t) = \frac{n_i(t)}{jS} \tag{2}$$

When service submissions are computed before an epoch starts, new instances for requested services are added (in the arrival order) to the head of the *Runqueue*.

When an epoch starts, the scheduler gets a service from the head of the *Runqueue* and runs it for one quantum. During the quantum the service instance may end its execution: in such a case it is moved to the *Expirequeue* to wait for the client request of the service computation result.

If the service does not terminate, the scheduler checks if a new quantum in the same interval can be allocated to the service: if the service *utilization time* is less than its priority at time t (i.e. $u_i(t) < p_i$), the service is put in the tail of the *Runqueue*, thus having another chance to run in the same or in the next interval of the same epoch. Otherwise it is suspended by the scheduler and put in the *Waitqueue*. In other words, a service is suspended if the ratio between the quanta used from the start of the epoch and the total elapsed quanta (including those passed in suspension), is greater than its priority.

When all quanta in the scheduling interval have been used, or no more services are in the *Runqueue*, the scheduling interval ends. Before the next epoch starts, the scheduler resumes all suspended services in the *Waitqueue* with the exception of threads whose suspension was explicitly requested by clients, that can be reactivated only by clients through *resume* requests.

4   Experimental Results

We performed some preliminary experiments with the scheduling policy by simulating the execution of service instances. The experiments were carried out to test the soundness of the scheduling algorithm implemented for the economy-based service provider of our case study. The scheduling algorithm is not evaluated against efficiency and performance metrics. In fact our purpose is to show how the proposed framework provides mechanisms to implement and experiment with a large variety of scheduling policies.

In the first set of experiments, services are submitted with randomly normal-distributed costs in the open interval $(0, 1)$. The results are showed in figure 3 that shows the utilization time assigned by the scheduler to ten services running for ten epochs varying the number of both quanta per interval and intervals per epoch, so the global execution time is constant (30 seconds). The results allow to identify a configuration of the scheduling parameters before mentioned that satisfies the requested service priorities. In fact, as a general result it is shown that when the number of used quanta is 3 or more times the number of requested services, the utilization time is close to the requested service priorities and the effect of the number of scheduling intervals is not relevant.

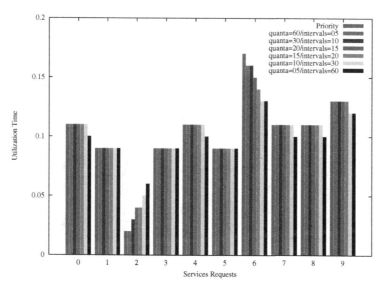

Fig. 3. Service utilization time varying the number of both the intervals and the epochs, with fixed system running time

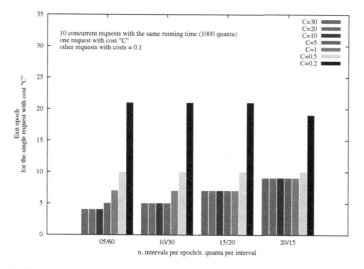

Fig. 4. Service execution time in the case of a single request with high cost

In the second set of experiments we evaluated how the service execution time varies by incrementing the associated costs, and consequently its priority.

We considered two situations: in the first there is one request with priority higher than the one associated by the provider scheduler as default (i.e. 0.1) to the other concurrent requests (see figure 4); in the second scenario 50% of the requests has priority higher than the default value (see figure 5). In both

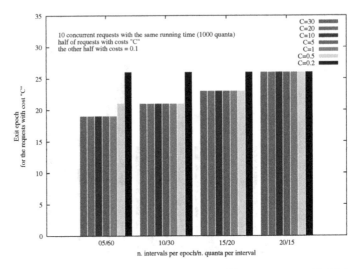

Fig. 5. Service execution time in the case of 50% of requests with high costs

scenarios we assume that the concurrent requests have the same execution time (1000 *quanta* of time).

The set of concurrent requests is limited to 10. As mentioned before, when the number of concurrent requests increases (more than one hundred), by assuming a minimal default cost of 0.1 it follows, by definition (1) that priorities are very small also if costs are one order of magnitude greater than the default. In this case the scheduling policies converges to a time-sharing policy without considering the required priorities.

In the graphs we show also the execution time changes according to different settings of scheduling parameters, i.e. the number of quanta per interval and the number of intervals per epoch. Like in the previous tests, the parameter values are set in order to guarantee the same epoch duration in all cases (300 quanta per epoch).

The graph of figure 4 reports how the execution time of a single high priority service request decreases by increasing its cost (the parameter C in the graph). The longest execution time for the service is 34 epochs corresponding to a service submission with the minimal (default) cost. From the graph we see how in this case by doubling the cost ($C = 0.2$) we obtain almost a 40% of reduction in the execution time. By increasing the cost up to ten times ($C = 1$) the default one, the runtime reduction ranges from 70% to 85% by reducing the number of scheduling intervals per epoch. Of course the simulation reproduces a synthetic test: we used it to show the expected execution time reduction in the best case, i.e. when our service submission has the highest cost in the service running set.

In the graph of figure 5 we report the execution time of half of the service requests, submitted with the same cost C. As a general comment of this test, the runtime reduction is minor than the previous case although it is less sensible to cost increases as well as the scheduling parameter settings. In fact the execution time gain ranges from 25% to 45% in the best case. The synthetic test shows that with many (50%) service requests all with the same cost greater than the default value, the limited gain is not significantly affected by increasing the cost.

Differently from the previous testbed, in the graphs of figures 4 and 5 we did not reported the measurements corresponding respectively to the scheduling parameters 30/10 and 60/05 because in such cases the number of requests is in the order of the number of quanta per interval, and so, as outlined in the previous experiment, there is no accounts of service costs.

5   Related Works and Conclusions

In this work we propose a service provider architecture based on continuation management to provide primitives to control web services execution and to implement service scheduling policies at application level. The primitives are offered by the service provider to external (client) applications through SOAP messages.

With this approach we may implement the service execution policies at two levels: the lower level relies on the service provider layer to implement local schedulers; the higher level can be a metascheduler that interacts with multiple service provider schedulers in a distributed setting to coordinate them by means of SOAP messaging.

Existing web service frameworks (Axis, WebSphere, etc.) make it difficult to implement a service provider architecture with preemption mechanisms of web services without a deep changing of the control patterns usually implemented as a built-in feature. This is because they usually obey to the *Inversion of Control* (IoC) programming pattern [10] widely used in most Java and object-oriented web-application environments. So, web service instantiation and life-cycle management cannot be fully controlled by programmers who add web services to the framework. For this reason, existing web service frameworks are not suitable to provide an application-level control of service execution supporting service suspension and resuming.

In [4] the authors propose a user-level framework for service execution scheduling. Our economy-based two-level scheduling algorithm is based on the one proposed in [4]. But we decided to split scheduling activities in two layers in order to interleave scheduling and communications activities. On the contrary, in [4] the scheduling epoch layer is introduced to measure the fairness of the scheduling algorithm, rather than actually use it for specific purposes.

In our work epochs are introduced as scheduling points when new service submissions are scheduled so that overhead due to priorities recomputing is limited. Furthermore the service scheduling framework proposed in [4] accomplish service (thread) suspension and resuming using the signals API of the underlying OS. Thus, although a user-level scheduler with a priority-based policy is proposed to control service execution, the system is depending on the underlying OS layer to properly work. In our system also the lower scheduling layer, i.e. the timesharing stage, is implemented at application-level by means of continuations programming.

So, the proposed continuation-based service provider features programmable and full control of generic web service executions that does not depend on the OS layer. Thus portability can be guaranteed across heterogeneous programming environments with explicit support of continuation capturing and resuming. This choice makes the framework flexible and easily adaptable for developing and experimenting scheduling facilities, policies and service-control in different service-oriented architecture applications.

We need to carry out more experiments that take into account the arrival of new service requests as well as the priority changes during execution. These tests will give us the possibility to study the scheduling algorithm behavior in more dynamic settings. In this scenario we are confident that the epoch size will be a relevant tuning parameter in order to adapt service utilization time to priority changes.

References

1. Foster, I., Kesselman, C., Nick, J., Tuecke, S.: The physiology of the grid: An open grid service architecture for distributed system integration. Technical report Open Grid Service Infrastructure WG (2002)
2. MacLaren, J., Sakellariou, R., Garibaldi, J., Ouelhadj, D.: Towards service level agreement based scheduling on the grid. In: Proceedings of the second European Across Grids Conference (2004)
3. Friedman, P., Haynes, C.T., Kohlbecker, E.E.: Programming with Continuations. In: Program Transformation and Programming Environments, pp. 263–274. Springer, Heidelberg (1984)
4. Newhouse, T., Pasquale, J.: A user-level framework for scheduling within service execution environments. In: Proceedings of the 2004 IEEE International Conference on Services Computing (SCC 2004), Washington, DC, USA, pp. 311–318. IEEE Computer Society (2004)
5. Abelson, H., Sussman, G.J.: Structure and Interpretation of Computer Programs, 2nd edn. MIT Press, Cambridge (1993)
6. Tismer, C.: Stackless python (2007), http://www.stackless.com
7. Giordano, M., Di Napoli, C.: A Continuation-Based Framework for Economy-Driven Grid Service Provision. In: Veit, D.J., Altmann, J. (eds.) GECON 2007. LNCS, vol. 4685, pp. 112–123. Springer, Heidelberg (2007)
8. Wooldridge, M.: Engineering the computational economy. In: Proceedings of the Information Society Technologies Conference (IST–2000), Nice, France (2000)
9. Buyya, R., Abramson, D., Giddy, J.: An economy driven resource management architecture for global computational power grids. In: Proc. of PDPTA 2000, Las Vegas, USA (2000)
10. Fowler, M.: Inversion of control containers and the dependency injection pattern (2004), http://www.martinfowler.com/articles/injection.html

Parallelization and Distribution Strategies of Large Bioinformatics Requests over the Grid

Eddy Caron, Frédéric Desprez, and Gaël Le Mahec

[1] University of Lyon, ENS Lyon, INRIA
[2] LIP. UMR 5668, ENS Lyon, INRIA, CNRS, UCBL, France
[3] LPC de Clermont-Ferrand, CNRS, IN2P3, UBP Université Blaise Pascal, France
`lemahec@clermont.in2p3.fr`

Abstract. This paper focuses on simultaneous scheduling of computation and data replication for life science applications on the grid. We present an adaptive algorithm based on the SRA algorithm (Static Joint Replication and Scheduling) [4] with more dynamicity for the jobs frequencies. The use of a linear program giving a databases mapping on the nodes and a jobs distribution schema, ensures us that our data placement and jobs distribution will be near the optimal solution, as long as the informations about the jobs frequencies are right. We validate our results with large jobs submissions simulations on a realistic platform.

1 Introduction

Since the eighties, biological databases have grown exponentially. The treatments or searches on databases that were taking few minutes can now take several days. Due to the geographical distribution of the life science laboratories and the computation power and storage capacity needs, grid computing is a good way to improve and simplify the resources sharing. In this paper, we will discuss how to distribute data and jobs among the nodes of a grid to improve the performance of the submission of bioinformatics jobs. In [4], the authors present a scheduling strategy called SRA (Static Joint Replication and Scheduling) based on the hypothesis that, if a large enough time interval is chosen, the proportion of a job using a data is always the same. This paper presents an adaptation of the SRA algorithm when these jobs proportions are varying.

The rest of the paper is organized as follows. In the next section, we describe the problem that our algorithm must deal with and we recall how the SRA algorithm is working. In Section 3, we present the algorithm itself. Section 4 is devoted to the experiments with comparisons to the SRA scheduling algorithms. The last section presents the conclusion and future works.

2 Problem Description

We have:

- $\{d_j\}_{j \in [1..n]}$: n databases of respective size $size_j$.

A. Bourgeois and S.Q. Zheng (Eds.): ICA3PP 2008, LNCS 5022, pp. 257–260, 2008.

- $\{S_i\}_{i\in[1..m]}$: m servers with m_i and w_i as storage and computational capacities.
- $\{a_k\}_{k\in[1..p]}$: p algorithms of linear complexity with $\alpha_k \times size_j + c_k$ the computational power needed to execute the algorithm a_k on d_j. Such a request is noted $R_{k,j}$.

The time to execute a request on a node depends on the size of the database. Each job is submitted to a *Resource Broker* which chooses a Computing Element to queue the job on it. When a job is queued on a *Computing Element*, it waits for the next worker node that can execute it, with a FIFO policy. The objective is to ensure the better throughput of the platform.

We present here a brief description of the SRA algorithm:

Let $\delta_i^j = \begin{cases} 1 \text{ if there is a replica of } d_j \text{ on } S_i, \\ 0 \text{ otherwise.} \end{cases}$

Let $n_i(k, j)$ be the number of requests $R_{k,j}$ to be executed on S_i.

Let $v_{k,j} = \begin{cases} 1 \text{ if } R_{k,j} \text{ is a possible request,} \\ 0 \text{ otherwise.} \end{cases}$

Let TP be the platform throughput.

The following linear program gives a data mapping on the servers and, for each kind of job, where they should be executed.

$$\begin{cases} \sum_{j=1}^{n} \delta_i^j \geq 1 & \text{Each data is on the platform.} \\ \sum_{j=1}^{n} \delta_i^j \cdot size_j \leq m_i & \text{Storage capacity is limited.} \\ n_i(k,j) \leq v_{k,j}.\delta_i^j \cdot \frac{w_i}{\alpha_k \cdot size_j + c_k} & \text{Computing capacity is limited.} \\ \sum_{k=1}^{p} \sum_{j=1}^{n} n_i(k,j)(\alpha_k \cdot size_j + c_k) \leq w_i & \text{Computing capacity is limited.} \\ \sum_{i=1}^{m} n_i(k,j) = f_{k,j} \cdot TP & \text{Requests frequencies.} \end{cases}$$

The integer solution approximation is then obtained by an approximation algorithm.

3   Dynamic Databases Redistribution and Job Scheduling

Using the SRA algorithm, when the frequencies of each type of request do not vary, we obtain very good results. But if the frequencies vary during the submission process, performance will significantly decrease. Our algorithm tries to correct this by observing each job frequency and recomputes the $n_i(k,j)$ jobs distribution values and the data placement matrix δ_i^j. Let us denote:

- N: the minimum number of requests to evaluate the frequencies.
- ε: the frequency variation threshold beyond which we decide to recompute the SRA linear program.

Algorithm 1. Dynamic SRA algorithm.

1: initialize($f_{k,j}$)
2: nb $\longleftarrow$ 0
3: δ_i^j, $n_i(k,j)$ $\longleftarrow$ SRA($f_{k,j}$)
4: **while** There is request $R_{k,j}$ to schedule **do**
5:      Add $R_{k,j}$ in $f'_{k,j}$
6:      **if** nb $\geq$ N && $\exists k,j$ such $|f_{k,j} - f'_{k,j}| \geq \varepsilon$ **then**
7:          δ_i^j, $n_i(k,j)$ $\longleftarrow$ SRA($f'_{k,j}$)
8:          Data redistribution(δ_i^j) (*if asynchronous data redistribution*)
9:          $f_{k,j} \longleftarrow f'_{k,j}$
10:          nb $\longleftarrow$ 0
11:          Reinitialize($f'_{k,j}$)
12:      **end if**
13:      Schedule $R_{k,j}$ according to $n_i(k,j)$
14: **end while**

The algorithm starts with the initialization of the frequencies and the data and job placement computing (l. 1 to l. 3). The main loop of the algorithm (from l. 4 to l. 14) starts with the record of the new job submission (l. 5). Then, if enough jobs have been recorded (nb $\geq$ N) and if a measured frequency is too different from the previously used one for the SRA algorithm ($|f_{k,j} - f'_{k,j}| \geq \varepsilon$), the algorithm recomputes δ_i^j and $n_i(k,j)$ (l. 7). If it is possible, the data redistribution can then be launched asynchronously by the algorithm. Otherwise, the job scheduling will cause the data transfers to reach the new data placement. The loop ends with the choice of a node to execute the job using the $n_i(k,j)$ values.

4   Experiments

In this section we present the results obtained on simulations using OptorSim [2], a grid simulator developed by the CERN for the DataGrid project [5]. The data used for the applications can be obtained from the platform or some external public ftp sites. The data sizes vary from 1 GB to 5 GB. Jobs are submitted with a rate of 1 job per 3.5 seconds. The data are distributed randomly among the nodes at the beginning of the process. For our experiments we used a network of 9 sites which have from 90 to 680 worker nodes of different computation power. Without correction of the data replication and job distributions over the nodes, the frequencies variations decrease the efficiency of the SRA algorithm (see Figure 1). The frequencies variations have few effect when the jobs submitted are not numerous. But, after few time, with a large set of jobs, the platform starts to saturate in spite of data replication. Then, the average waiting time of the jobs increases with the number of jobs submitted. By correcting the data and job distributions when detecting a significant change in the frequencies, our algorithm limits the platform saturation (see Figure 2).

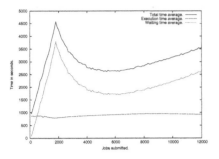

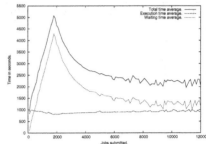

Fig. 1. Simple SRA algorithm   **Fig. 2.** Dynamic SRA algorithm

5   Conclusion and Future Work

In this paper, we proposed a dynamic job and data replication scheduling algorithm for the grid taking into account the specificities of the grid usage for bioinformatics. Using only some informations collected by the scheduler itself, this algorithm avoids the use of complex grid monitoring services and could be easily and effectively used in the context of bioinformatics grids.

In this paper, the database redistribution uses a fixed strategy to choose when and from where the data have to be transfered. The redistribution is itself a hard problem and we will study different strategies in a future work. Our algorithm will also be tested on Grid'5000 [1], a reconfigurable and heterogeneous grid dedicated to the computer science experimentations. We will use the DIET middleware [3] to which we already added an advanced data manager.

References

1. Bolze, R., Cappello, F., Caron, E., Daydé, M., Desprez, F., Jeannot, E., Jégou, Y., Lanteri, S., Leduc, J., Melab, N., Mornet, G., Namyst, R., Primet, P., Quetier, B., Richard, O., Talbi, E.-G., Touché, I.: Grid 5000: A Large Scale and Highly Reconfigurable Experimental Grid Testbed. International Journal of High Performance Computing Applications 20(4), 481–494 (2006)
2. Cameron, D.G., Carvajal-Schiaffino, R., Millar, A.P., Nicholson, C., Stockinger, K., Zini, F.: Evaluating scheduling and replica optimisation strategies in OptorSim. In: Proc. Fourth International Workshop on Grid Computing, 2003, pp. 52–59 (2003)
3. Caron, E., Desprez, F.: Diet: A Scalable Toolbox to Build Network Enabled Servers on the Grid. International Journal of High Performance Computing Applications 20(3), 335 (2006)
4. Desprez, F., Vernois, A.: Simultaneous Scheduling of Replication and Computation for Data-Intensive Applications on the Grid. J. of Grid Computing 4(1), 19–31 (2006)
5. Donno, F., Gaido, L., Ghiselli, A., Prelz, F., Sgaravatto, M.: Datagrid prototype 1. In: TERENA Networking conference (June 2002)

Designing an Architecture for Distributed Shared Data on the Grid

Dacian Tudor[1], Vladimir Cretu[1], and Wolfgang Schreiner[2]

[1] Politehnica University of Timisoara, Computer Science and Engineering Department,
Vasile Parvan Street, No. 2, 300223, Timisoara, Romania
{dacian,vretu}@cs.upt.ro
[2] Research Institute for Symbolic Computation (RISC)
Johannes Kepler University, 4040 Linz, Austria
Wolfgang.Schreiner@risc.uni-linz.ac.at

Abstract. Despite the continuous advances of the last years in grid computing, the grid computing programming paradigms are dominated by the message passing concept. There is little support for other paradigms such as shared data or associative programming. In this paper we analyze some of the existing solutions for grid shared data programming and highlight some of their drawbacks. We propose a new architecture and its core features as well as new evaluation means of its behavior in various scenarios including the next generation grid systems. In addition to the simplicity of our solution, we believe that it would allow us to easily apply further extensions.

Keywords: grid computing, distributed shared data, programming model.

1 Introduction

Although the number of networked machines has been constantly increased, the number of new distributed applications is still much lower. Some of the core issues that are faced by distributed applications are due to latencies, synchronization and partial failures. Only on dedicated grids ideal conditions can hold during the entire application lifetime. Next, the increasing heterogeneity and the greater difficulty to replace large spread legacy systems impose an important break on grid application development. One of the answers we believe to these challenges is in the grid programming model and more specifically in grid shared data programming.

In the grid landscape, there are very few solutions for large scale data sharing models. Solutions like the LOTS system [1], SMG [2] or Teamster-G [3] that addresses the shared memory problem at the grid level does not provide important information like detailed design, replication policies, mutual exclusion handling, and memory consistency specification. Besides the missing information, there is little evidence of their suitability or behavior in large scale grid computing. A new direction towards dependable distributed computing systems that aim to improve both data and service availability is aimed by Dedisys [4], which appears to focus on availability and fault tolerance at the system level rather than performance. Most advanced solution for grid

A. Bourgeois and S.Q. Zheng (Eds.): ICA3PP 2008, LNCS 5022, pp. 261.264, 2008.
© Springer-Verlag Berlin Heidelberg 2008

shared data programming that came to our knowledge is JuxMem [5], which is based on peer-to-peer middleware. One of its main drawbacks is the fixed replication scheme that bounds data replicas at creation time or when fault occur, and which does not consider the system dynamics such as data usage patterns.

We have noticed that there are few shared memory systems designed for the grid. Many of these systems were tested in particular environments that represent ideal scenarios of fast connected machines most of the times being grouped as high performance clusters. In search for a better approach, we aim to investigate the problem of distributed shared memory for grid systems and provide a system specification that addresses the following main points we found missing in most of the existing solutions:

(1) **Large scale system over large latency connections**, which are dominant between machines located at large distances.
(2) **Relaxed consistency and type coherence,** as we expect that relaxed consistency does not carry sufficient information on data usage.
(3) **Object oriented architecture,** as the most appealing concept for grid application programmers.
(4) **Quantifiable system validation and verification**, through formal methods as a proof of concept for the system model.

2 Abstract Model

Some of the previous attempts in designing distributed shared memory systems for the grid used logical mappings over one single large machine group. We believe that another split is necessary. We see this mapping as part of the system deployment, rather than a predefined mapping. In order to address thousands of nodes, we decompose the system into a federation of groups of abstract machines called universes. A universe is a logical collection of machine nodes which provides a hosting environment for distributed objects. Nodes are homogeneous and have a data storage capacity in memory and code execution capabilities. Each node can hold a certain number of objects so that the sum of all object weights held by the node shall not exceed the node s capacity. All existing universes form together the Grid Universe. Each universe is a continuously evolving entity together with its connections to the other universes. A universe groups together more physical machines which share the same communication paths, thus communication channels within universes are homogeneous and have known and constant characteristics. Communication between universes is unpredictable, unknown and dynamic.

We propose an object oriented model which provides interfaces for data encapsulation and a natural and convenient way to abstract data sharing objects. It supports the idea of objects residing in architectural different run-time systems like nodes in universes. The grid universe acts as a container for grid objects and provides means to create delete and locate grid objects based on a unique object identifier. The users do not operate directly on objects, but rather on object references. A grid object reference is a handle to a concrete grid object that provides the same interface as the object provides. A Grid Object has two identifiers associated with: the GID, which is associated by the system, and the OID which is given by the creator as a human friendly identifier. The OID is used to lookup a certain grid object. In order to decrease access time to grid objects from different universes, we make use of data replication concepts. If some configurable system conditions are satisfied, a grid object is replicated to other universe nodes, assuming that object state can be transferred from one process to another across a communication path.

3 System Architecture Selection

The main issue that our architecture needs to address is the problem of realizing mutual exclusion. We have chosen entry consistency as replica consistency specification for our system and we evaluated several possible solutions to realize the abstract model. In the following table, we summarize the characteristics of each of the four remaining candidates, where we highlight the negative characteristics of each solution by marking them in italic style.

Table 1. Solution Selection Criteria

Criteria	Centralized/N-T	Martin/N-T	Suzuki-Kasami/N-T	Grid N-T
Universe Scalability	High	High	High	High
Local scalability	*Low/Medium*	*Low*	Medium	High
Local obtaining time	*Low/Medium*	Medium/High	Medium	Low
Local resource demand	Low	*Medium*	*High*	Low/Medium
Independent processing	High	*Low*	*Low*	*Low*
Complexity	Low	*Medium*	*Medium*	*High*
Local dynamics	High	*Low/Medium*	*Low/Medium*	Low

The first solution is our main contribution and refers to a centralized algorithm inside each universe and a multi-token algorithm between universes derived from the Naimi-Trehel [6] algorithm that was adapted to satisfy entry consistency. The core motivation for this choice is its high local dynamics, higher capability to perform independently, a low resource demand and low complexity. We have traded the local scalability for all other characteristics as we believe that universes will have a limited number of nodes for typical deployment scenarios. The next two considered solutions are the compositional approaches described [7]. These are similar to the previous solution, the only difference is the mutual exclusion algorithm applied inside a universe. The last choice is the adapted Naimi-Trehel algorithm described in [8] which is applied on the grid scope. This solution requires a gateway node in each cluster in order to keep track if the token is held remotely or not. From this point of view, this design approach resembles our proposal. Based on the measurements of [8], it appears that the Naimi-Trehel algorithm is the most suitable algorithm between universes and it provides a reasonable trade-off between different classes or applications (highly parallel vs. low parallel applications) which supports the idea of our architecture proposal.

4 Conclusions

In this paper we have highlighted the problem of shared data programming on the grid and have pointed out that there is little research in this direction. We have introduced an abstract programming model that transparently defines the grid shared data items as grid shared objects. In addition to the relaxed entry consistency semantics, we consider different object types in order to exploit different synchronization schemes and reduce communications costs. We have proposed a mutual exclusion algorithm based on the Naimi-Trehel algorithm that is easy to adapt and extend in order to accommodate different interaction patterns.

A model of the presented system is currently being developed in order to be simulated and verified using a probabilistic model checker that would provide quantifiable results on the behavior of our system in various conditions. At the same time, a prototype implementation is being developed in order to confirm the findings through model verification and simulation.

References

1. Cheung, B.W.L., Wang, C.-L., Lau, F.C.M.: LOTS: a software DSM supporting large object space. In: IEEE International Conference on Cluster Computing, pp. 225-234 (2004) ISBN: 0-7803-8694-9
2. Ryan, J.P., Coghlan, B.A.: SMG: Shared memory for Grids. In: Proceedings of 6th IASTED International Conference on Parallel and Distributed Computing and Systems, pp. 439.451 (2004), http://www.cs.tcd.ie/coghlan/pubs/pdcs04-06072004-v1.pdf
3. Foster, I., Kesselman, C.: The Grid: Blueprint for a New Computing Infrastructure. Morgan Kaufmann, San Francisco (1999)
4. Osrael, J., Froihofer, L., Goeschka, K.M.: A Replication Model for Trading Data Integrity against Availabilit. In: The 12th Int. Symp. on Pacific Rim Dependable Computing (PRDC 2006). IEEE CS Press (2006)
5. Antoniu, G., Bougé, L., Jan, M.: JuxMem: An Adaptive Supportive Platform for Data Sharing on the Grid. Scalable Computing: Practice and Experience 6, 45.55 (2005)
6. Naimi, M., Trehel, M., Arnold, A.: A log (N) distributed mutual exclusion algorithm based on path reversal. JPDC 34(1), 1..13 (1996)
7. Sopena, J., Legond-Aubry, F., Arantes, L., Sens, P.: A Composition Approach to Mutual Exclusion Algorithms for Grid Applications. In: Proceedings of the 2007 International Conference on Parallel Processing (ICPP 2007), vol. 00, p. 65 (2007) ISBN 0-7695-2933-X
8. Bertier, M., Arantes, L., Sens, P.: Hierarchical token based mutual exclusion algorithms. In: IEEE International Symposium on Cluster Computing and the Grid, 2004. CCGrid 2004, April 19-22, pp. 539.546 (2004) ISBN: 0-7803-8430-x

Grinda: A Tuple Space Service for the Globus Toolkit

Sirio Capizzi and Antonio Messina

University of Bologna
Department of Computer Science
Mura Anteo Zamboni 7, 40126 Bologna Italy
{capizzi,messina}@cs.unibo.it

Abstract. In this article we present a service for the Globus Toolkit that implements the tuple space model, allowing applications to use it to coordinate their activities.

1 Introduction

There are several ways to coordinate tasks in a GRID middleware as, for instance, publish/subscribe systems or workflow engines. Another possible approach to coordinate tasks is the use of tuple spaces [1]. This model has been introduced several years ago and has been successfully used for the coordination of numerical applications. In this article we will describe our experience in developing a tuple space service named Grinda for the Globus Toolkit 4 [2]. This service is designed as coordination framework for applications and services. For example, it can be used by an index service to implement distributed indexes. Applications and services developed with Grinda can exploit interesting features like independence from network topology and the possibility to choose between different tuple space implementations, adapting the framework to the application requirements.

2 The Tuple Space Model

The Tuple Space model proposed by Carriero and Gelernter as coordination model for distributed application [1] is based on the concept of a virtual shared memory, the tuple space, on which the various hosts can operate using a limited number of powerful operations.

In the past years several tuple space implementation has been proposed. The most important are TCP Linda [3], the last incarnation of the original model, TSpace [4], JavaSpaces [5], GigaSpaces [6], Lime [7], Tucson [8] and many others.

The tuple space model we have employed in our system is inspired by JavaSpaces. It uses full fledge objects as tuples instead of the usual array structure. We have decided to use the JavaSpaces approach for two reasons: it simplifies the developing of applications promoting the reuse of existing objects, and it maps better into XML messages requiring less effort for the serialization. Moreover, our model supports subtype matching too.

A. Bourgeois and S.Q. Zheng (Eds.): ICA3PP 2008, LNCS 5022, pp. 265–268, 2008.

3   Service Implementation

The architecture of the Grinda service is composed by two main modules: a client-side module and a server-side one.

The main purpose of the client-side module is to hide the details of the communication with the server, in order to simplify the development of applications based on Grinda. It has been designed to be loosely-coupled with the service allowing the use of other libraries or programming languages. We have developed two different client-side modules: one in Java and the other in C++.

The server-side module contains the logic responsible for storing the tuples and for implementing the tuple space operations. It has been designed to be a Web Service deployable in the Globus Toolkit's container. Its architecture is based on the Factory Design Pattern used to create and manage configurations and tuple space objects.

Tuple spaces have been designed to be modular and share the same interface allowing different implementations to be developed. Until now, we have implemented two different types of tuple space: a transient and a persistent one. The first type uses spatial indexes to speed-up space operations whereas persistent tuple spaces have been implemented using an XML databases.

Tuple Serialization. The major difficulty in implementing Grinda service was the handling of different data types in tuples. Usually, web services developers have to deal with predefined data structures. In our case this approach cannot be followed because the service is unable to know in advance the data types employed. Therefore, we have simplified the serialization management, allowing developers to use their objects directly.

To convert data into XML we have used the XStream library [9]. Employing the Java reflection, this library automatically serializes objects in a XML representation following their own internal structure, without the need of specific serializers. If some data type still need a specific serializer, external plugins can be used.

Nevertheless, there are cases in which this translation to plain XML fails. For example, special encoding of binary data types or matching through the use of supertypes cannot be effectively achieved in this way. Therefore, special XML attributes have been added in these cases.

C++ Client. The automatic type serialization in the C++ client has been quite challenging. Actually, C++ does not implement a standard reflection API and RTTI is not powerful enough to support the automatic serialization of custom types. For this reason we have used the Qt4 Toolkit that provides the Meta Object System. It is a reflection API less evolved than the Java counterpart but still very useful for our purpose.

Since the Qt framework does not support SOAP or XML-RPC messaging, we have used the gSOAP 2.7.9 library, a little and embeddable library that allows to develop web services in both C and C++.

4   Test Results

We have performed some preliminary tests to verify the behavior of Grinda. In particular two different aspects have been measured: the latency of the system and its scalability. For the latter test two different types of applications have been employed.

The first type of application consists in using a brute force attack to guess an hashed password. This is an embarassingly parallel application that requires almost no communications during its execution. Thus the communication overhead is very limited.

The second test application is a plasma simulation performed porting in Grinda the MPI-based ALaDyn code [10] that implements a so called Particle In Cell (PIC) based simulation. The algorithm used is known to be not completely parallel and requires much more communications than the first application.

All our tests have been conducted on the same testbed: a 100Mbps Ethernet LAN composed by up to 64 Core Duo PCs equipped with Ubuntu Linux 7.04. This network was not dedicated because it is a student laboratory, but was the only choice we had to collect a medium-large number of hosts.

Latency Tests. The first test has measured the latency of the service and its dependency on the host number. Given a number of clients, the tests consist in calculating the average time spent for taking/writing the same tuple from/in a space. The average has been obtained from 1000 repeated tests. Figure 1a shows that the average time required by take operations seems to be absolutely independent of the network size, whereas write operations increase by a small factor, $\sim 20\%$, when the size grows. Probably this is caused by an higher overhead in instantiating all the objects required for storing tuples.

Scalability Test. As described before, the scalability has been studied on two different types of applications. In both cases, we have measured the average time required for computation as host number increase.

The purpose of the first application was to analyze the behavior of our service in a completely parallel application with a minimum communication overhead. Figure 1b reports performance time averaged over 100 run with respect to node

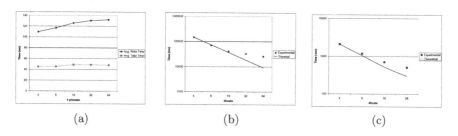

(a)   (b)   (c)

Fig. 1a. Latency test results. **Fig. 1b.** Results of the scalability test using the highly parallel application. **Fig. 1c.** Results of the scalability test for plasma simulation code.

number: it is clear that this application scale very well according to the theoretical limit, $\simeq N^{-1}$.

Figure 1c shows performance of plasma algorithm. Of course, the performance is worst with respect to the previous one. However this fixes the range of performance of the Grinda service.

5 Conclusion

In this article we have described our experiences in developing a tuple space service for the Globus Toolkit. This service can be used to implement distributed applications in a simple way, exploit interesting feature like automatic load-balancing. It provides automatic serialization of data types and its architecture is modular enough to support legacy applications too.

According to the test results we have collected, it seems that our service can provide good performance to both completely and non-completely parallelizable applications. However, these tests are only preliminary and a more deeper use and development of this service is needed in order to produce an industrial-strength product.

References

1. Gelernter, D., Carriero, N.: Coordination Languages and Their Significance. Communication of the ACM 35(2), 96 (1992)
2. Globus Alliance: Globus Toolkit 4 (2006), http://www.globus.org
3. SCA: TCP Linda (2006), http://www.lindaspaces.com
4. IBM Corporation: TSpace Specification (1999)
5. Sun Microsystem: JavaSpaces Specifications (2005)
6. Shalom, N.: Space-Based Architecture and The End of Tier-based Computing (2006)
7. Picco, G.P., Murphy, A.L., Roman, G.C.: LIME: Linda Meets Mobility. In: International Conference on Software Engineering, pp. 368–377 (1999)
8. Omicini, A., Zambonelli, F.: Tuple centres for the coordination of Internet agents. In: SAC 1999: Proceedings of the 1999 ACM symposium on Applied computing, pp. 183–190. ACM Press, New York (1999)
9. XStream Project: XStream Library (2007), http://xstream.codehaus.org
10. Benedetti, C., Londrillo, P., Sgattoni, A., Turchetti, G.: ALaDyn: a high accuracy PIC code for the Maxwell-Vlasov equations. In: Laser and Plasma Accelerators Workshop, Azores, Portugal (2007)

SuMo: A Framework for Prototyping Distributed and Mobile Software

Hervé Paulino

CITI / Departamento de Informática, FCT Universidade Nova de Lisboa, Portugal
herve@di.fct.unl.pt

Abstract. The current trend in the organization of computational systems is propitious to the definition of run-time infrastructures that embed distribution and mobility. Most of these grow from existent virtual machines that execute sequential or concurrent code. In this paper we present SuMo, a platform that factorizes all communication and mobility dependent operations into a reusable layer. Our purpose is to provide a framework to intuitively and easily extend existing virtual machines to execute mobile distributed computations.

1 Introduction and Motivation

The last few years has seen the proliferation of many programming languages featuring distribution and mobility. The gradual evolution of the computational systems to distributed environments, where mobility plays an crucial role, and the appearance of distributed process calculi, such as the Dπ-calculus [1], as a tool to model distributed computations, were two defining factors.

In many cases, these programming languages are simple extensions to already existing sequential or concurrent ones, incorporating constructs to move processes across the network, and to allow for remote communication and/or synchronization. Examples of such extensions are: DiTyCO (Distributed TyCO) [2], Mobile Ambients [3], Jocaml [4] and M-calculus [5] (based on Distributed Join [6]). The run-time support for these new distributed systems usually grows from existing infrastructures that execute local computations. Thus, all the effort goes into providing support for distribution and mobility.

In this paper we present SuMo (Support for Mobile distributed software), a platform that factorizes these distribution and mobility dependent operations in a reusable layer. We reason on which operations are required by our target systems, and to which degree these can be factorized. We then define the interfaces necessary for functionality standardization and abstraction, and provide full or partial implementations of the factorized operations, namely resource publishing and discovery, communication protocols, failure recovery, and so on.

The ultimate objective is to provide an intuitive framework for the easy and fast prototyping of these languages by embedding distribution in the original virtual machines. This allows to invest more in the implementation details that are real contributions to the community.

A. Bourgeois and S.Q. Zheng (Eds.): ICA3PP 2008, LNCS 5022, pp. 269–281, 2008.

In summary, we feel that the main contributions of this work to the area of middleware for distributed and mobile software are the following: (1) the factorization of the distribution and mobility dependent operations in a middleware that lives between the existent virtual machine and the outside world; (2) the design approach specially focused at existing virtual machines, trying to reduce the modifications to the indispensable (note that run-times may also be built from scratch); (3) modularity, the platform allows for many different types of architectures, message passing or shared memory driven; (4) full mobility support, weak and strong, providing the means for reliable communication, and; (5) extensibility, the platform is not self-contained, new functionalities, such as communication protocols or new events can be added.

Some work as already been done in this area [7], which features our collaboration. We, however think that this new approach is more powerful and simpler to use. A detailed comparison of our approach to the existing one will be given in section 4. The remainder of the paper is structured as follows: the next section reasons on which are the operations that can and must be factorized and, how this is done in the scope of the SuMo framework; section 3 presents a case study where we incorporate distribution and mobility into an existant virtual machine; section 4 compares our work with other proposals in the field, and; finally section 5 presents some conclusions and future guiding lines.

2   The SuMo Framework

In this section we reason about which are the distribution and mobility dependent operations that can and must be factorized and, how this is done in the scope of the SuMo framework.

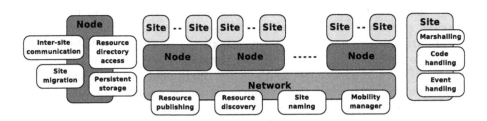

Fig. 1. The layered architecture of the SuMo framework

Our architectural approach is layered and service-based (Figure 1). The operations are encapsulated into services that, in turn, are structured in three layers: the *network layer* provides network-wide services, such as resource discovery; the *node layer*, composed of abstractions for regular network nodes (*nodes*) provides networking operations, such as remote communication, and; the *site layer* defines the computational units (*sites*) and how these interact with the remainder of the network, such as resource access.

2.1   The Network Layer

Interaction in distributed systems naturally depends on the awareness that a site has of the resources published by its counterparts, i.e., a Web browser must know where a target server is listening for requests. This information can be statically known, or discovered on-the-fly, where resource publishing and discovery plays a crucial role and requires some kind of directory service.

Resources published in such service must be uniquely identified in the network. A classic approach is the qualification with the hosting site's identifier. This requires some kind of site naming mechanism that can be simply the location of the node running the site, which imposes a one site per node restriction, or a symbolic identifier that has to be translated into the proper location.

One last concern is site mobility that introduces a problem in the management of the network's state coherency. Sites that have bindings to resources held by the site about to move will hold invalid references.

In the remainder of this subsection we will explain how SuMo copes with resource publishing/discovery, site identifiers, locations and site mobility.

Resource Publishing and Discovery. In SuMo the resource discovery and naming services are closely coupled, and from now on will be simply referred to as the *resource directory.* The framework fully implements this directory, providing the IResourceDirectory interface that allows sites to register and unregister their location, discover the location of their peers, publish a set of resources, bind to a set of resources, define new namespaces, and, in the presence of mobility, to inform the network that a migration is taking place and, later, to update their location,

Resources are represented in the framework by the Resource abstract class and identified by implementations of the IResourceIdentifier interface that, in turn, resort to site identifiers, implementations of the ISiteIdentifier interface.

Concrete instances of Resource must define resource compatibility, i.e., the mechanism that guarantees the absence of protocol errors when accessing the requested resource. This typically resorts to type information manipulation that is implementation dependent and thus not provided by the framework.

Site Identifiers. Implementations of IResourceIdentifier and ISiteIdentifier must define identifier equality. The framework provides a concrete implementations of these interfaces that cope with the most common use of identifiers, resorting to strings and denoting hierarchical networks. Flat networks can be seen as hierarchical network with a single namespace.

Hierarchical namespaces define overlay networks on top of the existant network topology. Figure 2 relates to a classic video streaming system where the available videos are categorized according to their style. In order to a site to receive the streaming of one given video it must register itself in the correspondent namespace. The leftmost figure illustrates the distribution of the sites along the network nodes. The trees of the right represent the three overlay networks, one for each available movie style.

In SuMo the media used to store the namespace's registry, e.g., hashtables (regular or distributed) or databases, is also defined by an interface (INameSpaceMedia).

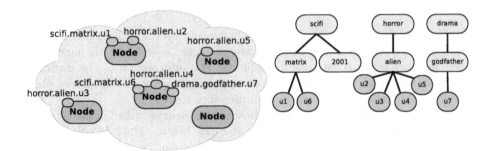

Fig. 2. Overlay network application example

Currently, only an implementation that resorts to an internal hashtable (HTNameSpaceMedia) is supplied.

The resource directory may be centralized, where all namespaces live in the same node, or distributed along the network. The later case requires communication between a namespace and its parent or sons. In SuMo all these details are encapsulated in class ResourceDirectoryProxy that, by also implementing the IResourceDirectory interface, provides all the operations available in the directory.

Locations. The current location of site is given by the Location abstract class. The choice of a class, in opposition to an interface, is due to the fact that locations must extend the Value base class for exchangeable values in the network (more on this later). Location must be concretely extended to provide any kind of localization protocols. This includes how the location listens to incoming connections, and how it provides the means for other sites to require a connection. Currently, SuMo provides a single concrete instance of Location: IPLocation, that resorts to the (node network name/IP address, port number) tuple used to identify ports in IP based communication protocols, such as TCP/IP.

Handling Site Mobility. We solve this problem by having a protocol that ensures reliable communication in the presence of logic mobility [8]. This results in a lazy reconfiguration of the network's topology. The attempt to establish a connection to a site that is no longer where expected throws an exception that triggers a connection to the resource directory. Once the new location is obtained communication may proceed.

This solution requires the locking of the moving site's information in the resource directory during the migration process. Thus, before migrating, a site informs the directory service of its intention, which causes the suspension every query related to the site until the new location is made public.

2.2   The Node Layer

A site executes in the boundaries of a node that provides for its execution environment, namely, dedicated and isolated flows of execution that ensure the privacy of a site's resources[1]. It is also desirable to abstract the site from all networking related details by providing, at the node level, a set of services that establish the interface between the site and the remainder of the network. For instance, sites running in the same node may communicate through shared-memory or TCP based sockets. With this approach the management of these details is entirely left to node, becoming completely transparent to the site.

In this perspective, the set of services provided by a node must include all the network operations a site requires, namely interaction with the resource directory, inter-site communication, site mobility and failure recovery. SuMo defines the interfaces and fully implements each of these services, requiring only the definition of the node's communication technology (or technologies if more than one is used).

Interaction with the Resource Directory. For this purpose the node must only feature a resource directory proxy of the kind described in the previous subsection. Only the root of the resource directory is known to the node and, thus, it is to that location that it will connect by default. However, as described in [8], sites may cache information about the location of the namespace of their peers. This information is passed to the node that uses it to reduce intermediaries.

Inter-site Communication. The node is responsible for managing site incoming and outgoing communication. A site may ask the node to send a single message or require a session. In the later case, the responsibility of managing the session is left entirely to the site. Messages are, thus, exchanged between nodes. This approach avoids having multiple threads, one per site, listening for incoming messages at a node. The downside is the fact that it may pose as a bottleneck for incoming traffic. Note, however, that the node only receives the message, delegating the responsibility of its handling to the to the target site. This means that, as soon as a message is delivered to a site, a new one can be received.

SuMo does not restrict the communication paradigm or protocol, it simply defines the interface that must be respected (IConnector). Currently, the framework only supplies one implementation, TCPConnector, that bases the communication on TCP sockets, bound to instances of IPLocation.

Site Mobility. In order to move to a new node, a site must be able to pause/resume its execution and to serialize/de-serialize its state. This forces every object that composes the state to be transferred to implement some serialization interface. The framework performs this task for every featured class and forces the user to do the same, by the means of either the java.io.Externalizable or the java.io.Serializable interfaces.

Once the serialization process is completed, the hosting node is called to perform the migration operation. The arrival on the new node automatically triggers the reconstruction of the site's state, binding it to the locally available instances of the node services, and the resuming its execution. A store-and-forward protocol is used, meaning that the serialized state is persistently stored

---

[1] The node launches a new flow of execution for each site it hosts. In turn sites may create their own flows of execution.

until the site's next migration. In other words, if a site originally running in node A migrates to B, and later to C, the state stored in A is only erased when the site is successfully restored in C. This ensures that at least two nodes have a copy of the site's state, providing an important tool for failure recovery.

Failure Recovery. The node provides a full implementation of a service (with interface IPersistanceService) for the persistent storing of a site's state, allowing for the recovery of previously stored states to, for instance, cope with hardware failures, or simply to rollback the execution.

The fact that the state of a migrated site is persistently stored in a node, until a new migration occurs, allows for the recovery of site even if, for any reason, the new node permanently crashes. It is only natural for this recovered state to be out-of-date, but it allows for the site to move to a new node and continue its execution. Picking in the previous example, if node C permanently crashes, the state in B can be recovered and the site can restart its execution in a new node D.

2.3   The Site Layer

A site is where actual computation takes place. It is an extension of an *original* virtual machine (VM) to handle distribution and resource mobility. Thus, a site running at some node must be able to perform computation and use the services provided by the node to interact with the remainder of the network.

In its original purpose, a VM would execute as a stand-alone computing element, and thus, with a self-contained execution environment. This contrasts with the deployment in distributed settings, where a computing element may affect and be affected by the remainder. A site must have the ability to trigger an action in one of its peers, such as remote method invocation, or simply request resources, such as code. We distinguish between the two because actions require some kind of computation (from a VM) while requests simply consult and collect data. In conclusion, sites must be composed of computing elements (VMs) and, at least one entity that uses the hosting node to manage remote interaction. We name this entity the *communicator*.

We now take a closer look on how the communicator must handle incoming actions and incoming/outgoing code (figure 3). The first requires the intervention

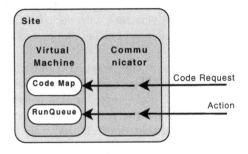

Fig. 3. Code requests and actions coming from the network

of the VM in order to execute the action and trigger the response. The second requires the access to the VM's code area, in order to retrieve or place the given code fragments. However, a VM is usually self-contained with all its data-structures protected from the outside world. Some kind of resource sharing mechanism that allows the communicator to access some of the VM's resources is required. Moreover, this implies the uniformity of the interfaces of these shared resources, since different implementations have distinct approaches.

In conclusion, this layer needs to address how a site is internally constructed by resorting to VMs and communicators, how resources can be shared among these, how the communicator handles incoming events, and last, but not least, how to implement some kind of marshalling procedure, possibly required to ensure the uniformity of the representation across sites.

Site Architecture. The internal architecture of a site is thus composed of at least one VM, that must extend the VirtualMachine abstract class, and of one *communicator*, concrete instance of the Communicator abstract class that is responsible for the interaction with the node, acessing the resources of the VM and marshalling. In figure 4 we present three distinct possible architectures for a site. The first is, perhaps, the more classic approach composed of a single VM and a single communicator. The second example illustrates a case where several VMs use a single communicator as the intermediate to manage their communication, local and remote. Finally, the third example is inspired in the Mikado membrane model [9] where one VM works as a membrane of the second, hiding its implementation details and filtering communication.

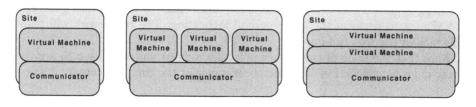

Fig. 4. Some possible architectures for a site

Accessing VM Resources. In most site architectures, resources, namely the code area and the queue of ready-to-execute tasks, of a VM must be accessed by other VMs or communicators. However, a VM is usually self-contained with all its data-structures protected from the outside world. To overcome this obstacle we define the IResourceSharer interface that must be implemented by every entity that wishes to have these access privileges. The VirtualMachine constructor receives the array of all the objects that want to access its resources. The granting is done by the VM, which allows to control who receives the accessing privileges.

The access to these shared resources must be uniform, which obliges the definition of interfaces, respectively ICodeMap and IRunQueue. Moreover, the type of elements placed in both structures must also be defined[2]. ICodeMap features methods to place and retrieve instances of CodeFragment, and IRunQueue must be a queue of instances of Frame.

Site Interaction. In SuMo inter-site communication is event driven. The messages exchanged are instances of the Event class that carries the event's data. Event discrimination in actions and requests is denoted by the ActionEvent and RequestEvent specializations of the the base class. These can, of course, be further specialized.

The handling of a code request transparently interacts with the code map to return the requested fragment. The download of code closures is also available, avoiding the posting of multiple requests. Only the code fragments that have not already been sent to the node performing the request are collected. The destination of every outgoing fragment is bookkept.

The framework does not impose any restrictions on the format of the code to migrate. The code serializing and de-serializing operations must be implemented by extending the CodeHandler abstract class that implements ICodeMap and provides the functionalities described in the previous paragraph. We want, however, to be able to migrate different kinds of data, such as a code fragment or an object (code plus data). For this purpose we define the IMigratable interface that defines the properties for *migratable* entities. Two concrete implementations MigratableCode and MigratableObject are provided.

Regarding actions, their handling begins by retrieving the code sent with the event (if any), passing it to the local code-handler that de-serializes and places it in the VM's code area. Next, the handling of the action itself is done by native code libraries, that are dynamically loaded on demand. For example, in order to allow for remote method invocation, a site must define a library that generates a VM task to perform the local method invocation. The framework will place this task in the VM run-queue.

Note that the code of the library is locally defined and its liaison to a given event must be encoded in the concrete instance of the communicator.

Marshalling. Before being dispatched to the target node, the data of an event (composed of instances of abstract class Value) may have to be marshalled, in order to be translated into a format understandable to the receiver. The procedure is not defined in the framework. Concrete instances of the communicator must supply it, by implementing the IMarshaller interface.

3   Case Studies

In this section, we present how the SuMo framework was used to implement the run-time system for the DiTyCO programming language [2,10], by extending the TyCO (Typed Distributed Objects) run-time [11] with support for distribution

---

[2] Note that internally the original representation may be kept. This however requires a transformation step between both representations.

and mobility of resources. Moreover, we present how the DiTyCO run-time was later used as the backbone for the one of the Mob programming language [12].

3.1   A Run-Time for the DiTyCO Language

DiTyCO is based on the TyCO calculus, which is a form of asynchronous π-calculus [13, 14], featuring objects, and process definitions as fundamental abstractions. Objects are sets of methods that are placed in channels. A method is selected by sending an asynchronous message targeted at the channel that holds the object. Thus, these messages are in fact method invocations. Process definitions allow for the abstraction of a process on a set of parameters, and enable recursion. Distribution was introduced in [2], by extended the language with lexical scoping for identifiers, located computations or *sites*, and code mobility (driven by lexical scope).

The Network Layer. DiTyCO networks are flat and the resources that a DiTyCO site exports are channels. Thus, there is one namespace for the whole network, and its location is usually referred to as *the name-server* (just as illustrated in figure 5). The nameserver solves the whereabouts of all the sites running in the network, and of the channels they export. Channels are represented by a concrete instance of Resource that defines channel equality by using the TyCO type unification algorithm. If the unification succeeds, the type of the channel in the name-server is replaced with the type resulting from the unification. Thus, the type locally inferred by the site that imports the channel can influence the type for the channel in the network.

The Node Layer. DiTyCO does not support site migration, thus nodes solely provide for interaction with the name-server and inter-site communication. All communication is done by resorting to the TCP protocol based connections provided by the TCPConnector class.

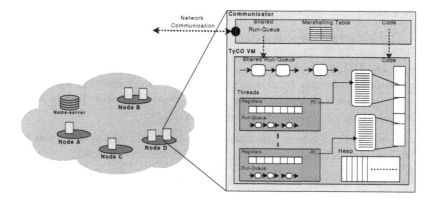

Fig. 5. The architecture of a DiTyCO site and network

The Site Layer. The run-time for DiTyCO is naturally built from the one for TyCO. Thus, the architecture of the site is simply complemented with the communicator (figure 5). The original virtual machine was altered to extend the VirtualMachine class, in order for the communicator to access to the VM's code area and run-queue. The code area and run-queue were slightly altered to be compliant with the ICodeMap and IRunQueue interfaces, respectively. The major alteration relates to the fact that fragments were originally mapped by their memory reference and, in context where code may migrate from site to site, the SuMo framework opts to map them by name.

To implement a concrete instance of the communicator we had to provide the event handling and marshalling procedures. Also required was the choice of the communication technology used in all network interaction, which fell on the already available TCP based.

Inter-site communication in DiTyCO regards the sending of messages (method invocations) or objects to remote channels, and remote instantiation of definitions. Sending a message or an object to a remote channel is an event that triggers an action at the target site. Two new action events where defined: (1) MessageEvent holds the arguments of a method invocation and its reception is handled by the tryReduceMessage library, and (2) ObjectEvent holds the object's free variables and its reception is also handled by a dedicated library, tryReduceObject, that places the object in the target local channel.

The remote instantiation of definitions uses a code downloading strategy, using the functionalities provided by the Communicator class. This includes the handling of CodeRequestEvent, and the methods featured in the CodeHandler class to handle incoming/outgoing code.

Regarding the marshalling procedure, in DiTyCO communication is driven by lexical-scope, meaning that every message or object targeted at a channel is sent to the site hosting that channel. This is implemented by keeping track of the channels exported to the network in a map, the *marshalling table*, that associates a the local channel to unique network-wide identifier (figure 5).

3.2   A Run-Time for the Mob Language

Mob is a high-level service-oriented mobile agent programming language [12]. It is compiled into DiTyCO, and thus it resorts the DiTyCO run-time. In reality it extends the DiTyCO run-time to include site migration across nodes, and to feature a number of other functionalities, such as the interaction with external programs, that are not in the scope of this paper. We will discuss how the DiTyCO run-time was extended to feature site mobility.

The Network Layer. Nothing was altered, the only difference is that Mob makes use of the migration handling capabilities of the resource directory.

The Node Layer. The node layer is also completely inherited from the DiTyCO run-time, making now use of the mobility service. The only requirement was to define how a DiTyCO site running a Mob computation is serialized and reconstructed. It this particular case, there are several functionalities required by the site that are common to every node, and thus, there is no need of migrating them. The state to migrate was defined accordingly, and the rebinding to the resources available locally is performed on arrival.

The Site Layer. Extends the inherited site layer with some new operations such as: (1) *remote site creation:* that creates a new site at a remote node, using the framework's remote launching facility; (2) *remote channel creation:* that creates a new DiTyCO channel at a given remote site by defining a new event handled by the NewChannelAt library, and, of course: (3) *migration:* that uses the lower layers to allow for DiTyCO site migration.

4   Related Work

Our work borrows some of the ideas discussed during the development of the Mikado-IMC [7] framework, on which we collaborated. However, while the IMC framework is more oriented in the development from scratch, our approach focuses more on the ability to extend existing virtual machines. This does not mean that both cannot be used to play both roles. It just leads to different conception ideas, that distinguish the frameworks. Moreover, SuMo structures the run-time environment in three layers, which allows for VM migration, i.e., strong mobility of computations, instead of only code and data.

The IMC framework is dedicated to incorporate mobility in virtual machines that use Java as their execution code. Thus, all the code migrated from one node to another is serialized Java byte-code, that is handled by a network class loader that fetches code on-demand. SuMo is not that bound to Java. It only uses the JVM as a middleware to support the run-time system. The native code of the VMs is not restricted. In fact, one of the components that must be implemented is the one that handles code serialization and de-serialization. This leads to a more general approach.

Regarding communication, in the IMC every binding has its own dedicated communication channel. In SuMo, all the connections directed at a node are handled by a single entity, the hosting node. For example, in TCP/IP based communication, a node has only one server socket.

The communication protocols are also easier to implement in SuMo. It is the simple implementation of an interface that sends and receives messages. In IMC, a protocol stack with session interfaces to forward messages between each protocol must be defined. Although, more general it adds a complexity factor that we do not think is necessary. Even the implementation of a simple protocol is time consuming.

5   Conclusions and Future Work

The framework has been used to implement the DiTyCO and Mob run-times, and is being used to implement other languages with distribution and mobility [15]. A embryonary version is currently the base for the run-time of the TyCO platform

[16]. The re-engineering of the platform with the new version has proved to be intuitive and simple, and will be included in upcoming releases. Experiences in the realm of virtual machine mobility have also been done in the scope of the Mob run-time. Thus, this kind of mobility is not restricted by the framework, in fact, we intend to supply general features for this support in the near future. The restriction can come, however, from the site itself, since it must be able to restart itself from a given state. This feature cannot be provided by the Mikado-IMC framework because of its close-coupling to Java, which does not allow users to access the run-time state.

Our future goals also include the development of higher-level APIs, in order to reduce even further the amount of code required to embed distribution into a virtual machine.

References

1. Riely, J., Hennessy, M.: Distributed Processes and Location Failures. In: Degano, P., Gorrieri, R., Marchetti-Spaccamela, A. (eds.) ICALP 1997. LNCS, vol. 1256, pp. 471–481. Springer, Heidelberg (1997)
2. Vasconcelos, V., Lopes, L., Silva, F.: Distribution and Mobility with Lexical Scoping in Process Calculi. In: Workshop on High Level Programming Languages (HLCL 1998). Electronic Notes in Theoretical Computer Science, vol. 16(3), pp. 19–34. Elsevier Science (1998)
3. Cardelli, L., Gordon, A.: Mobile Ambients. In: Nivat, M. (ed.) FOSSACS 1998. LNCS, vol. 1378, pp. 140–155. Springer, Heidelberg (1998)
4. Conchon, S., Fessant, F.L.: Jocaml: Mobile Agents for Objective-Caml. In: ASA/MA 1999, pp. 22–29. IEEE Computer Society (1999)
5. Schmitt, A., Stefani, J.B.: The M-calculus: A Higher-Order Distributed Process Calculus. In: Proceedings 30th Annual ACM Symposium on Principles of Programming Languages (POPL) (2003)
6. Fournet, C., Gonthier, G., Lévy, J.J., Maranget, L., Rémy, D.: A Calculus of Mobile Agents. In: Sassone, V., Montanari, U. (eds.) CONCUR 1996. LNCS, vol. 1119, pp. 406–421. Springer, Heidelberg (1996)
7. Bettini, L., et al.: A Software Framework for Rapid Prototyping of Run-Time Systems for Mobile Calculi. In: Priami, C., Quaglia, P. (eds.) GC 2004. LNCS, vol. 3267, pp. 179–207. Springer, Heidelberg (2005)
8. Paulino, H.: Reliable Communication in the Presence of Agent Mobility. In: Proceedings of the 12th IEEE Symposium on Computers and Communications (ISCC 2007). IEEE Computer Society (2007) (to appear in July 2007)
9. Boudol, G.: A Generic Membrane Model. In: Second Global Computing Workshop (2004)
10. Lopes, L., Silva, F., Figueira, A., Vasconcelos, V.: DiTyCO: An Experiment in Code Mobility from the Realm of Process Calculi. In: The 5th Mobile Object Systems Workshop (MOS 1999) (1999)
11. Paulino, H., Marques, P., Lopes, L., Vasconcelos, V., Silva, F.: A Multi-Threaded Asynchronous Language. In: Malyshkin, V.E. (ed.) PaCT 2003. LNCS, vol. 2763, pp. 316–323. Springer, Heidelberg (2003)
12. Paulino, H., Lopes, L.: A Mobile Agent Service-Oriented Scripting Language Encoded on a Process Calculus. In: Lightfoot, D.E., Szyperski, C.A. (eds.) JMLC 2006. LNCS, vol. 4228, pp. 383–402. Springer, Heidelberg (2006)

13. Milner, R., Parrow, J., Walker, D.: A Calculus of Mobile Processes (parts I and II). Information and Computation 100(1), 1–77 (1992)
14. Honda, K., Tokoro, M.: An Object Calculus for Asynchronous Communication. In: America, P. (ed.) ECOOP 1991. LNCS, vol. 512, pp. 141–162. Springer, Heidelberg (1991)
15. Martins, F., Salvador, L., Vasconcelos, V., Lopes, L.: MiKO: Mikado Koncurrent Objects. Technical Report 05081, Dagstuhl Seminar (2005)
16. TyCO: Typed Concurrent Objects (2003), http://www.ncc.up.pt/tyco/

A Debugger for Parallel Haskell Dialects*

Alberto de la Encina, Ismael Rodríguez, and Fernando Rubio

Facultad Informática. Universidad Complutense de Madrid
C/. Prof. José García Santesmases, E-28040 Madrid. Spain
{albertoe,isrodrig,fernando}@sip.ucm.es

Abstract. Due to its high-level nature, parallel functional languages provide some advantages for the programmer. Unfortunately, the functional programming community has not paid much attention to some important practical problems, like debugging parallel programs. In this paper we introduce the first debugger that works with any parallel extension of the functional language Haskell, the *de facto* standard in the (lazy evaluation) functional programming community. The debugger is implemented as an independent library. Thus, it can be used with any Haskell compiler. Moreover, the debugger can be used to analyze how much speculative work has been done in any program.

1 Introduction

The *functional* paradigm provides some advantages for the programmer. In particular, parallel functional languages are endowed with useful abstraction mechanisms like function composition and higher-order functions. The higher-order programming level provided by them allows to define the coordination of sub-computations in terms of the same constructions used in the rest of the program, which enables the definition and use of skeletons [1,2,5] to develop simpler parallel programs. Besides, since functional programs do not have *state*, side-effects are eliminated. So, the dependencies between processes are limited to obtaining the arguments needed to execute each function. These features ease the coordination issues and allow to define them in a natural way.

During the last years, several parallel functional languages have been proposed (see e.g. [13,5,12,4]). In particular, many of them are parallel dialects of the (lazy evaluation) functional language Haskell [10]. These extensions can be classified by level of control of parallelism, ranging from a completely implicit parallelism —for instance automatic parallelization— to an explicit parallelism where the programmer distributes the computation among a set of communicating processes that even may be located by the programmer himself at designated processors. The interested reader can find a detailed description of many Haskell dialects in [14], while an analysis of efficiency can be found in [8].

---

* Research partially supported by the MCYT project TIN2006-15578-C02-01, the Junta de Castilla-La Mancha project PAC06-0008-6995, and the Marie Curie project MRTN-CT-2003-505121/TAROT.

A. Bourgeois and S.Q. Zheng (Eds.): ICA3PP 2008, LNCS 5022, pp. 282–293, 2008.

An important weak point of all parallel Haskell dialects is that they lack debugging facilities. Thus, altough the efficiency results obtained are acceptable, it is sometimes difficult for the programmer to detect simple bugs. In this paper we will present the first debugger for a parallel Haskell dialect. In fact, our debugger works with any dialect whose compiler provides a very common primitive. Moreover, the debugger provides profiling information about the amount of speculative work done by the programs, an it also produces graphics allowing to analyze *races* between producer and consumer processes. In this paper we will concentrate on these features of our debugger. In particular, we will pay special attention to present the graphical outputs provided by our tool.

Let us remark that Haskell uses lazy evaluation. That is, it applies the *laziness* for deciding the computations to be executed in each moment. That is, a computation is performed only after it is detected that the result of that computation is required for continuing another computation that is already initiated. Let us note that pure laziness implies *sequential computation*. So, in order to allow parallel computations, parallel Haskell dialects introduce *eagerness* in different aspects. For instance, semi-explicit languages like GpH allow the programmer to use a `seq` operator to force the eager evaluation of parameters. Other more explicit languages like Eden creates new processes *eagerly*. Moreover, any newly created process is able to perform computations in parallel before its creator actually demands the result for continuing its execution. This feature, which is very useful for enabling parallelism, may cause that a program performs some computations that turn out to be unneeded. In fact, Eden processes are *speculative*: They perform computations under the assumption that they will actually be needed.

The uncontrolled speculation may be a source of inefficiency in parallel programs. In order to achieve a better use of resources and a higher performance, the programmer should be provided with a measure of the *unnecessary speculation* of a program. In this paper we present a method for comparing the speculative computations and the computations actually needed. Basically, the method consists in comparing the data actually needed by a process and the speculative data evaluated by processes launched by this process. Due to lack of space, we will only consider how to analyze the speculation in one parallel Haskell dialect (the Eden language), but dealing with other dialects is straightforward.

Unfortunately, making a functional program to show the results of partial computations in some points is not easy. Let us remind that, contrarily to an imperative program, a functional program does not have *state*. Thus, the observation of partial computations cannot be based on observing how some variables change, because variables do not exist in functional environments. Besides, due to the laziness of Haskell, the execution of a computation may turn out to be *unnecessary*, but a simple *observation* (e.g., writing a result in the screen or in a file) could create a false demand on such unneeded computation. Hence, observations must be defined in such a way that they produce a (neutral) result that is actually required only in the same situations as if the observations were not introduced. We will address this issue by using and extending *Hood* (*Haskell*

Object Observation Debugger [3]). This tool allows a programmer to observe the behavior of a Haskell program by inserting some calls to an *observation function* in the program. The observation function records the value returned by a function in some point of the program, but without creating extra demand. These functions will be the basis of our method to compare the useful speculation and the actual speculation in programs developed with parallel Haskell dialects.

The rest of the paper is structured as follows. In the next section we present the observation constructions of Hood and the basic ideas of its parallelization. Next, in Section 3 we present our method to assess the unnecessary speculation in a concrete parallel Haskell dialect. A case study is shown in Section 4. Finally, Section 5 contains our conclusions.

2 Basic Hood

In this section we show the basic ideas behind Hood. The interested reader is referred to [3] for more details about it.

As we have commented before, introducing observations in a lazy language can modify the order of evaluation, affecting to the overall computation. Fortunately, Hood allows the programmer to observe something similar to what can be observed in imperative environments. In fact, Hood allows the programmer to observe any intermediate structure appearing in a program. Moreover, we can also observe the evolution in time of the evaluation of the structures under observation. It is important to remark that Hood does not only observe simple data types. In fact, it can observe anything appearing in a Haskell program. In particular, we can observe functions. For instance,

```
observe "sum" sum (4:2:5:[])
```

will observe the application of function sum to its parameter, returning:

```
-- sum
 { \ (4:2:5:[]) -> 11 }
```

Note that what we observe can be read as *when the function receives as input the list 4:2:5:[], it returns as output the value 11.* The elements 4, 2 and 5 appear explicitly because they were really demanded to evaluate the output. However, when observing something like

```
observe "length" length (4:2:5:[])
```

we will obtain the following observation:

```
-- length
 { \ (_:_:_:[]) -> 3 }
```

That is, we are observing a function that when it receives a list with three elements it returns the number 3 without evaluating the concrete elements appearing in the list. Note that it is only relevant the number of elements, but not the *concrete* elements.

As it can be expected, higher-order functions can also be observed, but we do not show it due to lack of space.

2.1   Basic Ideas of the Parallel Implementation

Both the original sequential Hood library and our parallel extension have been implemented as libraries. Thus, our debugger can be used with any Haskell compiler and with any of its parallel dialects. Let us note that the main difficulties to implement our framework are in fact two intrinsic features of Haskell: The absence of state and the lazy order of evaluation. In order to deal with both features in a sequential environment, a monadic approach is used to guarantee that the order of evaluation is not modified. However, in the parallel case we need to observe *independently* the information concerning each process in the program. So, we need to take the control over where and when each tracing information is written. This requires to redefine some of the functionalities provided by Hood. In particular, we modify the tracing (sequential) monad to provide a new parallel-oriented monad. This monad creates several threads that independently deal with each part of the tracing information. The aim of this modification is to send the information collected in each processor to a different file. Since several processes can exist at the same time in the same processor, care must be taken to avoid inconsistencies in these files. In order to provide an efficient implementation of the observation mechanism, we enable the concurrent access to the report files of each processor. This feature requires the definition of critical regions where the simultaneous access to a file by several threads is restricted. By using a suitable concurrent implementation of the observation procedure, the required information is finally collected in the corresponding files. Then, our post-processing functions compute and organize the tracing information contained in the files, which concerns the speculative behavior of the program at each point. In particular, they match invoker and instantiated processes in pairs and compute the difference between computed data and required data for each pair.

3   A Sample Haskell Dialect: The Eden Language

Eden [5,9] extends the lazy functional language Haskell [10] by adding syntactic constructs to explicitly define and instantiate processes. It is possible to define a new *process abstraction* p by using the following notation that relates the inputs and the outputs of the process: p = process x -> e , where variable x will be the input of the process, while the behavior of the process will be given by expression e. Process abstractions can be compared to functions, the main difference being that the former, when instantiated, are executed in parallel.

Process abstractions are not actual processes. To really create a process, a *process instantiation* is required. This is achieved by using the predefined infix operator #. Given a process abstraction and an input parameter, it creates a new process and returns the output of the process. Each time an expression e1 # e2 is evaluated, the instantiating process will be responsible for evaluating and sending e2, while a new process is created to evaluate the application (e1 e2).

Once a process is running, only fully evaluated data objects are communicated. The only exceptions are lists, which are transmitted in a *stream*-like fashion, i.e. element by element. Each list element is first evaluated to full normal form and then transmitted. Concurrent threads trying to access not yet available inputs are temporarily suspended. This is the only way in which Eden processes synchronize. Notice that process creation is explicit, but process communication (and synchronization) is completely implicit.

Eden's compiler has been developed by extending the most efficient Haskell compiler (GHC). Hence, it reuses GHC's capabilities to interact with other programming languages. Thus, Eden can be used as a coordination language, while the sequential computation language can be, for instance, C. Performance results show that Eden programs can obtain *acceptable* speedups (see e.g. [9,8]).

3.1   Testing Speculation with Hood

In this section we present our method to assess the speculation of a parallel Eden program. The method is based on using the observation functionalities provided by Hood in specific points of the program under assessment, and it can be easily adapted to deal with other parallel Haskell dialects.

Let us recall that the application of `observe` to a term returns only the (partial) evaluation of the term that is actually *required* by other subcomputations in the context where `observe` is invoked. Hence, it gives us the (partial) term that is demanded in the context of the observation. When a process instantiates another process, the former process demands the computation of a term from the latter (from now on, *invoker* and *instantiated* processes, respectively). In order to perform our analysis, we need to consider the evaluation of this term at two different points. On the one hand, the observation of the term required by the invoker (in the context of the invoker) gives us the true necessities of the program at this point. On the other hand, the observation of the term constructed by the instantiated process (in the context of instantiated process) gives us the result of the speculated work performed by the instantiated process. By comparing both values, we can assess the amount of unnecessary speculation performed by the program at this point. In fact, if we obtain not only the final values of the term at both sides but also the order in which each part of the term is calculated, then we can infer not only the amount of unnecessary work but also the relative speeds of both parts. Hence, we can enrich the profiling capabilities of Eden.

3.2   General Scheme to Analyze Speculation in Eden

Let us remark that the speculative work can be done both by the invoker and the instantiated processes. For instance, the invoker process can instantiate a new process and afterwards can produce some values that this new process may or may not need. The values demanded by the instantiated processes are its *parameters*. In this case, the instantiated process takes the values computed by the invoker as long as it needs them, and the speculative work is performed by the invoker process.

Next, we present a general scheme to deal with any scenario where the speculative work of some processes has to be assessed. The basic idea is to redefine the basic constructions of the language to introduce observations. This redefinition performs all the required tracing issues in such a way that the programmer can forget any details concerning observations: He must just instantiate the processes he wants to analyze by calling the functions provided by the new constructors and introducing his function as parameter. Then, the system automatically reports any change on both its input and its output. By applying the new observation constructors to both an invoker and an instantiated process, all the needed information will be properly reported. Thus, if we want to observe the inputs and outputs of a process that computes a given function `f` then, instead of directly using `f`, we will call the following function `processObs` using `f` as parameter:

```
processObs f = process ins -> (observe "outsFromProcess" outs)
          where outs = f ins'
                ins' = observe "insToProcess" ins
```

The previous function defines a process with input `ins`. In order to observe the data that this new process receives from its creator and it actually *requires*, this parameter is observed by the second observation in the previous definition, labelled by `insToProcess`. After function `f` is normally applied to the input, the output `outs` is obtained. The observation of this term (first observation, labelled by `outsFromProcess`) reports the data this process transmits to its creator.

The previous function allows us to observe the treatment of inputs and outputs of the instantiated process. Similarly, we need a new functionality to observe the behavior of the invoker process. Next we redefine the process instantiation operator to include the observation capabilities. The new operator, based on the standard operator `#`, is `##`:

```
p ## actualParameters
  = observe "insFromProcess"
            (p # (observe "outsToProcess" actualParameters))
```

The new operator allows any process to instantiate a new process by using the standard one. Besides, two observations are introduced to report the inputs and outputs that the invoker process exchanges with the new process. Observations labelled by `insFromProcess` report the data that the invoker receives (and actually requires) from the newly instantiated process. Observations labelled by `outsToProcess` report the data that is sent from the invoker to the instantiated process (regardless of whether the instantiated process requires them).

The use of both new constructors leads to the general scheme depicted in Figure 1. By combining the new process abstractions `processObs` and `##` we obtain four relevant data. These data provide us with two critical measures concerning the usefulness of the speculation at this point of the program. On the one hand, the difference between `outsFromProcess` and `insFromProcess` gives us how much unnecessary speculative work was done by the new process. On the other hand, the difference between `outsToProcess` and `insToProcess` provides us a measure to know how much unnecessary speculative work was performed by the process creating the new instantiation.

Let us note that the definitions of `processObs` and `##` could be trivially extended to include extra parameters representing the strings that want to be used

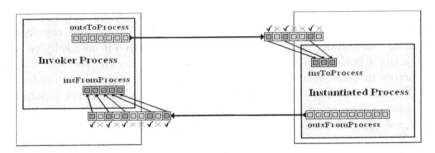

Fig. 1. Invoker and Instantiated Processes

for marking the inputs and outputs of the processes. Moreover, we can also include references to the processor where the process is actually being executed (denoted in Eden by `selfPe`). In addition to that, taking into account that `observe` can also observe functions, we can reduce the number of times we use `observe` by observing the functions themselves instead of looking independently to the inputs and outputs. Summarizing, the following definitions obtain all this information:

```
processObs str f = pf (observe  (str ++ ('_': show selfPe)) f)
   where pf f = process x -> f x
instProcessObs str p args =
   (observe (str ++ ('_' : show selfPe)) (\x -> p # x)) args
```

where `str` is a string parameter. Note that now the instantiation is performed by using a function (`instProcessObs`) instead of using an infix operator (`##`) because now we have to deal with three parameters (the string, the process and the arguments).

In fact, the framework can be easily applied to other general schemes and programming structures in Eden. In particular, all the skeletons defined in the Eden library have been trivially rewritten in terms of the new process abstraction and process instantiation operators. Hence, they inherit the capability to test the amount of speculative work. As an example, let us consider the most simple skeleton: The map skeleton can be defined in Eden as follows:

```
map_par f xs = [ (process x -> f x) # x | x <- xs] 'using' spine
```

This skeleton is trivially rewritten to include all the relevant observations. In particular, we can easily assign a different number to each of the taks of the list as follows:

```
map_parObs f xs = [ instProcessObs ("invoker"++show i)
                        (processObs ("childProcess"++show i) f)
                           x | (x,i) <- zip xs [1..]] 'using' spine
```

3.3   Dealing with Other Haskell Dialects

As the reader can imagine, in order to deal with any other parallel Haskell dialect it is only necessary to apply a scheme similar to that presented in the previous subsection. Let us remark that our basic parallel Hood library has been implemented as an independent library that can be used by any Haskell compiler. Thus, we do not need to modify the parallel Haskell compilers. We only need to encapsulate the basic constructions of each parallel dialect (process and # in the case of Eden) to introduce calls to the basic `observe` function in the appropriate places. This is quite simple, as most parallel Haskell dialects use very few extra constructions.

4   Analyzing Speculation: A Case Study

In this section we present the graphical feedback that can be obtained by using our debugger. In particular, we show how we can analyze both the final speculation of a program and the races between processes during runtime. As a running example, we will use the `linSolv` algorithm. This algorithm finds an exact solution of a linear system of equations of the form $Ax = b$ where $A \in \mathbb{Z}^{n \times n}, b \in \mathbb{Z}^n, n \in \mathbb{N}$. The algorithm presented here finds an exact solution and works over arbitrary precision integers. To find an exact solution for a given system of equations, `linSolv` uses a *multiple homomorphic images* approach. It consists of the following three stages: (1) map the input data into several homomorphic images; (2) compute the solution in each of these images; and (3) combine the results of all images to a result in the original domain.

This structure is particularly useful for operations on arbitrary precision integers. In this case the original domain is $\mathbb{Z}$, the set of all integer values, and the homomorphic images are $\mathbb{Z}$ modulo p, written $\mathbb{Z}_p$, with p being a prime number. If the input numbers are very big and each prime number fits into one machine word the basic arithmetic in the homomorphic images is cheap because fixed precision arithmetic can be used. Only in the combination phase, when applying a fold-based Chinese Remainder Algorithm (CRA) (see [7]), expensive arbitrary precision arithmetic has to be used to construct the result values.

Details about the implementation of `linSolv` in Haskell can be found in [8]. In brief, the main part to be parallelized consists in solving each of the homomorphic images, whose basic definition is: `xList = map get_homSol primes` where `primes` is an infinite list of primes, and `get_homSol` solves the system modulo a given prime. Thus, the basic parallel structure of the algorithm consists in performing all computations in the homomorphic images in parallel. It uses LU-decomposition followed by forward and backsubstitution to compute the solution in the homomorphic image [11]. From a speculation point of view, the main difficulty in the parallelization is that we have to make sure that new results are computed if primes turn out to be "unlucky", i.e. if the determinant of the input matrix A in the homomorphic image generated by this prime number is zero.

```
xList_all = map_farm get_homSol primes

xList = filter lucky xList_all
```

Fig. 2. Parallel `linSolv` (Eden speculative version)

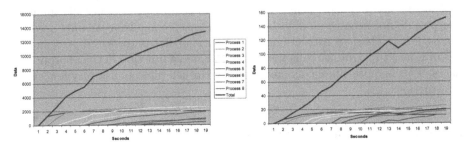

Fig. 3. 8 processes speculative version. Speculation in inputs (left) and outputs.

```
xList_all = map_farm get_homSol primes'

xList = filter lucky xList_all
xList_unlucky = filter (not.lucky) xList_all

(p_needed, p_spec) = splitAt ( 1 + toInt noOfPrimes) primes
primes' = p_needed ++ (additional xList_unlucky p_spec)

additional :: [Integer] -> [Integer] -> [Integer]
additional xs ys = zipWith (\ x y -> y) xs ys
```

Fig. 4. Parallel `linSolv` (Eden conservative version)

As we have to solve the linear system modulo several prime numbers, the most obvious parallel scheme is to use a `map_par` scheme so that an independent process is created for each prime. However, as a simple improvement, we can use a `map_farm` scheme so that we only create the same number of processes as processors are available in the system. So, in our first approach (shown in Figure 2) we just replaced the top level `map` by its parallel counterpart `map_farm`. Unfortunately, when using the `map_farm` version that includes observations, our tools detected a quite big amount of useless work. For instance, as shown in Figure 3, in a small system with 10 equations, 14000 useless data were computed. Obviously, this problem reduces the overall efficiency of the program.

Notice that the main problem in the first implementation is that we are using an infinite list without control. This is not a problem in a sequential Haskell version, because the laziness of the language guarantees that only the needed elements of the list are actually computed. However, the eagerness of the parallel version creates extra demand for all the elements of the (infinite) list. Thus, the programmer should take care of this issue to avoid creating too much speculation.

As a second approach, to avoid the potential waste of resources due to speculation we used a *conservative version* as shown in Figure 4. In this version the prime numbers are divided into those known to be needed (`p_needed`) and those which are only needed if some of the earlier primes are unlucky (`p_spec`).

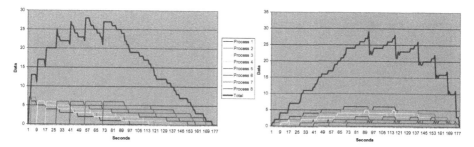

Fig. 5. 8 processes conservative version. Speculation in inputs (left) and outputs.

```
xList_all = map_rw get_homSol primes

xList = filter lucky xList_all
```

Fig. 6. Parallel `linSolv` (Eden semi-speculative version)

The function `additional` adds for each unlucky prime a new prime number to the task list `primes'`. Note in the definition of `additional` that, due to the demand-driven evaluation, the availability of unlucky primes in `xs` triggers the generation of one result element in `ys`. As it can be seen in Figure 5, by using this conservative version, the final amount of useless work was zero, even though now we are using a larger problem size. Unfortunately, this does not necessarily implies optimal speedups. The problem is that we have avoided useless work, but at the cost of reducing the average parallelism in the last part of the computation. Let us remark that the parallelism degree is good while the system is working on the **p_needed** primes. However, the generation of the **p_spec** primes is performed in a completely lazy form. Thus, they are only created when we are completely sure that they will be needed. This introduces sequentiality in the last stages of the computation. Fortunately, in most cases the number of unlucky primes is small, so that the length of **p_spec** is also small. Hence, the part of the computation where parallelism is reduced is relatively small. Anyway, in some cases this part of the computation can be more relevant. Therefore, we should try to avoid this problem.

Finally, we used a third solution where speculation was restricted but not completely avoided. In this sense, we used a variation of the task farm skeleton. More specifically, we used the replicated workers paradigm. A manager and a set of worker processes are created, and two tasks are initially released to each of the workers. As soon as any worker finishes a task, it sends the result to the manager, and a new task is delivered to the worker. The computation in the manager is demand-driven and triggered by the availability of result values. As soon as the manager has all the needed results it terminates all the worker processes. Notice that in this *semi-speculative version* the workers may be working speculatively on useless tasks, but only when the useful tasks have already been consumed and hence the degree of speculation is tightly limited. More details about the replicated workers skeleton can be found in [6]. Figure 6 shows the

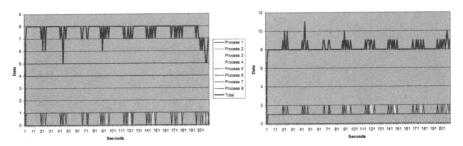

Fig. 7. 8 processes semi-speculative version (buffer size 2). Speculation in inputs (left) and outputs (right).

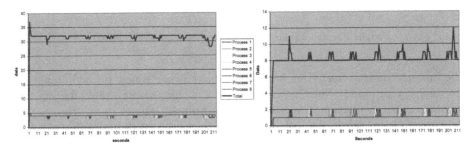

Fig. 8. 8 processes semi-speculative version (buffer size 5). Speculation in inputs (left) and outputs (right).

Eden code for the semi-speculative version of linSolv. The only modification to the sequential code is the use of a parallel replicated workers map (map_rw) instead of a sequential map over the infinite list of primes. By using this new version, only one useless message was sent by each process, as it can be seen in Figure 7. That is, the speculation was actually controlled.

Let us remark that in the semi-speculative version each process receives two tasks initially. In fact, we can consider that each process has an input buffer of size two. This buffer is used to avoid wasting time waiting for data. Let us consider using a bigger buffer to be sure that processes never get blocked waiting for data. Figure 8 shows the results obtained with a buffer of five elements. In this case, each process handles four useless data (buffer size minus one), while the number of elements in its input buffer is never less than three. That is, it is never waiting for data. Hence, it seems that a smaller buffer size (two or three) is enough for optimizing this problem.

Summarizing, we have shown how the graphical feedback provided by our tools allows the programmer to analyze the amount of speculative work done in the program. By using this information, the programmer can easily improve the performance of the implementation.

5   Conclusions

In this paper we have presented a debugger that can be used to analyze the amount of speculative work done in a parallel Haskell dialect. Moreover, the tool provides graphical information showing the *races* between producer and consumer processes. We have shown the usefulness of the tool with a concrete case study that consists in solving a linear system of equations.

As we have implemented the debugger as a library completely independent of the concrete parallel compiler, it can be used with any parallel Haskell dialect. In order to handle a concrete dialect, we only need to rewrite the basic constructions of the language to include appropriate calls to the basic function `observe`.

References

1. Cole, M.: Algorithmic Skeletons: Structure Management of Parallel Computations. Research Monographs in Parallel and Distributed Computing. MIT Press (1989)
2. Cole, M.: Bringing skeletons out of the closet: A pragmatic manifesto for skeletal parallel programming. Parallel Computing 30, 389–406 (2004)
3. Gill, A.: Debugging Haskell by observing intermediate data structures. In: Proceedings of the 4th Haskell Workshop. Tech. Rep. University of Nottingham (2000)
4. Kelly, P.H.J.: Functional Programming for Loosely-Coupled Multiprocessors. Research Monographs in Parallel and Distributed Computing. MIT Press (1989)
5. Klusik, U., Loogen, R., Priebe, S., Rubio, F.: Implementation skeletons in Eden: Low-effort parallel programming. In: Mohnen, M., Koopman, P. (eds.) IFL 2000. LNCS, vol. 2011, pp. 71–88. Springer, Heidelberg (2001)
6. Klusik, U., Peña, R., Rubio, F.: Replicated workers in Eden. In: Constructive Methods for Parallel Programming, CMPP 2000, pp. 143–164. Nova Science (2000)
7. Lipson, J.D.: Chinese remainder and interpolation algorithms. In: Symp. Symbolic and Algebraic Manipulation, SYMSAM 1971, pp. 372–391. Academic Press (1971)
8. Loidl, H.W., Rubio, F., Scaife, N., Hammond, K., Horiguchi, S., Klusik, U., Loogen, R., Michaelson, G.J., Peña, R., Rebón Portillo, Á.J., Priebe, S., Trinder, P.W.: Comparing parallel functional languages: Programming and performance. Higher-Order and Symbolic Computation 16(3), 203–251 (2003)
9. Loogen, R., Ortega-Mallén, Y., Peña, R., Priebe, S., Rubio, F.: Parallelism abstractions in Eden. In: Rabhi, F.A., Gorlatch, S. (eds.) Patterns and Skeletons for Parallel and Distributed Computing, pp. 95–128. Springer (2002)
10. Peyton Jones, S.L., Hughes, J.: Report on the programming language Haskell 98. Technical report (February 1999), http://www.haskell.org
11. Press, W., Teukolsky, S., Vetterling, W., Flannery, B.: LU Decomposition and Its Applications. In: Numerical Recipes in C: The Art of Scientific Computing, 2nd edn., Cambridge University Press (1992)
12. Scaife, N., Horiguchi, S., Michaelson, G., Bristow, P.: A parallel SML compiler based on algorithmic skeletons. Journal of Functional Programming 15(4), 615–650 (2005)
13. Trinder, P.W., Hammond, K., Mattson Jr., J.S., Partridge, A.S., Peyton Jones, S.L.: GUM: a portable parallel implementation of Haskell. In: Programming Language Design and Implementation, PLDI 1996, pp. 79–88. ACM Press (1996)
14. Trinder, P.W., Loidl, H.W., Pointon, R.F.: Parallel and distributed Haskells. Journal of Functional Programming 12(4-5), 469–510 (2002)

Introducing Aspects to the Implementation of a Java Fork/Join Framework

Chrysoulis Zambas and Mikel Luján

School of Computer Science, The University of Manchester
Oxford Road, Manchester, M13 9PL, United Kingdom

Abstract. When faced with the question of how will a program exploit the current and upcoming chip multiprocessors, many answers can be produced. Two of the most promising answers are: (1) frameworks or libraries where experts have encapsulated the parallelism, and (2) work stealing as a means of load balancing the work. This paper presents a study of whether aspect-oriented programming can benefit the implementation of a well-known Java framework for divide-and-conquer applications that relies on random work stealing. Despite different kinds of aspects being introduced, the performance evaluation shows no significant overhead due to their inclusion.

1 Introduction

Goetz announced in a recent article that one of the new additions of Java 7 will be a fork-join framework [6]. Furthermore the fork-join approach is actively being used by the new languages X10 [3] and Fortress [2] under development by the DARPA initiative on High Productivity Computing Systems. This paper presents a study of whether Aspect-Oriented Programming (AOP) can benefit the implementation of a well-known Java framework [11] for divide-and-conquer applications that relies on random work stealing. These applications solve a problem by recursively decomposing it into independent sub-problems, which can be executed concurrently, and whose output is the composition of the sub-problems' outputs. These applications take the general form illustrated in Figure 1.

Section 2 presents an introduction to AOP and AspectJ. The Java Fork/Join framework (FJF) is described in Section 3. The framework is improved by enforcing synchronization and parallelization protocols as aspects, by enabling a limited multi-inheritance relation and improving encapsulation of some internal interfaces. A further improvement is the development of aspects that help developers that use the FJF to prevent future bugs on their systems (see Section 4). The new framework using these aspects is evaluated for performance. Six benchmarks are used to evaluate whether the AOP version of the FJF pays an overhead versus the highly optimized Java framework (see Section 5). Finally, a summary of the paper is presented in Section 6.

A. Bourgeois and S.Q. Zheng (Eds.): ICA3PP 2008, LNCS 5022, pp. 294–304, 2008.
© Springer-Verlag Berlin Heidelberg 2008

```
result solve(Problem problem) {
    if (problem is small)
        directly solve the problem
    else {
        split problem into independent parts
        fork new subtasks to solve each part
        join all subtasks
        compose results from subresults
    }
}
```

Fig. 1. Pseudocode for a Fork/Join application

2 Background

Experience from object-oriented software development has produced examples where a *class* is not the best unit of modularization. There are concerns (functionality) that span more than one class, the *crosscutting concerns*. AOP introduces a new modularization unit, an *aspect*, to improve the separation of concerns. Crosscutting concerns can be implemented inside an aspect and maintained separately from other classes, instead of inserting them in the middle. AOP promises higher modularity and easier system evolution.

In a nutshell an aspect describes what needs to be done and where it needs to be applied. The "where" part determines the location in the normal execution flow of a program that needs to be altered to introduce the crosscutting concern. Examples of where AOP can be an improvement over Object-Oriented Programming (OOP) are characterized as:

- Code scattering: one logical functionality (concern) can not be implemented in just one class and pieces or repeated pieces of code are spread among multiple class.
- Code tangling: one class implements more than one concern.

AspectJ is an aspect-oriented extension of Java which generates standard bytecodes [1] and is considered the most mature AOP language. AspectJ defines two types of crosscutting concerns:

- Dynamic: The normal program execution flow is modified by adding a concern.
- Static: The static structure of classes, interfaces and other parts of the system is altered (e.g. introduction of a new object field, type-hierarchy modification, compile-time errors and exceptions changes).

The aspect is the main unit of AspectJ and contains all the code needed to implement dynamic and static crosscutting concerns. An aspect is made up of *pointcuts*, *advices*, and *introductions*. An aspect can also use any programming constructors available in Java classes.

```
class Hello {
    public static void print () {
        System.out.println ("Hello");
    }
}

aspect CountHellos
{
    int counter;
    private int Hello.val;

    pointcut helloPointcut (): call (* Hello.print (..));

    before (): helloPointcut () {
        counter++;
    }
}
```

Fig. 2. Simple aspect

An example is presented next to illustrate the different parts of an aspect. Figure 2 shows a simple aspect that counts the number of times the method `print` in class `Hello` is executed. The pointcut `helloPointcut` specifies the *join points* of the program corresponding to invocations of `print`. One pointcut can combine several join points. The main categories of join points are methods (including constructors), field access (access is only to data members), exception handler execution, and class and object initialization. During execution, each time the join point is reached the *advice* which increments the variable `counter` is executed before invoking the method. Furthermore, a new field is added to the class `Hello`, called `val` with the use of the *introduction* feature. An advice in AspectJ is similar to a method in Java, although there are three ways of executing the advice: before, after, or around the pointcut. The before advice body executes before the pointcut, while after advice bodies execute right after the pointcut execution. An around advice surrounds the pointcut and even can disallow the execution of the captured pointcut.

3   The Fork/Join Framework

This section introduces the Fork/Join Framework (FJF) developed by Lea (see [11] for more details). The key design issues for the framework include (i) lightweight classes for creating fork/join tasks, (ii) efficient task storage data structures, and (iii) efficient scheduling algorithms. Java itself provides the `java.lang.Thread` class that can be used to represent the fork/join tasks. However, this class is not used because the synchronization and scheduling of fork/join tasks are simpler compared to those of general-purpose threads;

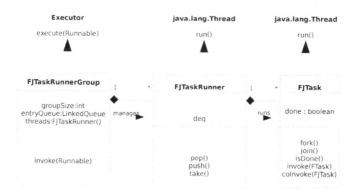

Fig. 3. UML class diagram for the FJF

fork/join tasks rarely need to block. Another reason is that the cost of creating, managing and destroying a Java thread might be greater than the cost of running a task.

Figure 3 shows a Unified Modelling Language (UML) class diagram of the FJF's key classes, methods and fields. The class FJTaskRunnerGroup manages a group of threads (instances of the class FJTaskRunner) that will run tasks. This thread pool is created at the start of the application and remains alive until the end. The number of threads in the pool (field groupSize) should be equal to the number of processors on the computer. It is then hoped that the operating system will map each of these Java threads to a processor. Although this is common in most operating systems, it is not guaranteed. The group has a task queue (field entryQueue) for storing tasks for the whole group. The class extends the Executor interface, which contains a single method execute(). This method is used to send a task for execution and return immediately. The method invoke() is used to send a task and wait for the task to be completed before returning.

The class FJTaskRunner extends the class java.lang.Thread class and its instances are the worker threads of the framework. Each task runner has its own task queue (field deq). All a thread does is pop tasks from this queue and run them. If it has finished executing all the tasks in its own task queue, it tries to steal some tasks from other task runners. If this fails, the thread then attempts to steal a task from the group wide task queue of the FJTaskRunnerGroup class. If it fails to steal any tasks it waits for a short time before attempting to steal again (new tasks might be added to the group queue, or other threads might spawn new tasks).

All fork/join tasks that will be executed by the framework must inherit from the abstract class FJTask. It implements the Java interface java.lang.Runnable which requires that its subclasses define the method run(). This method contains all the code to be run by the instances of FJTaskRunner. Its key methods include fork(), which arranges for the execution of a dependent task, and join(), which allows a task to wait for dependent tasks. The method `isDone()` is a completion status indicator. The methods `invoke()` and `coInvoke()` are used to execute one or more tasks and wait for their completion.

4   Applying Aspects

The AspectJ implementation of the FJF is illustrated in Figure 4. This implementation involved creation of four different aspects, which appear at the bottom of the figure.

4.1   InterfacesAspect Aspect

The first aspect, `InterfacesAspect`, implements the interfaces `Puttable`, `Takable`, `Channel` and `Executor`. These interfaces are not illustrated in the UML class diagram of the FJF as they represent internal mechanisms.

Hannemann et al. [7] explains that when software systems have role interfaces that need not be client-accessible functionality, then those interfaces are better to be declared inside an aspect and when needed, the compile-time declaration mechanism of AspectJ can be used. The `declare parents` construct is part of the AspectJ open class mechanism. It allows aspects to modify existing classes by attaching fields, methods or, as in this case, interfaces. These interfaces are not accessible by the client classes and thus simplifies and enforces the interface to the clients.

4.2   StaticWarnings Aspect

The second aspect, `StaticWarnings`, uses the compile-time warnings mechanism of AspectJ. The FJF can be extended, but there are many issues that must remain unchanged. For example, Lea explains that the method `isDone()` is

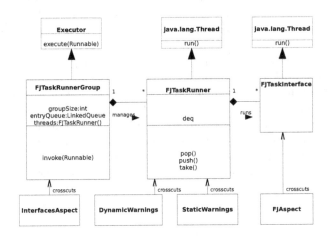

Fig. 4. UML class diagram for the FJF including aspects

"intended only to be called by FJTaskRunner." This means that only the worker threads can set tasks as finished. These issues are captured inside this aspect, and compile-time warnings are used, to help any programmers that need to extend the framework to avoid unnecessary bugs. The four warnings are the following:

- Warning 1: The method `FJTaskInterface.setDone()` should only be called by the `FJTaskRunner` class. In other words, only the worker threads should terminate tasks.
- Warning 2: The methods `FJAspect.yield()` and `FJAspect.join()` must never be called when a lock is held. This means, they must not be called by synchronized methods or when a lock is acquired through the `Lock` interface. This is because multiple tasks can be run by the same thread during a yield and since locks are held per-thread, the lock would not maintain the desired exclusion.
- Warning 3: The field `FJTaskRunner.active` should be accessed only by objects of the class `FJTaskRunnerGroup`. This is because this field records whether current thread may be processing a task or not.
- Warning 4: The last warning is that the size of the `FJTaskRunnerGroup` should be equal to the number of CPUs on the system. Lea [10] explains that this should guarantee better performance.

4.3 DynamicWarnings Aspect

The third aspect is called `DynamicWarnings`. This aspect prevents any race conditions that might be caused when threads (instances of the class `FJTaskRunner`) call their methods `take()`, `push` and `pop()` while not being the current thread. This is an example of how AOP can be used to enforce implementation protocols to prevent errors that might occur during runtime.

4.4 FJAspect Aspect

The fourth aspect is the `FJAspect` (see Figure 5) and replaces the implementation of the class `FJTask`.

In Lea's FJF implementation, any class that wants to be a task must extend the class `FJTask`. However, Java does not allow multiple inheritance. This can limit or compromise the implementation of a design. However, with AspectJ it is possible to replace an abstract class with an interface without loosing the ability to attach implementations to their methods. This is done with the inter-type declarations mechanism of AspectJ. The abstract class `FJTask` has a single boolean field, `isDone`, six static methods and seven methods. The interface `FJTaskInterface` and the aspect `FJAspect` replace the abstract class `FJTask`. Inside the `FJTaskInterface` all the non-static methods of the original `FJTask` are declared. The static methods are implemented in the aspect `FJAspect`. In this aspect also the boolean field `isDone` is declared and the implementations of the non-static methods are provided.

In this way, now the classes can implement the `FJTaskInterface` and extend any other classes if necessary. The mechanism used can be considered to be a limited form of multiple inheritance.

Fig. 5. UML class diagram for FJAspect

5   Performance Evaluation

The objective of the performance experiments are to understand whether there is a cost for using AOP in the implementation of the FJF.

The experiments are performed on a shared memory 8-core (i.e. 4 dual core) Opteron 2.4GHz machine running openSUSE 10.1 64-bit and JDK 1.6 64-bit with 1, 2, 4, 6 and 8 threads. The performance graphs report the speedup calculated against the sequential execution of the FJF without any aspect; i.e. OO implementation. The benchmarks are run 5 times and the average execution times are used in the graphs.

The first benchmark, Fibonacci, calculates the fibonacci number of 40. Figure 6 presents the speedup graph. The second benchmark implements a merge

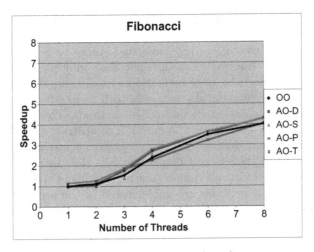

Fig. 6. Fibonacci benchmark

sort algorithm on an array of integers with 50 million elements (see Figure 7). The third benchmark, Integrate, performs recursive Gaussian quadrature for a given function integrating from 1 to 200 (see Figure 8). The fourth benchmark, matrix multiply, multiplies two square matrices of floats with size 2048 (see Figure 9). The fifth benchmark implements an LU decomposition on a matrix of doubles with size 2048 (see Figure 10). The sixth and final benchmark performs an iterative mesh relaxation, Jacobi, over a square matrix of doubles with size 2000.

In all the performance figures, AO-S represents the FJF using only the static aspect called StaticWarnings (see Section 4.2). AO-D represents the FJF

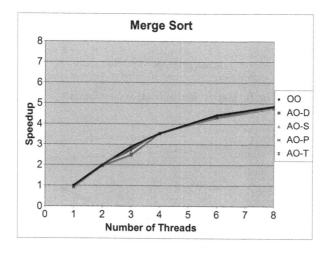

Fig. 7. Merge sort benchmark

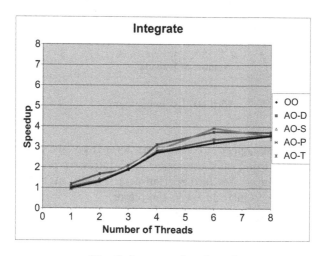

Fig. 8. Integrate benchmark

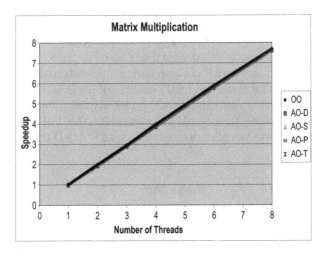

Fig. 9. Matrix Multiplication benchmark

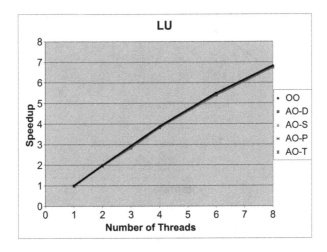

Fig. 10. LU benchmark

using only the dynamic aspect called DynamicWarnings (see Section 4.3). AO-P represents the FJF using only the aspect that improves programmability by improving the use of interfaces (see Section 4.1). Finally, AO-T represents the FJF using all the aspects introduced in the paper.

Although some differences in the execution times are observed in the graphs, these variations are within the standard deviation of the measured execution time. There is no indication that any of the AspectJ implementations of the FJF is introducing a noticeable overhead over the OO version.

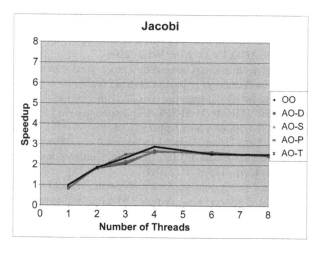

Fig. 11. Jacobi benchmark

6 Summary

This paper has illustrated that the implementation of the FJF can be improved using AOP. Specially interesting is the usage of aspects to enforce comments describing synchronization or parallelization protocols. The performance evaluation has showed that no significant overhead is paid for using AOP.

Our group has also investigated how to separate concerns in parallel scientific codes using AspectJ [8] which motivated a new join point for loops which was demonstrated by parallelizing loops [9]. Cunha *et al.* [4] developed Aspect-Oriented (AO) implementations of 8 concurrency mechanisms and patterns. These two papers are the closest related work. The FJF can be seen as the implementation of a concurrent design pattern. The first project that studied the relationship between design patterns and AOP was done by Hanneman and Kickzales [7] and then extended by Garcia *et al.* [5]. However neither of these papers addressed concurrency patterns.

References

1. AspectJ documentation (Last accessed, March 2008),
   http://www.eclipse.org/aspectj/docs.php
2. Fortress Programming Language (Last accessed, March 2008),
   http://projectfortress.sun.com
3. The X10 programming language website (Last accessed, March 2008),
   http://x10.sourceforge.net/x10home.shtml
4. Cunha, C.A., Sobral, L., Monteiro, M.P.: Reusable aspect-oriented implementations of concurrency patterns and mechanisms. In: AOSD 2006: Proceedings of the 5th International Conference on Aspect-oriented Software Development, pp. 134–145 (2006)

5. Garcia, A., Anna, C.S., Figueiredo, E., Kulesza, U., Lucena, C., von Staa, A.: Modularizing Design Patterns with Aspects: a Quantitative Study. In: AOSD 2005: Proceedings of the 4th International Conference on Aspect-Oriented Software Development, pp. 3–14. ACM Press, New York (2005)
6. Goetz, B.: Stick a fork in it (Last accessed, March 2008), `http://www.ibm.com/developerworks/java/library/j-jtp11137.html?ca=drs-`
7. Hannemann, J., Kiczales, G.: Design pattern implementation in Java and AspectJ. In: Proceedings of the 17th ACM SIGPLAN Conference on Object-Oriented Programming, Systems, Languages and Applications, pp. 161–173 (2002)
8. Harbulot, B., Gurd, J.R.: Using AspectJ to separate concerns in parallel scientific Java code. In: Proceedings of the 3rd International Conference on Aspect-Oriented Software Development, pp. 122–131 (2004)
9. Harbulot, B., Gurd, J.R.: A join point for loops in AspectJ. In: Proceedings of the 5th International Conference on Aspect-Oriented Software Development, pp. 63–74 (2006)
10. Lea, D.: Concurrent Programming in Java: Design Principles and Patterns. Addison-Wesley (1999)
11. Lea, D.: A Java fork/join framework. In: Proceedings of the ACM 2000 conference on Java Grande, pp. 36–43 (2000)

Analyzing Software Component Graphs of Grid Middleware: Hint to Performance Improvement[*]

Pingpeng Yuan, Hai Jin, Kang Deng, and Qingcha Chen

Service Computing Technology and System Lab
Cluster and Grid Computing Lab
Huazhong University of Science and Technology, Wuhan, 430074, China
hjin@hust.edu.cn

Abstract. Grid middleware is a kind of important service management tool and is composed of different interaction units. The units of a grid middleware do not interact in random ways and are very well connected. As shown in this paper, irrespective of the specific features of each grid middleware analyzed, the final outcome of grid middleware is a small world, hierarchical component diagram with well-defined statistical properties. These measurements of network are largely independent of the particular the application and indicated key execution path or key elements. Therefore, analyzing grid middleware structure can show a roadmap to tune performance of grid middleware. Based on analysis of those diagrams, the key components of grid middleware are outlined.

Keywords: Grid computing, Middleware, Performance, Small world.

1 Introduction

Grid middleware is a software stack designed to present disparate computing and data resources in a uniform manner, such that these resources can be accessed remotely by client software without knowing a priori the systems' configurations. Thus, development of grid middleware is a challenging activity that requires considerable expertise. Currently there are some grid middleware, such as Globus [1], UNICORE [2] and gLite [3]. However, due to some reasons, theirs performance is not so good that adoption of grid middleware is restricted to few domain.

Software, including grid middleware is composed of components which interact with each other. One of the aims of software development is to address the interactions of components. The action of software development leads to emergent software organizations whose structures lie outside the realm of explicit design. Performance of software is highly related with software structure. Understanding the structural features of software systems may provide models, metaphors, and tools to help us tune performance or reach better design.

Recently, after the underlying structures of many natural and artificial systems have been found to share many *scale-free* and *small-world* qualities, software systems

[*] This paper is supported by National Science Foundation of China under grant No.90412010.

A. Bourgeois and S.Q. Zheng (Eds.): ICA3PP 2008, LNCS 5022, pp. 305.315, 2008.

are identified as another important class of complex networks. Some research declared that the internal structures of software programs exhibit scale-free properties. For example, Myers [4] studied six open source software projects and showed that the networks formed by their class collaboration or call graphs showed approximate scale-free properties. Although, the research mentioned above declared properties of software networks were scale-free, few research based on software network analysis were performed on indicating how to improve performance.

The objective of the research is to enhance comprehension about the nature and the performance factors of grid middleware by quantitative measurement and structural analysis of existing grid middleware, and try to give some suggestion on performance optimization of grid middleware during development. Section 2 introduces the related work. Next section presents software graph and its topological measurement. In section 4, three kinds of grid middleware are introduced briefly. Section 5 firstly introduces how to obtain component graph from existing grid middleware, then describes statistics of component graphs of grid middleware. At the sane time, some discussion and comments about the implication on grid middleware development are presented. Finally, section 6 concludes the paper.

2 Related Work

Software is built up out of many interacting units and subsystems at many levels of granularity: subroutines, classes, source files, libraries, et al. Performance of software systems is tightly related with measures of software. Early measures of software were centered in intra-module aspects like program length or number of lines of code (LOC). Those measures cannot reflect complicated relationship between software units. Recently, there is a growing interest in analyzing software structure or software architecture measurement (inter-module). So, graph theory, which studies the properties of graphs, has been widely accepted as a tool to analyze software unit diagrams. The study of graph properties can be valuable in many ways for understanding the characteristics of the underlying software systems.

Current graph theory based research mainly focused on indicating statistical characteristics of software unit diagram. Many researches have found software unit diagram is scale-free network. Nathan LaBelle and Eugene Wallingford [5] analyzed complex networks in open-source software at the inter-package level and showed that the coupling of modules at this granularity creates a small-world and scale-free network. Valverde et al [6] presented the evidence for the emergence of scaling in software architecture graphs from a well-defined local optimization process. Alex Potanin et al [7] examined the graphs formed by object-oriented programs written in a variety of language, and showed that these turn out to be scale-free networks. Alexander Chatzigeorgiou et al [8] presented four different applications of graph theory concerning: the identification of *God* classes, clustering, detecting of design patterns and scale-freeness of OO systems. Spiros Xanthos [9] used spectral graph partitioning for identifying dense communities of classes (clusters) within an object-oriented software system.

To improve the underlying development processes, some research paid attention to software evolution. Sergi Valverde and Ricard V. Solé [10, 11] analyzed some large software applications and found software evolution is a small world. Luis Lopez-Fernandez et al [12] proposed the use of social network analysis for characterizing libre software projects, their evolution over time and their internal structure. Rajesh Vasa [13] presented recurring high-level structural and evolutionary patterns that had been observed in a number of public-domain object-oriented software systems and defined a simple predictive model that could aid developers in detecting structural changes. de Moura et al [14] showed that due to software growth in time, especially as a result of performance optimization of the program, software unit network has a small-world structure, as a consequence, to optimize language runtime systems and improve the design of future OO languages.

Other research investigated community network of developers. Patrick Adam Wagstrom et al [15] analyzed several methods of communication, a social networking site, project mailing lists, and developer weblogs, to understand the social network structure behind Free and Open Source Software (F/OSS) projects. This social network data was used to create a model of F/OSS development. Yongqin Gao and Greg Madey [16] studied the community network of the SourceForge.net to understand the open source software movement, to gain insights of the network development and its influence to individual development.

3 Software Graphs

Software is composed of many interacting units and subsystems at many levels of granularity. The interactions and collaborations of those units can be used to define graphs that form a description of a system. Here we use a broader unit definition that depends on the different granularity level. In package level, the unit is package, in class and method level, the units are class and method respectively. Unit dependency represents ways of information transfer between components. Designing software involves the definition of an information flow traversing a chain of related components. High software performance means efficient information transferring between components. This requires understanding the interactions among software units.

The interactions between software units are multidimensional and multifaceted, and representation of a software system typically involves a very complex space of interactions. In order to understand the interaction network, a graph $G=(V, E)$ for the software under consideration is defined. Let $V=\{v_i\}$ ($i = 1, f$, N) be the set of nodes and $L=\{(v_i, v_j)\}$ the set of links. Node of unit diagrams maps to a function or procedure in method level, a class in class level and a package in package level. Topological measurements of software graph include degree distribution, clustering, and betweenness. Here, we focus on those measurements related with performance. Those measurements include degree and betweenness. In the following, these measurements are presented briefly.

3.1 Degree

For each node i in a unit graph, there is both an in-degree k_i^{in} and an out-degree k_i^{out}. The performance of a unit is related with the performances of its dependency.

The in-degree and out-degree of a method are the numbers of called and calling. The in-degree and out-degree of a class are the sum of in-degree and out-degree of its methods respectively. Similarly, the in-degree and out-degree of a package are the sum of in-degree and out-degree of its classes. The in- and out-degree distributions $P^{in}(k)$ and $P^{out}(k)$ indicate the probability of finding a node with a specified in-degree or out-degree k, respectively, in a given graph. Many complex networks have recently been found to possess a power law distribution, where the probability, $P(k)$, of a particular node having a certain number of connections, k, decays with the power law $P(k) \sim k^{-\gamma}$, where generally $2 < \gamma < 3$.

3.2 Betweenness

Betweenness plays a key role in the characterization of complex networks, which can be used to quantify a node s importance. Betweenness of a vertex measures the control which a vertex has over interaction in the network, and can be used to identify key actors in the network. High betweenness indicates that a vertex can reach other vertices on relatively short paths, or that a vertex lies on a considerable fraction of shortest paths connecting pairs of other vertices. For software system, betweenness reflects the possible execution path needed to carry by the node, thus it can be used to predict the key nodes related with software performance.

4 Grid Middleware

There exist some famous grid middleware, for example, Globus Toolkit, UNICORE, gLite. In the following, we will introduce those grid middleware simply.

Globus Toolkit is a fundamental enabling technology for the grid. It includes core services, interfaces and protocols allow users to access remote resources transparently. In this paper, we only analyze GT4 Core and related packages. GT4 Core implements the *Web Services Resource Framework* (WSRF) and the *Web Service Notification* (WSN) family of standards. It provides APIs and tools for building stateful web services.

UNICORE (*UNiform Interface to COmputing REsources*) offers a ready-to-run grid system including client and server software. UNICORE makes distributed computing and data resources available in a seamless and secure way through intranets and internet.

gLite is the next generation middleware for grid computing. As part of EGEE project, gLite provides a bleeding-edge, best-of-breed framework for building grid applications tapping into the power of distributed computing and storage resources across the Internet.

5 Result Analysis

Grid middleware is built up out of many interacting units and subsystems at many levels of granularities: subroutines, classes, source files, libraries, etc. In order to improve the statistic analysis, we have constructed unit diagrams from a variety of grid middleware. The unit diagrams include method diagrams, class diagrams and package diagrams. The unit diagrams, especially method diagrams are very complex. In fact, the diagrams are not explicitly provided, but they can be constructed from source code. We analyze the source codes of Globus Toolkit 4 (GT4), UNICORE and gLite. Irrespectively which grid middle, method diagrams are the largest diagram among the diagrams of three levels. The class diagram of GT4 is shown in Figure 1. The nodes of this diagram are classes of GT4 and the links represented reference relationships between classes.

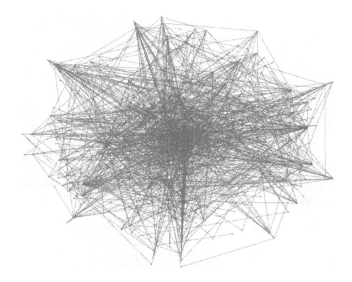

Fig. 1. Class diagram of GT4

5.1 Degree Distribution

We have examined the in-degree and out-degree distributions of three level units of three grid middleware and computed the un-normalized cumulative frequency distributions $P^{in}(k)$ and $P^{out}(k)$. The logarithms of these distributions according to different level have been plotted in Fig.2, 3, and 4. We do not see a great deal of difference among the same level diagrams of three grid middleware. In spite of the different designs, sizes of those grid middleware, their collaboration graphs show very similar properties.

The values of the exponents γ_{in} and γ_{out} are shown in the legends of Fig. 2, 3, and 4. In the method graph (Fig. 2), γ_{in} are 2.1347 (gLite), 2.1243 (GT4), and 2.0655 (UNICORE) respectively, and γ_{out} are 3.7553 (gLite), 3.3938 (GT4), and 3.4726 (UNICORE) respectively. In the class graph (Fig. 3), γ_{in} are 2.0671 (gLite), 2.1303 (GT4), and 2.0420 (UNICORE) respectively, and γ_{out} are 2.7437 (gLite), 2.7596 (GT4), and 2.6173 (UNICORE) respectively. However, in the package graph (Fig. 4), γ_{in} are 1.8437 (gLite), 1.8112 (GT4), and 1.97 (UNICORE) respectively, and γ_{out} are 2.0412 (gLite), 2.2576 (GT4), and 2.2067 (UNICORE) respectively.

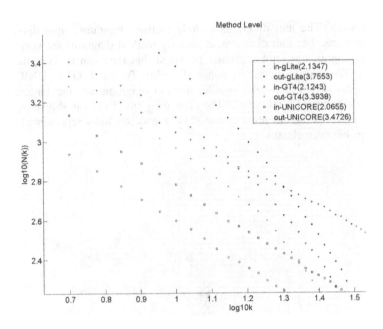

Fig. 2. Log-log graphs of the unnormalized cumulative in-degree and out-degree frequency distributions at method level

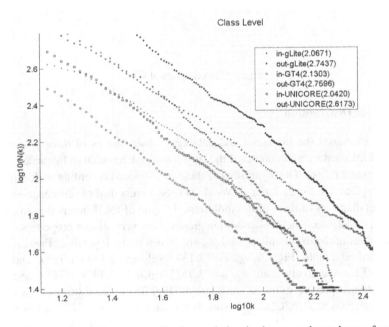

Fig. 3. Log-log graphs of the unnormalized cumulative in-degree and out-degree frequency distributions at class level

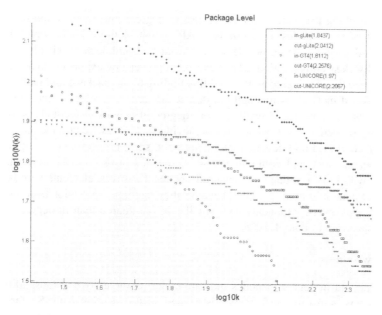

Fig. 4. Log-log graphs of the unnormalized cumulative in-degree and out-degree frequency distributions at package level

All distributions shown in Figure 2, 3, and 4 include significant linear ranges followed by a faster decay at large number of connections (k). This confirms Myers finding of the same phenomenon. According to those figures, these distributions reveal a power-law scaling region. The extents of the power-law regions are admittedly small, particularly for the out-degree distributions. Power-law fits for all 18 distributions have been carried out over the regions for which they exhibit scaling. Analysis of each graph shows clearly that distributions are approximately linear at each level. Package, class and method graphs are found to exhibit the same general properties. However, method degree distributions are found to be generally more linear over the entire data range than distributions at the package and class levels. Package- and class-level un-normalized cumulative degree distributions for three grid middleware look similar, with sparser information and slightly less linear structures.

Comparing γ_{out} and γ_{in} of three levels, we can find those values in package level are less than the values of the other two levels. The reason is that the definition of the package is not clear. We can also find that the out-degree exponent appears to be significantly larger than the in-degree exponent. The degree exponents, particularly in-degree exponents in the same level vary slightly. Out-degree exponents tend to have a larger varying range. Moreover, whether in-degree exponents or out-degree exponents tends to be smaller when the level is higher. For both sets of graphs, the in-degree distributions tend to extend to higher k; that is, it is more likely to find a node with many incoming links than outgoing links. One reason is, since the software development practices encourage the creation of small blocks of code (classes and methods) and significant reuse of those blocks within an application. The other reason is: after checking the nodes with the largest in-degrees and smallest out-degrees, we find most of those nodes are from Java API. Most of those nodes which have the smaller in-degree and larger out-degree are from grid middleware. This is also one of reason why class collaboration graphs exhibited power-law exponents that are smaller in out-degree than in-degree and extend this finding to the package and method levels.

Classes and methods with small out-degree are generally simple, since they do not aggregate other elements. However, if out-degree of classes or methods is too small, then many procedures are needed for achieving customers requirements. Thus, the performance of grid middleware may be not good since procedural call requires more CPU time, memory and communication overhead. Conversely, the performance of elements with large out-degree is generally better. However, elements with large out-degree are generally more complex because they aggregate behavior from many others. Thus, power-law exponents with smaller in out-degree than in-degree suggest a shallow spectrum of complexities.

5.2 Betweenness

Out-degree and in-degree of nodes indicate nodes complexity and reusability. From many aspects, software performance is related with execution path. So far, current connectivity metrics consider each node in the execution path to be equally important. However, for many execution path of a software network, some nodes can be more important than others. For example, a node with more execution paths can be considered important.

Betweennes is used to evaluate node s importance in a network. A node with high betweenness has great influence over flows in the network. While a node may have few direct connections -- fewer than the average in the network, it can also play a *broker* role in the network if it has one of the best locations in the network, for example, it is between two important constituencies. Without the node, the network would be cut off. A node holds a lot power over the outcomes in a network.

The top ten betweennesses of three level nodes of GT4 have been computed and are listed in Table 1-3. Different level nodes betweennesses of UNICORE are shown as in Table 4-6. According to Table 1, we can find nine of ten packages are about wsrf. In nine packages, five packages are about security, especially on authorization and authentication. The other four packages are about container, encoding, and configuration. Further checking Table 2 and 3, we can find most of class and method level betweenness are related with package level betweenness. However, there are some nodes betweenness which are not correspondent with high level betweenness, for example, *DelegationUtil*, *ManagedExecutableJobResource*, and *DelegationResource* of class level, *userHasPermissions_0* of method level. The reason why there exists inconsistency among betweenness of different level nodes is that betweenness of high level nodes is not the sum of betweenness of low level nodes. Analyzing Table 4-6, we can also find there exists inconsistency among three levels betweenness of UNICORE. In three levels of network, it is noticeable that package *com.pallas.unicore.client*, *com.fujitsu.arcon.njs.priest* and *JobContainer* class have larger betweenness. It indicates that those components are important nodes of execution paths in grid middleware. Therefore, developers of those grid middleware should pay more attention to those components if they want to improve the performance of grid middleware.

Table 1. Package Level Node Betweenness of GT4

Package	Betweenness
org.globus.wsrf.container	5103
org.globus.wsrf.impl.security.authorization	2978
org.globus.wsrf.config	2513
org.globus.wsrf.encoding	2313
org.globus.wsrf.impl	2000
org.globus.wsrf.impl.security.authentication.wssec	1274
org.globus.wsrf.impl.security.authentication.secureconv.service	1031
org.globus.axis.description	906
org.globus.wsrf.impl.security.descriptor	870
org.globus.wsrf.impl.security.authentication	738

Table 2. Class Level Node Betweenness of GT4

Class	Betwee-nness
org.globus.delegation.DelegationUtil	5547
org.globus.wsrf.encoding.ObjectDeserializer	3876
org.globus.wsrf.encoding.ObjectDeserializationContext	3230
org.globus.wsrf.config.ContainerConfig	3221
org.globus.wsrf.impl.ResourceHomeImpl	2759
org.globus.exec.service.factory.ManagedJobFactoryHome	2400
org.globus.wsrf.impl.security.descriptor.ResourceSecurityDescriptor	2356
org.globus.exec.service.exec.ManagedExecutableJobResource	2285
org.globus.wsrf.impl.security.descriptor.ServiceSecurityDescriptor	2265
org.globus.delegation.service.DelegationResource	2224

Table 3. Method Level Node Betweeness of GT4

Method	Betweenness
org.globus.wsrf.impl.security.descriptor.ContainerSecurityConfig.getConfig	5350
org.globus.wsrf.impl.security.descriptor.SecurityConfig.initialize	4435
org.globus.exec.utils.FaultUtils.makeFault	4305
org.globus.wsrf.impl.security.descriptor.ContainerSecurityConfig.getConfig_0	3686
org.globus.wsrf.encoding.ObjectDeserializer.toObject_0	3669
org.globus.wsrf.container.ServiceHost.getBaseURL	3521
org.globus.wsrf.encoding.ObjectDeserializer.toObject	3418
org.globus.wsrf.impl.security.descriptor.ContainerSecurityConfig.initialize	3357
org.globus.wsrf.container.ServiceHost.getBaseURL_0	3356
org.globus.cas.impl.databaseAccess.PermissionsEvaluator.userHasPermissions_0	3270

Table 4. Package Level Node Betweenness of UNICORE

Package	Betweenness
com.fujitsu.arcon.njs.priest	3213
org.openmolgrid.cli	3069
org.openmolgrid.cli.cliq	2530
org.unicore.ajo	2482
org.openmolgrid.client.plugins.meta	2084
com.pallas.unicore.resourcemanager	1338
com.pallas.unicore.client	1140
com.fujitsu.arcon.njs	788
com.pallas.unicore.requests	725
com.pallas.unicore.security	617

Table 5. Class Level Node Betweenness of UNICORE

Class	Betweenness
com.fujitsu.arcon.njs.priest.UspaceManager.Uspace	98818
com.pallas.unicore.container.JobContainer	94155
com.fujitsu.arcon.njs.actions.KnownActionFactory	92270
com.pallas.unicore.client.util.ClientPluginManager	71490
com.pallas.unicore.security.JobConverter	60219
com.pallas.unicore.client.explorer.SelectorDialog	56727
com.fujitsu.arcon.njs.priest.BatchTargetSystem	52685
com.fujitsu.arcon.njs.actions.EKnownAction	47187
com.fujitsu.arcon.njs.priest.Seminaries	44699
com.fujitsu.arcon.njs.priest.UspaceManager	41846

Table 6. Method Level Node Betweenness of UNICORE

Method	Betweenness
com.fujitsu.arcon.njs.streaming.DoStuff1.<init>	6146
com.fujitsu.arcon.njs.streaming.DoStuff1.listContents	4191
org.unicore.outcome.Outcome.<init>_0	3680
com.pallas.unicore.client.explorer.SelectorDialog.showDialog	3606
com.pallas.unicore.client.trees.JPATree.addGroupNodeAt	3562
com.pallas.unicore.client.trees.JPATree.checkContainers	3401
com.pallas.unicore.client.trees.JPATree.updateCurrentJob	3392
org.unicore.outcome.Outcome.<init>	3379
com.fujitsu.arcon.njs.streaming.DoStuff2.createCommands	3296
com.fujitsu.arcon.njs.actions.IncarnatedPortfolio.createExisting	3226

6   Conclusion

This paper analyzes the unit graph formed in GT4, UNICORE and gLite at the package, class and method levels and shows that those package, class and method-level collaboration graphs are nearly scale-free properties at each level analyzed. Previous studies mainly focused on class collaboration graphs, especially small linear ranges in graphs. This work extends that approach to both package and method levels for the three grid middleware. Based on analysis of grid middleware diagram, the key components of grid middleware, which are key performance factors of grid middleware, are outlined.

References

1. Globus Toolkit, http://globus.org/toolkit/
2. UNICORE (Uniform Interface to Computing Resources), http://www.unicore.eu/
3. gLite, http://glite.web.cern.ch/glite/
4. Myers, C.R.: Software systems as complex networks: Structure, function, and evolvability of software collaboration graphs. Physical Review E 68, 046116 (1~15) (2003)
5. LaBelle, N., Wallingford, E.: Inter-package dependency networks in open-source software. CoRR: Software Engineering, 0411096 (November 2004)
6. Valverde, S., Ferrer-Cancho, R., Solé, R.V.: Scale-Free Networks from Optimal Design. Europhysics Letters 60(4), 512..517 (2002)
7. Potanin, A., Noble, J., Frean, M., Biddle, R.: Scale-free Geometry in Object-Oriented Programs. Communications of the ACM 48(5), 99..103 (2005)
8. Chatzigeorgiou, A., Tsantalis, N., Stephanides, G.: Application of Graph Theory to OO Software Engineering. In: Proceedings of International Conference on Software Engineering, Shanghai, China, May 20-28, pp. 29..36 (2006)
9. Xanthos, S.: Clustering Object-Oriented Software Systems using Spectral Graph Partitioning. In: ACM Student Research Competition 2005, Grand Finals, Second Award (2005)
10. Valverde, S., Solé, R.V.: Hierarchical Small Worlds in Software Architecture, Santa Fe Institute working paper SFI/03-07-044 (2003),
    http://www.santafe.edu/research/publications/wpabstract/2003 07044
11. Valverde, S., Solé, R.V.: Logarithmic Growth Dynamics in Software Networks. Europhysics Letters 72(5), 858..864 (2005)
12. Lopez-Fernandez, L., Robles, G., Gonzalez-Barahona, J.M.: Applying Social Network Analysis to the Information in CVS Repositories. In: Proceedings of the 2004 International Workshop on Mining Software Repositories, Edinburgh, UK, pp. 101..105 (2004)
13. Vasa, R., Schneider, J.-G., Woodward, C., Cain, A.: Detecting Structural Changes in Object Oriented Software Systems. In: Proceedings of 2005 International Symposium on Empirical Software Engineering, Noosa Heads, Australia, November 17-18, pp. 479..486 (2005)
14. De Moura, A.P., Lai, Y.C., Motter, A.E.: Signatures of small world and scale-free properties in large computer programs. Physical Review E 68, 017102 (2003)
15. Wagstrom, P.A., Herbsleb, J.D., Carley, K.: A Social Network Approach to Free/Open Source Software Simulation. In: Proceedings of The First International Conference on Open Source Systems, Genova, Italy, July 11..15, pp. 16..23 (2005)
16. Gao, Y., Madey, G.: Network Analysis of the SourceForge.net Community. In: Proceedings of The Third International Conference on Open Source Systems (OSS 2007), Limerick, Ireland, June 2007, pp. 187..200 (2007)

Using Multi-core to Support Security-Related Applications

Wanlei Zhou and Yang Xiang

Deakin University, Melbourne, Australia

Outline

This tutorial introduces the challenges of modern security-related applications and the opportunities that multi-core technology brings. We envision that multi-core supported security applications will become the killer applications for next generation personal computers.

This tutorial is divided into four parts. The first part gives an overview of the multi-core technology. The related development of both multi-core hardware and software is introduced.

The second part gives the background knowledge of multiprocessing. Although multi-core technology has just emerged in very recent years, people have done research in multiprocessing for many years. Computer system technology, computer performance, computer architecture, and high-performance multiprocessing are discussed in this part.

Part three, security-related applications, is structured by the attacks and the defense systems. First, the Internet threats and attacks are introduced. Second, the defense systems or countermeasures and their effectiveness are discussed. We will see that unfortunately all these security-related applications are computing intensive applications, which can be difficult to run on today s personal computers without performance penalties, and cost huge CPU time and memory if they can. More inconveniently, they prohibit other applications running simultaneously or significantly slow down other applications.

Part four discusses how we can leverage the power of multi-core to support security-related applications. We will discuss five important research areas: partitioning and distributing workload of security-related applications, fine-grained multi-threading, smartly using the memory system, communications between cores, and new software architecture for multi-core. After that, we propose an innovative idea of software personal computer bodyguard that can protect future personal computers from various threats at all time and in real-time, with the support from multi-core. Finally, we point out future research directions and conclude this tutorial.

Target Audience

The audience of this tutorial includes researchers, practitioners, and technical workers who are interested in network and system security from academic, businesses and governments. No specific knowledge is required. Anyone with a basic knowledge of

A. Bourgeois and S.Q. Zheng (Eds.): ICA3PP 2008, LNCS 5022, pp. 316.317, 2008.

the Internet and computers will be able to understand the materials presented in the tutorial.

Bios of the Presenters

Professor Wanlei Zhou received his PhD degree from The Australian National University, Canberra, Australia, in October 1991. He also received the DSc degree from Deakin University, Victoria, Australia in 2002. He is currently the Chair Professor of Information Technology and the Associate Dean (International), Faculty of Science and Technology, Deakin University, Melbourne, Australia. His research interests include distributed and parallel systems, network security, mobile computing, bioinformatics and e-learning. Professor Zhou has published more than 170 papers in refereed international journals and refereed international conferences proceedings. Since 1997 Professor Zhou has been involved in more than 50 international conferences as General Chair, Steering Chair, PC Chair, Session Chair, Publication Chair, and PC member. Professor Zhou is a member of the IEEE.

Dr Yang Xiang received his PhD in computer science from Deakin University, Melbourne, Australia, in April 2007. He is currently with School of Management and Information Systems, Central Queensland University. His research interests include network and system security, and wireless systems. In particular, he is currently working in a research group developing active defense systems against large-scale network attacks and new Internet security countermeasures. He has served as guest co-editor for Journal of Network and Computer Applications special issue on network and system security, and the International Journal of Computer Systems Science and Engineering special issue on network attack and defense systems. He has served as PC co-chair for 2007 IFIP International Workshop on Network and System Security and PC member for many international conferences such as IEEE GLOBECOM 2006/2008 and IEEE ICC 2007. He is a member of the IEEE.

Symbolic Analysis for Increased Program Execution Performance

Kleanthis Psarris

Department of Computer Science
The University of Texas at San Antonio
San Antonio, TX 78249
psarris@cs.utsa.edu

Abstract. High end parallel and multi-core processors rely on compilers to perform the necessary optimizations and exploit concurrency in order to achieve higher performance. However, source code for high performance computers is extremely complex to analyze and optimize. In particular, program analysis techniques often do not take into account complex expressions during the data dependence analysis phase. Most data dependence tests are only able to analyze linear expressions, even though non-linear expressions occur very often in practice. Therefore, considerable amounts of potential parallelism remain unexploited. In this talk we propose new data dependence analysis techniques to handle such complex instances of the dependence problem and increase program parallelization. Our method is based on a set of polynomial time techniques that can prove or disprove dependences in source codes with non-linear and symbolic expressions, complex loop bounds, arrays with coupled subscripts, and if-statement constraints. In addition our algorithm can produce accurate and complete direction vector information, enabling the compiler to apply further transformations. To validate our method we performed an experimental evaluation and comparison against the I-Test, the Omega test and the Range test in the Perfect and SPEC benchmarks. The experimental results indicate that our dependence analysis tool is accurate, efficient and more effective in program parallelization than the other dependence tests. The improved parallelization results into higher speedups and better program execution performance in several benchmarks.

A. Bourgeois and S.Q. Zheng (Eds.): ICA3PP 2008, LNCS 5022, p. 318, 2008.
© Springer-Verlag Berlin Heidelberg 2008

Author Index

Lecture Notes in Computer Science

Sublibrary 1: Theoretical Computer Science and General Issues

For information about Vols. 1– 4743
please contact your bookseller or Springer